Tally-Ho

Tally-Ho

RAF Tactical Leadership in the Battle of Britain, July 1940

Patrick G. Eriksson

AMBERLEY

First published 2023

Amberley Publishing
The Hill, Stroud
Gloucestershire, GL5 4EP

www.amberley-books.com

British Library Cataloguing in Publication Data.
A catalogue record for this book is available from the British Library.

ISBN 978 1 3981 1162 2 (hardback)
ISBN 978 1 3981 1163 9 (ebook)

1 2 3 4 5 6 7 8 9 10

Typeset in 10.5pt on 13pt Sabon.
Typesetting by SJmagic DESIGN SERVICES, India.
Printed in the UK.

Contents

Dedication

To Douglas Bader, leader of 242 Squadron during the Battle of Britain (hereinafter the Battle), famous ace and later Group Captain, DSO and bar, DFC and bar; CBE in 1956 and knighted in 1976 for his work on behalf of the disabled. A parental gift of Paul Brickhill's biography of Bader, *Reach for the Sky*, was an inspiration in my youth. Later I corresponded with Bader and sent him golf balls, which he lost regularly. On a visit to Durban to open the Cheshire Home in that city, my parents ensured I was there and could meet him; what a powerful personality. I was much too overawed to let him know that I was the source of the golf balls, and when I informed him of this in a letter some time later, he quite rightly told me I was a clot. In an otherwise low-achieving youth, I regard being called a clot by Douglas Bader as a distinct accomplishment. Despite his sometimes controversial and difficult character, traits that are often highlighted now, he was a man of extraordinary courage and leadership ability; my first Battle of Britain hero, and still prominent among that pantheon for me.

To Air Commodore Alan Deere DSO, OBE, DFC and bar, New Zealander flight commander in 54 Squadron during the Battle, who, when I pestered him, very kindly went out to a bookshop and purchased a copy of his autobiography *Nine Lives*, signed it and sent it to me. A great hero of the Battle, he survived more catastrophic events over the course of two months of flying and fighting than any other member of 'The Few', but he kept coming back for more.

To 'Sailor' Malan, commander of 74 Squadron during the Battle and a major RAF tactical innovator then and later; he ended the war as Group Captain A. G. Malan, DSO and bar, DFC and bar, *Légion d'Honneur*. Post-war, he led the Torch Commando, an early anti-Apartheid movement of ex-servicemen in South Africa; my father was one of

250,000 members. Sailor died prematurely at fifty-two, of Parkinson's disease. Essentially a casualty of the 'Hometown Battlefield' embracing those who succumb one way or another, perhaps to Post-Traumatic Stress Disorder, once the wars are over.[1] To one among the many who have paid this price: my father-in-law whom I never knew, Major Willem Smit, veteran of the South African Corps of Engineers, South African 6th Armoured Division, Italy 1944-45.

To my parents who paid for flying lessons for me from age fifteen. I eventually soloed two years later after some twenty-two hours; a supreme day in my life, as for anyone fortunate enough to experience it, but I was a rotten pilot. However, my minor flying career brought home to me what had been achieved in the skies over southern England during the Battle of Britain in 1940, by young men just a few years older than myself, many of whom didn't have that much experience at all before being exposed to the realities of mortal combat.

Preface

The importance of the squadron leaders over southern England in that long autumn of 1940 who led the squadrons into battle, and their supporting flight commanders, has been rather neglected. The tactical abilities of these small unit leaders were critical in winning the battle and the many innovations and even experiments which they tried out during the active fighting merit a closer examination. The pre-war 'Fighter Area Attacks', founded on the notion that incoming German bombers over England would be unescorted due to the distance from their German home air bases, would prove to be almost totally unreliable; nobody then remotely thought France would fall, enabling enemy fighters to be based just across the Channel.

Air Chief Marshal Sir Hugh Dowding built the defensive system and made it work, before the war; he also prevented too many fighters from going to France. During the Battle of Britain (the Battle) he played the strategic role, adopting an attritional approach, keeping Fighter Command in business while minimising losses and emphasising knocking the German bombers down. This was directly related to small British fighter formations, essentially a squadron, and any raid would thus be attacked by a number of discrete squadrons; this approach reduced the possibility of catastrophic losses to RAF fighters and ensured a sequence of attacks on German formations giving rise to a lot of confusion for the incoming and outgoing raids. Dowding's subordinate Group commanders, mainly Air Vice-Marshal Keith Park of 11 Group, fought the actual tactical battle, deciding every day how many squadrons would be allocated to every raid, choosing those sectors to supply them; then sector controllers vectored their own fighters to the enemy formations, with hopefully a good tactical position (height and sun). Once contact was made, it was up to the squadron leader to decide what to do.

Participants in the Battle did not clearly see specific phases as starting and finishing, but rather experienced periods of more or less intensity as the fighting progressed; it is the historian writing after the fact who clearly sees campaigns, and phases thereof.[1] This also applies to Dowding, whose seminal report on his battle is written with hindsight and with specific phases in view.[2] Interestingly, Park's short and provisional report on the Battle to Dowding of 12 September 1940 has different and simpler phases compared to those of Dowding; Park's report may be viewed as essentially tactical at the 11 Group scale.[3]

While Dowding's strategic genius had placed the RAF in a position where they were about to fight a battle for which they were prepared, things were not as positive as it might have seemed. Firstly, the losses over France and Dunkirk had been serious, not just of aircraft but more particularly of well-trained pre-war professional fighter pilots, with lost squadron leaders and flight lieutenants being the most missed in the critical months to come. Secondly, RAF defensive thinking in the 1930s and dogma that was still held to be valid and important at least at its upper levels, had devised set-piece numbered area attacks; squadrons had been trained in these and imbued officially with their value. While the highly impressive achievements of British fighter production and the almost equally important repair organisation for damaged fighters in the UK redressed the losses in machines, there was no fast way of replacing highly trained and experienced pilots, especially tactical formation leaders, lost or wounded in combat. The pilot training sausage machine was functioning quite well, but neophytes were not the ideal replacements for lost veterans and professional airmen. When thrown into the deep end of the air battle raging over the British Isles, new squadrons and their mostly green pilots suffered appalling losses before they gained enough experience to become as deadly as their enemies. However, from a ruthless perspective, losses of inexperienced men would have been less serious than those of experienced veterans; gross levels of experience and thus fighting power for the RAF were lower than for the *Luftwaffe* when the Battle began, and thus while RAF losses of less experienced men on average had a lesser effect on overall fighting efficiency, those lost to the *Luftwaffe* on average had a more deleterious effect.

Another problem which would not be solved during the Battle, except extemporarily, was the vulnerability of the control rooms situated on sector airfields, many of which were totally or insufficiently unprotected, and the equally vulnerable small buildings on the coastal radar stations in the active battle areas. In time, these issues would be addressed, but during the Battle itself resort was had to moving operations rooms into – admittedly designated and partially prepared – alternative accommodations in villages near the sector airfields. Like all temporary and ad hoc arrangements, they were less than ideal, and communications proved especially difficult.

It is against this background that Dowding's strategy and Park's tactics (and those of 10 and 12 Group's leaders also to a lesser degree) would be applied. In broad terms, the *Luftwaffe's* strategy was entirely logical, with an endgame which should perhaps have been more expected by the RAF's leaders. The Germans began in July by largely attacking convoys in the Channel and along the east coast, naval assets at sea, and also attacking some coastal targets, particularly ports and naval bases, which climaxed with the great convoy battles of 8 August 1940. Then, starting from 11 August, coastal targets, radar stations, satellite airfields and ports, including also such targets within short distances of the coast, were assaulted. The attacks on airfields up to 16 August gradually moved further inland, to be followed by a shift to the key sector stations ringing London, attacks which began seriously on 18 August and continued until 5 September 1940. These achieved critical damage to the Fighter Command control system and to maintenance facilities on the ground, and in Park's and Dowding's considered opinions were exceedingly dangerous. From 28 August onwards, almost all the German single-engine fighters were concentrated in the general Pas de Calais region, to operate against the sector stations south, southeast, east and northeast of London. In Park's view, the change from 6 September to London as the main target, bearing in mind the first massive assaults on the city of 7 September, were something of a miracle, as equally perceived by Dowding, bringing much relief to an over-strained Fighter Command organisation, within 11 Group particularly.

More major London raids followed on 9 and 11 September, with a climax being reached in the effective defeat by Fighter Command of two massive raids on 15 September; two days later, Operation Sealion, the invasion of Britain, was indefinitely postponed by Hitler.[4] Raids on London would continue until the end of September 1940, a month that also saw some daylight raiders return in the west, under *Luftflotte 3*, many aimed at aircraft production targets. The shift to London as a major target was not just due to an accidental German night raid which lightly damaged the city on the night of 25 August, leading to British reprisal raids on Berlin, largely ineffective, except on the psyche of Hitler. Hitler and other Nazi leaders saw an intense assault on this major city, manufacturing, political and communications centre as being a potential war winner in its own right, and from as early as 16 August a major air attack on London figured in German invasion planning.[5]

The entire *Luftwaffe* strategy briefly outlined above formed a logical succession climaxing in the attacks on London, day and night, from 6 September, once the fighter stations surrounding the city had apparently been knocked out, at least in German thinking. London attacks were thus an intrinsic part of German invasion philosophy. Nazi invasions past and future at the time of the Battle of Britain encompassed major aerial assaults on capital and other major enemy cities: Warsaw, planned on day one already, albeit delayed in reality, Rotterdam, and to come – Belgrade, Moscow, Stalingrad.

This then was the German strategy. The German battle tactics showed a lot of adaptability and change over these several fraught weeks of intense aerial battle, and they have tended to be neglected in historical studies. The one feature often described is the common use of complex sets of fighter sweeps and light raids by Kesselring of *Luftflotte 2*, to mask attacks by small and fast formations of bombers. Here, German planning, both for single large raids and also for coordinated attacks west and east by *Luftflotten 3* and 2 will be examined briefly, and how these initiatives changed over the course of the Battle. Part of these German tactical matters was the evolving use of German fighters in their escort role and the divergence between fighters closely tied to bomber formations, appreciated by bomber crews and despised by fighter pilots, and those allowed to hunt for their opponents far and wide, appreciated by the aggressive fighter leaders. The latter aspects have been well covered in many previous studies. Less studied were highly successful *Jagdgeschwader* leaders, who, in their striving to increase their large scores, could leave bomber units exposed, despite strict orders from the top.[6] The question of the German bomber formations used has almost been ignored; an interesting RAF report from December 1940 describes the formation types observed by Fighter Command in detail and these compare favourably with formations described from German sources.[7]

German fighter formations (pairs or *Rotten*, and the double pair, known as a *Schwarm*) have enjoyed wide coverage in many histories of the Battle, as have the RAF vic-based pre-war fighter formations. However, a much larger range of RAF formations, either used regularly or experimented with, are obvious from study of Fighter Command squadron records and Intelligence Patrol Reports, and they deserve attention. What will form a core component of the present study is the tactical situation faced by the British fighter squadrons as they were vectored within sight of the German raids. Also critical, at the larger yet still tactical scale, was how well the controllers were able to place their squadrons, especially as regards height relative to raids (especially the bomber component thereof) and positioning of the generally twelve aircraft-strong RAF formations facing heavy odds, vis-à-vis the sun. While controllers did their level best in such matters, the radar seldom gave sufficiently accurate information on enemy numbers and even more critically, seldom a reliable height of enemy formations. Another factor was the placement of multiple attacking squadrons, especially assigning the higher performance Spitfire squadrons to tackle top cover escorts, thereby easing the approach of lower performance Hurricanes to the bombers, always the main target.

A complex set of decisions had to be made by the British unit leaders – facing odds almost always heavily against them – within a few seconds, while also flying their own aircraft and manoeuvring to maintain their own formation's integrity before the chaos of contact inevitably made a mess of everything for both sides. Sometimes there was just enough space and time to put in a rapid attack on a tight bomber formation and inflict damage to its cohesion and component aircraft, other times squadron leaders would have to split their small force so that part was ordered to take on the thankless task of distracting unavoidable escorts while their fellows went for the bombers. Things like Fighter Area Attacks were irrelevant in these situations, and in dealing with bomber formations, electing to fly in the tight 'vics' of three machines or more efficient and spaced-out 'finger fours' made little difference; however, against enemy fighters this would not hold true.

Luftwaffe tactics changed over the course of the Battle, in bomber formation sizes and escort tactics. Equally, the evolving tactics from RAF leaders in response, such as using single squadrons to attack, or pairs thereof, or even the large and cumbersome 'big wings' beloved of 12 Group. But at the heart of the Battle, and of this book, is the judgement shown by RAF unit leaders, the critical squadron leaders and their flight lieutenants, who had to assess the tactical situation facing them within a three-dimensional world wherein the machines were travelling at something like 200 or 300 mph (at least), and within moments make decisions that would lead to success or failure, high or low losses, and also their own personal survival to fight and lead another day, or their own demise.

The RAF unit leaders really had their hands full. Once airborne they had to follow the instructions of the sector controller, navigate the small formation, keep them in formation and change that formation once the enemy were close. When the enemy formation was sighted, there would be little time for them to think, decide and act; they would have to hope that the controller had placed them above the German bombers and even up-sun of the entire formation, but very often these aspirations would be dashed. Despite being only twelve fighters normally, but quite often even fewer, there were of course at most times other lone squadrons intercepting the same formation before or following their own interception, but coordination was practically non-existent. Later, paired squadrons were used by Park almost as a matter of course. As the German aircraft came into sight, the squadron leader would rapidly have to assess their bomber formation, how tight it was, whether there were any fighters flying alongside or even amongst the bombers themselves, and also observe – as much as cloud and the sun's glare allowed him to – where the escort was. This comprised normally a close escort, flying slowly and weaving near the bombers and thus less dangerous as they were not moving at combat velocities. Far more dangerous were the more remote escorts, higher than the bombers and mostly behind them. One of the most critical decisions of the unit leader would be to decide if there was enough space and time to put in a half-decent attack on the bombers before the escorts were upon them, and then also what attack method to employ: head-on, beam attacks or those from rear and quarters. In Dowding's overall battle of attrition, the squadron leader had to try and achieve a subtle balance between the aggressiveness needed to break up bomber formations, to damage aircraft and thereby allow follow-up destruction of stragglers, and the great importance of limiting one's own casualties.

In time and with experience, the advantages of a head-on attack became well known to unit leaders, and if it was possible to get ahead of the bombers and turn in on them without their escort interfering, a very fast closing speed attack could be made. Alternatively, a beam attack could be set up, which had its own difficulties as the turn into the flank of the bombers had to be well timed, and the shooting was almost entirely of a full deflection nature. However, despite many pilots struggling to be accurate in estimating how much offset or deflection to set before opening fire, when doing a beam attack on a large formation, one could spray bullets at the passing mass of bombers and almost certainly some would be hit. However, the reverse also applied and many RAF fighters could also be hit by return fire. Return fire was not a major risk for a high closing speed, head-on attack as often only a single forward-firing gun was available in most of the bombers, and this attack method also had the added advantage of often leading to breakup of bomber formations. Frequently, a planned head-on attack would end up being one from ahead and quarter, due either to imperfect positioning of the attacking squadron, or turns made by the bomber formation. For an attack from the rear or rear-quarter, the gap between bombers and higher-flying escorts to the rear had to be large enough to allow insertion of the squadron between bombers and escorts coming down from behind. A natural disadvantage of any rear attacks was a heavy, coordinated defensive fire from multiple gun positions. With beam attacks, defensive fire was often much less intense due to fewer beam-firing weapons and the inherent difficulties of deflection shooting for the bomber gunners using ad hoc extra machine gun fittings.

The medley of possible attack methods outlined above would flash through the squadron leader's mind as his small force approached the massed incoming German formations, typically stacked up vertically, higher to the rear, with bombers at the front and below, Me 110s behind and above and quite often between bomber *Staffeln* or *Gruppen*, or maintaining defensive circles over bomber formations, and finally further back and even higher, massed Me 109s. The RAF unit leader would have minutes at best, and often only tens of seconds to decide what to do, and then act to place his own fighters, possibly divide his formation, and then to attack. The attack itself would strive for maximum damage to the enemy at the least cost. The load of responsibility and concomitant strain placed on the shoulders of the squadron leader was thus orders greater than for his colleagues. Despite this, the leaders almost universally managed to carry on and to make these rapid decisions, upon which not only life and death depended for both sides, but also in the end, winning or losing the Battle of Britain in a cumulative sense over many weeks. One more thing, of course, would also have occupied the Fighter Command unit leaders in the air: flying his own aircraft, shooting at the enemy, keeping an eye on his tail and trying to stay alive himself.

Finally, regarding RAF fighter squadron leadership, the best were those attacking 'with intent' – i.e. with a serious determination to really do harm to a German bomber formation or Me 110 circle. Some leaders rather gratefully embraced Spitfire squadrons being instructed to go for the escort fighters and rather happily climbed up away from bomber formations and sought a favourable tactical situation to tackle some of the higher flying Me 109 escorts. Other leaders would attack a bomber formation but concentrate on stragglers at the back or sides and avoid tackling the solid part of a bomber formation and really splitting it up. They would thus happily pursue getting a victory or two but without exposing themselves to a full-on attack on a tight bomber formation with plenty of potential return fire.

Finally, there were the leaders who really came at things with intent, leading their fellows in a full-out head-on attack with the intent to really break up a bomber formation – with the speed of such events it was always pretty difficult to confirm a victory for any bomber you hit – the goal here was to split the bomber formation beyond any hope of maintaining their cohesion. Other leaders of this ilk would do the same thing through a serious beam attack, again with less chance of a personal victory but landing a blow on bomber formation cohesion and enabling others to go for the stragglers and small formations remaining after a successful break-up attack. Also, leaders who really went for a Me 110 circle, going right inside the circles and flying round in the opposite direction, firing. An RAF squadron leader or flight lieutenant leading a squadron into battle must thus be judged against a far more complex canvas than merely performing as an ace fighter pilot. Many leaders essentially had to sacrifice their own scoring ambitions to do their job properly, and to ensure the right balance between the success and casualties of their own men. Some reputations might thus suffer, judged against this more stringent set of duties, but some others might surprise in the enhancement of their achievements aside from just shooting down enemy aircraft.

This book is thus focussed on the squadron leaders and flight commanders who day-in and day-out performed these critical duties, and on unravelling the tactics they applied at such very short notice, in the air, against German bomber formations. Secondary weight will be given to German tactics, such as bomber formations, placement of their escort fighters about those bombers, and some attention will also be given to the role of sector controllers in placing their squadrons in the best positions relative to incoming raiders in order to assist the squadron leaders in their difficult tasks. To this end, the basic source data used is that from official RAF records, especially the Intelligence Patrol Reports/ Fighter Command Combat Reports – which give an overview of each action per squadron – the pilot's personal Combat Reports, the Squadron Operational Record Books, the Squadron Commander Reports on Flying Battle Casualties within the RAF Casualty Files (Air 81 records) and other sundry more ad hoc documents available from the UK National Archives. While any documentary source can include errors, documents completed soon after the aerial battles tend to be more accurate than the fallibility of human memory in the longer term; however, first- and second-hand more personal accounts are also considered in addition to the basis provided by the wealth of formal documentation. A number of texts are considered to provide a fundamental foundation to any study of the Battle of Britain and are utilised greatly in this book.[8]

Maps

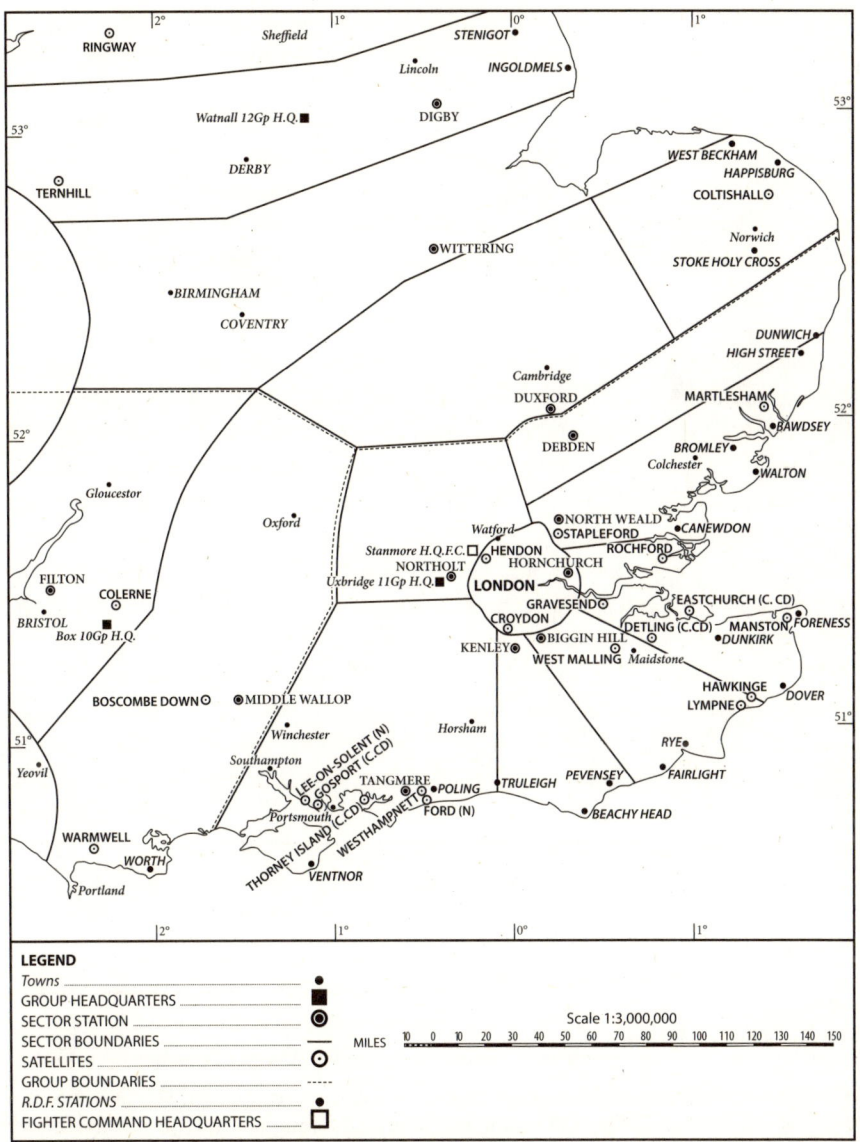

Map of 11 Group and more important parts of 10 and 12 Groups of Fighter Command; shows sector stations, sector boundaries, satellite airfields (N = naval, and C.CD = Coastal Command airfields) and radar (RDF) stations. Redrafted and simplified from an original in: James, T. Cecil G., *The Battle of Britain* (Abingdon: Routledge, 2012) which is itself a reproduction of an original, Sheet 1 of Map 115, compiled and drawn at the Air Historical Branch of the RAF.

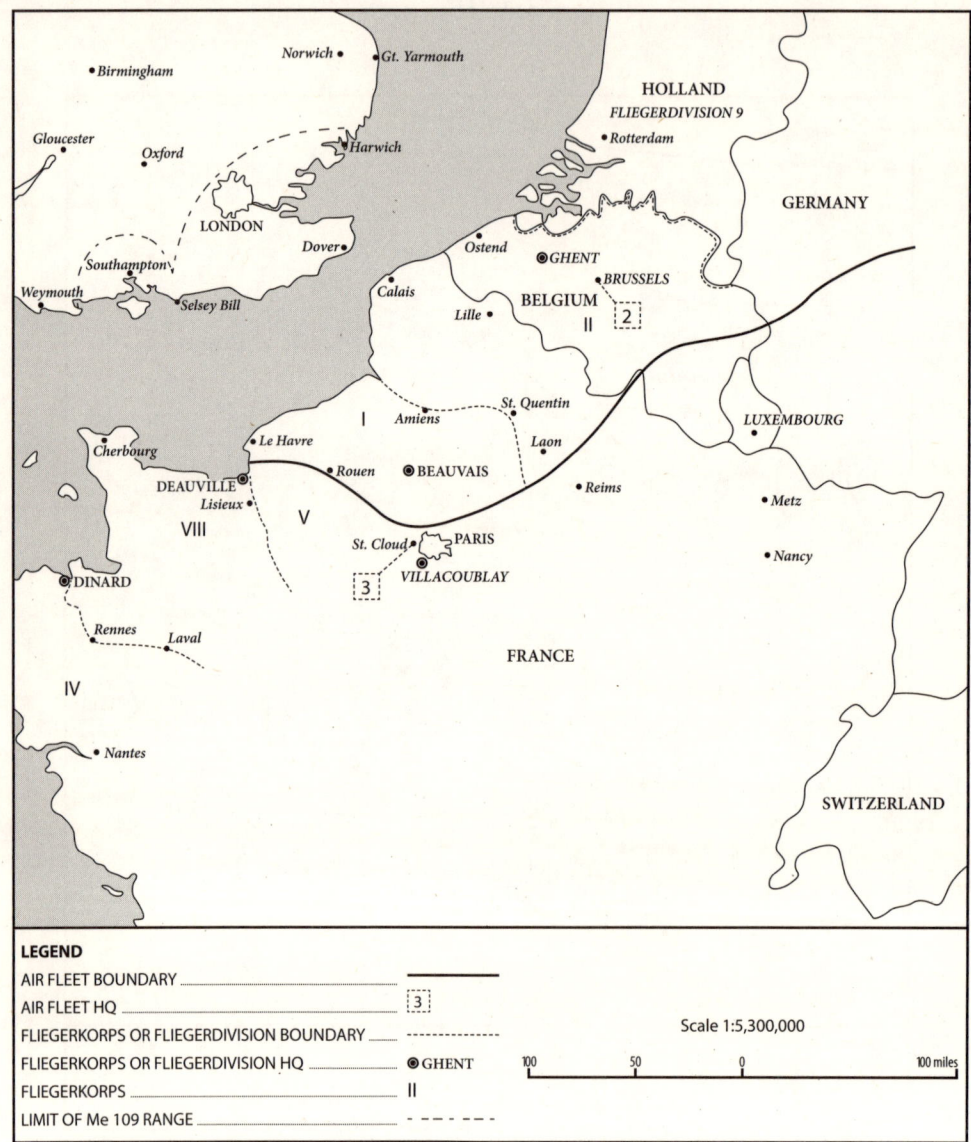

Luftflotten 2 and 3 base areas in Northern France, their component subdivisions into *Fliegerkorps* or *Fliegerdivisionen*, and the limit of the range of the Me 109 fighter, for the general Southampton area and for the London region. For the former area, note the very limited penetration possible. Simplified and redrafted from a map headed 'German Forces in the Battle of Britain', in Overy, Richard, *The Battle of Britain: the myth and the reality* (New York: W. W. Norton, 2002) (pp. 166-167).

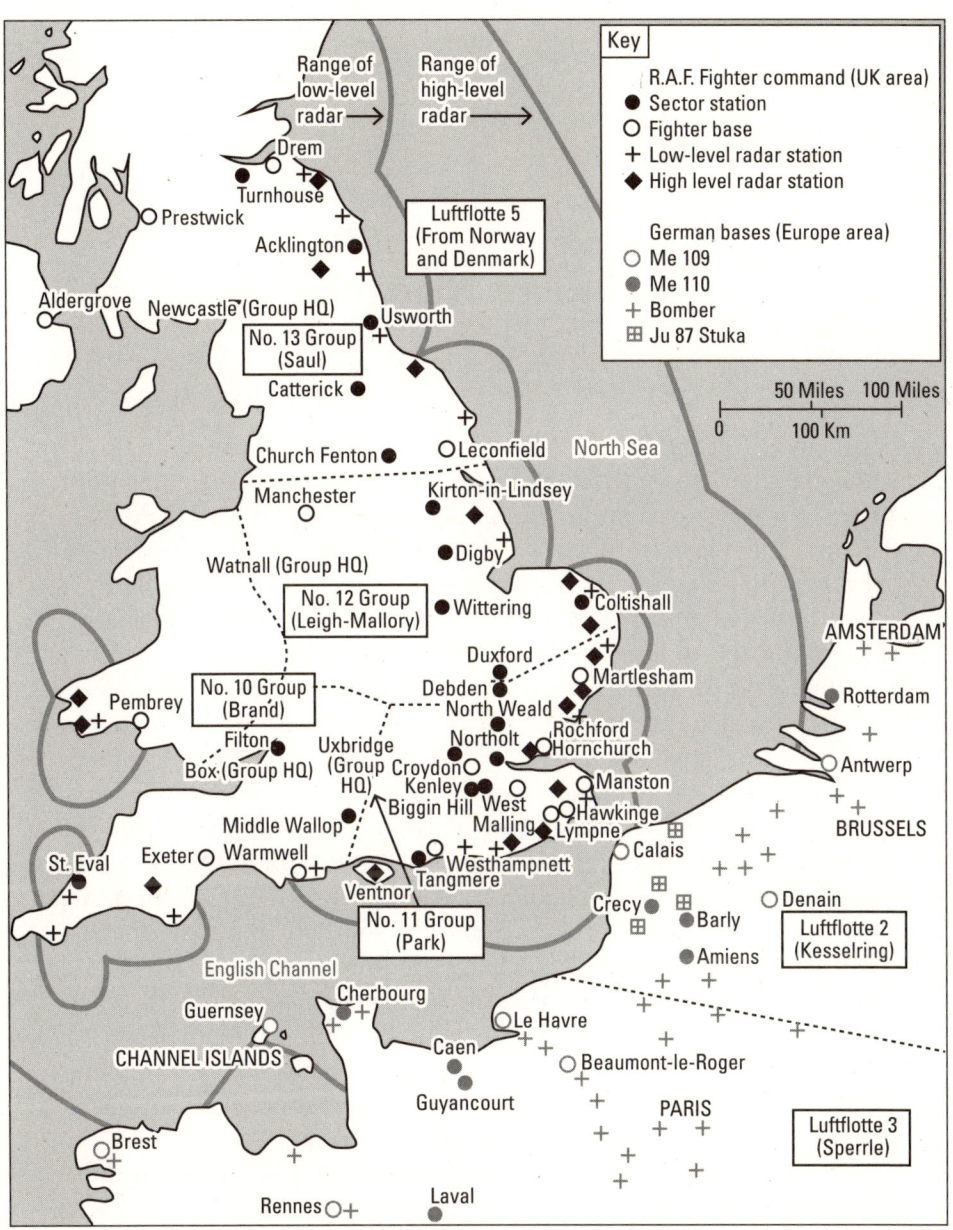

Fighter Command, RAF and *Luftwaffe* dispositions for the Battle of Britain. For July 1940, most German incursions originated in the Pas de Calais region (Stukas and Me 109s) for the Straits of Dover and surrounds, or for the Western Channel, from the Cherbourg peninsula. From: Eriksson, Patrick G., *Alarmstart* (Stroud: Amberley, 2017).

1

The Learning Curve of July 1940:
The First Nine Days

Most books on the Battle of Britain begin their narratives on 10 July 1940, the date chosen by Dowding to mark the official beginning of the Battle, a notable exception being *Battle over Britain* by F.K. Mason.[1] The first nine days of July are also examined below in some detail as they already illustrate many of the persistent realities of the Battle. It was relatively common for small RAF fighter formations, normally a section of three, to intercept lone German bombers during July, and the first nine days of the month already set the scene. These bombers were either reconnaissance machines or regular bomber aircraft on armed reconnaissance missions, mostly against shipping in the Channel and off the East coast of the British Isles, or inland targets of opportunity.

From 1 to 9 July 1940, a total of twenty seven bombers and one reconnaissance Me 110 were destroyed by Fighter Command, with three more bombers damaged and another ten slightly so.[2] These actions and their casualties occurred right around the southern and eastern coasts of Great Britain, the victories being credited to twenty-four fighter squadrons, with 603 Squadron getting four and 616 Squadron, three; one Hurricane was lost to return fire (its pilot safe) and ten more damaged.[3] Immediately, the perils of attacking even lone bombers became obvious; bombers attacked later in the Battle when in formation with coordinated cross-fire would be much more lethal targets to tackle. What is interesting for these twenty-seven lone German bombers shot down during July's first nine days is that, on average, they were attacked by 2.93 RAF fighters, with a lower average of 2.1 fighters needed to damage a single bomber. This directly relates to two major factors: rifle calibre machine guns in the attacking fighters hindering infliction of major damage to the bombers, and the range at which fire was made on them was also of great importance. For nineteen of the German machines destroyed (eighteen bombers, one Me 110), detailed RAF records in the form of the

Intelligence Patrol Reports (IPRs) exist, revealing that an average of 4,797 rounds of ammunition were expended on each destroyed bomber. IPRs are available for only five of the damaged German bombers, indicating an average expenditure of 2,400 rounds of ammunition on each. There is no meaningful difference in average ammunition expenditure per different type of German bomber, or even the Me 110, which ranged from 4,411 to 5,629 rounds.

Some of the IPRs from the first nine days of July 1940 supply interesting information on the excess ammunition supplies carried by the fighters of eight individual Spitfire squadrons spread across all four groups of Fighter Command (Chart 2), which were supposed to be fixed at 2,400 rounds (300 rounds per gun) per machine, irrespective of whether Hurricane or Spitfire: they varied from 2,450 to 2,588, with two much higher exceptions – 74 Squadron carried 2,720 rounds and 603 Squadron a whopping 2,780-2,800.[4] As always happens at the sharp end, squadrons based on their own battle experience, and at the discretion of squadron commanders, wanted to maximise ammunition supplies for fighting; in the greatest increase in supplies carried, for 603 Squadron at 2,800 rounds, this would have provided an approximate three extra seconds of firing – enough for a single relatively short burst. While obviously an important factor in improving battle capability, such overloading of the ammunition tanks would have carried the risk of possibly increased gun stoppages.

While one must always treat statistics with the caution they deserve, particularly here where the number of data points is small for 1–9 July 1940, it is already obvious from this brief discussion that destruction of a lone bomber needed attacks of between two and three British fighters which used about two-thirds of their available ammunition, assuming 300 rounds per gun, eight guns. This equates to about thirty-two seconds of firing time, which is approximately equivalent to complete use of ammunition for two fighters. Fighter Command aircraft successfully attacking a bomber generally applied attack ranges of 300 yards or less to open fire: just over three-quarters of successful attacks by individual fighters applied this, and the other quarter opened fire further away (data from IPRs). Interestingly, but bearing in mind small amounts of data as already discussed for the 1–9 July period, bombers which were only damaged rather than being destroyed were attacked mostly from ranges of 350 yards or greater.[5] Destruction of lone bombers thus necessitated multiple British fighters getting in close and expending large proportions of their ammunition. A single attack by one fighter would only bring down a bomber in exceptional circumstances.

Applying this apparent principle to attacks on massed German bomber formations still to come in August-September 1940, it can logically be assumed that numbers of attacking fighters and their ammunition expenditure would likely be even higher to achieve success, reflecting added difficulties due to cross-fire from many defensive weapons in the bombers as well as the very real threat from escort fighter attacks. There was thus less time for making an attack on a bomber, meaning more attacks by individual fighters would likely be needed, and the dangers inherent in all such attacks would be orders greater than when only a single bomber is being assaulted. This is the real explanation for over-claiming against German bomber formations, as each of several necessary attacking fighters might well claim the lethal damage for himself that is really the result of a communal and cumulative effort. In most cases, a brave pilot getting in close to fire on a bomber in an escorted formation would probably often be able to put out one engine and inflict other damage on aircraft systems (e.g., hydraulics in He 111s particularly) and often wound crewmen as well, but this would usually not suffice to bring the bomber down.

Attacking massed bombers from astern would generally be the most dangerous method as this favoured maximum combined defensive fire, and the closing speed of the fighter would be affected by the forward speed of the target; escort fighters could easily inflict serious casualties on attacking RAF fighters whose attention was fixed on their targets. This common, yet poor tactical situation, arose at least partly from the so-called Fighter Area Attacks, which mostly entailed attacks from rear and rear-quarter, prescribed by the Air Ministry and assiduously practiced in peacetime. Beam attacks, implying full deflection, or lesser deflection very often in reality were harder to achieve, but meant much less effective defensive fire, made things harder for escort fighters to react, and avoided much of the armour protection carried by the bombers and installed for attacks from astern; if the fighter missed a target he would almost certainly hit another as the formation streamed past his firing aircraft at approximately right angles, or an acute angle. While the installation of side-facing machine guns did lower the effectiveness of this attack method, these ad hoc gun positions were never very efficient.

Best of all, in terms of effects on German bomber formations would be a head-on attack; also difficult to perform as the squadron leader had to place his aircraft in the right spot ahead of the German formation. Fire from ahead was often lethal in the unprotected glassed-in cabins of the bombers, defensive fire was negligible and forward-facing armour protection generally lacking in the German target aircraft. Approach speeds during a head-on attack were very high, firing interval was concomitantly short, and a breakaway above or below (better) was necessary before collisions occurred. Most effective, especially in breaking up and terrifying German bomber formations, was if the attacking fighters kept going right through the rapidly approaching bomber formation, but obviously this brought an increased risk of collision. In time, beam and head-on attacks would become much more commonplace as Fighter Command's expertise and experience grew, and on 15 September 1940 they reached an acme, coincident with the serious defeat of the *Luftwaffe*, which triggered cancellation of the invasion by Hitler two days later.

The first beam attack on a lone bomber in early July, was performed by three Spitfires of 602 Squadron on the first day of the month already, and two days later a 54 Squadron trio led by F/Lt 'Wonky' Way showed a new initiative when launching simultaneous astern and beam attacks on a bomber.[6] Thereafter combinations of astern, quarter and beam attacks on lone bombers became much more common.[7] However, coordinating a simultaneous delivery of such attacks as 54 Squadron had achieved was not repeated very often, with the different attack methods much more often following one upon the other as incoming fighters in line astern each took up the attack in succession. 602 Squadron achieved another first, on 7 July, when they made beam and head-on attacks on a bomber.[8] Many highly innovative tactics thus emerged right at the beginning of the Battle already, quite often more by chance than planning, but vital lessons were thus learned, and in time these tactics could and indeed would be more broadly applied at flight and squadron level by able squadron leaders.

The first proper raid employing an escorted bomber formation to attack a British target and which was opposed by RAF fighters, took place on 4 July 1940. The target was a small shipping convoy of about nine vessels passing through the Straits of Dover in an approximately north to north-eastwards direction.[9] The raiding force was made up of eighteen Do 17s from all three *Staffeln* of II/KG 2, flying in vic formations line astern, with an escort of two Me 109 *Gruppen*, II/JG 51 and I/LG 2; the bombers were at *c.* 6,500 ft and the weather was cloudy, which hindered accurate bombing and also led to difficulty in maintaining their formations.[10] The raid was intercepted by eight Hurricanes of 79 Squadron from Hawkinge at about 14h30.[11] Despite the presence of a large Me 109 escort, some of the Hurricanes were able to get to the bombers, at least three being seen by II/KG 2 crewmen to dive down at them, and two of the bombers were damaged and in each the observer and the radio operator were wounded.[12] The one Dornier at least was well shot up, with over 100 bullet holes in it and the starboard engine was put out of action.[13] The two crewman positions where casualties were inflicted in each bomber and the loss of the starboard engine in the one, suggest an attack from above on the starboard quarter or beam. German claims encompassed two Hurricanes at *c.* 14h45 by 5/JG 51, and another by I/LG 2 a few minutes earlier.[14] These were clearly somewhat over-optimistic when balanced against the single Hurricane shot down and a few bullet holes in another (see below). A second claim by I/LG 2 was rejected at unit level already.[15]

Soon after, the Me 109s of *II/JG 51* came down, and Sgt Harry Cartwright DFM, an experienced pilot from flying over France recently, friend and wingman of P/O Donald Stones, was shot down and killed over St Margaret's Bay.[16] Stones had also managed a brief attack on the bombers and then fought one of the Me 109s at low level above the Dover RDF station, being hit by a few bullets.[17] As no one amongst the 79 Squadron survivors made any claims, the two damaged Do 17s can logically be credited to Sgt Cartwright.[18] His demise at the hands of the fighter escort was probably due to his keeping up the attack on the bombers long enough to damage two of them significantly, at his own peril and indeed, at the cost of his life; being an experienced and successful pilot he must have known the risks implicit in attacking an escorted bomber formation.

This very first escorted bombing raid in the Battle already raised one of the inherently insoluble problems in the Battle of Britain, for both sides. If the German fighters were too close to the bombers, they became vulnerable themselves due to reduced speed and also rather ineffective for the same reason. Thus, the German fighters tended to place themselves several thousand feet above the bombers and generally behind and could therefore retain fighting speed through weaving and moving around above their charges. Their RAF opponents knew that the gap between escort and bombers provided an opportunity to make an attack on the bombers, but at great risk to themselves as the German escort would inevitably descend on them with height and speed advantage while they were aiming at their targets. Timing in such situations became critical and was a very important aspect of tactical leadership for both sides, but particularly for the RAF fighters. Their leader could use a few of his limited number of fighters to take on and distract the escort, a dangerous and thankless task but if carried out with determination and aggression, they often survived; alternatively, the leader could opt for a fast, single attack on the bombers followed by a dive beneath them or to either side to get out of danger. All of this, of course, neglected the dangers from the bomber's own gunners, no insignificant factor, especially if the bomber formations were well trained in coordinating fire in a formation.

Later in August 1940, due to continuing complaints from the bomber crews, Göring would insist on a close escort of fighters flying right next to them, or even in some cases, using Me 110s mostly, flying amongst the bombers. Neither side would ever nullify the inherent dangers they faced from the various permutations of this conundrum. However, each individual pilot in the lonely and cramped confines of his cockpit made his own decisions and choices in finality; Harry Cartwright was the first RAF fighter pilot in the Battle of Britain to face this situation, and he made his decision, which damaged two bombers and wounded four crewmen, thereby reducing both aircraft and men available to *II/KG 2*, and he died doing it. While available documents provide no answer, S/L John Joslin, recently appointed to command 79 Squadron, probably led his unit; the leader had done his job well in this first case, as a brief attack was carried out on the bombers despite a large and well-placed escort.

That evening, 4 July, F/O Desmond McMullen led a section of 54 Squadron Spitfires flying from Rochford in very cloudy weather on a patrol over the Deal-Dover area at 18h38-19h45; they had lost their number 2 member in the murk when the remaining two aircraft were bounced very briefly from slightly above and astern by unidentified aircraft and slightly damaged.[19] Soon after, McMullen had a snap shot in cloud at an enemy twin-engined, twin-tailed aircraft, presumably either a Dornier or Me 110.[20] Nine Hurricanes of 32 Squadron were also up on patrol at the same time, flying in three vics over Dungeness, when they lost formation in cloud and emerged on the other side in some disarray to observe six Me 109s some 2,000 ft above them, who dived down. A dogfight ensued.[21] One section in particular became involved in the combat; P/O Grice being hit in the rudder, port aileron and having his engine seize on him, managed to force-land wheels-up near Manston at Pegwell Bay, while P/O Gillman's Hurricane was hit in the glycol tank but he got it down at nearby Hawkinge airfield.[22] Both Hurricanes, although seriously damaged, were repairable and both pilots unhurt.[23] The third member of the section, P/O Smythe, claimed hits on the Me 109 responsible for downing Grice, seeing glycol pouring out but lost sight of it in the melee as it dived away; he then turned on another Messerschmitt attacking him and shot it down into the sea off Pegwell Bay, killing *Uffz.* Schiller of *2/LG 2*.[24] *I/LG 2* flew a free chase quite far inland that evening, claiming to have reached the outskirts of London, and *2 Staffel's Leutnant* Geisshardt claimed one of the Hurricanes shot down, while Schiller's Me 109 is recorded as having fallen near Hawkinge at *c.* 18h55.[25] Seeing as no other German claim was made for the second Hurricane of 32 Squadron shot down, this may have fallen to Schiller.

5 July 1940, apart from a couple of successful actions against lone bombers, saw a rather unusual encounter in the evening between a pitifully small formation of three Spitfires of 64 Squadron and what was apparently a full *Gruppe* of Me 109s, presumably *II/JG 51*, although elements of *2/JG 51* may also have been involved.[26] Official records record that the mission was an operational patrol off Rouen, but this particular city lies some 50 km inland from the French coast, and that piece of coast is over 100 km across the Channel from the southern English coast.[27] In a vivid account of this action provided by Sub Lt Frank Dawson-Paul, a stalwart and very able fighter pilot from 64 Squadron, he records pursuing a Me 109 over the French coast and right over the town of Calais.[28] This location would make more sense. In

the event, Dawson-Paul records their being vectored over the Channel to intercept a reported fifty-plus enemy aircraft, which they duly spotted and identified as about thirty-six Me 109s flying at *c.* 24,000 ft; the three lonely Spitfires, some 4,000 ft lower, duly and very bravely climbed after them and saw the enemy eventually form a circle at *c.* 32,000 ft.[29] These are very strange tactics for an entire *Gruppe* of Me 109s with height advantage and in greater numbers to pursue.

Dawson-Paul, despite having poor control at that altitude, which favoured the Me 109 entirely, drew away from his two comrades and flew around the centre of their circle against their circling direction, but when he opened fire on one of them, the recoil caused his Spitfire to flick into a stall from which he recovered some 2,000 ft lower down.[30] Still somewhat disoriented, he was bounced by one of the Me 109s who damaged his Spitfire and then carried on diving; Dawson-Paul finally caught up with him over Calais, and as he levelled off and fired, he saw a large piece come off from the rear of the Me 109 but was then thrown into a somersault by German flak exploding very close by, and beat a hurried retreat.[31]

Two German pilots from *4/JG 51* had made claims for Spitfires, *Leutnant* Hohagen making one north of Hythe and *Ofw* Illner a second west of Le Touquet at *c.* 20h52.[32] P/O Milne from the 64 Squadron section was shot down and posted missing, supposedly near Rouen, but probably in the Channel nearer the scene of action described above, and Dawson-Paul's Spitfire was damaged by an Me 109 and/or flak, presumably somewhere between Calais and the British southeast coast; he managed to land safely at Hawkinge.[33] While a Me 109 of *2/JG 51* damaged 30% in a crash-landing has been interpreted as having been damaged by Dawson-Paul in this engagement, this is unlikely; up until 12 July 1940, *I/JG 51* was still based in Holland, at Leeuwarden, before its move to the Pas de Calais on 12 July.[34] There are thus no known *Luftwaffe* losses to associate with this action. What is unexplained about this entire action is why the controllers would have sent a mere section of three Spitfires across the Channel to intercept a raid identified as more than fifty enemy aircraft, and which turned out to be an entire fighter *Gruppe*; this was essentially a potential suicide mission.

On 7 July 1940, with a convoy proceeding up the Channel from south of the Isle of Wight at about midday, reaching the Dover Straits by *c.* 21h30 in the evening, Kesselring kept his *Luftflotte* 2 Me 109s flying over the southern Kent and French coasts most of the day, preparatory to the main raid on this convoy in the Dover straits.[35] These German sweeps and fighter enticements were countered by Air Vice-Marshal Park keeping a guard over his coastline with orders to avoid fighter combat if possible.[36] Three Spitfires of 54 Squadron were scrambled from their forward base of Manston at about 13h00 and intercepted a lone He 111 of *4/KG 4*, which they damaged slightly and wounded a crewman.[37] However, one of Kesselring's watching *Staffeln*, 7/*JG 51*, was close enough at hand to bounce the 54 Squadron section and damage all three Spitfires; while F/O McMullen, the section leader managed to put his damaged aircraft down at Manston, P/O's Coleman and Campbell had to force-land their Spitfires near Deal, writing them both off, and all three pilots were slightly wounded.[38]

7/*JG51* made four claims in all, 3 to 4 miles south of Dover between 13h05 and 13h10; presumably two of them reflected a double claim on a single aircraft as all four were confirmed by the German adjudication system.[39] In contrast, F/Lt Alan Deere, in his autobiography, describes this action as having begun with the 54 Squadron section tackling a group of Me 110s which crossed the south coast near Dungeness and then being jumped by the Me 109s as they were about to attack the twin-engined fighters.[40] Either way, whether the bait was a lone Heinkel or a formation of Me 110s dangled enticingly over Dungeness, this ambush by a *Staffel* from *JG 51* probably owed much to the philosophy of the current *Kommodore*, Theo Osterkamp. This was, very simply, to conjure up any stratagem whereby the RAF fighters could be manoeuvred into a tactically vulnerable situation and then attacked by surprise from above, skewing losses heavily against the British.[41] He felt that a 5:1 loss ratio was essential for the Me 109s to prevail.[42]

A fairly large German attack on a convoy off Folkestone in the late evening of 7 July by forty-five Do 17s drawn from *II* and *III/KG 2* and escorted by *II/JG 51* led to something of a fiasco in the RAF reaction.[43] Although radar had given adequate warning, the British reaction was rather slow; a three-Hurricane convoy patrol from 79 Squadron was late, as was a flight of six Spitfires from 64 Squadron and another six from 65 Squadron.[44] The Dorniers arrived in several formations, flying at about 8,000 ft with *II/JG 51* at about 12,000 ft; B Flight of 65 Squadron approached the coast between Dover and Folkestone at 12,000 ft.[45] Their rear section, Green led by F/O Proudman, let the leader F/Lt Gerald Saunders know that they had seen enemy aircraft through the clouds below and Saunders ordered them to lead the way, and his Blue Section then followed them down. On emerging from a cloud layer, Saunders and his three Spitfires found themselves alone between two cloud layers – Green Section had vanished and were not seen again.[46] In the same moment, between five and nine Me 109s dived onto their tails and the three Spitfires broke up and fought several combats over a wide area; Saunders and F/Sgt Franklin each claimed Me 109s off Calais, and the latter observed some Me 109s escorting bombers back across the Channel and attacked the escort, supposedly shooting down another Me 109 *c.* 10 miles off the English coast.[47]

II/JG 51 claimed five Spitfires shot down, all confirmed, in the Hastings-Dungeness-Folkestone-Dover area between 20h20 and 20h55 and must be assumed to have shot down all three Spitfires of Green Section, 65 Squadron.[48] Three Hurricanes of 79 Squadron led by S/L Joslin, directed to carry out a convoy patrol off Folkestone, were suddenly bounced from the rear and their leader shot down in flames. When the two wingmen, P/Os Stones and Parker, turned to meet their attackers, they saw that they were Spitfires and noted their markings, which turned out to be those of 65 Squadron.[49] John Joslin had been shot in the head and fell from his diving machine before it crashed just west of Dover, and landed some 250 yards away from it.[50] The three machines of Green Section, 65 Squadron, went missing off Folkestone,[51] but whether they or Blue Section had shot down Joslin by mistake remains unknown. A section of 54 Squadron near Dungeness clearly saw Spitfires and Hurricanes chasing each other in and out of the clouds at about 5,000 ft, while another section of the squadron saw some aircraft in the distance in the same general area and sent one Spitfire to investigate, which had a brief and inconclusive engagement with a Me 109 and was also briefly fired upon by a Hurricane.[52] The cloudy weather and many small British formations in a small area obviously led to some deadly confusion, never mind the actions of the Me 109s. The *Luftwaffe* claims data indicates that the combat between Proudman's Green Section and 5 and 6/JG 51 took place over quite a wide area.[53] The three claims for Me 109s shot down into the Channel by Saunders and Franklin of Blue Section, 65 Squadron, were not supported by any loss or even damaged Me 109s recorded on the *Luftwaffe* side.[54]

With both 79 and 64 Squadrons' aircraft having been at *c*. 8,000 ft, those of 65 Squadron were at about 12,000 ft,[55] so the controllers had got the interception largely right, despite its late timing; what went wrong, apart from it being late? The cloudy weather certainly played a role in 65 Squadron being badly bounced, and S/L Joslin of 79 Squadron was a victim of friendly fire. A limited success was achieved by the seven Spitfires from 64 Squadron, also vectored onto this raid and who managed to catch some of the retreating Dorniers near the French coast, where they claimed two shot down: one each by Sub Lt Dawson-Paul and F/O Jeffrey, mistakenly identifying them as Me 110s. Both force-landed damaged at nearby airfields, where Dawson-Paul's victim was written off and carried a wounded crew member.[56] As the two Do 17s were from two different *Gruppen*, it is likely that they were stragglers from the returning bomber formations. Overall, despite good positioning by the controllers of the intercepting RAF formations, little was achieved in terms of a solid attack on the bomber formation; Fighter Command's learning curve was steep.

A large convoy passed through the Straits of Dover soon after midday on 8 July 1940, and radar stations picked up enhanced aerial activity over the Pas de Calais from about 12h30 onwards; Blue Section 610 Squadron led by F/Lt Bill Warner took up station over the convoy at about 14h00 and soon after intercepted a *Staffel* of Dorniers 6 miles off Dover.[57] Sgt

Else claimed damage to one bomber and silenced its rear gunner, but their combined cross-fire shot P/O Raven down in flames; he survived ditching but unfortunately drowned. However, the attack led to the Do 17s dropping their bombs wide of the ships.[58] The three Spitfires thus succeeded in their objective of avoiding damage to the convoy. This small action had provided the first opportunity for RAF Fighter Command to attack an unescorted enemy bomber formation; faced for the first time with the reality of an oft-theorised situation, the 610 Squadron section may have first considered and possibly tried to apply the so-called Fighter Area Attacks so beloved by the pre-war higher echelons of the RAF. These were formalised, numbered attack methods, based on vic-formation sections of three aircraft, flights of six and squadrons of twelve machines, and were drummed into the pilots to the exclusion of any other tactical wisdom, including that forgotten already from the First World War where the vast majority of those in higher command had cut their fighting teeth.[59]

Red and Green Sections of 610 Squadron took off just before 15h00 and were told to patrol Tenterden, then sent to Dungeness and finally given a vector of 50° from there, which took them to about 5 miles south of Hythe where the convoy then was.[60] They were thus dispatched as reinforcements to the convoy escort. It was good controlling as they intercepted seven Do 17s from *III/KG 2* and an escort of twelve Me 109s from *I/LG 2* at *c.* 15h45; the bombers were at about 6,000 ft.[61] Red Section carried out a number 3 Fighter Area Attack, i.e. from the rear, with section in line abreast, on the leading section of four Do 17s, while Green Section did a number 1 attack, from below and behind, on the slightly higher-flying rear three Do 17s.[62] Basically, the two sections of 610 Squadron came at the bombers more or less straight from behind, Red Section directly at the leading section of four Do 17s while Green Section, behind them, pulled up to fire at the rear section of three Dorniers.[63] The Me 109 escort did not stop these attacks and one was claimed by P/O Pegge who saw it diving away, shovelling out black smoke;[64] this often signalled a Messerschmitt using full boost to get away but *7/JG 51* did suffer a 12% damaged Me 109 which force-landed in France with a wounded pilot.[65] *I/LG 2* saw no British fighters,[66] and may thus have been a high escort or top cover for *JG 51* closer escorts. P/O Pegge observed one Dornier with a smoking engine and several of the 610 Squadron pilots saw their rounds hitting the bombers but with no visible effect.[67]

Their attack showed two things: it was possible to get at escorted bombers if a fast approach was made and the escort was initially too far away; secondly, the lack of success of those who fired and saw their bullets hit home perhaps reflected the rigidity of the 'Fighter Area' methodology and probably also indicated too great a range. After all, the numbered attacks went along with a recommended standard range of *c.* 400 yards (favoured originally by Dowding, who later changed his mind), which harmonisation distance was applied early in the war until the reality of combat experience showed it to be too far, Colin Gray of 54 Squadron and Sailor Malan in 74 Squadron, both flying out of Hornchurch Sector Station, took the lead as early as July in reducing it to *c.* 250 yards.[68]

At about the same time as 610 Squadron was fighting the Dorniers, nine Hurricanes of 79 Squadron were bounced by free-chasing Me 109s off Dover.[69] This was typical of the tactics favoured by *Luftflotte 2* commander Field Marshal Albert Kesselring, who kept a set of airborne threats, both bombers and fighters, airborne over and off the Pas de Calais and Straits of Dover through much of the day. From these, free-chasing Me 109s, Ju 87s and small Do 17 formations could launch raids against British coastal targets, covered by direct escorts and a complex plethora of single-engine fighter formations, which became a *Luftwaffe* feature over the Straits.[70] Initially, P/O Donald Stones led a section of Hurricanes of 79 Squadron up from Hawkinge, but some five minutes later reinforcements of two more sections were sent up to join him and he ended up leading the entire formation.[71] After about an hour on patrol without meeting any enemy aircraft, the Squadron was ordered to land and refuel, and as they turned back to Hawkinge, were hit in a perfect bounce by *7/JG 51*, which picked off the two rearmost Hurricanes while the others did not even notice their dispatch.[72] The Me 109s had come down through a cloud layer above the Squadron, lying at about 8,000 ft; both Hurricanes went down in flames. P/O Wood managed to bail out into the Channel but died of his terrible burns before anyone could get to him, and F/O 'Tubby' Mitchell force-landed in a field near Dover but was trapped in his machine unable to open the hood and died in the flaming wreck.[73]

Revenge was exacted by Red Section of 74 Squadron, led by Sgt Mould and sent to patrol between Manston and Deal. They were able to surprise a *Schwarm* of four Messerschmitts from below and pursued them to low level over the hills and valleys inland from Dover-Folkestone.[74] One was shot down by Sgt Mould and force-landed near Elham, the first Me 109 to crash on British soil, and its pilot *Lt* Böhm of *4/JG 51* was taken prisoner; the other was chased out to sea trailing white smoke, presumably glycol, as witnessed by a pilot of 32 Squadron some minutes later.[75] This one made it back to France lightly damaged.[76] Three Hurricanes of 32 Squadron had been dispatched just after 15h00 to reinforce the convoy's protection; one had engine trouble and had to land while another Squadron aircraft appears to have joined the remaining two.[77] As their patrol ended at *c.* 16h00, nearing Hawkinge to land they engaged small formations of Me 109s that lightly damaged the aircraft of P/O Grice, while P/O Smythe was attacked by six *9/JG 51* Me 109s and his engine died after the first burst of the leader of the second trio; this German pilot then sat behind his helpless machine but did not fire.[78]

Thought to have been *Oblt* Arnold Lignitz, he was either a chivalrous enemy or had no more ammunition.[79] Smythe managed to stretch his glide to Hawkinge aerodrome but crash-landed, writing off his aircraft.[80]

Nine Spitfires of 65 Squadron were sent in to the Dover area as reinforcements by the controllers, S/L Desmond Cooke leading as Blue 1, closely followed by his successor, S/L Sawyer flying in the Blue 2 section spot.[81] They intercepted small formations of disorganised *JG 51* Me 109s at *c.* 16h00 and S/L Cooke followed some into a large cumulus cloud; S/L Sawyer narrowly avoided being shot down by four others.[82] F/Sgt Franklin actually saw Blue 1 being stalked by a Me 109 below him, attacked it and claimed it shot down in the sea, probably that lost by *7/JG 51* 8 miles out over the Channel, *Uffz* Schneiderberger killed. S/L Cooke, due to hand over command that very day to Sawyer, was not seen again.[83] The British fighter lost in this final set of actions related to the convoy fell to *Oblt* Fözö from *4/JG 51*.[84]

In the evening, 54 Squadron dispatched two Me 109s over south-east Kent, one each from *III/JG 51* and *I/LG 2*.[85] F/Lt Way led three sections of 54 Squadron, and climbed his Blue Section, in the lead, up to two unsuspecting Me 109s, firing at each in turn himself from 200 and 250 yards respectively; the first gave off glycol from a damaged radiator and the second dived down and *Lt* Striberny of *I/LG 2* bailed out unhurt about 5 miles north-west of Deal where he was taken prisoner, the machine crashing at Sandwich.[86] Striberny's *3/LG 2* could only raise five machines for this mission, which was apparently to escort a small Do 17 formation, possibly from *KG 2*.[87] The limited numbers available to *I/LG 2* may explain why they were operating closely together with aircraft from *III/JG 51*. Another pilot from 54 Squadron, P/O Garton, soon after saw a Me 109 making for France, then turn back over the Channel and make for some cloud cover over the English coast between Deal and Dover; he gave it two very short bursts before it vanished in the clouds, subsequently crashing near Hawkinge killing the pilot.[88] The fact that it had turned back for England in mid-Channel suggests it was already damaged, probably by F/Lt Way, and in that state a couple of short bursts by Garton were enough to finish it off.

The marauding Me 109s were no longer having things all their own way, as the RAF fighter pilots rapidly adapted to their methods of surprise attacks from above, especially dangerous in cloudy weather such as had characterised 8 July. What is interesting in the British fighter squadron documents from this day is that the Me 109s seemed to have flown in threes as much as in pairs. Soon enough, Fighter Command and 11 Group would strive to limit such fighter versus fighter combat over the sea in the Pas de Calais-Dover area, to concentrate on bomber formations and preserve precious fighter aircraft and pilots. With their higher numbers and predilection for fighter bounce tactics, these combats had distinctly favoured *Fliegerkorps 2* led by the wily Kesselring, advised by that experienced World War 1 ace and tactician, *Oberst* Theo Osterkamp.

On 9 July 1940 the first encounters with formations of Me 110s in the Battle occurred, adding another dimension to the bombers and Me 109s met thus far. Excluding encounters with lone bombers performing reconnaissance or single aircraft bombing missions, the first action began around the southern part of the Isle of Wight. Red Section of 43 Squadron was scrambled from Tangmere at 11h42, led by S/L George Lott; they were directed by the controller to proceed to St Catherine's Point on the southern tip of the island, there to intercept six aircraft proceeding westwards at about 5,000 ft.[89] It was excellent controlling as once there they saw six Me 110s and got close to them approaching from behind before they were seen; the Messerschmitts promptly turned round to meet them head-on.[90] Led courageously by Lott, the three Hurricanes, though faced with the fearsome nose-mounted armament of the Me 110s, kept on, jinking as they went.[91] S/L Lott suffered a direct hit on his front armoured windscreen from one of the Me 110s, which sent splinters into his right eye, blinding it, but he managed to dive away and bailed out from only 700 ft once over land, near Southampton.[92]

His two wingmen went for the Me 110s, Red 2 following one into cloud where he lost it; Red 3, P/O Carey hit another Me 110, putting its port engine out of action but got no chance to finish it off as the others broke up and three attacked him.[93] He made a claim for one damaged Me 110 and broke off from the three fleeing Me 110s, who were faster than his Hurricane. This first encounter with a small formation of Me 110s by RAF fighters over English waters on 9 July shows the *Zerstörer* to have been rather more effective than they are often portrayed; at the cost of a single lightly damaged Me 110 they had dispatched a much nimbler Hurricane and ensured its pilot, an experienced squadron leader, was out of the Battle and indeed future combat. Facing the Me 110's fearsome front armament was something to be avoided if possible, especially in view of the greatly superior manoeuvrability of the RAF's fighters, which made such attacks unnecessary.

While various sources have related 43 Squadron's action to *III/ZG 26*, the location of the fight was rather too far west logically to have involved this *Geschwader*.[94] It is more likely to have been *V/LG 1*, which was closest to the area of action, being based at Caen and often flying from airfields in the Cherbourg area.[95] Indeed, this *Gruppe* is known to have flown two missions escorting Ju 87s, apparently into the Plymouth area where one small steamer was sunk and another damaged.[96] One of these missions was definitely in the evening, with one Me 110 lost, for which details of the operation are available.[97] This fight with 43 Squadron may thus have been related to its earlier mission. Quite often, German aircraft that were damaged in combat where such damage could be relatively easily repaired were not reported in the German loss documentation; minor damage to a *V/LG 1* Me 110 can thus be inferred for 43 Squadron's P/O Carey.

Just to complicate matters further, the Luftwaffe losses documentation[98] includes an error, showing three Me 110s of *III/ZG 26* as having been lost on 9 July 1940, and another damaged, and this is logically also then given in many books published on the Battle. In actual fact, only one of those Me 110s was lost on 9 July, but in a later action than that with 43 Squadron, plus the damaged one presumably hit in the same later action, which occurred over the Thames Estuary; the other two actually were shot down on 10 July, along with another lost and one more slightly damaged on that same day.[99] The crew of the Me 110 lost on 9 July was soon fished out of the Channel by a He 59 floatplane of the efficient German air-sea rescue service; they were lucky that the Channel waves allowed a landing to be made.[100] RAF rescue services were much thinner on the ground, and based on limited numbers of fast launches and local lifeboat resources, augmented by fishermen and other vessels who happened to see an aircraft coming down into the water.

Meanwhile, towards the east, a large northbound convoy was assembling in the Thames Estuary in the later part of the morning of 9 July 1940 and had been observed by German reconnaissance aircraft, resulting in the British radar system detecting a build-up well behind the Pas de Calais area.[101] A Flight of 151 Squadron from North Weald with their intrepid station commander, Wing Commander Victor Beamish flying on the wing of the leader, F/Lt Hugh Ironside, lifted off at 13h36 and climbed hard through scattered clouds.[102] Soon enough and after only a couple of controller instructions they were faced with the first fully fledged raid of the Battle, seeing about 40 bombers, He 111s and Ju 88s with about 60 Me 110 and 109 escorts behind and above, the whole formation stepped up from *c.* 12,000-20,000 ft.[103]

The bombers were actually Do 17s from *III/KG 2*, and *I/LG 2* may have been part of the escort, although mission times given do not match for the latter.[104] Ironside appeared unfazed by all this, and split his pitifully small force into its two sections of three, one diving for the bombers and the other turning for the massive escort, at *c.* 13h45-14h00; however, the German escort was there promptly and none of 151 Squadron managed to get at the bombers and all ended up fighting the large escort.[105] Documentation on this encounter is thin but F/Lt Ironside's logbook pages for 9 July are on the web, and therein he briefly describes meeting about 100 enemy aircraft over the convoy and attacking the Me 110s and Me 109s at *c.* 10,000 ft. At first his guns would not fire but later in the action he claimed a Me 109 at about 17,000 ft after seeing its petrol tank apparently blow up.[106] He also observed that P/O Hamar and F/O Forster shot up two of the Me 110s, but that their destruction was not certain.[107]

From *Luftwaffe* casualty documentation, one Me 110 of *III/ZG 26* was lost along with its crew, which is credited to Beamish, Forster and Hamar, while another suffered 50% damage, presumably from one or two 151 Squadron pilots.[108] The gunner on the latter aircraft may have panicked, apparently bailing out over the sea on the return flight, being posted as missing.[109] Two Me 109s were claimed by F/O Milne and Midshipman Wightman of 151 Squadron, but no Me 109 losses related to this fight can be traced in *Luftwaffe* loss records, and Wightman was himself shot down in the sea but rescued unhurt by a trawler.[110] F/Lt Ironside's Hurricane suffered a cannon shell strike which shattered his cockpit, wounding him in the face and sending glass splinters flying into one eye, but he made it home, his machine only lightly damaged.[111]

151 Squadron's attack, with only six aircraft against maybe a hundred enemies, nevertheless had the desired effect, the bombers splitting into six formations, only one even finding the convoy and no ships were hit directly, but two were damaged, presumably by near misses.[112] *III/KG 2*, in optimistic contrast, claimed three ships sunk, three damaged.[113] 151 Squadron were an intrepid and aggressive lot, as was their station commander, and a strong anti-German feeling ran through the unit as a result of a flight commander shot down at Dunkirk who made it on to a ship only to be sunk by an e-boat, which then proceeded to finish off most of the survivors in the water by machine gun fire, only 24 out of over 500 souls on board being saved.[114]

The same convoy was subjected to another large attack about two hours later, another massive stepped-up formation again being intercepted by a single unit, 65 Spitfire Squadron, whose tactics were rather different to those employed by 151 Squadron. How to attack a well-escorted bomber formation and to get to fire at the bombers before the escort could stop them would remain an ongoing problem for the RAF fighters. Once the Battle began in earnest in mid-August, it became common for the 11 Group commander AVM Park and his controllers to try and direct the higher performance Spitfires to higher altitude expressly to take on the German escorts and thereby allow the Hurricane squadrons to tackle the bombers under better conditions.[115] However such successful coordination of RAF squadrons under the intense fighting of August and September 1940 was not often perfectly achieved, and a critical factor in eventually winning the daylight battle would remain the necessity of attacking bomber formations despite their escorts, and in splitting small RAF squadron formations of about twelve fighters into two parts as attempted by 151 Squadron on 9 July. Generally, such attacks would almost automatically result in casualties, which would become serious as the method was perforce practised repeatedly as the days wore on. Such squadrons as were prepared to maintain such tactics aggressively were critical to the RAF winning what was in the end a contest of attrition. It was this set of circumstances which led to the emergence of alternative tactics such as the head-on attack, difficult to perform with very limited firing time at high closing speeds, or attacks from the beam, where deflection shooting skills were required. Beam attacks had the advantage of effectively bypassing rear-facing armour for bomber crews and engines. The German solution of mounting extra defensive machine guns on the sides of their bombers' cockpits was not very effective, especially for Ju 88s where rear defensive armament was placed within the upper cockpit perspex cover that formed the entire cockpit roof, and if the latter was lost in combat or jettisoned by a nervous gunner for a possible bail-out, then the guns went with it.

Seven Spitfires of 65 Squadron lifted off just after half past three that afternoon and were vectored onto the raid off North Foreland.[116] Meanwhile, nine Hurricanes of 79 Squadron were harrying a *Staffel* of Me 109s off Dover at *c.* 15h35-15h40, which were probably part of a sweep in advance of the raid itself.[117] Although 79 Squadron claimed one destroyed, one probably so and a damaged Me 109, none can be identified in German loss records.[118] Interestingly, P/O Stones pursued his Me 109, claimed as damaged, emitting black smoke, to the French coast, and turned away just before the coast itself was crossed.[119] 79 Squadron had been patrolling Hawkinge at 15,000 ft when they spotted the *Staffel* of Me 109s about 10 miles out to sea.[120] Midshipman Birrell similarly chased his Me 109, claimed as a probable to the enemy coast, having seen pieces come off under his attack; he had first engaged east of Dover, as did P/O Millington who was convinced his victim had been destroyed over the Channel.[121] Interestingly, Millington also recorded that his Rotol-propellor Hurricane using full boost easily overtook the Me 109. Fighter Command was already learning how to adopt the *Luftwaffe's* fighter tactics, and the Me 109s in this case seem to have fled in some disorder for home with aggressive opponents chasing them right back to their own side of the Straits of Dover.

65 Squadron, with only seven Spitfires, flew a formation of pairs and a vic, with two aircraft of Blue Section leading followed by Red Section of three, and at the rear, two aircraft of Yellow Section.[122] In the North Foreland area shortly before about 16h00 at 10,000 ft they sighted the organised convoy raid of about seventy enemy aircraft flying towards the Thames Estuary at heights from 8,000-14,000 ft; the stepped-up formation was comprised of v-shaped vics of five, seven and nine machines, three vics broad and in line astern.[123] The *KG 2* Dornier *Gruppe* flying at the base of the formation was protected by a good-sized escort of Me 110s and Me 109s, flying above and to the sides of the bombers.[124] F/Lt Gerald Saunders led his seven pilots in a climb for position to 16,000 ft and, finding himself slightly above some Me 109s of the escort, attacked. His pilots became involved with several small groups of the Me 109s, flying in pairs and vics of three, and claimed two

shot down confirmed and three probables; one pilot attacked a Me 110 about 5,000 ft lower down.[125]

In return, *Stab I/LG 2* claimed one Spitfire over the mouth of the Thames Estuary at 16h04, while *5/JG 51* claimed two at 15h55-16h00, north-east of Margate.[126] *I/LG 2* claimed two Hurricanes at *c.* 15h30, but neither appears to have been accredited; they may also have related to the earlier action with 151 Squadron, specifically the shooting down of Wightman of 151 Squadron discussed earlier.[127] Only one Spitfire was actually hit, by a single cannon shell in the wing and was only temporarily unserviceable, so German claims were exaggerated.[128] Analogously, 65 Squadron's claims against Me 109s, two confirmed, three probables, have to be balanced against a single Messerschmitt and pilot of *5/JG 51* lost 5 miles north-east of Ramsgate at *c.* 16h00.[129] While these fighter-versus-fighter combats were going on, the bombers, estimated by ground observers to be seventy-five in number, serenely unloaded their bombs, inaccurately, on a lone, small ship sailing for the river mouth.[130] Interestingly, the Spitfires of 65 Squadron were carrying excess ammunition, one pilot firing 2,468 rounds.[131]

The scene shifted in the evening of 9 July to the west, with a raid mounted by twenty-seven Ju 87s of *I/StG 77* on a convoy off Portland.[132] Initial radar data supplied to the controller suggested only a three-plus enemy aircraft raid, although this was later updated to an additional formation of six-plus enemy machines and that information was passed on by the controller to the single section of Spitfires of 609 Squadron aloft and on their way; the three RAF pilots were thus expecting only a small formation and had been informed it was at the cloud base.[133] The section, led by F/O Peter Drummond-Hay, was thus not expecting an escort and the interception was actually made just above the clouds, about 15 miles south-east of Portland Bill.[134] The second message was not received by the 609 Squadron section,[135] possibly due to the distance from Middle Wallop sector station and the cloudy weather upsetting radio reception. P/O David Crook was the first to spot an enemy aircraft, a Ju 87, and as he notified the section leader, the latter went for this straightaway; Crook also saw about nine Me 110s *c.* 3,000 ft higher than the bombers and observed that they were coming down.[136] Despite repeated attempts to warn the section leader who was unaware of this development and concentrating on the Ju 87s, there was no reaction from either Green 1 or 2, and F/O Drummond-Hay was last seen some distance away to the south isolated by some of the escort; he did not return.[137] Green 2 tried to help but was kept away by the Me 110s; P/O Appleby had followed his leader, attacking the second Ju 87 in a vic of three but was himself set upon by three of the Me 110s from approximately the beam or quarter.[138] He reported that their fire was accurate but used too little deflection, and he was thus able to out-climb them and drop on their tails from the clouds; he fired over the nose of one of the Me 110s and it flew into his fire, and later attacked a Ju 87, claimed as a probable, and fired short snap bursts at other enemy machines with no visible results.[139]

Meanwhile, Green 3, P/O Crook had cannily waited until the attacking Me 110s got to about 600 m range behind him and had opened fire, before violently diving into cloud to avoid them.[140] Flying in and out of the cloud, he fired at a Ju 87, claimed damaged, and a Me 110, then destroyed another Stuka, having followed the Ju 87 down to sea level and seen it hit the sea.[141] It is likely that he was responsible for the one Ju 87 lost, that of the *Gruppenkommandeur Hauptmann* Freiherr von Dalwigk, he and his gunner both missing.[142] The Me 110 *Staffel* escorting the Ju 87s, *13/LG 1* was led by *Oberleutnant* Glienke and on the way back over the Channel the engines of his aircraft were seen to lose power and it lost height before ditching; the crew were fortunate to be rescued by the *Luftwaffe*.[143] Glienke had also made one of the two claims for Spitfires shot down by *V/LG 1* off Portland at about 19h30 at a height of *c.* 800 m.[144] *I/JG 2* also claimed two Spitfires, south of Portland at *c.* 19h30 though these were only apparently credited as probables.[145] The loss of Glienke's Me 110 can be ascribed to either P/O Appleby's fire as discussed above, or possibly to F/O Drummond-Hay's last and fatal combat with the twin-engined fighters, or even to both. The convoy attacked by the Stukas appears to have suffered damage to two steamers. [146]

At about the same time, one of several Me 109-escorted He 59 rescue seaplanes looking for downed *Luftwaffe* crewmen happened to be near a convoy off the east coast of Kent and was unfortunate enough to be sighted by a flight of 54 Squadron near the Goodwin Sands.[147] The latter had been sent to patrol south of Deal and were in search formation, Red Section at 9,000 ft and Yellow Section at 4,000 ft.[148] On sighting the He 59, escorted apparently by four Me 109s, F/Lt Deere directed Yellow Section to take the seaplane, he and his Red Section providing top cover; Yellow 1 and 2 attacked the He 59, forcing it down on the Goodwin Sands, while Yellow 3 got mixed up with the Me 109s. [149] This particular He 59 was searching for the *II/JG 51* pilot lost earlier, and had flown from Boulogne via Calais to the Ramsgate area.[150] F/Lt Deere, seeing the Me 109s interfering with Yellow Section, came down with Red 2 to help, while Red 3, Sgt Lawrence was left up at *c.* 9,000 ft as a final top cover; as Red 1 and 2 went down, another dozen Me 109s appeared, circling at low level and Red 2 and Yellow 3 fought them.[151] Alan Deere, Red 1, took on the original four escort Me 109s, and having shot down the rear Me 109 at relatively low level into the sea with two bursts, then climbed for height intending to attack the He 59 that he had seen land on the sea.[152] As he did so another Me 109 tried to get on his tail and they got into a dogfight, ending up charging at each other head-on; neither would yield and the Me 109 collided with Deere's Spitfire as it flashed just overhead, flattening two of his three propeller blades and pushing in the cockpit hood.[153] The Me 109 managed to get home with minor damage.[154] Deere had an amazing escape: his engine seized, then caught fire but he managed to put the Spitfire down in a field and as the flames took hold, broke his way through the damaged and jammed cockpit hood with his hands.[155] It would appear that Deere, in climbing to attack the force-landed He 59 floatplane, got mixed up with one of the twelve Me 109s which reinforced the original escort of four machines, and that these were also the ones involved with Red 2, 3 and Yellow 3.

The most interesting tactical initiative taken in this action by 54 Squadron flight leader Alan Deere was to have left Red 3 up higher as a top cover: Sgt Lawrence dived down and attacked one Me 109 seen on the tail of a Spitfire, seeing it plunge into the sea in flames, zoom-climbed back up and did the same to a second Messerschmitt, again behind a Spitfire; he claimed one Me 109 shot down and another as a probable.[156] Despite this, the Me 109s were too many and Red 2, P/O Evershed went missing and Yellow 3, P/O Garton was killed.[157] F/Lt Deere in the heat of his own actions had heard P/O Garton screaming for help, his Spitfire aflame and with four Me 109s on his tail, but could do nothing to assist.[158] Garton's aircraft crashed at Sandwich, Kent at 20h35.[159] *4/JG 51* claimed four victories, two confirmed, two awarded only as probables, as against 54 Squadron's three aircraft and two pilot losses.[160] Alan Deere had collided with the Me 109 flown by *Ofw* Johann Illner of *4/JG 51*, who was one of the pilots awarded only with a probable victory by the *Luftwaffe* system; presumably this reflects the fact that his own machine was not seriously damaged, 10% only, and got home.[161] *II/JG 51* lost one Me 109 and pilot in the sea off Dover against the two confirmed claims of 54 Squadron.[162]

The early fighting in July 1940 against the Me 109s was very hard and RAF fighter losses in combats mostly taking place over the sea were high. 54 Squadron was one of those hard-fighting units that took heavy losses in July, but as can be seen they were learning fast, and in August they fared much better against the German escort fighters as a result of their experience and adapted tactics, and with much of the fighting shifting to being over the land. Where previously Me 109 pilot losses over the sea had been tempered by the *Luftwaffe's* efficient airborne and seaborne rescue services, the much less efficient RAF service resulted in disproportionate pilot casualties in the unforgiving waters of the Channel and North Sea. The battle of attrition, at least for fighter-versus-fighter actions thus swung in favour of the RAF once the large and persistent inland raids of August began. In September, as inland penetrations grew in distance even more as London became the prime target, the German aircraft and their crews ended up even further behind in the attrition statistics.

2

10 July 1940: The Official Start of the Battle of Britain

10 July 1940, a day marked by a large raid on a west-bound convoy off Folkestone-Dungeness, and for the first time with an adequate number of RAF fighters being dispatched to oppose it, was chosen by Dowding as marking the official beginning of the Battle of Britain.[1] The large convoy, codenamed Bread, had left the Thames Estuary and sailed around the North Foreland, and not long after at about 10h30 was sighted and reported by a reconnaissance aircraft with a massive escort approximating an entire *Gruppe* in strength, including aircraft from 4 and *5/JG 51*.[2] While the reconnaissance machine has been equated with a casualty in the *Luftwaffe* loss records from *4(F)/121*, this *Luftwaffe* unit was based at Caen-Carpiquet airfield, a base falling under *Luftflotte 3* and lying some 200 km to the south-west of the North Foreland.[3] It is very unlikely that a reconnaissance machine from one *Luftflotte* would be used on a mission by another *Luftflotte*, *Luftflotte 2* in this case, and far more plausible that the latter *Luftflotte* would have used one of their own. More confusion arises from the fact that the Do 17 from *4(F)/121* belly-landed near Boulogne, well within the *Luftflotte 2* area and only about 50 km south of North Foreland.[4] Compounding an already confusing situation, none of the intercepting British fighters involved in the action against this reconnaissance aircraft or its escort claimed to have even damaged the Dornier.[5] That no RAF claim was made suggests the possibility that the particular (probably *Luftflotte 2*) reconnaissance aircraft on this mission actually got away without any meaningful damage, its large escort having done its job effectively, and that the *4(F)/121* Dornier was brought to grief by another RAF squadron. This will be discussed further.

74 Squadron's A flight led by P/O Freeborn and dispatched from nearby Manston intercepted this German formation at about 10h50, and despite attacking from a height advantage they became

involved in fighting the escort, claiming two probably shot down and four damaged Me 109s; nobody from 74 Squadron claimed specific damage to the lone Dornier.[6] *JG 51* claimed three Spitfires shot down east of Ramsgate soon after 11h00; two Spitfires were in fact damaged and force-landed, one at Manston, while *5/JG 51* lost an Me 109 and pilot who disappeared into the Thames Estuary.[7] Bearing in mind the disparity in numbers, 74 Squadron had done very well.

Nine Spitfires of 610 Squadron had been scrambled to intercept a *Staffel*-strength fighter sweep from *III/JG 51*, which came in near Dover about 11h15, and S/L Smith's aircraft was hit and was further damaged when it crashed in landing at Hawkinge.[8] The *III/JG 51* made three claims for Spitfires north-west of Dover.[9] 610 Squadron claimed two probable Me 109s but none were lost.[10] Their incursion was probably to cover the retreat of *II/JG 51*, a tactic much used by the astute Albert Kesselring, leader of *Luftflotte 2* later in the Battle; at this early stage it would have been on the instructions of the equally wily *Oberst* Theo Osterkamp, *Kommodore* of *JG 51* and also in charge of the as-yet limited German fighter units in the vicinity of the Pas de Calais. Known affectionately as 'Uncle Theo' he had been a major ace in the First World War with thirty-two victories, with another six scored early in the Second as the *Kommodore* of *JG 51*.[11]

To pick up again on what might have happened with the Do 17 P of *4(F)/121* that crash-landed near Boulogne after suffering 60% damage and being written off from fighter attack, with a dead observer, wounded radio operator and one other wounded crewman, several sources reveal a much more complex possible solution.[12] The dead observer, *Oblt* Somborn was indeed a member of *4(F)/121*.[13] At this time many reconnaissance units were busy converting from Do 17s to Ju 88s, such as *4(F)/121* and *1(F)/123* in *Luftflotte 3*, for example; *2(F)/123* and *3(F)/31*, in contrast, still operated only the Do 17.[14] While a Do 17 of *4(F)/121* did fly a reconnaissance sortie early that morning, over Worthy Down airfield from 05h00–08h00, it landed safely; however, another Do 17, from *1(F)/123* also flew a reconnaissance mission early the same morning, with an assigned target route Oxford-Portsmouth-Isle of Wight-Swindon, and this aircraft struggled back to France with 250 bullet holes, a dead observer and two wounded crew members.[15] While the dead observer is confirmed as belonging to *4(F)/121*[16] and the machine apparently to *1(F)/123*, the inherent conundrum is not necessarily that unusual. German units did quite often 'borrow' machines from each other, particularly within the same *Geschwader*, and thus carried a crew which did not come from the same sub-unit (*Gruppe* or *Staffel*) as the machine. Within the relatively few long-range reconnaissance units in *Luftflotte 3* this could easily have applied.

There is one more possible complication: *1(F)/123* was based inland at Tussous-le-Buc, very close to Tussous-le-Noble and Guyancourt airfields.[17] This lay in the western outer suburbs of Paris about twelve kilometres south-west of an area of the city and its outskirts known as Boulogne Billancourt. Possibly, the reconnaissance machine that belly-landed near 'Boulogne' may have been near this Boulogne (Billancourt), very close to its home base of Tussous-le-Buc. The latter airfield was the main base for *Luftflotte 3*'s reconnaissance units. *4(F)/121*, in contrast, was based at Caen-Carpiquet.[18] The ongoing conversion of *4(F)/121* would not likely have been on the forward base at Caen Carpiquet, but logically would have taken place at the main reconnaissance base for *Luftflotte 3*, namely Tussous-le-Buc; there were several other major air bases very close by (Tussous-le-Noble, Guyancourt) and some of these also housed facilities from the French aero industry, thus making an ideal and plausible location for conversion of a unit like *4(F)/121*. Presumably, the latter unit remained based at Caen Carpiquet, sending a few crews back to Tussous-le-Buc for conversion.

So it is possible that on 10 July 1940 an extra crew was needed for a second reconnaissance mission (detailed above) in addition to that over Worthy Down, and they might have called on a crew undergoing conversion at Tussous-le-Buc. This crew may well have borrowed a Do 17 P from *1(F)/123* at that base. Once they had been in action, and returning with a damaged aircraft and crew casualties, they might well have made for Tussous-le-Buc from whence the aircraft had been borrowed, and seeing that Paris was close by, better situated for medical care than Caen Carpiquet. This would provide a logical explanation for a crew from *4(F)/121* manning a machine from *1(F)/123* and belly-landing it near 'Boulogne' (Billancourt).

Whatever the precise unit designation of the Dornier that belly-landed 60% damaged and with significant crew casualties, this had been caused by a section of 145 Squadron Hurricanes led by F/Lt Dutton; this intercepted it at *c.* 06h15 several miles south of Southampton, thus within the area of its designated reconnaissance route, damaging it but not bringing it down immediately, and so claiming only a probable victory.[19] What they had done to the reconnaissance Dornier and its crew also lived up to F/Lt Sailor Malan's cold-blooded dictum that it was often better to send back a seriously damaged German bomber with dead and wounded crew than to merely dispatch it;[20] Malan was the leading light of 74 Squadron and took over as its very effective leader on 8 August 1940.[21]

About an hour earlier, at 05h20, off Winterton on the East coast, three Spitfires of 66 Squadron were vectored onto a Do 17 of *II/KG 3* which was climbing when first seen.[22] The leading Spitfire attacked as it got to about 17,000 ft and just before opening fire he saw it jettison its bombload; he fired 2,663 rounds, significantly more than the normal ammunition load of 2,400 rounds, but received accurate return fire from the ventral gunner who hit his machine five times including one bullet in the armoured windscreen, causing him to break away.[23] The second Spitfire attacked next, experiencing no return fire, and with no apparent damage caused, the third fighter went in from astern firing from 300 down to 50 yards; this time the port engine caught fire and the Dornier went down but levelled out and a final attack by the same pilot left the starboard engine also burning and it plunged into the sea and disintegrated.[24] The third pilot expended 2,600 rounds, again a significant extra load of ammunition.[25]

Green Section of 242 Squadron was sent to relieve another squadron section on convoy patrol off Lowestoft and on arrival, *c.* 07h50, saw ships' anti-aircraft fire and a He 111 climbing into cloud; Green 1, P/O Eckford attacked it from astern and above at *c.* 15,000 ft and fired all his ammunition in a single long burst.[26] The enemy broke away in cloud trailing white smoke; on his return to the convoy and the section, a He 111 was seen again at *c.* 08h20, disappeared again and then was spotted about 4 miles south-east of the convoy.[27] Sub Lt Gardner, Green 2, dived and fired from astern, then made a beam attack from about 25° above, seeing the port engine out of action and port undercarriage leg come down, and following a third attack the Heinkel hit the sea; he saw one survivor crawl onto the wing.[28] Eckford expended 1,800 rounds and Gardner 1,600.[29] The aircraft belonged to 7/KG 53 and none of the crew survived in the longer term; despite mention of two Heinkels in this action, there was probably only the one, which was attacked by the two pilots separately.[30]

Three Spitfires of Green Section 92 Squadron were patrolling over Barry, southern Wales, *c.* 10 km south-west of Cardiff, at 4,500 ft when at *c.* 11h15 they spotted a Ju 88 at about 10,000 ft, but it disappeared in the clouds before anyone could get near.[31] Green 2 was subsequently vectored to the south-east and after fifteen minutes, near Exeter by then and as he turned back to return to base, he spotted a He 111 at *c.* 10,000 ft and put in two astern and one beam attack, seeing a large piece detach from the top of the fuselage and white smoke from the starboard engine, following which the Heinkel went into a spiral dive and disappeared.[32] He had expended 1,600 rounds from about 150 yards range.[33] No relevant He 111 or Ju 88 appears in the German losses for the day.[34] A reconnaissance Do 215 of 2/*Aufkl. Gr. Ob.d.L.* was lost on this day, crashing and burning out at Le Havre, killing three and injuring a fourth crew member, including a German war correspondent.[35] This

Gruppe specialised in high altitude strategic photo-reconnaissance work, and this loss may have been an operational accident as damage due to flak at high altitude is unlikely, and the 92 Squadron action was at *c.* 10,000 ft. A war correspondent would also probably have been more likely to fly a less dangerous mission.

A large raid was now put together to attack convoy Bread as it traversed the narrow straits between Dover and Calais; this comprised forty seven Do 17s of *I* and *III/KG 2*, escorted by around thirty Me 110s of *III/ZG 26* and fourteen Me 109s of *III/JG 51*, with *I/LG 2* in company.[36] These aircraft were seen to be stacked upwards in a three-tier formation, with the bombers at *c.* 4,000 ft, the Me 110s at *c.* 8,000 ft and the Me 109s at *c.* 12,000 ft, when intercepted by RAF fighters.[37] A report by F/O Henry Ferris of 111 Squadron clearly noted that the Dorniers were arrayed in three formations, one behind the other.[38] The convoy by then was off Dungeness-Folkestone, and as the attack on the ships began, pilots from 56 Squadron met the Me 110s off Folkestone and P/O Page observed the *Zerstörer* begin to form a protective circle, with the Me 109s higher up following suit.[39] This tactic of adopting a Me 110 circle, often with top cover Me 109s, became a standard way of operating for these heavy fighters, and was first seen over Britain on this day. However, it was not just for protection, but also provided a fighter cover that was difficult to attack effectively. By circling it maintained a protective cover in a chosen area for a short period, while bombers lower down would pass over and bomb the target with relative impunity as few would be brave enough to tackle them seriously while faced with such a daunting fighter cover above. Once the last bombers had departed for safer shores, the circles would break up; any attacks on the bombers could easily be met by detaching some of the circling fighter cover to deal with them while the raid was still in progress. The RAF would have to learn how to deal with these circling Me 110s, which they did achieve quite soon, as will be seen.

Following the costly reconnaissance mission that successfully spotted convoy Bread, the Germans put together a large raid to attack the ships and contribute to the general aim of stopping Channel traffic and the intended blockade of supplies into the United Kingdom. Planning was led by *Oberst* Fink and *Oberst* Theo Osterkamp, *Kommodoren* respectively of *KG 2* and *JG 51* and responsible for coordinating bomber and fighter operations over the Straits of Dover and adjacent areas.[40] Twenty-two Do 17s from *I/KG 2* and another twenty-five from *III/KG 2* flew in separate formations, *I Gruppe* stacked up behind *III Gruppe*, with Major Adolf Fuchs, commander of *III/KG 2*, leading the raid, with a direct escort provided by Major Schalk's *III/ZG 26*.[41] Interestingly, the Me 110s started off flying with the bombers at the same altitude of about 4,000 ft, and judging from RAF reports discussed below, some stayed until just before the bombing before climbing up to join a circle.[42] A higher flying protection was provided by fourteen Me 109s of *Hauptmann* Trautloft's *III/JG 51*, as well as *I/LG 2* probably providing a more indirect escort higher still.[43]

Study of the relevant RAF records and other sources cited here enables the German plan to be unravelled; it was complex, thus typically German, and relied on almost perfect timing by all units concerned. While the Me 110s were to accompany the bombers as close escort as they came across the Channel from France towards the convoy, then sailing south-west of Dover and lying approximately due south of Folkestone, as the bombing was about to begin they were to leave them and form a short-lived circle off Folkestone. Me 109s from *III/JG 51* were to form the upper part of this circle. Often misunderstood as 'defensive circles', reflecting an overstated respect for the prowess of British fighters, these circles were actually there to provide a higher-flying presence of a formidable force of fighters above or close to the target, be it over land or sea. Sometimes the circle would be just before the target along the bombers' route, in other cases just past the target and along the route as here, where the circle formed over the Channel off Folkestone just to the north-east of the convoy. The Me 110 part of these circles had an inherent and very important role: far from protecting themselves from the danger of the more nimble RAF fighters, they were there to take over protection of their bombers once the more capable but very short-ranged Me 109s had had to turn for home. They would then fly back above and behind the vulnerable bombers flying at a lower level and often including damaged aircraft carrying casualties, never mind formations by now broken and scattered. Also, as the German bombers reached the target, they would be flying beneath this circling protective umbrella thus being shielded from many attacks – it took a brave or foolhardy British fighter leader to make a serious assault on the bombers while also flying directly beneath such a threat.

From the RAF side, according to the philosophy of AVM Park and fully supported by his chief, Dowding, single British fighter squadrons would be directed onto incoming raids, being guided by their individual sector controllers to the interception itself; this was intended to limit fighter casualties while setting in motion an unpredictable set of successive assaults on the German formations in quick succession.[44] According to the German plan detailed above, the incoming British fighters were supposed to be attracted to the elevated circling fighter formations, effectively a trap as their height advantage gave them the initiative to attack at will and relatively safely. The confusion and disturbance of well-laid *Luftwaffe* plans by several small British fighter formations descending on them from different directions and at varying altitudes, often within minutes or relatively short intervals of time, was an added bonus of the overall 11 Group philosophy, and so it would prove on 10 July 1940. All the various German components of this large raid would be assaulted, with a sharp and effective attack on the bombers by 111 Squadron being delivered despite all the escort fighters disposed so carefully, while the fighters themselves, especially the Me 110s, would be drawn into conflict and suffer relatively serious losses for little gain. In July, flights rather than full squadrons were often dispatched by the controllers, as on the 10th.

British radar noted a concentration of radar returns behind Calais at 13h20.[45] Five minutes before this A Flight of 32 Squadron had been dispatched from Biggin Hill to patrol above the ships and once in place there, saw the incoming raid at 13h35.[46] The sheer size of the raid led them to request reinforcements, but these were already on the way: a further three Hurricanes, Green Section of 32 Squadron led by F/O Humpherson, were able to join up with their comrades.[47] As they did so, they observed about sixty incoming bombers in waves, each of about twenty machines disposed in vics line astern, making for the convoy.[48] The leader of A Flight saw the convoy being bombed, did not note any hits and the bombers then turned for France; due to 32 squadron's aircraft being at about 11,000 ft while the bombers were at *c.* 4,000 ft and flying in and out of clouds with intermittent rainstorms, they were able to play no role in interfering with the *Luftwaffe's* activities before Humpherson's section picked out a straggler from the retreating bombers on their way back over the Channel.[49] They damaged this Dornier and left it in mid-Channel at about 3,000 ft and gliding at *c.* 105-110 mph.[50]

The arrival of the third section of 32 Squadron, and almost concomitantly of the *Luftwaffe* raid above the convoy, occurred at about 13h40-13h45; further reinforcements from 74 Squadron were ordered up from Manston at the same time and in the next quarter of an hour until *c.* 14h00 elements from 74, 56, 111 and 64 Squadrons arrived over the Straits of Dover area and joined the action, all within minutes of each other.[51] There was thus much activity and combat within the space of only a few minutes, and aircraft speeds shifted the action rapidly; in all of this there was thus implicit danger for battle plans that relied on good timing, although the *Luftwaffe's* plan worked quite well that day. The incoming Dornier bombers would have been cruising at about 3.8-3.9 miles per minute, on a par with the Hurricanes being vectored in from the British side; Me 110s were faster at about 4.75 miles per minute and fastest of all were the Me 109s and Spitfires cruising at *c.* 5 miles a minute.[52] Basically, within the German plan, there was a bombing attack on the convoy directly south of Folkestone, while a Me 110-Me 109 circle formed just to the north-east off Folkestone and the bombers were to fly close to Dover and then back to the French coast near Calais. Within this framework, the Dorniers would have taken slightly over three minutes to fly from their aiming points over the ships to Dover, with Me 110s and Me 109s taking about two and a half minutes for the same distance. With relatively minor air combat once the Geman formations were on their way back over the Channel – the attack of 111 Squadron on the rear Dorniers – action between the circling Me 110/109 fighters and 56/74/64 Squadrons would all have taken place within only a few minutes, probably between three and five minutes only. And this was in a relatively small area from south-west of Folkestone through to the Dover area, a stretch of about 12 or 13 miles. Aerial combat was thus a very fast activity, and no wonder participating pilots only got fleeting glances at any specific aircraft, including those they shot at; this goes a long way to explain multiple attacks on the same aircraft, especially for larger twin-engined machines like Dorniers or Me 110 *Zerstörer*, which seldom fell to a single attack where the RAF was using .303 inch machine guns only.

RAF records and the other sources given here suggest that as *KG 2* came up with the convoy, so the Me 110s and Me 109s surged ahead to form the circle about 5-6 miles to the north-east, off Folkestone. In rapid succession the circle was assaulted by six Hurricanes of 56 Squadron who went for the lower Me 110s, to be rapidly followed by 74 Squadron, which dived through the lot, 110s and 109s from above, with 64 Squadron appearing on the scene as the circle broke up and the Me 110s followed the bombers rapidly disappearing over the narrows of the Channel back to France and safety.[53] This complex engagement between elements of three RAF squadrons and the Me 110-Me 109 circle over several minutes basically overlapped with the assault of 111 Squadron on the rear elements of *I/KG 2*'s Dorniers; there was a collision between a 111 Squadron machine and a Dornier, which was also witnessed from above by a pilot from 74 Squadron enmeshed in the fight off Folkestone with the German fighter circle.[54] The violence of air combat, against the rear of the Dorniers after they had bombed the ships and against the *Luftwaffe* fighter circle dissipated within only a few minutes, leaving a few retreating machines being chased back over the Channel, as high speeds and highly varying directions taken by aircraft in mortal combat ensured that the dense tangles of fighting machines soon became dispersed over wide areas, exposing pilots to the strange yet almost universal phenomenon of suddenly being alone in their patch of the sky. The latter of course, only for the survivors, able to return to their bases. The dead had passed in a few minutes and their remains and those of their machines lay scattered across the seabed or surface waters of the Channel mostly, with a few in France.[55]

It is perhaps pertinent now to examine briefly the individual experiences of each Squadron as their leaders rapidly made their decisions on how to tackle the enemies they met. B Flight of 56 Squadron was ordered off from Manston,[56] a forward base used by various squadrons to place them closer to where action was likely from across the Channel. They were led by F/Lt 'Jumbo' Gracie, one of the squadron's characters and a forceful leader to boot; after being vectored to Dover, within five minutes of arrival there the enemy formations were seen 3 to 5 miles to the south-west, attacking the convoy.[57] 56 Squadron's Hurricanes were at about 8,000 ft and ran into the escort now forming the circles off Folkestone, with the Me 110s at the same approximate altitude.[58] Gracie's plan was to try and get above the fighters and then dive through them on to the bombers now coming up beneath the forming circles, but this was thwarted by the sheer number of German fighters.[59] Gracie then put his sections in line astern and climbed, and on getting above the Me 110s he led his small force against about fifteen or twenty of them flying in a left-hand circle.[60] He fired a long burst at a Me 110, observing bits of the tail become detached, which was also seen by two flight members, a third watching the *Zerstörer* spinning out of control towards the sea; Gracie himself had also seen one crewman bale out.[61] Even a few moments taken to observe the fate of a victim invited danger, and Gracie's machine was hit from behind and belched oil, petrol and glycol; he was lucky that the Merlin engine kept going long enough to get him back to Manston, where it finally seized at 500 ft and as the Hurricane also became enveloped in smoke a crash-landing was inevitable, writing off the aircraft, but the pilot walked away from this one.[62]

One of Gracie's pilots, Geoffrey Page, actually saw the Me 110 circle forming as the Hurricanes climbed, and then he was diving through the centre of the circle, firing at two Messerschmitts before climbing vertically up the other side to make a second attack against the rotation of the Me 110s.[63] In his excitement he fired rather wildly and some of the Me 110s broke from the formation; by this stage the Me 109s from the upper circles were coming down and wild dogfighting with them began.[64] As so often happened in these brief yet fierce air battles, Page now found himself completely alone except for a lone Me 109 and the two intrepid pilots went for each other head-on, narrowly avoiding a collision.[65] Page claimed a probable Me 109[66] but had done better than he knew. His opponent, *Oberfeldwebel* Artur Dau of 7/JG 51, recorded his side of the story:

In order to avoid a collision, shortly before impact, I pushed my machine beneath the Hurricane. In this moment I felt a blow in my aircraft and then concentrated on reaching the French coast. I had been hit several times, my engine was damaged and I could no longer see ahead. Then the engine gave up the ghost and I could only orientate myself by looking through the side panels of the canopy; the front of it was completely covered with oil. As I still had a lot of altitude I managed to reach the French coast by gliding. I wanted to try and reach the airfield at Boulogne but missed this by a short margin and had to land in a field; I attach a picture of this forced-landing and as can be seen my aircraft was fully burnt out. I had got away with it without any injury.[67]

In all, B Flight of 56 Squadron had claimed a second Me 110 destroyed by Sgt Whitehead[68] – but possibly shared with Gracie[69] – plus another probably destroyed, and three Me 109 probables including Page's victim.[70]

Eight Spitfires from 74 Squadron, up from Manston, had arrived in the Dover area just as things got going, and climbing to 12,000 ft saw about twenty Dorniers attacking the convoy at *c.* 4,000 ft, with an estimated forty Me 110s circling above at 8,000 ft and around forty Me 109s circling above them at 12,000 ft; the sum of all these machines looked to the pilots like a three-layer formation.[71] F/Lt Measures led 74 Squadron's Spitfires into a brief climb above the circles followed by a spiral dive down the centre of the rotating enemy; a series of individual combats ensued with what were reported as Do 17s, Me 110s and Me 109s.[72] Measures himself, while engaged in attacking a Me 110 and then a Do 17, also observed a Me 109 collide with either a Dornier or *Zerstörer*;[73] this could only have been F/O Higgs of 111 Squadron impacting with a Dornier of *I/KG 2* underlining once again how the many actions involved in this raid all occurred within a few minutes of each other. In the swirling confusion of this confrontation the pilots of 74 Squadron reported five attacks on Do 17s, and three each on Me 110s and Me 109s. While many were inconclusive, Measures hit a Me 110 and saw its port engine smoke, and three individual pilots saw fire and smoke emitted from the starboard engine of the Do 17s they attacked.[74] All claims against Do 17s were most likely actually made against Me 110s, and the three reported attacks on a 'Do 17' with its starboard engine on fire probably related to three pilots attacking the same Me 110. One of the three was hit by enemy fire in return and crash-landed at Lympne.[75] In total, 74 Squadron claimed a Do 17 (sic), a Me 109 and three damaged Me 110s.[76]

Six Spitfires of 64 Squadron scrambled from Kenley to provide reinforcements for the battles in progress off Folkestone flew at maximum speed and managed to get there in time to see the large dogfight in progress, with Me 110s beginning to break from their circles.[77] As they were flying at only 4,000 ft, 64 Squadron engaged damaged aircraft falling out of the fight and those leaving it to return to France and safety. They claimed four destroyed and two damaged, the star performer being Sub Lt Dawson-Paul who caused one Me 110's port engine to catch fire and watched it ditch, shortly thereafter dispatching another into the sea, from which the gunner bailed out and was picked up by a destroyer.[78] Some of the *Zerstörer* were harassed all the way back to the French coast.[79]

Overlapping with the combat between the circling German fighters and successive attacks by 56, 74 and 64 Squadrons, was the attack made on the German bomber formation by 111 Squadron. Nine Hurricanes had left Croydon to proceed to forward base at Hawkinge, but were diverted to intercept the Dorniers attacking the convoy south-west of Folkestone.[80] It is quite often claimed that 111 Squadron made a head-on attack on the Dorniers and the squadron is supposed by some to have charged through an anti-aircraft barrage to attack the bombers.[81] Taken together these two suppositions make for rousing material, but while they might be based on 111 Squadron's operational record book entry for 10 July 1940, this supposed source of a head-on attack has been misread. While the 111 Squadron operational diary does indeed state that the Hurricanes approached a formation of about twenty four Dorniers head-on, in the very next sentence the diary goes on to state that the Squadron flew past the formation and then turned in and attacked from astern.[82] The same train of events is given in more detail in the 111 Squadron Intelligence Patrol Report.[83] The Squadron was at 8,000 ft when they reached the convoy and the Dorniers were flying in vics, line astern, stepped up from 4,000 ft.[84] As 111 Squadron approached approximately from head-on but several thousand feet higher up, they flew over the convoy and saw the first formation of Dorniers, *III/KG 2*, bomb the convoy; then as they flew down the side of the second formation, comprising stepped-up vics of *I/KG 2*, also descending, as they turned in to attack them from the rear they saw their bombs go down as well.[85] S/L Thompson makes it quite clear that as they turned in behind the Dorniers, all naval anti-aircraft fire ceased.[86]

Despite it not being a head-on attack pushed fearlessly home through an intense anti-aircraft barrage, nevertheless 111 Squadron's attack was an impressive one. Putting his three sections in line astern, Thompson led them all in from directly behind in a classic example of a Fighter Area Attack No. 5, he himself singling out the port aircraft of the rear section or vic of Dorniers and putting in a five seconds burst while closing to only 50 yards.[87] No damage was visible except for a thin trace of vapour from the starboard engine.[88] Meanwhile F/O Ferriss led his section into the starboard part of the rear vic of bombers.[89] He then saw a straggler behind the first bomber formation, ahead of the one he was attacking and led his section after this aircraft; despite a long pursuit over the Channel this German machine was able to maintain a steady 300 mph[90] and got away, and was almost certainly a Me 110 rather than a Dornier. S/L Thompson having broken away from his first attack to the left, returned for another assault and was a witness to F/O Higgs colliding with a Dornier and both aircraft diving seawards out of control. As he attacked another Dornier himself, he saw about 100 yards ahead the crew of another bomber bailing out.[91] The four parachutes were also seen by several other squadron members.[92] Thompson then attacked yet another Dornier after four other squadron pilots had fired at it and gave it the rest of his ammunition very close in at about only 25 yards range, apparently without any effect.[93]

111 Squadron correctly assessed that Higg's collision was a definite loss of a Dornier, as was that of the one whose crew had bailed out; two or three additional machines were thought to have been badly damaged by attacks carried out by seven of the Hurricane pilots.[94] Two damaged Dorniers were in fact claimed by the squadron.[95] They lost one machine of their own, F/O Higgs killed, and two more damaged: Sgt Carnall belly-landed his machine at Hawkinge while F/O Ferriss's aircraft was damaged in combat against several Me 109s out over the Channel.[96] As was always the case with any air action, claims made by both sides were inflated. This almost always reflected the confusion of fast-paced and intense combat rather than any innate dishonesty on the part of the pilots involved. On the German side *I* and *III/KG 2* claimed that they had sunk a cruiser, damaged another, dispatched four merchant ships with a further three damaged; all this for the real loss of a single steamer of a mere 446 tons.[97] Aerial victories over thirteen Hurricanes and nine Spitfires were claimed, seven of the total of twenty-two being made by *III/JG 51*, two by *I/LG 2* and a rather astonishing twelve by *III/ZG 26*.[98] These twenty-two claims relate to total RAF fighter losses of two Hurricanes: F/Lt Gracie of 56 Squadron whose aircraft was written off after crash-landing at Manston, while F/O Higgs of 111 Squadron was killed in a collision with a Do 17 of *3/KG 2*. Three fighters were damaged, one from 74 Squadron and two from 111 Squadron.[99] The role played by the second Me 109-equipped Gruppe, *I/LG 2* remains unclear in the sources; they appear to have been an indirect escort and their two victories were claimed over the mouth of the Thames Estuary relatively late in the entire battle.[100] When 74 Squadron had first sighted the enemy near the convoy, they had reported two parallel lines of fighters at 12,000 ft;[101] these may conceivably have been *I/LG 2*, who did not apparently become involved in the circling mass of German fighters off

Folkestone. Some reports suggest that the Hurricane of 111 Squadron piloted by F/O Higgs was in fact first hit by *Oberleutnant* Walter Oesau of *7/JG 51* before losing control and colliding with a Do 17.[102]

The RAF was more circumspect in their claims over *Luftwaffe* aircraft. The fighter pilots involved in the aerial combat around convoy 'Bread' claimed three of the Dorniers with another probable and two damaged, six Me 110s plus one probable and five damaged, and one Me 109 and three damaged for a grand total of ten victories.[103] Against these claims were *Luftwaffe* casualties of two Do 17 total losses, one being shot down by fighters and anti-aircraft fire off Dungeness with only one wounded survivor being rescued; the other was the machine which F/O Higgs collided with, an aircraft of *3/KG 2* carrying the *Staffelkapitän* who was the observer, and which fell into the sea close to the Dungeness Roads Buoy.[104] The observer and the radio operator survived to become POWs; they lost a wing in the collision and the violence of this led them to think they had been hit by anti-aircraft fire.[105] Another three Dorniers were damaged but made it back to France; one carried two wounded crew members, another a dead and a wounded airman and had 190 bullet holes in it.[106] The third aircraft force-landed near Marquise, and at 70% damage was written off. One crewman was dead on board with another two wounded.[107] Three Me 110s were lost from *III/ZG 26* off Folkestone and one slightly damaged; in two aircraft the pilots both survived wounded to become POWs, despite one of them, *Oberfeldwebel* Willi Meyer, being thrown out of the machine by the impact when it hit the sea.[108] No one survived the loss of the third Me 110; two damaged Me 109s from *7/JG 51* made it back to force-land in France, but one burnt out and was written off.[109]

With the Germans trying a new tactic on 10 July 1940, an examination of its relative success makes sense. A relatively large force of forty-seven bombers had been despatched to attack a convoy in the Straits of Dover. Accompanying them were between sixty-two and seventy-four fighters, most of which went ahead once the convoy was sighted and formed a set of circles just to the north-east of the convoy; the bombers could pass under the protection of this circling umbrella as they finished bombing and began to turn off target. Theoretically, this should have worked well; the fighter circles reaching from about 8,000 to 12,000 ft and thus well above the bombers, between 4,000 and *c.* 5,000 ft, would have attracted many of the British fighters being vectored in to the raid, and would also have provided high cover for the bombers at the same time, with height and thus speed advantages if RAF fighters went for the bombers. Much of this did in fact happen, with 56, 74 and 64 Squadrons all going unhesitatingly for the circling fighters; strangely, 32 Squadron at *c.* 11,000 ft on convoy patrol did not manage to tackle any of the formations, fighters or bombers, except for one section fighting against a retreating straggler. From the RAF side, for the first time in July a relatively large number of fighters was committed against a raid, with thirty-two of thirty-eight fighters directed to the raid entering combat. While still utilising flight-strength formations, often of six and on this day up to eight or nine machines, the RAF was not yet using the Dowding system to full effect, which was designed around employing a squadron of twelve aircraft at a time. This would change soon enough.

The *Luftwaffe* fighters did nothing to stop the only effective attack made on the Dorniers, that by 111 Squadron who caused fairly severe casualties. Seeing as 111 Squadron came in to attack the bombers while the German fighter circles really had their hands fairly full with 56 and 74 Squadrons, there was little time or opportunity to do anything much about the attack on the bombers. 64 Squadron came in late and got amongst the Me 110s from the circles as these dived out of the fight and made to go back across the Channel. The RAF tactics of sending in a set of separate squadron elements, between six and nine aircraft each, from different directions and under different sector controllers and at different times, was really an inherent product of the Dowding system, which could only effectively handle one or two squadrons from a specific station at a time – any delay in putting together larger RAF formations would have been fatal in combating rapidly moving incoming German formations. An unanticipated advantage from the Dowding system, related also to the high speeds which the RAF fighters flew towards their targets under the controller's orders, was that many if not most of the scrambled fighters arrived within a short space of time. Their arrival in small packets had the effect of cumulatively overloading the fighting capabilities of the German formations, tying up lots of the fighters in manoeuvring and fighting, while others arriving within minutes of each other were relatively free to attack the bombers with less danger of fighter interference.

Thus 56 Squadron, the first unit to tackle the fighter circles, was itself badly outnumbered and achieved little – apart, of course, from distracting the German fighters and making some of them fight. While that was still going on, the next fighters from 74 Squadron arrived, and the circling fighters were now much more involved in their own battles and had little attention left for their charges, the Dorniers. The second Me 109 *Gruppe* of *I/LG 2* seems to have been too far away from all of this or chose not to be involved until near the end of the action.

Most inefficient of the lot were the Dornier bombers; RAF intelligence gleaned from the captured *Staffelkapitän* of *3/KG 2*, the machine with which F/O Higgs of 111 Squadron collided, that the bombers were carrying twenty 50 kg bombs,[110] hardly likely to do fatal damage to most ships, and by only sinking one small ship of less than 500 tons they revealed their inexperience in the exacting business of attacking moving ships on the high seas. There was little point in losing three bombers, three Me 110s and a Me 109, plus four damaged aircraft, along with highly trained crewmen dead, captured, missing and wounded, while the target escaped almost unscathed and while the RAF defenders lost two fighters, one pilot and three damaged aircraft.

The RAF units had been well controlled, with 56 Squadron being vectored in at the height of the circling Me 110s, and 74 Squadron at the height of the top circles of Me 109s; sensibly 64 Squadron was sent in at only 4,000 ft to catch their enemies as the circles dissipated and German fighters dived out to return home. 111 Squadron had been guided in at 8,000 ft, perhaps a bit too high for their bomber targets, but the extra height was easily used in a fast and effective attack on the Dorniers from behind. The basic German failure had been insufficient escorts, not close enough to the bombers to protect them adequately. This was to remain the major stumbling block to the *Luftwaffe* for the remainder of the Battle: fighters close enough to the bombers to keep them safe were themselves vulnerable due to perforce having to fly and weave at very low speeds, while the best potential for effective attacks on incoming RAF fighter formations was to be had from positions some way away from the bombers and at several thousand feet higher. This conundrum for the *Luftwaffe* would never be adequately solved and as escorts multiplied and became ever more complex, the overall formations became larger and clumsier, and often had difficulty in combating small RAF formations coming in at variable heights and from different directions within a short space of time.

So despite published accounts to the contrary, 111 Squadron did not make a head-on attack on the German bomber formations on 10 July; when they came in at *c.* 8,000 ft in an approximately head-on approach towards the Dorniers which were at 4,000-5,000 ft altitude, this orientation had not been planned by either controller or S/L Thompson, and their height relative to the bombers was too much for a potential rapidly-decided head-on attack. Such attacks were best made at the same level as their targets as the closing speed was already very high, leaving only a few seconds for aiming and firing before a breakaway to the side, over or under the bombers was needed. Perhaps their experience against this raid encouraged 111 Squadron to consider better ways to attack bomber formations, such as from head-on, but it is equally possible that they were already thinking that way and were just not able to carry out such an attack against this raid. There is no documentation to indicate exactly when this squadron under S/L Thompson's effective leadership actually decided to adopt the head-on attack as their standard method.

3

11 July 1940: Shipping Raids in the Western Channel

Shortly after dawn, German reconnaissance activity began over the Eastern and Central Channel areas, Thames Estuary and off the coast of East Anglia; one Do 17 was shot down off the latter coast.[1] Two Spitfires from a section of 66 Squadron sent up at 05h17 to patrol Winterton, were vectored to the south-east of Yarmouth; as the clouds were heavy and thick, Blue 2 was sent to the top of the clouds, while S/L Rupert Leigh, Blue 1, went below the cloud and saw two Do 17s being fired at by a convoy's escort.[2] Leaving one Dornier fleeing rapidly east having already bombed, he attacked the other just below the clouds at about 06h00 and at *c.* 2,500 ft, and gave it two bursts, 1,600 rounds, in thick cloud and rain squalls but saw no results, and the rear gunner put one bullet in his oil tank.[3] This same aircraft appears to have been intercepted very soon after by a single Hurricane from 242 Squadron, about half a mile off Cromer and at a height of *c.* 1,500 ft, in equally bad visibility with low cloud and rain; S/L Douglas Bader made a head-on attack followed by a stern attack, giving two- and six-second bursts respectively, but then lost the enemy in the poor visibility, having also seen the rear gunner fire back briefly.[4] The Observer Corps saw a Do 17 crash into the sea off Cromer at the same time as Bader's claim.[5] A Dornier 17P weather reconnaissance machine from *Wekusta 26*, lost with its crew of four, fits this shared claim.[6] With expenditure of something close to 4,000 rounds by the two squadron leaders,[7] success had been achieved.

S/L Peter Townsend, commanding 85 Squadron, had been sent up from Martlesham Heath through low-lying mist at 05h30 to intercept a German intruder but found nothing; he then maintained a patrol between Martlesham and Felixstowe and at 06h30 saw a single Do 17 ahead and about 1,000 ft above him, close to Felixstowe.[8] As much as he tried to get himself into a good position for an attack, the Do 17 used its height and speed plus extensive cloud cover to evade his attentions; to stop it getting clean away, Townsend carried out an attack from below and behind.[9] The enemy rear gunner shot back with 'cannon' (so described, but actually machine gun) fire at 600-700 yards, while Townsend waited until he was about 400 yards away before opening up a series of three to four bursts while closing to 200 yards or even less.[10] The squadron leader was then almost blown out of his seat by an explosion in the cockpit between his legs, which he surmised might have been his glycol tank exploding; he bailed out successfully over the sea, his Hurricane plunging into the deep about 5 or 6 miles off Felixstowe, and he was rescued none the worse for his immersion by a naval trawler and landed at Yarmouth.[11]

The Dornier was from *4/KG 2* and three of the four-man crew were relatively lightly injured by Townsend's hail of bullets; they were out on an armed reconnaissance sortie and had dropped some of their bombs on shipping in Lowestoft harbour.[12] The Dornier belly-landed at Arras St Leger, 50% damaged, with 220 bullet holes in engines, fuel tanks and many in the cabin, which was a shambles.[13] Once more, the same situation for most attacks on German bombers pertained: it normally required more than one attacking fighter, and the rifle calibre ammunition did not easily score lethal damage; attacking pilots had to get in really close. Once again, return fire from the bomber had been effective.

Convoy attack south of Portland, c. 07h30-08h20

A convoy sailing east across Lyme Bay and nearing a position south of Portland Bill by about 07h30 was to prove an early focus for *Luftwaffe* attack, repeated later in the day.[14] At this time a section of Hurricanes from 501 Squadron, Middle Wallop, was sent aloft on convoy patrol, and soon afterwards radar detected two formations of German aircraft off Cherbourg, proceeding northwards.[15] The Middle Wallop controller scrambled five Spitfires of B Flight of 609 Squadron from Warmwell soon after, to reinforce the three machines from 501 Squadron, which being closest were vectored towards the enemy.[16] Clouds hampered the three lonely Hurricanes in finding the convoy but descending below the clouds they saw the ships about 8 miles south of Portland Bill, and that they were being bombed, the attackers leaving when they saw the Hurricanes approaching.[17] The section leader then climbed above the clouds over the convoy and was intercepted by at least a *Staffel* of Me 109s, resulting in a dogfight and almost straight away the two surviving members of 501 Squadron's Green Section noticed a parachute descending; after landing they realised it must have been Sgt Dixon, who was missing.[18] The section had met the enemy just before 08h00, which comprised nine or ten Ju 87s at 7,000 ft, with about twenty Me 109s at 12,000 ft and half a mile behind the dive bombers.[19]

The German attackers are believed by one source at least to have been about ten Ju 87s from IV/LG 1 (see discussion below) escorted by *III/JG 27*;[20] this much more plausible identification of the Me 109s is confirmed by a claim made for a Hurricane shot down south of Portland by *Oblt* Franzisket of *7/JG 27* at about 08h03.[21] While Sgt Dixon had managed to bail out of his stricken Hurricane *c.* 10 miles south-east of Portland at 08h00, he drowned and the Weymouth lifeboat sent out to find him was unsuccessful; his body later washed up on the French coast and he is buried in Abbeville.[22] At about 08h05, 609 Squadron intercepted the same enemy raid,[23] F/Lt Barran leading his five Spitfires to about 15 miles south of Portland before spotting nine Ju 87s at about 8,000 ft, the dive bombers being in line astern and apparently gliding to attack a ship.[24] It is likely the Stukas had throttled down just prior to turning over and diving down on their targets, air brakes out to slow them down in their steep dives.

'Pip' Barran had obviously not yet seen the Me 109 escort lurking in the sun, estimated later by survivors as two squadrons in number, at 12,000 ft, as he skilfully led his flight line astern and placed them between the sun and the Ju 87s. While he led his own Blue Section down to the attack, he wisely left the two Spitfires of Green Section behind as a safeguard.[25] Alas, his skill and caution were for naught as the relatively large number of Me 109s, hidden in the sun, dived down and engulfed the small number of Spitfires at *c.* 08h15; not overly concerning themselves with the two look-outs, most of the Messerschmitts went for the leading section, its third member and only survivor, P/O Blaney reporting later that his first intimation of trouble was seeing bullets passing his windscreen.[26] His immediate breaking off of his own attack, concomitant evasive action and warning to his colleagues were to no avail except for himself; his sharp turn revealed no enemies on his tail.[27] P/O Mitchell, Blue 2, last observed diving behind his leader for the Ju 87s, was not seen again, but his body was given up by the sea, washed ashore at Newport, Isle of Wight, several days later.[28] His demise is ascribed to *Oblt* Dobislav of *9/JG 27* who claimed a Spitfire shot down south of Portland.[29]

The fact that P/O Jarvis Blaney saw no more Me 109s after his first evasive turn suggests that they performed the classic *Luftwaffe* bounce tactic of a fast dive onto the enemy, pulling out beneath their tails, firing and pulling back up to altitude. Blaney himself descended and found a Ju 87 at 1,500 ft at which he fired while closing in from 200 to only 50 yds, and watched it go into the sea, and then circled one ship that had been hit.[30] By 08h20 all the Germans had disappeared. The two members of Green Section flying rear-guard were lucky; suddenly finding themselves with Me 109s all around and seeing Blue Section under attack, they next found themselves close to a number of Ju 87s after presumably diving away from the Messerschmitts.[31] They each briefly had a go at a Ju 87, F/O Little, Green leader firing at one which fell on its back shedding small pieces, and his wingman P/O Curchin seeing two Me 109s on his tail just in time as he closed with a dive bomber. He managed to avoid them and by now quite low he found that all the Stukas had vanished, and he could see the remaining Me 109s already about 10 miles away heading home.[32]

As Pilot Officers Blaney and Curchin turned for home, they both observed a Spitfire obviously in serious difficulties, flying slowly towards the southern coast and pouring smoke; getting closer they saw it was the aircraft of F/Lt Barran.[33] About 5 to 6 miles south of Portland Bill, the engine finally stopped and the pilot was observed to bail out and his parachute to deploy successfully.[34] However, that was almost the final effort of the stricken pilot, P/O Blaney observing no reaction from the pilot in the water when he circled him; soon afterwards when a boat found him and hauled him inboard, F/Lt 'Pip' Barran died.[35] He had been hit twice in his right leg, was badly burned and suffering from the shock of his wounds and his immersion in the water.[36] The cold waters of the Channel alone could quickly sap the life of downed RAF pilots; lacking dinghies in 1940, they often did not last even half an hour before losing consciousness. A man with gunshot wounds and burns from a fire in his aircraft, despite his trying to reach the coast before his dying engine quit on him, had little chance if he fell into the water; it was a miracle he even managed to bail out.

This entire action of five Spitfires of 609 Squadron against a small escorted formation of Ju 87s underlined once again the truth of that old adage, 'beware of the Hun in the sun'; this was no mere comic-book statement but one very much rooted in fact, both in the First World War when it was coined and equally so in the Battle of Britain. The problem remained basically the same for the RAF fighters over England in 1940, only the details and relative complexity changing: how to approach the bombers and deciding which were the real target for the defenders against the efforts of the escorting German fighters. The risks were always there, and almost every time in order to get within effective firing range of the bombers, the escort had to be hazarded. Some leaders tried to mitigate this basic truth by sending pathetically small numbers of their fighters (three to six, generally) to try and distract the escort long enough for the other machines to get in a brief attack on the bombers. This was precisely what F/Lt Barran had done on 11 July 1940. Although all knew that an escort was likely there, behind and above the bombers and hiding in the sun as best they could, if they could not spot them then they could never be sure how far away they were and if their height and distance offered a shot at attacking the bombers. If unsure, as in this case, another approach would have been first to go for more altitude before diving down on the bombers and flying through any intervening escort fast enough to largely nullify them. However, the *Luftwaffe* often had more than one escorting formation and a top cover would then still endanger the RAF attackers.

A final review of the Me 109-escorted Stuka attack on the convoy south of Portland: 609 Squadron survivors claimed one Ju 87 shot down into the sea by P/O Blaney and another probably destroyed by F/O Little.[37] No potential *Luftflotte 3* casualties are given in the *Luftwaffe* loss lists, but these do contain two casualties suffered by *IV/LG 1*: 11 *Staffel* lost one machine and crew, with another suffering 10% damage. The former was placed over Dover and the latter off that same port and force-landed at St Inglevert in the Pas de Calais.[38] While these two losses would admirably fit the claims of 609 Squadron, and while one source ascribes this raid to nine to ten Stukas from this *Gruppe*,[39] there is a problem. *IV/LG 1* was part of *Luftflotte 2*, and was stationed in the Pas de Calais, its operations being carried out over the Straits of Dover area in general.[40] Although not impossible, it is rather unlikely that a *Gruppe* stationed across the Channel from Dover and forming part of one *Luftflotte*, would operate almost at the opposite end of the Channel operational area, near Portland, and under the auspices of another *Luftflotte*. Furthermore, *Luftwaffe* loss records clearly locate both *IV/LG 1* casualties near Dover.[41] Which Stukas the 609 Squadron flight might have met is thus unknown and whether they actually caused casualties at all, despite each claiming RAF pilot firing their full ammunition load of 2,400 rounds, must remain unresolved.[42]

Analogously, while plausible *Luftwaffe* claims exist for the 501 Squadron Hurricane of Sgt Dixon and the 609 Squadron Spitfire of P/O Mitchell, none has been preserved for F/Lt Barran, almost certainly a victim of *III/JG 27* as well.[43] This may suggest that the action between one or more Me 109s of *III/JG 27* and F/Lt Barran did not result in a German claim that was strong enough to allow confirmation, even as a probable, no such claim thus being preserved in the relevant records.[44] This in turn suggests that F/Lt Barran put up a good fight before being able to get away, albeit badly wounded, from his opponents in a damaged machine and heading north for the coast, which he never reached.

A lone German reconnaissance Do 17 P from *2(F)/11* was lost and its crew of three killed when it was shot down at *c.* 10h14, about 20 miles south of the Isle of Wight; it had been flying west and may have been trying to relocate the convoy attacked in the raid discussed above.[45] It had been intercepted by a flight of 601 Squadron led by F/O Rhodes-Moorhouse, who together with P/O Bland and F/O Doulton was responsible for its demise.[46]

Attack on Portland harbour, and convoy, c. 11h30-12h20

Radar apparently either did not detect this attack before mid-Channel or plotted it erroneously as a single aircraft, and when it suddenly became apparent in the central Channel area, controllers at 10 and 11 Groups had to rush to catch up.[47] In the western part of the Channel, south of the Isle of Wight and Portland, the French coastline was out of effective radar range and the *Luftwaffe* could thus build their bomber formations and escorts without being detected until about mid-Channel when they suddenly appeared on the radar screens.[48] Add to this the standard four-minute time lag between raid detection and plotting thereof at group or sector headquarters, controllers had little time to react and establish where the Germans were headed before scrambling fighters to tackle them.[49] This contrasts with the Straits of Dover region where radar could follow raid build-ups over and even inland from the Pas de Calais and also see them coming well in advance towards the Thames Estuary. While 11 Group had something of an advantage in this regard, the much shorter Channel crossing there effectively meant there was also precious little time to get at the bombers before they crossed the English coastline.[50]

A Flight, 601 Squadron, led by F/Lt Sir Archibald Hope, were the nearest unit, who were at the time being vectored onto an outgoing reconnaissance machine which had flown over central and southern Wales earlier; by waiting to intercept such missions on the way out, Fighter Command controllers were able to determine which part of the enemy coast they were heading for.[51] Three Hurricanes of 87 Squadron from Exeter were already on patrol somewhere over Lyme Bay, and they along with another six Hurricanes from 238 Squadron, Warmwell, who were patrolling over that base, were directed to Portland.[52] A section of 501 Squadron Hurricanes and nine more from 213 Squadron, Exeter, were rapidly scrambled, respectively at 11h42 and 11h50 to help, along with B Flight 601 Squadron from Tangmere, up at 11h55. These three formations would not engage the enemy, however.[53] There were thus several Fighter Command units all converging on the general Portland area: A Flight of 601 Squadron from the east would be first on the scene, 87 Squadron's section from the west arriving not long after, and 238 Squadron's machines saw action a bit later, more to the east-north-east of Portland.

An innovative and interesting new escort technique was used by the *Luftwaffe* in this raid; *Geschwader Kommodore* of ZG 76 Major Grabmann had given his men strict orders to protect the Stukas from RAF fighter attack, even at the sacrifice of their own aircraft and lives, as recalled by 9/ZG 76 *Staffelkapitän Oblt* Gerhard Kadow.[54] This eyewitness, who would survive the day as a prisoner of war, was more fortunate than several of his fellow III/ZG 76 comrades, and clearly described the escort philosophy applied: the seven Me 110s, all that was serviceable of Kadow's own *Staffel*, were assigned to the right flank of the Stukas at an altitude of *c.* 12,000 ft. Another *Staffel* had the left flank but at 18,000 ft was not immediately available to support their lower flying colleagues, nor the Stukas.[55] They were also flying some distance behind the dive bombers, as observed by F/Lt Hope of 601 Squadron, the first unit leader to see the enemy formation.[56] III/ZG 76's third *Staffel*, described by Kadow as the close escort, was in fact tasked with giving close escort support to the Stukas after they had bombed and were pulling up at low level and thus flying slowly, at their most vulnerable.[57]

With the Stukas flying at *c.* 14,000-15,000 ft,[58] the closest Me 110 escorts were those of 9/ZG 76 who were flying a couple of thousand feet lower than them. The idea behind this placement was no doubt to have escorts on the spot as the Stukas slowed to bomb, turning and diving down for their targets at Portland; thus, as the dive bombers entered their dives and slowed with their air brakes, protection from British fighters attacking from above, viz the six Hurricanes of A Flight, 601 Squadron, was provided immediately – the dive bombers would soon have descended to the level of 9/ZG 76 and then below them. Of course, it was also tough on these seven Me 110s as they would be faced with attack from superior altitude by more manoeuvrable single-engined fighters; *Kommodore* Grabmann's envisaged possible sacrifice was about to become reality, and four of the Messerschmitt *Zerstörer* would not return, three of them from the vulnerable 9th *Staffel*.[59] This also explains why most of the pilots of the 601 Squadron flight which first sighted and attacked the German raid, either immediately or soon after diving on the descending Stukas, met Me 110 escorts.[60] The second British unit to arrive over Portland, the three Hurricanes of 87 Squadron, witnessed a couple of Hurricanes in combat with Me 110s and noted that the latter seemed to be trying to form a defensive circle.[61]

As already stated, A Fight of 601 Squadron were the first to be vectored onto this raid, detected somewhat late. F/Lt Sir Archibald Hope, their twenty-eight-year-old leader, was the 17th Baronet of Craighall, Scotland, an Oxford graduate and chartered accountant.[62] His combat report below gives an admirably clear exposition of the interception and also illustrates the excellent leadership of a skilled tactician; he had no hesitation but acted promptly and cleverly.[63]

I was leading A Flight on patrol over Portland Bill at 16,000' at 11.33 when we sighted a large formation of E/A to the west (about 1 mile) flying north. I counted 21 Ju87 and then observed about 5 formations in vic behind stretching right out of sight. Each formation of 7 a/c at least. The leading E/A were about 14,000', the rear ones at 16,000', the same as us. The E/A were getting into line astern and then turning right and diving. I turned right and my Flight got into line astern also. There were no 110s above me so I turned left and we all attacked the mass of

Ju87s below us. I opened fire on one at about 300 yds. Its rear gunner ceased to fire and it turned and slipped over to the left disappearing in a most peculiar manner. I then pulled up on two more 87s about 200′ above and 200 yds away and fired a 4 sec burst at one which appeared to fall away to the right, out of control. I carried on and at once saw one Me110 ahead of me at which I finished my bullets. There were three other 110s just above me on the right so I dived to sea level and came home. A cine film was exposed. No E/A were observed to crash. All the 87s had long range tanks on the wings, rather larger but the same shape as those on a long-range Hurricane. They were coloured pale green or green blue below with black crosses. The Me110s were standard camouflaged. The Me110 escort appeared very inefficient to me. They were only about 1,000-1,500 feet above the 87s and were ½ to 5 miles behind. As the bombers turned east and formed line astern the 110s also turned east and were completely out of position when we attacked from the north west. [E/A = enemy aircraft; a/c = aircraft; 200′ = 200 feet]

Interesting criticism of the mishandling of the Me 110 escort, almost from one professional to another! F/Lt Hope's wingman F/Sgt Pond also recalled the incoming enemy aircraft flying north-east and then turning to the east to attack Portland harbour; as he, too, plunged into the melee of diving Stukas he encountered an Me 110 flying towards him and being pursued by a Hurricane, and Pond gave the German twin-engine fighter a brief burst from the beam as it sped past.[64] F/O C. J. H. Riddle, one of two brothers serving in 601 Squadron and leading Yellow, the second section behind F/Lt Hope and F/Sgt Pond, also shot at a Ju 87 but was too close and broke off almost immediately, watching it turn over and descend out of sight.[65] Very wisely, he remembered to look in his mirror then, just in time to see three Me 110s firing at him from very close astern, and he did a half roll, diving to 5,000 ft and with a steep aileron turn successfully lost them.[66]

His number two in Yellow Section, P/O Chaloner-Lindsey who would have been flying behind Riddle, also dived down onto the descending Ju 87s. Patrick Chaloner-Lindsey, a pre-war short service commission entrant, was unfortunate enough to be involved in a three-aircraft collision on 17 August 1939, but when he realised one of his passengers lacked a parachute, and despite a badly broken leg and head injuries, he eschewed bailing out himself and was able to land the machine safely; for his troubles he received a mere letter of appreciation from higher authority.[67] His combat report of 11 July 1940, the only one he would submit before his death in action fifteen days later, not only makes interesting reading in itself as he immediately met an Me 110 upon diving into the melee, but also serves as a brief memorial to a brave man.[68]

I was No 2 Yellow Section. We attacked Raid off Portland, diving to the attack. I got on the tail of an Me 110 and closed to 100-150 yds and opened fire keeping on a burst of 5 seconds. I observed tracer entering the e/a. I broke away and climbing up delivered a beam attack, I again observed tracer entering the fuselage of e/a, he then slipped away towards the sea. At 50 to 60 ft, the port engine was on fire. As he was about to hit the sea another Hurricane put a burst into him and he went straight in and sank immediately.

After his fleeting shot at a Messerschmitt 110, F/Sgt Pond attacked a Stuka diving down towards the Portland harbour mole and was only able to keep up with it by using his boost cut-out to get within *c.* 200 yards; after a few seconds the rear gunner stopped firing back but then he had to break away and did not see it crash.[69] The headlong dive of A Flight of 601 Squadron into the midst of the diving Ju 87s and Me 110s of *9/ZG 76*, upset their aim and the Stuka attack on Portland harbour at 11h53 was ineffective as a result, with only a single merchant vessel slightly damaged and the harbour itself virtually unscathed.[70] At least six claims against Ju 87s by 601 Squadron's A Flight are recorded: one confirmed by F/O Cleaver, five probables and one damaged.[71] The raid on Portland had been made by *III/StG 2* escorted by Me 110s from *III/ZG 76* and only one dive bomber was lost, with two NCOs missing after their machine crashed into the Channel off Portland Harbour mole.[72] It is thus likely that F/Sgt Pond attacked the already mortally hit Stuka sent down by F/O Cleaver; an uncontrolled dive to destruction without using dive-brakes would explain why Pond needed to use his boost over-ride to catch up with this machine. As to the many probables claimed against Ju 87s by 601 Squadron's pilots, the ability of the Stukas to manoeuvre in unusual fashion, especially with dive-brakes out when diving, might explain those misinterpretations; see descriptions in F/Lt Hope's combat report above.

It is evident from the following combat report excerpt written by S/L Dewar, leader of the 87 Squadron section, that they intercepted the incoming German raid very soon after 601 Squadron's A Flight had arrived on the scene: this is supported by his observation that German aircraft were diving towards ships as the 87 Squadron machines approached, and that he saw two other Hurricanes in action with Me 110s.[73]

Hurricanes at 5,000 ft. West of Weymouth, sighted 9 enemy aircraft approaching Portland from the south at 15,000 ft approx. Commenced to climb going south to get in between E.A. and sun. Saw 9 more E.A. and one group of about 12 Me110s as we were going up. Got level and up sun of enemy at about 12,000 ft. As we approached some aircraft dived to attack shipping. Enemy did not appear to be aware of our presence. Saw two other Hurricanes attacking and swung into 110s which seemed to be flying to form a circle. Saw a Hurricane diving and turning slowly with 110 on his tail, put four burst in 110. On last burst port engine appeared to blow up. Aircraft flicked onto its back and dived almost vertically. Owing to presence of numerous E.A. I did not watch this aircraft hit the sea, but I feel certain it must have gone in about 4 miles east of Shambles. Method of approach was line astern then 'free for all'. Fire brought to bear from astern, with full deflections, as aircraft was turning. The aircraft had the normal markings.

The manoeuvres of the section led by S/L Dewar were very effective, in placing them at about the same level as the Me 110s, but up-sun from them, thereby also placing the Me 110s, already troubled by attack from some of the 601 Squadron Hurricanes and apparently trying to form a circle to defend themselves, in an even worse tactical position. Surprise was also achieved, an extremely valuable commodity in combat. S/L Dewar attacked the Me 110s directly over Portland harbour, having just seen the Stukas diving towards shipping there; his approach from the south was unexpected for intercepting British fighters. As with F/Lt Hope's leadership, John Dewar's guiding of his small formation into a tactically advantageous position was exceptional. This was hardly surprising for someone as experienced as he; a Cranwell graduate with high ratings from that establishment, the thirty-three-year-old Dewar had led 87 Squadron over France with outstanding skill and returned to the United Kingdom to be decorated with the DSO and DFC.[74] He appears to have shot his Me 110 victim off the tail of a Hurricane, presumably one from 601 Squadron; both F/Lt Hope and F/O Riddle from this squadron reported diving away from pursuing Me 110s.[75] The Shambles mentioned in Dewar's report excerpt above refers to a treacherous sandbank about 3 miles east-south-east of Portland Bill, marked by a lightship until 1 August 1940 when it was deactivated and the crew withdrawn, the vessel itself being towed into Portland harbour for the duration.[76]

S/L Dewar's excellent leadership and tactics enabled his section to perform beyond their numbers. His number three, P/O Jay, described how a Me 110 went straight across in front of him in a steep turn as he dived to the attack; having given it a burst it dived away, followed by Trevor Jay who gave it rather long bursts on the way down and saw how it hit the sea at more than 300 mph without ever trying to come out of the dive.[77] Jay was to lose his life near the end of the Battle of Britain, still aged only nineteen.[78] Dewar's number two, meanwhile, F/O Dick Glyde, gave an Me 110 nearest him two deflection bursts, then proceeded to get on its tail and as the Messerschmitt turned gently, he fired once more, this time closing in from 200 to only 80 yards.[79] The fighter lost power as thick white vapour came out of both engines and Glyde managed a last burst just before overshooting.[80] But then Glyde was himself hit from behind, three rounds passing through his starboard wing tip and a fourth through the rear panel of his cockpit canopy, a close escape; he quickly half-rolled out of the line of Me 110 fire, diving steeply away.[81] The initial surprise attack led by S/L Dewar had thus seriously hit three Me 110s, at no real damage to the 87 Squadron trio, and two of them would soon do even more damage.

B Flight of 238 Squadron, having been patrolling their base at Warmwell, were vectored to Portland at 11h55, just after Portland harbour had been bombed. As they approached Portland, they observed anti-aircraft fire at 5,000 ft, some 5,000 feet below them.[82] F/Lt Walch put them into line astern and climbed towards a combat they could see south of them, about 3 miles away.[83] Getting closer Walch observed a Me 110 at about 10,000 ft diving towards a ship off Portland Bill; ordering Green Section to stay above as protection against any escort fighters, F/Lt Walch took Blue Section into the attack on the lone Me 110, which turned towards him.[84] He fired two three-second bursts from overhead at a range of *c*. 300-200 yards, and after Blue 3 had also fired, Walch made a second attack from the beam and then closed in from astern from 250 to only 50 yards, seeing the Messerschmitt straighten out, white smoke issuing from one engine.[85] This then caught fire and the Me 110 dived with Blue Section following and seeing their shared victim crash into the sea.[86]

This same Me 110 seems also to have caught the attention of F/O Glyde of 87 Squadron, as he escaped an attack from the rear by a Messerschmitt, as described above. After this lucky escape, Glyde had a good look around and spotted a Hurricane attacking a Me 110 at *c*. 6,000 ft, and he joined the party, firing several apparently unsuccessful deflection bursts before yet another Hurricane joined in.[87] As the hapless Me 110 descended further, to *c*. 3,000 ft, trying also to escape seawards, Glyde applied his boost cut-out to catch up again and from slightly above and closing from a range of 250 yards to 100 yards, let fly again and saw white vapour coming out of the one engine.[88] Once more he had another and even more fortunate escape as the plucky rear gunner put a bullet through the central panel of his cockpit hood, which ended up hitting the armour plate just behind his head.[89] Glyde fired again at the Messerschmitt and saw it ditch, apparently still under control, near a light ship east of Portland Bill, the machine sinking within half a minute; he saw no one emerge.[90] As will be seen, he was probably mistaken in this last impression.

The light ship was the Shambles vessel referred to earlier and would almost certainly have been the ship seen by F/Lt Walch of 238 Squadron. F/O Glyde, 87 Squadron clearly referred to two other Hurricanes being involved; a third additional Hurricane attacker, logically, would have been

P/O Chaloner-Lindsey of 601 Squadron, who also saw a lone Me 110 hit the sea with an engine on fire, and who had done the initial damage to this aircraft at the start of the battle when A Flight of 601 Squadron dived onto the descending Stukas and the escorting Me 110s of 9/ZG 76.[91] Three separate claims, by Chaloner-Lindsey 601 Squadron, F/O Glyde 87 Squadron and F/Lt Walch's Blue Section 238 Squadron thus all appear to refer to the same Me 110 which ditched off the Shambles.[92]

Interestingly, there is a German account of this loss. *Lt* Jochen Schröder led the second *Schwarm* of only three machines instead of the usual four, of Me 110s in 9/ZG 76, escorting Ju 87s to attack shipping at Portland harbour, and flying at about 12,000-14,000 ft when attacked by Hurricanes.[93] His rear gunner, *Gefreiter* Franz Sorokoput, shouted a warning just as bullets hammered the Messerschmitt, shattering the instruments and setting the starboard engine on fire.[94] Presumably, this would have been the first attack, by P/O Chaloner-Lindsey. Using the engine fire extinguisher and diving for 5,000 ft, Schröder managed to get the fire out, but soon after they were attacked again, gunner Franz Sorokoput pluckily almost dispatching F/O Glyde but being himself badly wounded in these final attacks, by Glyde and F/Lt Walch; Schröder managed to ditch successfully a couple of miles offshore of one of the Portland breakwaters and got his wounded comrade out of the rapidly sinking machine and inflated his mae west for him.[95] Schröder himself was dragged down underwater as his aircraft sank, as he was still attached by a microphone lead but he managed to rip off his helmet and swim back to the surface, where he was rescued not long after; however his gunner had by then disappeared and was never found.[96]

There is a *Luftwaffe* account for another of the four Me 110s lost in this battle, flown by the *Staffelkapitän* of 9/ZG 76, *Oberleutnant* Gerhard Kadow.[97] He first met RAF fighters over the coast and after breaking away from an initial head-on encounter was almost instantly attacked from the rear by two more fighters; these hit both engines which became almost useless thereafter.[98] Although Kadow claims both engines stopped after this first assault by the three fighters, his further actions before a final forced-landing at Grange Heath near Lulworth at *c.* 12h10[99] suggest he still had some power available. His first three attackers can logically be identified as Green Section of 238 Squadron, left above as cover against escort fighters when F/Lt Walch led his Blue Section down onto a lone Me 110, as described earlier, who claimed a shared Messerschmitt 110.[100] While these three Hurricanes of 238 Squadron saw that Kadow's machine was done for and ceased firing while still following him,[101] two more Hurricanes got involved.

S/L John Dewar of 87 Squadron whose partial combat report was given above, after leaving one Me 110 almost certainly badly hit, flew a full circle to assess the battle he was involved in, and also to clear his tail of two more Me 110s. He saw a bomb exploding near ships in Portland harbour, two German aircraft diving towards the ground and one more Me 110 apparently still pursuing him.[102] Dewar's second Me 110 claim, also against that flown by *Oblt* Kadow which force-landed on Grange Heath, would have been met initially while it was over a position somewhere east of the Shambles.

Two further Me 110s of *III/ZG 76* were lost in this Portland raid, the machines flown by *Oblt* Hans-Joachim Göring, nephew of the *Reichsmarschall*, with gunner *Uffz* Albert Zimmermann, and *Lt* Friedrich-Wolfgang Graf von und zu Castell with gunner *Gefr* Heinz Reder; both crews perished.[103] Graf Castell, from *7 Staffel* had bravely gone to the assistance of Göring from his higher-flying escort position, having seen Göring from *9th Staffel* fighting several British machines. The latter was last seen plunging vertically in flames, while his would-be saviour plunged into the sea.[104] Graf zu Castell's aircraft is the only possible candidate for the Me 110 seen by P/O Jay of 87 Squadron to dive into the sea at over 300 mph,[105] as Göring's came down on land.

Trevor Jay had seen an Me 110 flying in a steep turn in front of his Hurricane as he dived into the Messerschmitts behind his leader, S/L Dewar.[106] Jay gave it a burst as the Me 110 dived, followed by the Hurricane, which gave it several fairly long bursts on the way down.[107] Obviously the crew of this particular Me 110 were either dead or incapacitated, as no attempts to bail out or return fire were seen by Jay and it plunged straight down into the sea at high speed.[108] It is quite possible this was the same aircraft attacked by his 87 Squadron colleague F/O Glyde, who had fired three bursts at an Me 110, the third from only 80 yards and which was followed by the German fighter giving off thick white vapour as it slowed markedly, before Glyde got in a final burst prior to overshooting.[109] Seeing as the three 87 Squadron Hurricanes were flying in line astern, with Glyde number two, he would have arrived at the fight momentarily before Jay. The vapour and loss of power observed by Glyde as he closed right in suggest sudden throttling back by the Me 110 pilot, something he would have needs done before diving steeply away. Perhaps Glyde's final burst hit the crew, or one of Jay's bursts as the Messerschmitt dived to its destruction, we will never know. No German Me 110 pilot would willingly have gone into a full-out dive with throttles still wide open, as this aircraft was well known for stiff controls, particularly being very difficult to pull out of any kind of a dive.

Göring and Zimmermann's flaming machine crashed at high speed directly into a rocky height on the island of Portland, the Verne citadel, where it and its human cargo were immolated; no trace of either man was ever found and they remain missing to this day.[110] Both these *III/ZG 76* Me 110s fell at *c.* 12h00,[111] right at the beginning of the fight between the

Me 110s and the British fighters, encompassing a few from 601 Squadron, three from 87 Squadron very soon after, and some minutes later six from 238 Squadron. The most likely candidate for the demise of Göring and Zimmermann was S/L Dewar, the first 87 Squadron member to pounce on the Me 110s of 9/ZG 76. In his combat report excerpt, Dewar described giving an Me 110 four bursts and then seeing its port engine apparently blowing up, and immediately afterwards the Messerschmitt flicked onto its back and dived almost vertically away. Presumably the port petrol tanks had exploded and this would have started a major fire, and the crew were, like Graf Castell and his unfortunate gunner, either incapacitated or dead, and the machine thus never pulled out of its final dive to destruction on the Verne citadel's rocks. That the Me 110 flicked over into a dive after Dewar's fourth burst suggests the crew had been hit.

There is a problem with this interpretation of Dewar as the logical victor: in his combat report he states that he felt sure the Me 110 had gone in some 4 miles east of the Shambles sandbank.[112] However, Dewar's claim was right at the beginning of the fight, which began over Portland itself and he himself describes in the second part of his combat report seeing a bomb land near a ship in the harbour;[113] this argues against a location some 7 miles to the east of Portland, i.e. 4 miles beyond the Shambles. In addition, Schröder's Me 110 ditched only about 2 miles offshore of Portland about five minutes after the loss of the Me 110s of Göring and Graf Castell.[114] One should also remember that combat reports were filled in immediately after landing, with excited pilots clustering around the squadron intelligence officer as they did so; in this environment mistakes were common enough. Dewar's second Me 110 claim, that flown by *Oblt* Kadow which force-landed on Grange Heath, would have been met initially while it was over a position somewhere East of the Shambles. S/L Dewar may thus in the excitement of the moment of reporting confused the two locations, over Portland and east of the Shambles.

The anti-aircraft gunners at Portland harbour, mostly on the Verne heights, claimed three victories during the aerial battle,[115] which logically would equate to the two Me 110s of Göring and Graf Castell and the lone Stuka of *III/StG 2*, which all fell close to or on Portland itself.[116] It is also possible that the explosion seen by S/L Dewar on Göring's port wing when the engine exploded was an anti-aircraft hit; the degree to which anti-aircraft fire contributed to the loss of these three German machines cannot be determined.

While *III/ZG 76* lost four Me 110s and their crews, they claimed two Hurricanes, one each by *Oblt* Kaldrack and *Oblt* Tonne.[117] Two Hurricanes were in fact damaged but repairable, that of F/Lt Walch 238 Squadron, by Me 110 forward fire and rear gunner bullets as already described, and that of F/Sgt Pond whose machine was hit several times by friendly fire from his own squadron, 601, as detailed below.[118] The fact that the two Hurricane claims by *III/ZG 76* do not appear in the *Luftwaffe* claims list[119] suggests they were not confirmed by the relevant authorities. Significantly, it would appear that two of the Me 110s that were shot down fell victim to five attacking fighters each, a third to two RAF fighters and just one probably to only one attacker; and the contribution of Portland anti-aircraft fire is unknown. Me 110s thus seem generally to have required multiple attacking British fighters, and seldom fell to a single attacker.

There was another Stuka raid associated with the dive bombing attack on Portland harbour by *III/StG 1*, tasked with bombing some ships apparently hugging the English coast; their leader, *Hauptmann* Mahlke commented favourably on their fighter escort which rendezvoused on time.[120] *V/LG 1* had been scheduled to provide escort to Ju 87s on their way to Weymouth Bay at noon, but their mission was scrubbed due to excessively cloudy weather conditions.[121] Presumably they were part of a larger planned escort. In the event, Mahlke's *Gruppe* found only a single vessel sailing some 15 km south-east of Portland, HMY *Warrior*, a converted luxury yacht of 1,120 grt and 284 feet long, used to provide escort for Royal Navy submarines on passage between Portland and Portsmouth naval bases.[122] Even though attacked by an entire *Gruppe*, strong and unexpected winds below 3,000 ft badly upset their aim and no hits were claimed.[123] Those on the helpless yacht experienced this attack somewhat differently, recording being bombed by over fifty aircraft, but probably only thirty, the norm for a *Gruppe*; one bomb did hit, passing right through the vessel, killing one man and sinking the ship.[124] *III/StG 1* certainly did not seek out shipping hugging the coast, but appear to have bombed the first vessel they sighted, about 15 km south-east of Portland in open waters.[125]

Possibly in reaction to the ingress of this unexpected associated raid, there was some rather confused vectoring of British fighters. F/Sgt Pond of 601 Squadron, after having followed a Ju 87 in its dive down into the sea off Portland harbour earlier, became involved in the confusion and when he tried to join up with a Hurricane section thereafter, they mistook him for an enemy and turned onto his tail when he came up behind them.[126] They were actually the section of 501 Squadron which had been scrambled to meet the German raid but did not intercept. One of them, P/O Hewitt, opened fire on Pond's machine, damaging his air speed indicator, flaps and one aileron but he managed to get back to base at Tangmere without further harm.[127] Hewitt claimed an enemy Hurricane on his return.[128]

A small raid on Portsmouth countered, c. 18h00

At about 18h00 the dockyard at Portsmouth was bombed by a small formation, comprising twelve He 111s of *I/KG 55*, escorted by about a dozen Me 110s of *III/ZG 76*.[129] It was detected at 17h46 flying over the Channel directly north of Cherbourg; 601 Squadron had been on patrol over their base at Tangmere for about half an hour already and a few minutes after detection 145 Squadron at nearby Westhampnett was ordered up as well, taking off at about 18h00, as the bombs were actually falling on Portsmouth,[130] 601 Squadron was vectored to the Southampton area as the raid's course suggested either that city or Portsmouth as the likely targets.[131] The German raid progressed across the Channel directly northwards and once over the Needles at the western end of the Isle of Wight they turned north-eastward up the Solent, heading straight towards Portsmouth.[132] Coming south from Southampton, twelve Hurricanes of 601 Squadron led by F/O Rhodes-Moorhouse intercepted about halfway up the Solent opposite the north-west coast of the Isle of Wight. They counted the twelve bombers, flying in vics of three machines, line astern, and noted the escort of Me 110s higher up.[133] While Rhodes-Moorhouse led one flight for the bombers at about 18,000 ft, he ordered the other to climb and take care of the escort several thousand feet higher; a running fight then ensued up the Solent towards Portsmouth.[134]

There is a fascinating eyewitness account from the small bomber formation by *Oberleutnant* Siegfried Schweinhagen, the observer who was flying in the lead aircraft of the last bomber vic, coded G1+LK.[135] As Schweinhagen watched the Needles pass by about 16,000 ft below and his pilot turned in the direction of Portsmouth up the Solent, he saw the Me 110s surge ahead after sighting approaching dots from the Southampton area.[136] In the few minutes before the Heinkels reached their target area, the six Hurricanes of 601 Squadron did their best to hinder their progress; their claims against *I/KG 55* are confusing as four different sets of relevant records which have been preserved provide highly variable numbers of bombers destroyed, varying from one to four, or probably destroyed, between four and six.[137] Suffice to say that 601 Squadron must at least have hit several He 111s and certainly distracted them as their target rapidly came up ahead, as the bombing only caused slight damage to Portsmouth, which suffered about twenty bombs dropped and the chosen target, the floating dock, escaped unscathed.[138]

F/Sgt Pond, 601 Squadron, in the heat of the moment while making an attack on a Heinkel from the rear, saw his victim explode and debris hit the adjacent machine as the action continued on over Portsmouth harbour itself.[139] Pond then appears to have hit the adjacent machine, which later crashed on East Beach, Selsey.[140] This aircraft was in fact that in which *Oberleutnant* Schweinhagen was flying and his report has it that his left wingman was hit by anti-aircraft fire and the Heinkel went straight down and into the harbour.[141] Bearing in mind that they were flying at about 16,000 ft, any anti-aircraft hit must needs have been by a reasonably large shell that would logically have caused an explosion, especially if a bomb had been detonated in the aircraft. This could have been what F/Sgt Pond observed, but equally one of his bullets could also have detonated a bomb on the Heinkel and caused a violent explosion, which Schweinhagen interpreted as an ack-ack hit. Either way, the Heinkel would almost certainly have been blown to bits and scattered wreckage and the bodies of the unfortunate crew should then have been observed in the harbour itself, and none were reported. This aircraft, G1+HK, is reported as missing along with its crew, having crashed into the Channel off Selsey Bill.[142] How to reconcile such a discrepancy is not obvious, but it is possible that this machine was hit by an anti-aircraft shell, dived rapidly away following a more limited explosion and managed to make it a few miles out over the Channel off Selsey Bill, where it met its end. It has also been credited to 145 Squadron in such a location[143] during the attack of that unit on the Heinkels which followed on that by 601 Squadron; this subsequent action is described below.

Siegfried Schweinhagen and G1+LK, just after having bombed the harbour, were attacked from behind by two fighters of 601 Squadron, which inflicted mortal damage and he did not report any collision with the vanished left wingman's aircraft; as they left the Portsmouth peninsula behind them heading south for the coast, both engines were on fire, the one undercarriage leg hung down indicating the loss of hydraulic fluid and both dorsal and ventral rear gunners were badly wounded.[144] While the action between one flight of 601 Squadron and the Heinkels had been going on, about 7,000 ft above them, the other flight had tackled the dozen or so Me 110s of the escort, which initially formed a circle.[145] Not much information is available on this part of the battle, but one Me 110 was claimed shot down[146] and two Hurricanes were claimed by *III/ZG 76*, who suffered no casualties themselves.[147] But as the raid, its escort and the attackers of both from 601 Squadron approached Portsmouth harbour, the anti-aircraft defences opened up on everybody, and the one Hurricane lost by the squadron has been ascribed to this in many sources.[148] Another reference ascribes the loss of this machine to a bullet received in the gravity tank of the Hurricane during an attack on the bombers over the Channel off Selsey Bill, and that the pilot bailed out badly burned and wounded.[149]

There is an account by the pilot concerned, Sgt Arthur Woolley, which appears to be a formal report on his bailing out on 11 July 1940, and under rather special conditions at that.[150] While he was, fortunately, only slightly burned and had suffered some broken ribs, Woolley was indeed brought down by a hit in the gravity tank, but from one of three cannon shells which hit his Hurricane while in combat with some of the Me 110s.[151] As the aircraft caught fire he bailed out at about 23,000 ft, opening his parachute within seconds; as he was temporarily blinded by burning petrol and deafened from the noise of the cannon strikes, he was blissfully and very fortunately unaware of the extreme peril he was facing.[152]

Another of the cannon shells had exploded in the middle of his 'chute, which he was sitting on, as did all RAF fighter pilots at the time of the Battle, causing numerous splinter holes in the canopy.[153] Safely on the ground on the north-western part of the Isle of Wight, only then did he see that his parachute was somewhat the worse for wear but still had worked perfectly; the Irvine Company had reason to be proud of that 'chute.[154] Later, after his discharge from hospital and a more careful examination of his parachute on the squadron, about 50 round bullet holes, very different in appearance to those from the splinters, were noted; in addition it was clear that the bullet holes had not resulted from hits while the 'chute was still folded but had been caused once it was opened.[155] Arthur Woolley thus had a very strong case for having been shot at while hanging helplessly, temporarily blinded and deaf, beneath his parachute canopy. One can only suspect the Me 110s of *III/ZG 76*, which had suffered the loss of four of their own aircraft and crews earlier in the day, with five dead including one of Göring's nephews.[156] The plunge of his burning Hurricane and his bailing out was seen by Siegfried Schweinhagen in *I/KG 55* Heinkel G1+LK as this aircraft flew up the Solent towards Portsmouth.[157]

145 Squadron, having taken off as the bombs fell, saw anti-aircraft fire ahead, as well as two groups of enemy aircraft high above as they lifted off. S/L Peel led them in a climb for the enemy and they turned after them as the bombers were flying south-south-east away from Portsmouth.[158] By the time they got up to the bombers, 145 Squadron could see only one or two of the escort still in view as the Me 110s put on speed and vanished across the Channel leaving the bombers behind.[159] 145 Squadron thus found the Heinkels unprotected as they closed, with eleven bombers still in formation.[160] They were soon reduced to ten as the Heinkel G1+LK with Siegfried Schweinhagen aboard could not keep up and lost height fast as their comrades kept to their southerly course for France; at this stage they were attacked by Hurricanes from all sides,[161] which must have belonged to 145 Squadron.

As the two seriously wounded gunners aboard the machine could not have survived ditching, the fast failing Heinkel was turned back to port where a large beach lay behind them.[162] It being low tide, a successful crash-landing was made on the wide expanse of sand exposed on East Beach on the eastern side of Selsey Bill.[163] With both engines smouldering, three of the crew, all wounded, managed to extricate themselves from the aircraft, and despite warning of imminent explosion, soldiers bravely helped them to remove the two gunners, one already dead and the other mortally wounded; *Oberleutnant* Schweinhagen and the others just got out in time, as the fire reached the petrol tanks in the wings and the wreck exploded and largely burnt out (Illustration 41).[164] Though almost certainly a victim of both 601 and 145 Squadrons, G1+LK is credited to P/O Wakeham and P/O Lord Kay-Shuttleworth of the latter unit.[165] Presumably they had delivered the coup de grace to an already doomed bomber; this is how over-claiming so often resulted in fast-moving and complex aerial action, and normally with no deliberate intent.

The Heinkel G1+HK that F/Sgt Pond believed to have exploded under his fire and which *Oberleutnant* Schweinhagen thought had been hit mortally by anti-aircraft fire as his wingman dropped rapidly out of formation and appeared to have fallen into Portsmouth harbour, seems to have nevertheless made it away over the Channel. P/O Storrar of 145 Squadron, having become separated from his comrades in their initial attack on the retreating Heinkel formation, noticed a lone bomber trailing white smoke making off to the south-south-west, which he caught up with south of St Catherines Point on the Isle of Wight.[166] After a single rear attack the machine belched black smoke, the undercarriage dropped and Storrar saw it land on the sea with two crew members managing to escape and perch on a wing.[167] I/KG 55 suffered only two total losses in this action and this machine could only have been G1+HK, missing with its crew of five, in the waters of the Channel.[168] F/Lt Dutton of 145 Squadron also claimed a He 111 shot down[169] and might have damaged the Heinkel before Storrar found it; thus each was likely unaware of the other's role in its destruction.

S/L Peel had led 145 Squadron in an attack from the rear against the retreating Heinkel formation near Selsey Bill.[170] Despite being hit by return fire and his aircraft being badly damaged, Peel held on and chased a bomber out over the sea for 25 miles across the Channel, claiming it as a probable; his Hurricane made it back close to the coast but he was forced to ditch south-west of Selsey Bill, fortunately being seen by the coastguards.[171] He was lucky to be rescued just in time by the Selsey lifeboat in a semi-conscious state.[172] A second Hurricane also pursued a He 111 out to sea and suffered damage to its glycol cooling system; F/O Branch managed to get back to base where his engine seized, but he got it down in one piece.[173] In all, 145 Squadron claimed three Heinkels and one Me 110 destroyed.[174] While the loss of two bombers, G1+LK and G1+HK have been dealt with already, a third He 111 force-landed at its base at Villacoublay in south-western Paris where it was written off, 80% damaged;[175] possibly, S/L Peel accounted for this machine or at least partly so, with F/O Branch.

It was at this stage in the Battle that the RAF instituted some concrete action to improve the very inadequate air sea rescue situation, in view of the many pilots ending up in the sea due to the nature of the combat during July, dominated by maritime and coastal targets.[176] Arrangements were set in train with the Admiralty for motor craft to patrol actively close inshore when aerial action was happening, and additionally over three hundred small craft controlled by the Royal Navy were given general instructions to keep watch in their areas when aerial battles were in train.[177] The RAF's direct response involved stationing fast launches at the 11 Group coast, one at Calshot in the Solent, and two each at Newhaven, just west of Beachy Head, and Ramsgate, just south of North Foreland; although controlled by Coastal Command, requests through the relevant Coastal Group headquarters could be speeded up through phone calls directly to the launches' home stations.[178] Finally, in early September 1940, several Lysander aircraft were specifically stationed in 10 and 11 Groups, Fighter Command, to search for downed pilots and help to guide small craft towards them.[179] The Royal National Lifeboat Institution vessels also performed sterling service throughout the Battle.

In summation, the evening *Luftwaffe* raid on Portsmouth reflects rather poor planning: the bomber formation was too small to inflict serious damage on its dockyard target; the escort was too small to be effective, bearing in mind the inferiority of the Me 110 against both RAF fighter types. While the Me 110s did in fact distract half of the first squadron to attack, 601 Squadron, the other flight and very soon after 145 Squadron pitted eighteen fighters against just twelve bombers. To lose three bombers from twelve represents a catastrophic loss rate of 25%. Damage in Portsmouth was limited and mostly to civilian targets, while the targeted floating dock escaped unharmed. Both British squadrons appear to have made rear attacks on the small bomber formation, though the documentation on attack method remains somewhat vague.

In reality, eighteen RAF fighters pitted against twelve effectively unescorted Heinkels should have led to a greater slaughter. The first two bombers damaged, G1+LK and G1+HK, seem also to have attracted quite a few other fighters, a common feature throughout the Battle. The controllers did a good job, placing both British fighter squadrons favourably for attack on the bombers, and at approximately the right altitudes to do so; the force used was appropriate, and one squadron, 601, was in position and able to attack the bombers before they bombed. Undoubtedly, they, together with the strong anti-aircraft barrage over a major naval base, distracted the bomb-aiming. The second squadron, 145, was ideally placed to decimate a retreating small formation of effectively unescorted bombers and might well have done so if many of the Hurricanes did not latch onto two already mortally damaged bombers. Both sides were obviously still learning – but the RAF won this battle reasonably comfortably.

4

12–15 July 1940: Activity Shifts to Dover Straits and East Coast Convoys; *EGr 210* Enters the Fray

12 July 1940: triple convoy attack off east coast

The only bombing raids on 12 July were a set of unescorted *Luftwaffe* attacks on convoy FS219 'Booty', comprising thirty-eight ships, mostly relatively small coasters varying from 230 to 3,168 tons. It left the Tyne Estuary the day before and was due to arrive at Southend, at the entrance to the Thames Estuary, on the 12th.[1] This convoy was to be assaulted three times, approximately 15 miles east of Aldeburgh, between *c*. 08h40 and 09h10.[2] A total of nineteen RAF fighters engaged a reported twenty-one He 111s of *KG 53* and three Do 17s of *KG 2* over the convoy and its environs.[3] With all the aerial combat taking place several miles out to sea, casualties from machines that were shot down were high.[4]

The German plan had obviously to take into account that the target was far beyond Me 109 escort range, and no Me 110s, which could easily have covered the relevant distance, were assigned either, as convoys generally in their experience thus far only had small escorts, mostly of two to three British fighters. By the time any RAF reinforcements had been scrambled, climbed and reached the convoy, the Germans intended to be long gone. To this end, the three bomber formations were to attack the convoy in quick succession within the space of about thirty minutes.

Luftwaffe intelligence was very poor throughout the Battle[5] and they seem to have had little understanding that most sector stations had forward airfields to which fighters were sent almost daily to be that much closer to potential action. Hurricanes from 17 and 85 Squadrons from Debden were indeed placed at Martlesham Heath, ideally situated to defend the convoy, as this airfield was only 12 miles from Aldeburgh. The third British unit to be involved was 151 Squadron, which was at its North Weald sector station, but with controllers forewarned by radar (and the Dowding defensive system was as yet still largely a mystery to the *Luftwaffe*), they were sent off just after 08h30 and made the distance of more than 70 miles to the convoy, by then off Orfordness, in under half an hour. This was fast enough to let them catch the third German formation.[6] Poor intelligence and concomitant poor planning ensured that these unescorted bombers would be effectively countered, suffer significant casualties, and cause little damage to the convoy: one ship sunk, one damaged.[7]

Six Hurricanes of 17 Squadron were put up at about 08h00-08h15 as direct convoy protection.[8] They were split into three pairs of fighters by the Debden controller, one patrolling over Dunwich, another off Aldeburgh and the third pair off Orfordness, each separated by about 6 or 7 miles.[9] At the time of the first *Luftwaffe* attack on the convoy, the pair of P/O Manger and Sgt Griffiths were directly over it, with P/O Pittman and Sgt Fopp to the north and F/O Count Czernin and P/O Hanson to the south. These dispositions were good enough to ensure each successive incoming *Luftwaffe* formation was met by one of them. At about 08h40 Manger and Griffiths were at 10,000 ft above convoy Booty's ships when they sighted twelve He 111s of *II/KG 53*, flying in a single open vic formation a couple of thousand feet lower down; as the Heinkels had dived unexpectedly out of some clouds they were able to bomb the convoy and cause the abandonment of the *c.* 2,000-ton *Hornchurch* by its crew, which later sank off the Aldeburgh Light Vessel about 12 miles north-north-east of Aldeburgh itself.[10] Bent on revenge, P/O Manger led Sgt Griffiths in line astern into a dive for the Heinkels, and singled one out which had broken away from its formation, attacking from astern and below in a Number One attack; Manger opened fire at 350 yards, closing to 50 yds with a single long burst.[11] The bomber slowed down, both engines aflame and shedding debris, and the undercarriage dropped as it glided down into cloud; as Griffiths followed up with another long burst of about nine seconds, he saw the bomber start to disintegrate.[12] The Heinkel of *II/KG 53* fell into the North Sea where it and its crew disappeared.[13]

Expecting more of the same and as no doubt also registered with radar warning, 11 Group rapidly sent in reinforcements, initially three Hurricanes of 85 Squadron from North Weald, but which were already at the Martlesham Heath forward base.[14] At the same time, the northern 17 Squadron pair over Dunwich were ordered south, and having about the same distance to fly as the 85 Squadron trio they got there slightly ahead, as they were already at altitude when summonsed.[15] North Weald also put up ten Hurricanes of 151 Squadron – which had a long way to go – and 12 Group added nine more fighters, but these did not intercept.[16] Interrogation of *Luftwaffe* survivors from the second formation, now closing with the convoy, revealed that the whole of *8/KG 53*, nine machines, had taken off from its French base at Mouvaux, Lille area, and assembled into a formation comprising three *Ketten* in vics line astern headed north over the sea for the convoy off Aldeburgh.[17] The three Heinkels making up the rear vic included the machines flown by *Fw* Böte and *Fw* Baumeister, the latter carrying *Oberleutnant* von Brocke as observer, who was also the intelligence officer of *III/KG 53*.[18] The observer was often the aircraft commander in *Luftwaffe* bombers and this machine was thus probably leading the *Kette* also, with a member of the *Gruppe* staff on board.

It was von Brocke's machine that attracted the attention of P/O Pittman and Sgt Fopp of 17 Squadron who had sighted the nine He 111s approaching the convoy about 15 miles off Aldeburgh at *c.* 8,000 ft; they had climbed up and placed themselves behind the last vic of Heinkels, and finding one straggling a bit, they made a series of quarter attacks on the machine with deflection taken into account.[19] The luckless He 111 made off to the south with the two Hurricanes in hot pursuit, continuing their quarter attacks, who were rewarded by seeing the undercarriage of the bomber drop and the port engine stream petrol and eventually stop; the aircraft crashed into the sea near a trawler which they had just tried to bomb, surely an act of desperation, whose captain nevertheless picked up three wounded survivors. Only the pilot lived, the two others being buried at sea the next day.[20] The Heinkel had fallen into the sea about 4 miles east-north-east of the Slipwash Light Vessel, off Orfordness.[21]

There were some other actors in this drama, flying in a number of 500 Squadron Coastal Command Ansons, also patrolling near Orfordness; just before the attacks by 17 and 85 Squadrons on *8/KG 53*, the Anson crewmen observed the leading three He 111s about to attack the ships and one Anson, MK-L, courageously climbed to engage as the balance of six more He 111s appeared.[22] Having seen the engagements with the 17 (Pittman and Fopp) and 85 Squadron pilots, the crew of this machine had the experience of passing almost head-on past the Heinkel under attack and as it flashed by the turret gunner on the Anson opened fire and watched as the Heinkel ditched in the sea, some survivors emerging.[23] Under the impression that they had shot this aircraft down and not having seen all the attacks made by P/O Pittman and Sgt Fopp on this bomber as it descended mortally hit towards the sea, the Anson crew quite understandably claimed the victory as theirs;[24] thus does innocent over-claiming occur.

Another Anson of 500 Squadron, coded MK-D and flown by F/O Whitehead, is reported as shot down by the same Heinkel in this action, with three crew killed and one survivor, Sgt Smith, taken prisoner.[25] This machine in fact crashed into the estuary of the Maas River at Pernis just outside Rotterdam in Holland, at about 23h30 the previous night, where the three bodies of Whitehead and two of his crew were recovered and Sgt Smith captured.[26] The loss of this Anson is ascribed to an attack by Heinkel bombers, which might explain why it has been taken as a victim of the convoy Booty actions where other aircraft of 500 Squadron were in fact engaged peripherally.[27]

As the two 17 Squadron pilots Pittman and Fopp had picked off their Heinkel from the rear vic, the bombers had been descending for their attack on the convoy and with the breakaway of the Baumeister/von Brocke Heinkel, the other two machines in the vic were left adrift of their comrades. It was at this stage that the three Hurricanes from 85 Squadron arrived on the scene at about 7,000 ft; spotting the He 111s attacking the convoy, Sgt Jowitt led his section in a dive from approximately abeam the remains of the rear vic of bombers now flying at about 6,000 ft.[28] Jowitt must have been hit by return fire, as he crashed into the sea off Felixstowe to the south and was posted missing.[29] P/O Bickerdike, on his first operational mission, and Sgt Rust avenged him by setting the nearest Heinkel on fire, seeing it dive away in trouble.[30] Bickerdike was unable to follow his victim as another Heinkel attacked him,[31] possibly the lone survivor of the rearmost vic. Sgt Griffiths and P/O Manger, the first 17 Squadron pair to see action were still in the vicinity of the convoy, and the former reported seeing four Heinkels flying eastwards at about 4,000 ft, with one of them about 500 yards behind the other three.[32]

Having by now bombed the convoy, it was logical that the Heinkels, making for home, would want to put on all speed to escape and thus dived to put more distance behind themselves and the danger zone. Griffiths opened up on the trailing bomber, presumably already damaged by 85 Squadron's attack, from about 250 yards and closed in to only 50 yards seeing both engines on fire and the machine enter into a spiral dive into the sea, where it sank in about fifteen seconds with no sign of any survivors.[33] This aircraft can reasonably be tied to the second machine lost by 8/KG 53 that crashed into the North Sea about 10 miles north-north-west of the Aldeburgh Light Vessel, from which the pilot, *Feldwebel* Böte and the radioman *Fw* Hartmann, both wounded, were in fact rescued.[34] Under interrogation the two survivors let slip that their aircraft had carried twenty-six fifty kilogram bombs as well as two extra defensive machine guns mounted in the side windows of their Heinkel.[35] Hartmann was lucky to survive, he being the only crew member whose position lacked armour plate protection, with 85 Squadron's beam attack probably responsible for hitting at least some of those who did enjoy rear-facing armour plate.[36]

The third and final attack on convoy Booty was made by a small number of Do 17s from *II/KG 2*; while several sources discuss greater numbers of attacking bombers,[37] the intercepting RAF fighters only reported one vic of three Dorniers.[38] Amongst the *Luftwaffe* casualties was *Hauptmann* Erich Matchetzki, *Staffelkapitän* of 5/KG 2[39] so it is likely that all three machines were from the same *Staffel*. In a remarkably accurate piece of controlling, North Weald sector got the ten Hurricanes of 151 Squadron to make a perfect interception of the very small formation of three Dorniers at 6,000 ft off Orfordness as they made to attack the convoy[40] at about 09h00. Theoretically, it should have been a massacre, with ten Hurricanes boring in on only three bombers; however, the Dorniers kept a tight formation and fought back with heavy and almost perfectly coordinated return fire, which was to prove devastating.[41] The 151 Squadron formation comprised three sections of three Hurricanes each, led by their feisty commanding officer, S/L 'Teddy' Donaldson, plus the additional machine of Wing Commander Victor Beamish, station commander at North Weald, who kept his own Hurricane always available and which was maintained mostly by the ground staff of 151 Squadron.[42] Teddy Donaldson led his first section into the attack, as graphically described in the relevant Intelligence Patrol Report:[43]

> S/Ldr Donaldson attacked with No. 1 Section, having ordered No. 5 attack, but owing to a sharp turn by e/a only he himself got in an attack. This took the form of fire from 300 yds direct abeam closing to 30 yds. astern. Bullets hit the e/a but no results were seen. During this time both rudder cables of his Hurricane were shot away, the rotol spinner was hit and a bullet hitting the engine sump caused oil to pour all over the a/c making it very difficult to see. S/Ldr Donaldson managed to get back to Martlesham by opening throttle to swing a/c left and closing to swing right. The engine stopped about 50 feet off ground when landing but he got down safely although the starboard tyre was shot through. An explosive bullet had burst inside the fuselage of his machine. [No. 5 Fighter Command Area Attack = directly from astern, sections in line astern, each machine following the one in front]

Donaldson may have done better to have spread out his own fighters into section abreast (in an 'official' No 3 attack) to spread the bombers' return fire and to expose them to a much greater weight of fire from the Hurricanes. He took considerable risks and exhibited a remarkable display of flying skill and bravery to land successfully at base without further damage and thereby save his aircraft; many other pilots would simply have bailed out under the circumstances. S/L Donaldson used the engine torque (to the left) to swing the Hurricane by adroit use of the throttle.

151 Squadron was well known for its excellent leadership; with inspiration provided by Donaldson and Beamish, they were an aggressive bunch. No less of a tiger than Donaldson, W/Co Beamish bored in next on the same left hand Dornier and ignoring the heavy return cross-fire came in from slightly above to gain some speed and from dead astern and, by now level with his target, riddled the German bomber; the return fire stopped, the undercarriage dropped and the port engine blew up as it broke away from its two companions.⁴⁴ Beamish also managed to fly his badly damaged Hurricane safely back to North Weald, while four of his fellow pilots finished off the crippled aircraft and watched it crash into the North Sea.⁴⁵

F/Lt R. L. Smith flying the two-cannon Hurricane and his number two 'Buzz' Allen attacked the remaining two Dorniers, but the cannons didn't fire due to a broken compressor; Smith saw Allen press on into the attack before losing sight of him.⁴⁶ F/O Allen's Hurricane was also badly hit by the Dorniers' return fire, with serious damage to his engine, which seized a few minutes later; it was seen to ditch and man and machine to vanish from sight immediately.⁴⁷ P/O Hamar pursued the remaining two Dorniers, silencing return fire from the rear gunners and as he flew homewards he saw the Dornier the squadron had shot down still floating but already partly submerged.⁴⁸

The final act in the set of convoy attacks on Booty by the *Luftwaffe* was carried out by F/O Count Manfred Czernin and P/O Hanson of 17 Squadron. Observing 151 Squadron in action against the Dornier vic, they joined in and singled out the leader of the vic and chased it down to low level as it made out to sea eastwards.⁴⁹ They made a number of quarter-astern and head-on attacks on this hapless machine, leaving it struggling and flying slowly just above the waves of the North Sea.⁵⁰ This Dornier was lost, four crew missing including the *Staffelkapitän 5/KG 2, Hauptmann* Erich Machetzki.⁵¹ So two of the three Dorniers in the attacking vic were lost in fighting near the convoy, by then off Orfordness: one with Machetzki aboard crashed into the North Sea and the other fell into the water near the convoy.⁵² Exactly who shot down which of these two machines is unsure, but 151 and 17 Squadrons appear to have got one each.⁵³ Two sources each describe crewmen casualties from one of these Dornier aircraft, who appear to be confused with survivors from one of the 8/KG 53 Heinkels lost, that shot down by P/O Pittman and Sgt Fopp of 17 Squadron earlier.⁵⁴

Overall, the three successive attacks made on convoy Booty within the space of about half an hour must be judged a failure, reflecting poor planning predicated on weak *Luftwaffe* intelligence. Each of the three German bomber formations was intercepted and suffered severe casualties. Losses given as percentage of total sorties were: twelve He 111s *II/KG 53* (8%); nine He 111s *8/KG 53* (22%); three Do 17s *5/KG 2* (67%). Against the background of something like 5% loss often being considered the maximum rate a unit could stand and still operate effectively, these were catastrophic losses. Only one ship was lost and one damaged, while two RAF fighters and their pilots perished, with two machines seriously damaged. It was particularly the well trained and courageous gunners aboard the three Dorniers of *5/KG 2* who performed best in the entire action, whose deadly cross-fire caused one Hurricane to be lost and two severely damaged as they essentially bored in one at a time in-line astern. The leadership of 151 Squadron while equally courageous as the Do 17 gunners, was perhaps a bit too gung ho, exposing as it did each incoming fighte, in turn to the combined firepower of all three bombers. One aircraft and pilot lost with two machines heavily damaged was too high a price for the one Do 17 shot down by 151 Squadron; this was not the proportionate battle of attrition envisaged by Dowding and Park.

The one noticeable feature of the RAF defence was the outstanding fighter direction, especially by the North Weald and Debden controllers; every single formation, no matter how small, dispatched by 11 Group from these two sectors did in fact intercept a German formation over the sea. In contrast, no interceptions resulted from the two small formations launched from 12 Group stations,[55] neither of which had further to go than 151 Squadron.

12 July 1940: numerous single aircraft actions

For the rest of the day, the cloudy and rainy weather restricted *Luftwaffe* activity to lone raiders and reconnaissance incursions, from Scotland through to Cornwall. At about 10h00 a section of 609 Squadron led by F/Lt Howell with F/O Edge and P/O Curchin claimed a probably destroyed Heinkel He 111 some 3 miles east of Portland Bill.[56] This was most likely a 50% damaged He 111 of *Stab/StG 3* which force-landed at Cherbourg with three wounded crew members.[57]

Almost three hours later, at 12h55, Yellow Section of 603 Squadron, P/O Gilroy leading Sgt's Caister and Arber, respectively numbers 2 and 3, was scrambled after an intruder; they spotted a single He 111 at 10,000 ft north-west of Aberdeen, flying south-east.[58] Climbing to intercept, Yellow 1's first, long burst of ten seconds was made from the starboard beam, to quarter and then from an astern position, as he closed from *c.* 300 yards to 50 yards; the Heinkel's undercarriage dropped and oil splashed onto

P/O Gilroy's windscreen, while rear gunner return fire ceased.[59] Many more attacks were made by all three Spitfires from beam, astern and from above, as the Heinkel descended in a spiral, while also trying to climb very slowly at times. Yellow 2's windscreen was also splashed with oil.[60] When the enemy was seen to be out of control and over Aberdeen, Gilroy called the ceasefire, but the Dyce controller, receiving reports from pilots on the ground that the He 111 was climbing, ordered them to continue to attack, which they did, the last burst being from Sgt Arber when the Heinkel was at about 300 ft. It crashed into Aberdeen's new ice rink, killing all four aboard.[61] The Spitfires were carrying 2,800 rounds apiece, an extra 400 per machine.[62] While Aberdeen anti-aircraft guns claimed a hit on the Heinkel's tail (disputed by the Spitfires), navy ack-ack, as was their wont, fired indiscriminately into the fight.[63] The three fighters reported firing a total of 6,749 rounds; three attackers and that many rifle calibre rounds was pretty much what it took to bring down a German bomber; the Heinkel was from *9/KG 26*.[64]

The next action against a lone German machine, most likely on an armed reconnaissance flight as it carried bombs, took place about 15h40 off Chesil Beach near Portland, and involved the tragic loss of P/O Duncan Hewitt, a native of New Brunswick, Canada. No relevant Dornier 17 casualty exists in the German Quartermaster General Loss Returns.[65] His demise appeared to be due to the slipstream of the enemy flying ten feet above the sea, which was rough in the generally poor weather with low clouds and rain. P/O Hewitt was seen to hit the water, and at 250 probably mph his Hurricane disintegrated. His body was later seen floating next to a half-opened parachute, and was not recovered.[66] The terrible blow to his parents was arguably made worse by officialdom following standard procedures, as laid out in an extract from a letter to his father:[67]

I am directed to inform you that a metal box containing a cake, and posted at Rothesay, N.B. at the end of May last and addressed to your son has just been forwarded to this section, who normally deal with the kits and personal effects of officers and airmen of the Royal Air Force. The kit and effects of Pilot Officer Hewitt are at present in safe custody at the Central Depository of the Royal Air Force at Colnbrook, nr. Slough, Bucks, and authority to release them for forwarding to you will be given by Accounts 13 (Effects) after action to presume death for official purposes has been taken. In the meantime I am to enquire as to your wishes regarding the disposal of the cake. The tin has not yet been opened but, providing the cake is still edible, it is suggested that it might be handed over to an organisation in London who look after the welfare of young colonial Royal Air Force officers in the United Kingdom. No action will be taken pending receipt of your reply.

Twelve Hurricanes of 43 Squadron had been sent aloft from Tangmere to intercept an incoming raid at about 15h43;[68] it must have given a radar return somewhat greater than a single aircraft, otherwise a full squadron would not have been dispatched. The hapless Heinkel 111 from *Stab/KG 55* was dispatched by no fewer than six pilots: S/L Badger, F/Lt Dalton-Morgan, P/O De Mancha, P/O Gorrie, P/O Upton and Sgt Ayling.[69] In the event it would appear that the main damage was inflicted by Tom Dalton-Morgan, who led his Blue Section to make the first attack on the He 111 at about 8,000 ft over Southampton Water; he went in first and attacking from astern and closing to 100 yards, he watched the starboard engine blow up.[70] He found himself in a cloud of smoke and small debris for a few seconds afterwards, and after the rest of his section had a go, he made a second similar attack, this time seeing fine debris and black smoke come from the port engine.[71] The Heinkel was now only capable of gliding and force-landed 4 miles north of Fort Nelson, ending up in a hedge at about 16h30.[72] It came down near the Horse and Jockey Pub at Hipley (Illustrations 38 and 39), north-west of Portsmouth,[73] no doubt to the great joy of the patrons that Friday afternoon.

This machine had been on an armed reconnaissance mission, carrying both bombs and three large cameras, and an aerial photograph of oil tanks found on board may have been of the objective; it had dropped its bombload of sixteen 50 kg bombs as it was attacked, and was heavily armed with six MG 15 machine guns.[74] The pilot, *Fw* Möhn, was unhurt, but two crew members were wounded while the observer, *Oblt* Walter Kleinhanns was grievously wounded and died later in hospital.[75] Tom Dalton-Morgan numbered the famous buccaneer Sir Henry Morgan amongst his ancestors.[76]

At *c.* 16h40. F/Lt 'Sailor' Malan led Red Section of 74 Squadron on an intercept of a single He 111 about 15 miles north-east of Margate at about 8,000 ft; they found the Heinkel bombing a ship from about 6,000 ft with anti-aircraft fire giving the enemy away easily.[77] As the He 111 turned away, Malan ordered Sgt Mould and P/O Stevenson, respectively Red 2 and 3, into line astern, along a course of 80⁰.[78] A succession of attacks from astern by all three pilots followed, with Red 2 making a second set of attacks, by which time the port engine was in flames and the starboard one was smoking badly. The undercarriage of the Heinkel had also dropped and return fire had ceased. Red 2 then saw it crash into heavy seas.[79] Return fire was experienced as very heavy in the beginning, apparently from rear upper and lower gun positions and two side blister positions also; Malan opened fire from 500 yards already, an unusual distance for him but then closed to 300 yards and fired more bursts closing to 200 yards.[80] Oil from the Heinkel splashed on his windscreen and mainplane, and then his two wingmen closed in, firing bursts from *c.* 400-350 yards, closing to 200 yards, with Sgt Mould making the final attack from 350 yards, closing to 100 yards.[81]

There is no suitable loss of a He 111 to fit this combat in the German casualty listings, only a 40% damaged He 111 of *III/KG 53* that crash-landed at Katwijk airfield in Holland after having an engine die during an operational flight.[82] A course of *c.* 80⁰ from a position about 15 miles north-east of Margate will finish up close enough to Katwijk airfield and it is conceivable that *III/KG 53* may have sent out a machine to search for survivors from the three *KG 53* aircraft lost in the earlier convoy raid off Aldeburgh between *c.* 08h40 and 09h10. What is noticeable in the 74 Squadron Intelligence Patrol Report is the intense return fire put out by this aircraft, inducing all three pilots to open fire from relatively longer range than they would normally have done. Despite carrying more rounds than usual, 2,720 per aircraft as opposed to the normal 2,400, and using 7,240 of them between the three Spitfires,[83] the range may have worked against their efficacy. Though Red 2 claiming to have seen the Heinkel crash into heavy seas from a low altitude, the weather this day was generally cloudy and rainy, and he may have seen splashes from the Heinkel ditching its remaining bombload in the waves, which he confused with the machine itself crashing.

At almost the same time, far to the west, a Ju 88 approached St Eval aerodrome at *c.* 16h30, dropped nine bombs near a hangar, which did no damage, and 234 Squadron, the resident fighter unit, scrambled Blue and Yellow Sections.[84] The retreating Junkers was attacked briefly by P/O Lawrence, who got in a single quarter deflection burst of one second from *c.* 225 yards range, seeing bullets enter the lower gun position; P/O Gordon followed this up with a long burst from the beam and two short ones from astern, his own aircraft being hit by one bullet that snapped a rudder cable.[85] P/O Gordon observed bullets hitting the starboard engine before the Ju 88 vanished in the clouds. Although two ground witnesses later described seeing an enemy bomber coming out of cloud in the direction of Trevose Head, some eight kilometres north of St Eval, with black smoke pouring from the starboard engine,[86] no Ju 88 is listed from any Ju 88 unit this far west in the German losses.[87] The two 234 Squadron pilots claimed the Ju 88 as unconfirmed. The *Luftwaffe* loss lists are not 100% complete and sometimes when damage was less severe and the machine repairable at the unit itself, no loss was reported; sometimes it was simply administrative inefficiency or papers got lost.

About an hour later, the final interception of a German machine in a small action on 12 July took place, by six Hurricanes of 145 Squadron, south of St Catherine's Point, Isle of Wight.[88] The 145 Squadron pilots reported a small formation of Ju 88s escorted by Me 110s, P/O Yule claiming a Ju 88 destroyed in an action in and out of cloud, as low as

700 ft above the sea.[89] This was probably a Ju 88 of *I/KG 51*, which crashed at Villaroche and was written off, killing the crew of four.[90] While the 145 Squadron pilots also claimed three of the escorting Me 110s as damaged,[91] none were; *V/LG 1* recorded escorting an armed reconnaissance by a single Ju 88 off the Isle of Wight, with merchant ships being attacked and action with 'Spitfires'.[92] This appears to have been a new practice by the *Luftwaffe*, to escort an armed reconnaissance machine even in cloudy weather favourable to such single aircraft missions; obviously the casualties to lone raiders were becoming of some concern to them, on 12 July 1940 these amounting to three destroyed and two damaged aircraft, the loss of thirteen crewmen and another three who returned home wounded.

13 July 1940: three convoy raids, not four

There were three 'real' raids this day, two by Stukas discussed later, and the other marking the first combat mission of *EGr 210* (*Erprobungsgruppe*, 'Test Group') in the Battle. At *c.* 11h45, eight bomb-carrying Me 109s and ten Me 110 bombers escorted by four others of the *Gruppe* attacked shipping in the Thames Estuary reported earlier by reconnaissance.[93] They claimed hits on four ships totalling some 20,000 tons, but it appears that no merchant vessels were in fact lost.[94] While the *Erprobungsgruppe 210* history states that additional escort was provided by *I/JG 52*, that *Gruppe* was stationed in Germany at the time.[95] RAF fighters did not intercept this raid and the attackers suffered no combat losses,[96] although one Me 110 crash-landed at St. Omer, 45% damaged.[97] The latter casualty being listed under this date may reflect confusion emanating directly from entries in the *Luftwaffe* Quartermaster General Loss Returns, this particular aircraft being listed under 20 July 1940 with a handwritten 'correction' (?) to 13 July 1940 right next to it; there is a more comprehensive discussion of this loss and these records more generally under 20 July 1940.[98]

In foggy weather, single aircraft tried to attack ships off Portland. A trio of 501 Squadron Hurricanes, P/O Gibson, P/O Parkin, P/O Hairs, claiming a Dornier 17 between 09h15 and 10h00 south of St Albans Point (sic, St Alban's Head?), 3 miles south-west of Swanage. This may have been a Dornier of *4(F)/14* which force-landed 10% damaged at Caen after being subject to fighter attack, its crew unhurt.[99] A few minutes before 11h00, the readiness section at Tangmere, Blue Section of 43 Squadron, was scrambled after a 'bandit' plotted by radar at low level south of the Isle of Wight.[100] F/Lt Tom Dalton-Morgan led his section in formation to the attack, and he carried out several individual attacks, experiencing no return fire from the Ju 88.[101] By now well beyond 10 miles off the English coast, a limit Fighter Command tried not to exceed to minimise losses of pilots in the unforgiving sea, one engine was afire and the other smoking as the hapless Junkers descended rapidly, apparently still under some control, and after a final combined attack it ditched off the French coast. They saw two crewmen clamber into a circular dinghy.[102] However, the normally efficient German sea rescue service did not succeed in saving them and all four crew were declared missing; amongst the *Luftwaffe* casualties of the day, this can only have been the Ju 88 of *II/KG 51*, which failed to return from a mission.[103] Dalton-Morgan himself learned long after the war that this machine from *6/KG 51* was captained by *Oblt* Fritz Kesper.[104] It was a gallant crew, whose gunners managed to hit both of Dalton-Morgan's wingmen, P/O Gorrie's machine sustaining a hit in the petrol tank and that flown by P/O De Mancha hits in the port wing and aileron.[105]

At about 12h45, F/Lt L. C. Withall, who had only joined 152 Squadron as B Flight commander the previous day, led three Spitfires against a Ju 88 flying near the Dorset coast; he fired and hit it but lost the enemy in clouds, though his port wing was covered in oil from the obviously damaged Junkers.[106] Squadron records note only that Withall's attack had no result.[107] However, *III/KG 51* had one of their Ju 88 aircraft 20% damaged in a combat with RAF fighters, which landed at Rouen, crew unhurt.[108] The location was *c.* 100 km north-west of their base at Etampes-Mondesir;[109] this could well have been the victim of F/Lt Withall's attack.

13 July 1940: the raid that wasn't

A British convoy sailing westward was due to arrive off Portland and then to sail on into Lyme Bay at about 15h00; however, it was delayed due to having zigzagged.[110] Three Spitfires of 609 Squadron operating from their forward base of Warmwell were flying low at 4,000 ft to the west of Swanage, looking for the convoy.[111] With radar warning of approaching *Luftwaffe* aircraft, twelve Hurricanes of 238 Squadron, also flying out of Warmwell, were sent up at 14h45 to cover the Portland area[112] and thus covering both that naval base and harbour as well as the convoy. The approaching German formation was made up of *V/LG 1*, which lifted off in France at 14h38, escorting a reconnaissance Do 17P to Portland.[113] This formation has quite often been misinterpreted as an incoming raid of fighter-bomber Me 110s of this *Gruppe*, intent on attacking the convoy,[114] but their unit history makes their actual intended role clear.[115]

There appears to have been one reconnaissance Dornier with the Me 110s and another about 10,000 ft lower.[116] German planning perhaps used the opportunity provided by the high Dornier and its strong Me 110 escort to slip in a second reconnaissance machine in the hope the upper formation would distract and indeed attract any defending fighters from the RAF. As will be discussed, however, there might only have been one Dornier, at about 10,000 ft. This Dornier was seen approaching Portland and in fact overflew the harbour,[117] which was its probable mission, while the higher Dornier was probably intended to locate the convoy. It was by no means an unusual mission for *V/LG 1*, which undertook six such escorts between 1 and 13 July 1940.[118] The twelve reconnaissance machines lost over and around the UK in the first twelve days of July[119] no doubt raised concerns for their vulnerability over a well-defended island.

V/LG 1 duly formed a circle about 6 miles south of Portland,[120] under which umbrella the higher Dornier could easily and relatively safely do its intended convoy location job but leaving the lower reconnaissance Dornier much more vulnerable. The official intelligence summary report of the action noted that the Me 110s made no attempt to come to the aid of the lower Dornier, and that they avoided diving below 10,000 ft in the subsequent fighter combat.[121] However, having a circling Me 110 fighter formation at altitude over a specific spot close to an intended target was standard operating procedure in many ways and was a German tactic already seen on 10 July off Folkestone, and would be repeated in many future raids, especially in August 1940. In most of these cases, the Me 110s tried to maintain altitude and attract opposing fighters up to their level where the Me 110s had an inherent advantage of height rather than attacking RAF formations seen at lower levels and even climbing up towards them. Certainly, on 13 July *V/LG 1* made no attempt to interfere with the clearly visible British fighters climbing up towards them other than to change the direction of their turns to try and get behind the RAF sections as they closed in on them.[122]

When the *Luftwaffe* formation came in, 238 Squadron was above the Portland area at about 11,000-12,000 ft.[123] F/Lt Walch leading B Flight was senior to his Australian compatriot leading A Flight, F/Lt Kennedy, by a few months;[124] as anti-aircraft fire from the Portland defences drew attention to the Me 110s about 10,000 ft higher up, Kennedy was ordered to take his Red Section and engage an observed incoming Do 17 about 1,000 ft below them, while the remaining three sections of Hurricanes climbed to take on the Me 110s.[125] The Dornier reconnaissance machine, probably flying out of Jersey in the Channel Islands, was heading for the coast in a shallow dive as Kennedy put his section in line astern and chased it across Chesil Beach as it made for some oil tanks in the harbour; the anti-aircraft guns there let fly and the Dornier appeared to drop a bomb near a gun site.[126] F/Lt Kennedy closed in on the other side of the harbour to close range, putting out one engine and silencing the rear gunner in two attacks from astern; his two wingmen then pursued the Do 17P from *2(F)/123* and opened fire as it lost height rapidly and turned back towards the land, flew over Portland Bill and turned once more, towards Chesil Beach again, where it crashed into the sea close alongside.[127]

Kennedy meanwhile had been seen to break away sharply after his initial attack and dive towards the coast; ground eyewitnesses were later reported as having seen a combat with Me 110s at low level and a RAF fighter flying off at very low level and probably damaged while apparently being pursued by a second machine, and in trying to reach base at Warmwell running into some high tension cables and crashing fatally.[128] It would appear very likely that Kennedy had been wounded by return fire and his Hurricane damaged also by the Dornier he attacked, this leading to his rapid breakaway and dive for the coast towards the north-north-east where Warmwell lay. His Hurricane is reported as stalling and crashing trying to avoid electric cables at Southdown Farm, Littlemore, on the northern outskirts of Weymouth, during his landing approach.[129] The Hurricane in fact crashed at Littlemayne Farm just outside West Knighton, just over a mile from Warmwell airfield, about a mile north of high-tension cables lying to the south and about 3 miles away from Littlemore.[130] After pulling up to avoid the cables, Jack Kennedy would have had only ten to fifteen seconds before his stalled machine hit the ground, assuming a slower speed in its likely damaged state.

When Red Section of 238 Squadron was detached to pursue the Do 17 reconnaissance aircraft, the other three sections of the squadron climbed up to the circling Me 110s of *V/LG 1*; the RAF fighters took up positions about 1,000 ft above the circle and as much as possible between the Messerschmitts and the sun.[131] The job of the Me 110s was of course to maintain their circle at high altitude thereby providing an umbrella for the reconnaissance aircraft to fly in for its mission and then to fly out again, when it would be accompanied by the twin-engined fighters back across the Channel. They were thus not going to break up the circle until the time was right. According to the intelligence summary report, 238 Squadron's pilots initially waited above the *Zerstörer* for single aircraft to break away from the formation.[132] Thereafter, many attacks were made between 20,000 and 17,000 ft, 238 Squadron's pilots finding that all the Me 110s did left-hand turns and the Hurricanes could easily turn inside them, when the German fighters made good targets as they banked steeply in their turns.[133]

The only conclusive attacks were by Sgt Batt whose victim dove into the sea, P/O Considine whose long full deflection burst at a turning Me 110 caused it to dive steeply with its port engine afire, and thirdly by P/O Urwin-Mann who also attacked a turning Me 110 which was last seen diving away for France with white smoke pouring from an engine.[134] Batt described climbing a couple of thousand feet above the circle and then diving into its middle, firing, after which he pulled up at full throttle for another go.[135] He then observed P/O Covington expose himself to danger by attacking from below the circle and knocking out a Messerschmitt, thereby breaking up the circle, which then fled in complete confusion.[136] His memory must have been at fault in his book as Covington in fact only joined 238 Squadron on 20 August 1940[137] and he possibly confused him with P/O Considine.

The German account of this action makes for interesting reading. They reported an initial combat with 'Spitfires', no doubt 238 Squadron's Hurricanes, in another example of the oft-repeated error of Spitfire snobbery; with no casualties yet suffered, they reformed and set out back across the Channel, but one Me 110 flown by *Lt* Eisele of *15 Staffel* lagged behind,[138] most likely damaged in the combat. It was then seen to be shot up in a brief attack by Spitfires, damaging both engines, and it glided down and turned on its back; one of the crew bailed out but got hung up on the tail unit and the aircraft crashed upside down into the Channel and vanished with both crew members, about 9 miles south of Portland.[139] Despite stating that no casualties were suffered in the first action against 'Spitfires', no doubt meaning that no machine was destroyed yet, a machine of *14 Staffel* flown by *Lt* Krebitz had in fact been badly damaged and he badly wounded; despite a bullet lodged in his shoulder blade with another two through a calf and a foot, he managed to fly back to land successfully but his machine was written off and he spent months recovering.[140] Another Me 110 of *15 Staffel* returned to base severely damaged, 50%, with one crewman wounded, and a fourth Me 110 of the *Gruppe* was slightly damaged and one of the crew wounded.[141]

With further distance to travel and more height to gain to get at the Me 110s, the section from 609 Squadron at *c.* 4,000 ft west of Swanage, attacked from above and up-sun of the Messerschmitts, only two of the pilots being involved, the third breaking off from the combat with a faltering Spitfire.[142] Clearly this was the second attack described by *V/LG 1*, and the section leader F/O Dundas claimed a Me 110 shot down in a brief encounter; this would logically have been the aircraft flown by *Lt* Eisele, almost certainly already damaged by 238 Squadron.[143] Both Dundas and his wingman P/O Miller described firing at a Do 17, the latter pilot firing most of his rounds into it; several members of 238 Squadron including Sgt Batt saw this aircraft flying out to sea losing height rapidly and with an engine on fire.[144] The Me 110s claimed by Sgt Batt and P/O Considine were both reported to have dived steeply away with visible damage and could well have been the same machine, most likely that of *Lt* Krebitz, severely wounded and thus very likely to have dived steeply away, before recovering control at lower altitude and managing to fly back to France despite severe loss of blood.[145]

P/O Urwin-Mann's claimed Me 110 victim was last seen diving towards France with an engine on fire, a description that almost perfectly matches that of P/O Miller of 609 Squadron when claiming a Do 17 probably shot down.[146] They may well have fired on the same aircraft, and it would also tie in well with the 50%-damaged Me 110 of *15 Staffel*, which managed to return to base, badly damaged.[147] The combined Intelligence Patrol Report for 238 and 609 Squadrons on this action,[148] is rather scathing about the tactics of the Me 110s, as the following short excerpt makes clear. 'The Me's made no attempt to go to the rescue of the lower Do. when it was attacked. They seemed content to stay circling round in a wide formation. The Me's seemed to do nothing but left-hand turns.'

Mistaking an Me 110 for a Do 17, and vice versa, occurred many times in the Battle; so there may well not have been a second Do 17 reconnaissance aircraft at all, in which case *V/LG 1* had displayed a selfish indifference to the fate of their charge. While the IPR summary report credits three 238 Squadron pilots with conclusive attacks, Batt, Considine and Urwin-Mann,[149] five of their comrades were co-claimants to their victims.[150] While this action was no raid at all, tactics around the Me 110 circle formation were interesting. F/Lt Walch leading nine of his Hurricanes above the circling Me 110s does not seem to have had any useful ideas as to how to tackle his enemy, with the majority of the 238 Squadron pilots waiting for single aircraft to leave the circle before attacking. This was not likely to happen any time soon as the Me 110 crews fully realised that their safety lay in maintaining the circle and keeping their protective umbrella intact. It was the initiative of one pilot, P/O Considine, who finally took some considerable risk and attacked the circle from below, knocking out one *Zerstörer* and leading to the breakup of the large circle, which wrought the change. Sgt Batt also showed a better way to tackle such circles, by diving steeply into their midst and pulling back up again to repeat the tactic. This was similar to tactics applied against circling Me 110s by 56 Squadron on 10 July under the leadership of F/Lt 'Jumbo' Gracie, and those used by F/Lt Measures of 74 Squadron on the same day.

13 July 1940: two Stuka convoy attacks near Dover

From various but by no means all sources, it is clear that there were two actions against shipping off Dover this day, one in the afternoon between about 15h50 and 16h30, and perhaps as late as 16h45, and the other in the early evening between *c.* 17h30 and 17h50, possibly *c.* 18h00.[151] The first German raid was directed at Convoy CW 5 not long after it had departed from Dover with a single escort, the First World War destroyer *HMS Vanessa*.[152] This raid comprised a small formation of Ju 87s from *II/StG 1*, given variously as six, nine or twelve in number.[153] The escort was provided by nineteen Me 109s *of II/JG 51* led by the *Staffelkapitän* of *4th Staffel*, *Oberleutnant* Josef Fözö; the latter probably provided the most accurate count of his charges, at six Ju 87s.[154] The Stukas took off from the Pas de Calais while the escort were based at Desvres, some 20 km further south.[155] The latter would thus have flown roughly northwards, a few miles inland and approximately parallel to the coastline at Boulogne and northwards, and would presumably have met up with the Stukas, flying essentially north-west from the Calais area, towards Dover, before mid-Channel between Calais and Dover.

The 11 Group controller had sent the eleven Hurricanes of 56 Squadron from their forward base at Rochford at about 15h30, on what was termed an 'offensive patrol' over the Channel.[156] P/O Geoffrey Page was one of the pilots flying on this mission and describes the squadron being ordered, firstly, to patrol the French coast near Calais at 12,000 ft, and subsequently being instructed to fly a 'sweep' from Calais to the south and about 3 miles off the coast.[157] It was rather unusual for an 11 Group squadron to be ordered to thus trail their coats at relatively low altitude so close to the Pas de Calais coast, close to which were based sufficient Me 109s to cause them great trouble, and especially Hurricanes to boot, less capable of handling the dangerous Me 109s. However, the controller knew that the convoy and its single destroyer escort had just put out from Dover and was very vulnerable and further destroyer losses could hardly be afforded at this critical, early pre-invasion stage of the Battle. Page himself, later in the mission sighting HMS *Vanessa*, then understood the orders.

Essentially, while the Stukas were lumbering into the air and forming up over Calais, and their Me 109 escorts were starting to proceed northwards for their rendezvous with them north-west of Calais, quite unknown to them, they were actually being accompanied a few miles off the coast by 56 Squadron's Hurricanes. If they did see a fighter formation to their port side, flying northwards like them, the Me 109s might well have thought it to be German, and providing extra escorts. The RAF controller was thus being clever and even innovative, and it worked initially, as will be seen.

The squadron was led by its most experienced pilot, F/Lt 'Slim' Coghlan; the relatively recently appointed new C/O, S/L Manton, wisely let this situation persist for a while, as he gained experience of the fighting.[158] This was truly a mark of excellent leadership on Manton's part. Page was flying in the third section of the squadron formation, and having flown southward off the French coast for about a quarter of an hour, they were ordered to get back to Calais and speeding up, this they did, within about seven minutes; as they got there they spotted the small formation of Ju 87s setting out from the coast of France and flying towards Dover, dead ahead of them and a little lower.[159] As Coghlan skilfully led them in a dive onto the Ju 87s someone spotted a dozen Me 109s above and behind the Stukas, which had not yet noticed the Hurricanes – they were after all coming from the wrong direction for British aircraft.[160] F/Lt Coghlan had succeeded in placing his Hurricanes in the ideal attack position,[161] but as always the risk of retaliation was there and it would come soon enough from the higher flying escort of Me 109s.

Being behind and above Coghlan's Red Section, Geoffrey Page had a good view of his leader opening the attack on the Stukas, his chosen target giving off a large puff of smoke, then flames, and dropping slowly from its formation; the dive bombers seemed paralysed for a moment, then they jettisoned their bombs, rolled onto their backs and dove seawards, hotly pursued by the vengeful Hurricanes.[162] Not far behind them, the Me 109 escorts followed in their turn; the escort leader, *Oberleutnant* Fözö recording being warned of enemy aircraft over mid-Channel and subsequently saw sixteen to twenty Hurricanes (only eleven were present as noted), which had placed themselves behind the Stukas, in firing positions, and thus directly between the dive bombers and their close escort.[163] This very nicely sums up the eternal dilemma for Fighter Command formation leaders: to get at bombers they almost always had to put themselves into certain danger, between their prey and its escort. Only beam attacks and head-on approaches tended to obviate this.

F/Lt Coghlan had just enough time to hit a Stuka well and see it beginning to smoke before he spotted two Me 109s closing in behind and had to break away.[164] Turning tightly, Coghlan managed to get behind a Messerschmitt himself and thought he had struck home, but it was not so, and then his own aircraft was hit.[165] From the German perspective, *Oblt* Fözö and several of his comrades fired at the Hurricanes and watched as three left their formation, two apparently dropping straight down and one seen to glide towards the water, giving off heavy smoke.[166] These three Hurricanes were ascribed to initial attacks by *Oblt* Fözö, *Uffz* Buder, also of 4/JG 51, and *Hpt* Tietzen, *Staffelkapitän* 5/JG 51 at *c.* 16h26-16h30.[167] Fözö next observed a Hurricane chasing a Ju 87 making for the French coast, with an Me 109 behind the former, in turn pursued by a second RAF machine, behind which Fözö placed himself; the entire line astern 'formation' was descending towards the water.[168] The *Oberleutnant* then saw the damaged Stuka crash on the beach at Wissant, followed by *Fw* John in the leading Me 109 sending the front Hurricane into the Channel, one wing sticking up above the waves briefly before disappearing, and then saw his own victim drop like a stone, apparently into the Channel close to John's victory.[169] Despite John's victim having thus been witnessed by his leader, he was awarded only a probable victory, as was *Fw* Tornow of *4th Staffel* and Tietzen's second claim was also thus classified; Fözö was awarded a second confirmed victory, timed a few minutes after his first claim.[170]

For their part, 56 Squadron put in claims: two Stukas destroyed by F/O Brooker and Sgt Cowsill, five probables by F/Lt Coghlan, S/L Manton, Sgt Hillwood, Sgt Baker and Sgt Smythe, as well as an Me 109 destroyed by F/Lt Coghlan and another probable by P/O Page. All claims were made off Calais.[171] *II/StG 1* in fact had two machines damaged, one crash-landing on the beach at Cap Gris Nez and despite serious damage was repairable, while the other made it to Norent Fontes airfield where it force-landed, 30% damaged; both crews were unhurt.[172] There were no Me 109 casualties. The many claims by 56 Squadron do not readily allow assignment of casualties to individual pilots; however, Sgt Cowsill was apparently seen to shoot down a Ju 87 (or, rather, to damage it) before his own demise.[173] 56 Squadron lost two Hurricanes and pilots in the sea, while F/Lt Coghlan, who was slightly wounded, put his damaged machine down at forward base. Sgt Baker's aircraft was also damaged by the German aircraft and although he had to force-land it at *c.* 17h00 at Rodmersham, just south of Sittingbourne, he was unhurt and the aircraft repairable.[174] While Sgt Cowsill's Hurricane has been ascribed to *Fw* John and recorded as having gone into the sea off Calais at 16h45,[175] the relevant casualty report signed by S/L Manton tells a different story:[176]

> Whilst on an offensive patrol on the afternoon of the 13th July, 1940, 741936 Sgt. Cowsill, J.R. was shot down over the English Channel. In Hurricane N. 2432 he came down in the sea approximately 2 miles from St. Margarets Bay. A motor torpedo boat immediately proceeded to this area but was unable to find any trace of the pilot or aircraft with the exception of a small piece of plywood bearing the number of the aircraft. No further details are available.

Sgt Cowsill was thus able to struggle back across the Channel before crashing in the sea off St Margarets Bay, 4 miles along the coast, north-east of Dover. He may well have had his machine severely damaged and/or been wounded himself by attacks from *II/JG 51* off Calais, as related by the account of

Oblt Fözö discussed above.[177] Sgt Baker's Hurricane may have fallen victim to *Hpt* Tietzen, whose claims were both several minutes later than the rest by *II/JG 51*.[178] F/Lt Coghlan's damaged Hurricane has been ascribed to the initial attack of the *II/JG 51* Me 109s, possibly that flown by Fözö.[179] Sgt Whitfield, the other fatality in 56 Squadron would appear to have gone into the Channel off Calais, probably due to the fire of either *Fw* John[180] or *Oblt* Fözö, or even both of them. In the relevant casualty report for Sgt Whitfield, he is reported to have descended into the sea some 10 miles off Calais[181] near a destroyer, which could only have been HMS *Vanessa*.

There is one other witness account of this action that might possibly also explain at least one German claim. P/O Page of 56 Squadron, reported above as having witnessed his formation leader F/Lt Coghlan hit a Stuka and then seeing the rest of them diving vertically for the sea after jettisoning their bombs, rapidly rolled his Hurricane onto its back and spiralled down after them.[182] Getting on the tail of one, he fired a long burst and saw something fall off as his Hurricane swept past the Stuka, unable to dive slowly as the dive bomber could with its dive brakes.[183] Pulling out above the water, Page was attacked by a couple of Me 109s who tried to stop him returning to England as his fuel ran down; he finally got away by using his boost cut-out and flying straight over a destroyer, HMS *Vanessa*, rolling as he went so they would not fire at him.[184] His sudden drop in pursuit of the Stukas does to a certain extent match *Oblt* Fözö's description of two Hurricanes dropping when the *II/JG 51* Me 109s attacked the squadron.[185]

The second *Luftwaffe* attack on the same convoy off Dover, carrying coal and escorted by HMS *Vanessa*, was made on the order of *Kanalkampfführer*[186] *Oberst* Fink who sent in some Ju 87s, probably from *IV/LG 1*,[187] escorted by *III/JG 51*.[188] The fighters were due to meet their charges at 17h00, and *Oberst* Theo Osterkamp, the fighter leader on the Channel front at this stage and commander of *JG 51*, the main unit there, took off some ten minutes later, as he wanted to see the British warship which had been reported in the Channel.[189] The RAF response was to put up 54 Squadron, reported variously as nine or twelve Spitfires, and eleven more of 64 Squadron.[190] The former were ordered up from forward base at Rochford and vectored out over the Channel off Deal and then towards Calais and the latter left from Kenley, flying in over Dover to the Channel.[191] Neither Spitfire squadron reported any contact with the Stukas; the small Stuka formation, while not hitting any ships, did manage to place one bomb only six yards astern of HMS *Vanessa* that damaged her propellers and she had to be towed to safety by another destroyer.[192] One Ju 87 of *10/LG 1* was 30% damaged in the attack and the gunner badly wounded, at *c.* 17h30 – presumably by anti-aircraft fire from the destroyer – but made it back to base.[193]

54 Squadron probably reached the vicinity of this raid first, having come presumably from Rochford,[194] while 64 Squadron, coming from Kenley[195] had further to fly. Blue Section of 54 Squadron, flying rearguard to the unit and led by F/Lt Way, while on a vector from a position over the Channel off Deal towards Cap Gris Nez at 15,000-12,000 ft, spotted two Me 109s about 5 miles off Deal at *c*. 6,000-8,000 ft.[196] While Way claimed the one Me 109 'probably damaged', P/O Gray latched onto the second Messerschmitt and pursued it relentlessly over the sea right down to almost sea level, firing from 300 down to 150 yards, watching as it fell, smoking; his claim was confirmed by F/Lt Way and Sgt Smythe, 56 Squadron, on his way home across the Channel from their earlier action.[197] While the Rochford Intelligence Officer opined that this Me 109 was from the earlier action involving 56 Squadron, the Me 109 unit involved with 56 Squadron, *II/JG 51*, suffered no losses, not even a damaged machine, and additionally, the very limited fuel endurance of the Me 109s would not have allowed flying in both actions, separated in time by thirty to forty-five minutes.[198] The escort of the Stukas in the second raid, however, did lose a single Me 109: *III/JG 51*'s *Lt* Lange was shot down over the Channel in action with Spitfires south of Dover at *c*. 17h30 and killed.[199]

64 Squadron, having arrived over Dover at 20,000 ft and orbiting the town observed some twenty Me 109s approaching from rear and slightly above, and Sub Lt Dawson-Paul broke formation and fired at a pair of Messerschmitts.[200] The two Me 109s dived steeply, pursued by another 64 Squadron Spitfire, F/O Woodward, but one of the Me 109s managed to get on this Spitfire's tail, and Dawson-Paul dived down onto him and attacked from almost head-on, fired and saw smoke pouring out.[201] The German fighter then rolled onto its back, but the canny Dawson-Paul did a stall-turn and hit him again, and claimed to have seen the pilot bail out and his machine crash into the Channel, witnessed also by F/O Woodward.[202] During this fighting between the Me 109s of *III/JG 51* and 64 Squadron, *Oblt* Lignitz claimed a Spitfire shot down south of Dover at *c*. 17h25, and *Oberst* Theo Osterkamp, *Kommodore* of *JG 51*, claimed a probable victim in the Dover area.[203] However, no Spitfires fell victim to Me 109s during this battle, nor did any Messerschmitt pilot bail out either.

What 64 Squadron did suffer was a rather bad-tempered Sergeant pilot, Arthur Binham, whose machine had been hit by the Dover anti-aircraft batteries during the combat with the Me 109s, at *c*. 17h45. He managed to make it to nearby Hawkinge airfield where he belly-landed.[204] There is another account by Sub Lt John Sykes of exactly the same thing happening to him;[205] however, other standard sources on the Battle do not mention such a loss. The aircraft concerned, L1075,[206] is given as having been lost on 9 July 1940 in another standard source.[207] That volume lists the brief history of every single Spitfire built, but confusingly, in another entry has this same aircraft issued to 610 Squadron on 14 August 1940 from a maintenance unit.[208] Clarity on this second 64 Squadron loss to Dover anti-aircraft fire is thus distinctly lacking, but the account by the pilot concerned is first-person testimony.[209] Either way, none of this really helps explain the two German claims, nor Dawson-Paul's claim for an Me 109 shot down.

There is, however, a fascinating account by one of the German pilots concerned, *Oberst* Theo Osterkamp of *Stab/JG 51*, that offers some support for Dawson-Paul, or at least for a British fighter hitting his Messerschmitt, and also explains the claim for a Spitfire made by Osterkamp.[210] As already related, Theo Osterkamp, a *Pour le Merite* winner and air ace from the First World War still flying in action in his second global conflict, had followed in the wake of the *III/JG 51*-escorted Stuka raid on the convoy off Dover as he wanted to see the British warship at sea. As Osterkamp proceeded north and then over the Channel he was above solid clouds at *c.* 12,000 ft, but then they disappeared and he was suddenly exposed in broad daylight.[211] By about 17h30, over mid-Channel he saw a large ship south-west of Dover, which seemed to be too broad for a merchant vessel; he thought he was looking at a British monitor, having seen them from the air in the First World War.

As he flew over this supposed monitor, he saw no Stukas – they had in fact already bombed and departed – but saw something glinting in the sun out of the corner of his eye, which he interpreted as his fighters from *III/JG 51*.[212] Before he could collect his thoughts he was surrounded by British fighters, all apparently firing at him and one succeeded in hitting him on top of his engine and he smelled burning in his cockpit, presumably from up ahead. Instinctively he turned away, banking steeply, only to see a Spitfire loom up directly in front of him, less than 50 metres away; fully expecting an imminent collision, as a last resort he instinctively pressed all his gun buttons.[213] Lo and behold, he heard a dull explosion in front of him, thought he saw a single wing flash past, his machine rattled and shook, and he dived steeply down from 12,000 ft to 4,500 ft, when he began to pull out desperately. Only some 600 ft above the sea he managed to pull the Messerschmitt out of its dive and was relieved to find himself alone. Fortunately, the burning smell had gone but his engine rattled horribly; when he gently opened the throttle it got even worse, but he was close to Boulogne by then and put down at Le Touquet.[214] After landing he found that there was a bullet hit in one propeller blade, but over half of each propeller blade had been shot off, so his interrupter gear must have been hit and damaged. Exactly twenty-three years before, to the day, on 13 July 1917, Osterkamp had shot off his own propeller blades in combat! [215]

Theo Osterkamp's claim for a probable Spitfire, made as he desperately opened fire before an apparently imminent collision with such an aircraft, can be explained by his having almost collided with one of 64 Squadron's aircraft as it was hit by friendly anti-aircraft fire. Perhaps also, Sub Lt Dawson-Paul's claim can be reconciled with the damage to Osterkamp's Messerschmitt. These things are always imponderables, but the speed at which events in aerial combat occur can lead to many an optical error. One further optical aberration needs to be addressed here, namely *Oberst* Osterkamp's observation of a British monitor: only one such vessel was available in UK waters during 1940, namely HMS *Erebus*, which had sailed to the main Royal Navy base at Scapa Flow in August after a refit. Several faults, the weather during her working up again, and target practice delayed her dispatch to Dover until late in September 1940.[216] It is possible that what Osterkamp glimpsed from an altitude of *c.* 12,000 ft, was the disabled destroyer HMS *Vanessa* being aided by some other vessel alongside, giving the impression of a single broad vessel of war such as a monitor.

Overall, the two small Stuka raids on the convoy off Dover this day, while only damaging a destroyer – serious enough at this anxious pre-Invasion time – also saw escorting Me 109s dispatch two Hurricanes and their pilots and damage another two, one of which force-landed, all from 56 Squadron. Their own losses amounted to three damaged Stukas, one of which force-landed, and a single Me 109 and pilot. Both sides over-claimed appreciably: RAF claims totalled two Stukas and three Me 109s confirmed, as well as five Stukas and one Messerschmitt escort probably destroyed; German fighters claimed four confirmed Hurricanes and a Spitfire, and three Hurricanes and a Spitfire probably shot down. The overriding point of it all was that 56 Squadron's Hurricanes were able to stop the bombing of the convoy in the first raid, but they paid the price through their own not inconsiderable losses.

14 July 1940: single convoy attack off Folkestone

This day saw just one aerial action, a raid by escorted Stukas on a convoy off Dover (Illustration 21), which demonstrates how over-claiming can occur and can sometimes be explained. Three RAF Squadrons took part, 151, 615 and 610, and they each saw action against the raiders made up of three *Gruppen*: IV/LG 1 Ju 87s, and Me 109s from III/JG 3 and II/JG 51.[217] 151 Squadron claimed two Me 109s by S/L Donaldson and P/O Hamar, and one probable by F/Lt RL Smith; 610 Squadron's P/O

Litchfield claimed a probable and a damaged Me 109; 615 Squadron claimed two confirmed Ju 87s by F/Os Gayner and Collard, and another unconfirmed from P/O Hugo. In comparison, German losses amounted to two Stukas and their crews, one Me 109 destroyed and its pilot wounded, another 40% damaged.[218] For the *Luftwaffe*, claims of three Hurricanes by *Hpt* Tietzen 5/*JG 51*, *Oblt* Priller 6/*JG 51*, and *Ofw* Illner 4/*JG 51* and one probable by *Oblt* Stange 8/*JG 3* are set against one Hurricane and pilot lost, P/O M. R. Mudie who died of wounds next day, and two more damaged, those flown by F/O Collard and P/O Roberts, all three casualties being from 615 Squadron.[219]

There are two inconsistencies. While only one Stuka loss is given in one authorative source, a second was clearly lost, its dead crew listed, one of whose bodies was later washed up along the Dutch coast.[220] Secondly, *Oblt* Stange 8/*JG 3* is listed as the claimant for a probable Hurricane in one source while the unit history records the victor as *Ofw* Trebing of *Stab III*/*JG 3*.[221] It is of course possible there were in fact two claims by *III*/*JG 3*, one of which was rejected by the *Luftwaffe* victory confirmation system, so not making it onto the official list but being still shown in the unit history. While all major sources give only the destroyed Hurricane of 615 Squadron in their loss lists, the relevant Intelligence Patrol Report for the squadron clearly lists another machine as unserviceable upon landing, and several bullet holes in a third.[222]

615 Squadron was the first into action, its Red Section of S/L Kayll, P/O Montgomery and P/O Mudie having been sent up earliest from its forward base at Hawkinge, being in position over the convoy off Folkestone-Dover at 15h00; this squadron had sent thirteen Hurricanes forward from Kenley two hours before, one above the normal complement of twelve as a spare if another aircraft malfunctioned.[223] S/L Kayll and his two wingmen saw the incoming raid of about forty Ju 87s, initially at 12,000 ft with some Me 109 escorts about a thousand feet higher up; the section climbed and attacked the Stukas who were just starting their dives on the convoy.[224] Kayll and Montgomery fired several bursts at various Ju 87s but could not assess any results due to attacks by other Ju 87s as well as from some of the escorting Messerschmitts,[225] one of which was able to surprise P/O Mudie who was shot down in flames at *c*. 15h00. He managed to bail out but was terribly burned with gunshot wounds to the face; despite being rescued by an MTB and admitted to Casualty Hospital in Dover, he died early the next morning having also suffered severe shock.[226] His machine plunged into St Margarets Bay.[227]

As *II*/*JG 51* was rather experienced in fighting over the Channel by this time, and in view of *III*/*JG 3* having only arrived at their new base of Guines in the Pas de Calais on 12 July 1940,[228] it would most likely have been the *JG 51 Gruppe* who took on the escort function, with relative neophytes *III/JG 3* probably flying top cover. As *III/JG 3* fell under the control of *Stab/JG 51* on their arrival at the Channel,[229] this decision would have been up to *Geschwader Kommodore* Theo Osterkamp. *II/JG 51* claimed three victories, all south-east of Dover over the sea, whereas *III/JG 3* claimed a single probable victory, *c.* five kilometres north-east of Folkestone,[230] over land. This also supports *II/JG 51* having attacked Red Section of 615 Squadron. The earliest claim was by *Hpt* Tietzen, *Staffelkapitän 5/JG 51*, at 15h10, fifteen and twenty-five minutes respectively prior to the other two claims of this Gruppe; *III/JG 3*'s probable was claimed at 15h15.[231] Tietzen may thus have shot down P/O Mudie.

While the engagement of Red Section 615 Squadron with Ju 87s and Me 109s was going on, the remaining nine machines of the unit took off from Hawkinge to help out, starting about 15h00; however, it is reasonably clear from squadron records that each of the remaining three sections appear to have operated separately, as they each took off and gained height over their forward base.[232] Yellow Section were still at low altitude when they spotted some dive bombers and did not hesitate, as an excerpt from the Intelligence Patrol Report (IPR) of 615 Squadron details:[233]

Yellow Section when about half a mile off Dover at 3000 feet saw bombs being dropped on the convoy. They at once engaged a section of Ju.87's which were just below them. Yellow leader (F/O Gayner) attacked No. 3 of the enemy aircraft from astern. After several short bursts the enemy aircraft turned from side to side then went into a left hand diving turn. Pilot then jumped out by parachute and enemy aircraft crashed into the sea. This was seen by both Yellow Leader and Yellow 2 (Flying Officer Collard – Yellow Two) attacked No. 2 enemy aircraft after first short burst the enemy aircraft turned left. Then did a diving turn to the right enabling Yellow 2 to get another burst at 200 yards closing to 50 yards. The enemy aircraft turned over on its back and dived into the sea. This was seen by both Yellow 2 and Yellow 3. Yellow 2 on the way home was attacked head on by a Ju.87 but Yellow Two managed to fire a short burst as the enemy passed, but did not observe the result of his fire. He was then attacked by 2 Me.109's but by steep diving and turning he managed to get back to Hawkinge although he had several bullet holes in his machine. Yellow 3 (P/O Hugo) attacked 1 enemy aircraft astern after a short burst the rear gunner ceased firing, the enemy aircraft went into a vertical dive. Yellow 3 had to pull away but delivered another attack on the same enemy aircraft after three more short bursts, the right wing of the enemy aircraft caught fire. The enemy aircraft then glided down to the sea, turned over when it hit the water. Yellow Three circled round, nobody appeared to get out of the machine, which soon sank. On the way home Yellow 3 ran into 15 Ju.87's. He engaged one head on but did not see the result.

Yellow Section claimed three Stukas, as outlined above, but only two were lost from *IV/LG 1*.[234] Yellow 1 and 2 appear to have attacked soon after each other and there are some similarities in their accounts, although they are not identical. Their two claims, being witnessed, were recorded as confirmed; Yellow 3's claim on the other hand, being unwitnessed was taken only as 'unconfirmed'.[235] P/O Hugo, being alone at the time, also describes a different end for his claimed Ju 87, that it glided down into the sea on fire, turning over when it hit the Channel waters. Bearing in mind the three claims have to be equated with only two available losses, it would not be unreasonable to suggest F/O's Gayner and Collard may have hit the same Stuka, and P/O Hugo a second. The hits by a couple of Me 109s, or at least one of them, on F/O Collard's Hurricane could explain one of the *II/JG 51* claims for a Hurricane over the Channel south-east of Dover.[236]

Blue Section of 615 Squadron was probably next off from Hawkinge, followed by Green Section; while the latter saw nothing after take-off, Blue Section tried to get at some Me 109s it had spotted but was unable to make contact.[237] Presumably the Me 109s were higher, and Blue 2 became detached during this, and on rejoining his section was attacked by several Messerschmitts which shot up his Hurricane badly, but P/O Roberts made it back to forward base at Hawkinge where his machine was declared unserviceable, and he was uninjured.[238] The one machine of 615 Squadron shot down with P/O Mudie mortally wounded and the two damaged can explain the three claims by *II/JG 51* made over the sea and south-east of Dover.

The two other 11 Group fighter squadrons involved in this aerial battle around Dover, the ten Hurricanes of 151 and twelve Spitfires of 610 Squadrons, were sent up from their respective stations, Rochford at 15h00 and Biggin Hill at 14h58.[239] Applying cruising speeds of the two aircraft types and distances to be flown from their bases to the Dover area suggests they would have arrived close together, and times of their attacks as recorded in the IPRs point to 151 Squadron having got into the fight a few minutes ahead of 610 Squadron.

151 Squadron were ordered to intercept a large German force reported west of Dover. Flying at 12,000 ft and proceeding down-sun, at *c.* 15h20 they observed anti-aircraft bursts near seven Me 110s above 14,000 ft.[240] They also saw a large enemy formation, probably comprising Me 110s, which turned round and made for France. As the Squadron prepared to take on the seven observed Me 110s, two Me 109s were seen to detach

themselves from a group of five at *c.* 17,000 ft and dive on P/O Forster's Hurricane, which was still catching up with 151 Squadron due to slow refuelling at Rochford. Forster was able to evade the fire of the first Me 109 through a tight left turn; the reaction of his Squadron Commander is recorded in the 151 Squadron Intelligence Patrol Report:[241]

> P/O Forster's critical position was appreciated by S/L Donaldson, who at once attacked the leading 109 from level port, firing one long burst from 100 yds to nought. The E/A at once flicked on to its back, but S/L Donaldson continued to fire 2/3 seconds. With smoke pouring from it the 109 dived steeply in inverted position and crashed at position estimated to be near Temple Ewell, N.W. of Dover. Witnessed by and confirmed by W/C. Beamish and Midshipman Wightman.

As is obvious from this, 151 Squadron's commander immediately went to his man's aid and attacked the Me 109 from very close quarters at almost full deflection, obviously hitting it and at least damaging it. S/L Donaldson's concern for his own men must have given them confidence in his leadership and in aerial battles generally. P/O Hamar took on the second diving Me 109, turning inside it. The Messerschmitt then made a left-hand climbing turn, not a strongpoint manoeuvre of this aircraft type, and Hamar was easily able to close in and gave it a six seconds burst with deflection of about 45° from 250 yards down to fifty; the 109 straightened out and dived, Hamar giving it another six-second burst from only fifty yards down to point blank range, seeing an explosion in front of the cockpit and the Messerschmitt dived steeply down pouring out white smoke.[242] P/O Hamar then had to break away but P/O Forster saw it crash into the ground.[243] The IPR describes how F/Lt R. L. Smith had taken his section above the rest of the squadron and saw a Me 109 being chased by a Hurricane (presumably Hamar) and being in a position to cut the corner, he fired a brief two-second burst from 200 yards to almost point blank range at the Messerschmitt from beam to quarter as it straightened out from a turn, and then pulled up to avoid hitting the pursuing Hurricane, which passed beneath him. Smith followed the diving 109 down to about 7,000 ft when it was still giving off puffs of smoke; he was flying the squadron's unique two-cannon Hurricane in this action.[244]

It is inferred here that some Me 109s from *III/JG 3* were involved with 151 Squadron; they claimed a probable Hurricane (maybe two) about 5 km north-east of Folkestone at *c.* 11,000 ft at 15h15.[245] Two Me 109s became casualties, both from 8/JG 3: one pilot was wounded and bailed out off Boulogne, a second Messerschmitt was damaged 40% and managed to belly-land at Wissant.[246] While these German losses can be reconciled with the two Me 109 claims of 151 Squadron, S/L Donaldson's confirmed and P/O Hamar's unconfirmed, F/Lt Smith's probable Me 109 claim[247] was likely against the same aircraft attacked by Hamar. There is no Hurricane loss for the probable claim (or perhaps two claims, Stange and Trebing?) of *III/JG 3*. As mentioned, this claim or claims were located 5 km north-east of Folkestone,[248] which is close to Temple Ewell. What then did the RAF pilots Donaldson, Forster, Beamish, Wightman see on the ground in this general area which made them think an enemy aircraft had come to grief there? The same might also apply to the German claimant(s). There is a possible solution.

There was a railway line running through Temple Ewell from the station there to nearby Dover, and in the Dover area were a number of long-range artillery pieces, including three mobile railway guns, 13.5-inch First World War naval guns worked by the Royal Marines Siege Regiment, Dover, which could fire projectiles up to 37 km, well beyond the Channel narrows between Dover and Calais.[249] If one or more of these weapons had been placed on the railway line nearer Temple Ewell at that time and day and had fired a shell, then an observer in the air at about 12,000 ft who thought he had just dispatched an enemy aircraft to its doom, can be forgiven for interpreting such a large gun flash as the explosion when the downed machine hit the ground. This misconception might apply equally to 151 Squadron and *III/JG 3* pilots making or witnessing victory claims.

The twelve Spitfires of 610 Squadron arrived soon after 151 Squadron in the area of the combats at about 15h20 and initially patrolled over Hawkinge at *c.* 10,000 ft. They then appear to have turned towards the north-east and begun climbing, as Green Leader P/O Litchfield next saw three or more aircraft diving steeply in line astern and passing the right rear of the Spitfire squadron, by then at about 15,000 ft.[250] As the squadron was alerted to these aircraft, the four sections turned and Litchfield then saw two or more Me 109s at about 8,000 ft and dived steeply on to them from the rear. He almost blacked out as he pulled up behind one; his two wingmen did momentarily black out and lost contact.[251] Just prior to 610 Squadron's arrival on the scene, 151 Squadron had sent two Me 109s steeply down, both apparently damaged, in the same area. It is thus distinctly possible that these plus one or two pursuing Hurricanes of 151 Squadron, those of Smith and/or Hamar, were the machines seen diving steeply behind 610 Squadron by P/O Litchfield. While there is some possible discrepancy in the relative altitudes, 151 Squadron apparently being at somewhere between 12,000 and 14,000 ft, while 610 Squadron by then had climbed from 10,000 to 15,000 ft,[252] the recorded differences are not very large and in the heat of combat and pursuits, pilots may well have made inaccurate estimates of their altitudes.

P/O Litchfield of 610 Squadron, now alone after his two wingmen had blacked out and lost him, fired several bursts at the one Me 109 as he crossed the Kentish coast. After the third burst the Messerschmitt dived steeply away again, and after the next showed a spurt of flame followed by thick smoke.[253] Litchfield then saw the second Me 109 come to help the first and easily outmanoeuvred it and gave it two bursts, seeing it climbing away for France, also smoking. To his credit, Litchfield is quoted in the IPR as noting that this smoke might just have been 'normal exhaust gasses'.[254] This would also make sense for a Me 109 that was climbing away; one with a seriously damaged and smoking engine would be more likely to dive away. It is thus postulated that Litchfield's two claims for a probable Messerschmitt and then for a damaged Me 109 may have been made against two aircraft already damaged by 151 Squadron and diving away from that action, only to be caught up by Litchfield. These two double-claimed Me 109s would then equate most likely with the two casualties suffered by *8/JG 3*, the more seriously hit machine being that whose wounded pilot bailed out off Boulogne, and the less damaged aircraft making it back to France and a belly-landing at Wissant.[255] The only real alternative would be to disallow the claims by either 151 or 610 Squadrons, or only allow them one each. However, the details described in the two Intelligence Patrol Reports suggest that both squadrons did in fact hit and damage two Me 109s each, supporting the suggested double-claims. In this case, there is no question of over-claiming but rather only of sharing a destroyed Messerschmitt and another damaged and belly-landed.

The dive-bombing attack by the Stukas of *IV/LG 1* on Convoy CW 5 led to the loss of *Island Queen,* a 779-ton commodore ship carrying coal bound for Cowes on the Isle of Wight; hit off Folkestone Gateway Lightship, despite being towed by a trawler she sank, three crew members dying in the attack.[256] Two more coasters were damaged, one seriously, set on fire and having to be towed into port.[257] Bombing results against the convoy were thus rather limited. There was a German radio claim later in the day of the sinking of an 11,000-ton vessel.[258]

15 July 1940: convoy attack off Essex, Suffolk

Amongst the various sources, there is a measure of confusion about a convoy attack north of the Thames Estuary. Some accounts have the raid being carried out by fifteen Do 17s of *KG 2* from *Fliegerkorps* II, with Hurricanes from 56 Squadron (and also from 151 Squadron in two sources) thwarting the raid and all bombs falling wide of the target ships.[259] While pilot reports suggested a dozen Do 215s attacking a convoy off Orfordness at about 14h15 this day,[260] it was most probably a small group of Me 110s from *EGr 210*.[261] Ten of their Me 110s had indeed attacked a convoy, locality given in the Thames Estuary (sic), sinking a 2,855-ton vessel (four crewmen lost) near the Aldeburgh Light Vessel and badly damaging a smaller ship in the same area, which later sank. They reported seeing a flight of Spitfires but suffered no losses.[262] The two merchant ships were part of convoy FN223 that had earlier departed from Southend bound for the Tyne where the surviving vessels arrived on 17 July; both were hit some 10 miles south of the Aldeburgh Light Vessel and both were taken in tow but sank off Harwich, the *Heworth* losing four crewmen and the Polish *Zbaraz* none.[263] Do 215s were essentially reconnaissance machines at this time and were unlikely to have been employed on a bombing mission, but *EGr 210* were part of *Fliegerkorps II*, and their Me 110s, suddenly appearing out of the murk could easily be mistaken for Do 215s, which had a much less bulbous nose than Do 17s and more closely fitted the 'flying pencil' appellation applied to the Dornier bombers in general.

The 'Spitfires' reported by *EGr 210* were Blue Section of 56 Squadron, led by F/Lt Gracie who had been ordered off from the forward base of Manston to escort the convoy.[264] The weather was poor with rain clouds at 2,000-3,000 ft and visibility was bad. Suddenly they saw nine to twelve 'Do 215s' about half a mile away through the murk, diving in vics line astern or echelon on the convoy.[265] While Gracie and F/Sgt Higginson reported firing at a few Dorniers and the former was fired at in turn, and Higginson claimed one shot down unconfirmed and Gracie a probable, there were no losses and *EGr 210* didn't even report any action with RAF fighters.[266] The third pilot in the 56 Squadron section, F/O Michael Constable-Maxwell, was more moderate in his assessment of this encounter, assigning only probable victories to his two compatriots and suggesting they drove off the bombers.[267]

The Messerschmitt pilots from *EGr 210* didn't need any encouragement to leave the scene, their remit being rapid bombing attacks rather than air fighting. The *EGr 210* formation comprised two machines from the Staff Flight and eight from 2 *Staffel*; they departed from St Omer as a forward base at 14h00[268] and applying a cruising speed of *c.* 4.75 miles per minute would have reached the area offshore of Harwich by approximately 14h14, almost the exact time reported by 56 Squadron for the bombing of the ships.[269]

F/Lt Roddick Smith led a section of Hurricanes from 151 Squadron aloft from the forward base at Manston, a full fifty minutes after the 56 Squadron section had taken off from there; Smith's section intercepted a lone Do 215 off Harwich which they chased in and out of the thick clouds.[270] Smith, flying the two cannon Hurricane of 151 Squadron, and Sgt Atkinson giving it several short bursts before it disappeared in the thick weather, sharing a claim for a damaged Dornier.[271] No such damaged machine is included in known *Luftwaffe* losses for the day. A Hurricane of 245 Squadron claimed a damaged Do 17 between 17h00 and 18h00 off Turnhouse, but again none can be identified in German losses for the day, which equated in total to only two machines which were shot down, a Heinkel of *2/KG 26* and a Ju 88 of *4/LG 1*.[272]

Two Spitfires of 603 Squadron were vectored onto a lone bandit which radar had located off Peterhead and at 12h12 they sighted it only 500 ft above the sea under very cloudy conditions almost down to sea level.[273] P/O Stewart Clark got in the first attacks, from astern and closing to 100 yards and using all his ammunition, while P/O Morton attacked second, using astern-quarter attacks; the only observed damage to the enemy aircraft was that it lost oil, covering Stewart Clark's windscreen and upon landing, it was also found all over the wings and propeller.[274] In fact, the Heinkel from *2/KG 26* ditched about 50 miles offshore, one crewman dead from the Spitfres' attack. Four survivors managed to get into the dinghy, one wounded; they were rescued by a fisherman two days later, by which time the dinghy had drifted to about a mile off Fraserburgh,[275] some twenty kilometres to the north-east of Peterhead. About an hour later, at *c.* 13h20, a section of 213 Squadron intercepted a reconnaissance Do 17 north of Portland which they attacked, claiming it damaged.[276] However, return fire from the enemy aircraft hit the Hurricane of Sub Lt Bramah near Dartmouth, wounding him badly in the arm; he bailed out and was fortunate to be rescued from the sea by the destroyer HMS *Scimitar*.[277]

There was one other set of bomber incursions this day, into the west of England and Wales. The airfield at Yeovil was lightly bombed by a small formation of *Luftflotte 3* bombers who slightly damaged a hangar and the runway, but the Westland Aircraft Works there was untouched.[278] Bombs also fell at Avonmouth and at St Athans airfield, both about 35 miles north of Yeovil, and a Spitfire of 92 Squadron is thought to have dispatched a Ju 88 of *4/LG 1* near Cardiff some three hours after Yeovil was attacked.[279] The Yeovil attackers might thus also have been from this *Geschwader*; this was an unusual target at this early stage of the Battle, being the location of an aircraft factory producing the Whirlwind fighter.[280]

In a separate action, P/O Holland of 92 Squadron, on a lone patrol, was vectored onto a Ju 88 at 9,000 ft over Porthcawl at *c.* 17h10; the enemy aircraft dived at high speed into cloud layers and Holland dived after it, firing from astern with very little deflection and closing to 200 yards used all his ammunition.[281] Pieces were observed detaching from the fuselage of the Junkers, but Holland made no claim and nothing was recorded in the Squadron's Operational Record Book either.[282]

Late in the evening on a sortie from 18h45 to 19h40, a section of Hurricanes from 145 Squadron intercepted a Do 17 a couple of miles South of Selsey Bill and two of the pilots claimed it as a probable victory;[283] once more no suitable Dornier victim appears in the *Luftwaffe* losses. It is just possible that the *4/LG 1* Ju 88 discussed above fell to 145 Squadron's attack. The base of *II/LG 1* at Orleans-Bricy[284] in France lay south-east of Selsey Bill, closer to that area than the Bristol Channel area where 92 Squadron's lone Spitfire had operated. The *Luftwaffe* loss list merely states that this Ju 88 failed to return from an operational sortie.[285] Six Hurricanes of 145 Squadron had been scrambled and Green Section sighted a lone Do 17 and one pilot from the section managed to find it amongst cloud layers and pursued it about 30-35 miles out to sea, leaving it with a burning starboard engine and wing, but with the rear-gunner still firing.[286] This IPR also describes how the other two Hurricanes of Green Section found another lone Do 17, West of Selsey, and gave it a few short bursts in amongst the thick clouds with no apparent effect. All three pilots possibly attacked the same machine.

There were no German claims for 15 July 1940.[287] Though two bombers were shot down, with rather fleeting attacks made in very bad weather where claims were essentially for damaged or probable victories, no damaged German aircraft being recorded in the loss listings is understandable. Some German machines were probably hit and slightly damaged, but if repairs were effected at unit level, then often such damage was not recorded in official casualty lists. The claim for a Dornier unconfirmed by F/Sgt Higginson of 56 Squadron, made against the *EGr 210* Me 110 raid, is harder to explain, as he stated that he saw it hit the sea;[288] possibly one of the Me 110s he was chasing had a bomb hung up after the brief shipping raid and managed to jettison it during his chase. Such an explosion in the sea just behind a rapidly retreating enemy machine just above sea level could easily enough provide a false impression of an enemy shot down into the drink.

5

16–19 July 1940: Small Raids in Western Channel; Dover and Shipping Attacked by *EGr 210* in East

16 July 1940: small airfield raid, Lee-on-Solent

A section of 603 Squadron led by F/O Ritchie, with P/Os Morton and Stewart Clarke, was vectored onto a lone He 111 from *9/KG 26* in very hazy, misty weather, 10 to 20 miles north-north-east of Fraserburgh, at 18,000 ft and attacked at 16h06.[1] Each pilot made a number of attacks, mainly from astern, with a few from quarter-astern and one from beam to astern, closing in to between 150 and 50 yards, with a total of 7,910 rounds fired.[2] This means each Spitfire was carrying significantly more than the standard ammunition load of 2,400 rounds per aircraft. The hapless Heinkel ditched *c.* 25 miles out with two survivors being seen to get into their dinghy, who were rescued and became PoWs.[3] Return fire from the bomber was kept up for much of the attack, resulting in one armour-piercing round in the wing of one of the Spitfires.[4] This once again underlines how in most cases the rifle calibre machine guns carried by the RAF fighters necessitated the expenditure of much ammunition, and that from close range, to achieve success against the German bombers.

Between 16h40 and 18h04, a Ju 88 of *6/KG 54* at *c.* 3,000 ft was shot down by three pilots of 601 Squadron between the Needles, Isle of Wight and the mainland; two survivors, one wounded, were rescued.[5] F/O Rhodes-Moorhouse had led seven Hurricanes of B Flight, 601 Squadron up from Tangmere, and they sighted three Ju 88s, one being promptly dispatched into the sea by Rhodes-Moorhouse and another also attacked by him but with no visible results, the two bombers then making off for France.[6] While it would appear that the Junkers 88 was shot down by a section of three Hurricanes led by Rhodes-Moorhouse and this machine was observed to jettison its bombs and then ditch in the Solent, the B Flight leader claimed to have seen the other one he attacked plunge straight into the sea from 9,000 ft and disappear completely.[7] However, only one bomber was lost, perhaps another one had dived away steeply and also jettisoned bombs, giving an impression of a total loss such as seen by Rhodes-Moorhouse. These actions were apparently against a small Ju 88 formation which attacked Lee-on-Solent airfield where they destroyed a Royal Navy machine on the ground.[8] Perhaps a slightly larger formation than just a *Kette* of three Ju 88s from *II/KG 54* actually made up the raid, some being intercepted and turned away by 601 Squadron's attack before being able to drop their bombs, and a few others getting away in the murk and making the attack on the airfield. The *Luftwaffe* also reported a *Stab/KG 2* Dornier 17 being damaged in combat but making it back to St Inglevert aerodrome in the Pas de Calais, where a successful crash-landing was made.[9]

17 July 1940: single aircraft actions and a small bounce

Poor weather continued and as a result there was little action. Shortly after midday, a lone Dornier 17 on reconnaissance near Kenley was intercepted by two Hurricanes of 615 Squadron, and minutes later by a single Spitfire of 64 Squadron, and claimed damaged, but got away.[10] While no suitable loss can be found in German records, the last casualty mentioned above for 16 July may have been reported for the wrong day, and may in fact be the aircraft damaged in the Kenley–Redhill area on 17 July.[11]

A full-strength 64 Squadron was sent up for a patrol, 13h22-14h20, over Beachy Head;[12] during July 1940 unless there was a radar plot of a relatively significant incoming raid, such large British fighter formations were unusual. On this afternoon there was an especially dangerous combination of clouds and sun streaming through in between, just right for an ambush, which is precisely what happened. One can only speculate why 64 Squadron was vectored to Beachy Head, but possibly they were placed there to cover the return of two small Blenheim formations from 236 Squadron, sent out to sweep the Calais-Boulogne sector.[13] In point of fact, two Me 109s from *3/JG 2* were scrambled to chase after the Blenheims but in the bad weather conditions did not find any enemy aircraft.[14] *Lt* Helmut Wick and his wingman *Oblt* Pflanz then carried on towards the north across the Channel and through a break in the clouds thought they recognised the Isle of Wight, when in fact they were seeing Beachy Head, which resembles to a certain degree the southern half of the Isle of Wight. Beachy Head lay almost directly across the Channel from *I/JG 2*'s base at Beaumont-le-Roger.[15] The experienced and aggressive Wick spotted the Spitfire formation in between the clouds and skilfully stalked them, making maximum use of cloud and sun; he thought there were fourteen Spitfires[16] but in reality there were twelve. F/O D. M. Taylor was flying as a weaver on the left of the squadron,[17] normally placed behind and above the squadron formation, with a companion weaver to the starboard side also. This might explain Wick's estimate of fourteen Spitfires – two weavers protecting what he might have thought was a complete squadron of twelve.

In any event, Wick had little trouble in diving on F/O Taylor and riddling his Spitfire from only 40 yards range and without this being seen by any other squadron member; in his excitement and with explosive cannon strikes at very close range, *Lt* Wick claimed the Spitfire simply exploded into pieces.[18] Taylor was fortunate in being able to force-land near Hailsham at *c.* 14h00,[19] some 12-13 km north of Beachy Head, and was seriously wounded with metal fragments in the head, body, right arm and right leg.[20] Unfortunately, there is no Intelligence Patrol Report preserved for this action of 64 Squadron, nor any Squadron Commander's Report on Flying Battle Casualty for the wounded Taylor and his Spitfire being shot down and written off.

S/L MacDonell, a caring and well-respected leader of his Squadron, upon taking command on 26 July soon changed the tight vic formations in use in 64 Squadron to a much more loose arrangement.[21] While this undoubtedly was a great improvement and left them much less vulnerable to attack,[22] they still used weavers flying above and behind the Squadron as an extra precaution against being surprised and bounced. These methods, while helping, did not prevent a skilled surprise attack from succeeding, especially when clouds and sun combined to favour ambush; Wick's successful bounce of F/O Taylor was not seen by anybody else in the remaining eleven Spitfires of the Squadron.

Not all RAF fighter squadrons in the Battle of Britain made changes to the tight vic formations, and those made by MacDonell stand to his credit. In any case, no fighter formation, not even the much-vaunted 'finger four' or *Schwarm* of two pairs invented by the German pilots Mölders and Lützow in the Spanish Civil War,[23] was a panacea providing significant protection against surprise attack. Even later on, during 1941-2 when RAF sweeps and small, heavily escorted bombing raids on Northern France clashed regularly with *JG 2* and *JG 26* in that region, and both sides were using the *Schwarm* as the standard formation, the *Luftwaffe* units still made use of a top cover *Rotte*, or pair, strongly akin to the 1940 RAF weavers.[24] They had a special air force slang term to describe these top-cover mission assignments: *Holzaugenrotte* ('wooden-eyed pair'), and their use continued into the Battle of Germany also.

S/L John Peel led six Hurricanes of 145 Squadron to intercept a lone German bomber in the clouds near St Catherine's Point, Isle of Wight at *c.* 15h30; they claimed to have damaged a Ju 88 but were probably responsible for hitting a Heinkel of *Stab/KG 27*.[25] This was in fact lost in the Channel about 30 miles south of Bognor Regis,[26] killing all aboard. It was carrying the normal crew of five plus the *Kommodore* of *KG 27, Oberstleutnant* Georgi.[27] Despite being hit by return fire from the bomber, S/L Peel was able to return to base, his aircraft damaged.[28]

A missing Spitfire of 603 Squadron, F/O Peel killed, was thought to have been an accident, most likely engine failure, while on a patrol begun at 07h27.[29] *I/KG 51* lost a Ju 88 and its crew of four, described in the loss lists as having been shot down over the Channel; this may have been a victim of the second patrol of the Calais-Boulogne sector by two Blenheims of 236 Squadron, referred to above.[30] However, this operational area would have been unusual for *KG 51*, part of *Luftflotte 3* which generally operated further west. A He 111 of *II/KG 27* force-landed at Le Blanc in France and was damaged 35%, about 100 km west-south-west of its base at Bourges[31] in unoccupied France; it may have been an operational accident rather than the consequences of combat.

18 July 1940: *Oberst* Osterkamp's tactics, RAF tactical responses, and German ace fixation

The day's action began with a multi-part German tactic that probably owed much to the influence of *Oberst* Osterkamp, *Kommodore* of *JG 51*[32] and to the weather. The *Luftwaffe* by this stage were aware that British radar could pick them up over the Pas de Calais as raids assembled, and often used this fact to their advantage.[33] With a convoy approaching the Dover Straits and cloudy conditions, a German raid was to be expected anyway, and they did not disappoint.[34] The assembly of aircraft behind the French coast was duly noted by British radar and 11 Group were notified of the build-up by *c.* 09h00.[35] As a result, twelve Spitfires of 610 Squadron, led by F/Lt Brian Smith, were scrambled from their forward base at Hawkinge at 09h37.[36]

The *Luftwaffe* assembly of a raid over the Pas de Calais almost always had the Me 109 escorts and top cover at high altitude already before they crossed the French coast, which is where they generally picked up any bombers they were to escort; as a result by the time they reached a nearby target such as Dover or a convoy in the Straits they were well placed at superior height to intercept and interdict RAF fighters still frantically straining for altitude after taking off from a nearby forward base such as Hawkinge or Manston. The German fighters almost always had an altitude advantage. If the British fighters had taken off from their sector stations, such as at Biggin Hill, Hornchurch or Kenley, resulting in distances of about one and a half times that covered by the Me 109s to reach the Dover area, they would have had time to gain altitude on the way, but may well have arrived too late to intercept a rapid Stuka raid. Thus the need for forward bases close to potential targets, but with the concomitant disadvantage of not gaining enough height.

While this conundrum applied in early July, the RAF learning curve by the 18th had progressed beyond a tame acceptance of the way of things. F/Lt Smith's leadership was an example of the innovations made by Fighter Command pilots themselves to address tactical disadvantages imposed by the realities of geography and warning times provided by the radar system. With a German formation having been reported on radar as heading from around Gravelines on the French coast, between Calais and Dunkirk, and making towards Ramsgate, instead of heading for Dover Smith put his men into a steep climb along a heading inland rather than towards the coast.[37] This soon became almost standard practice for veteran leaders of fighter squadrons, many flying reciprocal courses before reversing them at altitude and heading along the ordered vector for the raid itself. Over the Channel and Dover area that morning, dangerous conditions existed, with cloud layers at approximately 3,000 ft, 6,000 ft and 10,000 ft.[38] F/Lt Smith did the right thing in placing his squadron below the top cloud layer[39] and they duly intercepted nine to twelve Me 109s at *c.* 10h00 about 10 miles off the French coast.[40] But here their luck ran out; the German formation was exclusively Me 109s, with no bombers present,[41] and they must have been able to see 610 Squadron through the top cloud layer. The *Luftwaffe* pilots had more tricks up their sleeve, living up to Osterkamp's maxim of using all kinds of subterfuge to surprise the RAF fighters and aim for the desired 5:1 loss ratio, British to German, as can be seen in an exerpt from the relevant casualty document for P/O Litchfield:[42]

> This engagement with enemy took place between the French and English coast, the actual intercepting being brought about between layers of cloud at 9,000 feet. Pilot Officer P. Litchfield was leading Green Section who met three M.E.109's, turning to attack, this section were themselves attacked by some M.E.109's. Pilot Officer P. Litchfield was last seen following a M.E.109 into a cloud. No. 3 in his section reports seeing an unidentified aircraft dive into the sea, and sink 6/10 miles off Dover.

Hauptmann Tietzen, *Staffelfkapitän* 5/JG 51 claimed the Spitfire[43] and obviously sent in a few of his men first to distract Green Section, normally the last section in a RAF formation, and lead them away from their colleagues, while he and other Me 109 pilots performed the bounce on P/O Litchfield. This was typical *Luftwaffe* fighter arm thinking: surprise the enemy, set up some sort of ambush for one of them, and perform the bounce on that aircraft. The formation leader was almost always the one to perform the actual attack and then gain the victory, protected by his own men above and behind him; thus, the kill rate was kept up, own losses were minimised and *Luftwaffe* aces rapidly grew their scores. The thinking was that by increasing the number of aces and their scores, then they must win as they destroyed many more enemies than their own losses.

In this specific example, only one pilot in a *Staffel* actually opened fire and attacked an enemy, and it needs to be remembered that an entire German fighter *Gruppe* was in the air at the time.[44] It was uneconomic use of fighters, but supported the German fixation with aces begun in the First World War and worship of Manfred von Richthofen, a history to be repeated in the Second World War. The RAF approach would have been to attack an entire German *Staffel* by stealth if possible and promote a much more general battle, where casualties to both sides were much more likely. The latter approach formed part of the battle of attrition vision for the struggle over the British Isles as appreciated by Dowding and Park. *Hauptmann* Tietzmann himself was to live for another month exactly before perishing in combat, having brought his score to twenty, and another seven in Spain. He received a posthumous *Ritterkreuz*.[45]

18 July 1940: a low-level attack on trawlers

Very soon after the previous action, *1/EGr 210* lifted off from their forward base at St Omer at 10h15, their Me 110 C-6s heading for the area of the Thames Estuary and further north, flying at sea level on an armed reconnaissance mission.[46] They suddenly came across about ten ships in a convoy off Lowestoft, and without any hesitation *Oberleutnant* Lutz, the *Staffelkapitän*, led them to attack. Due to the speed of the assault, only weak anti-aircraft fire was met and the Me 110s claimed two 1,000-ton ships on fire.[47] It seems likely that *EGr 210* had attacked a group of naval anti-submarine and mine-sweeping trawlers off Harwich: four trawlers, HMTs *Lady Madeline, Spene, Cape Finisterre* and *Stella Leonis* reported damage and casualties due to bombing and strafing.[48] *EGr 210* obviously had an inflated idea of their success in this 'convoy' attack.

Just after bombing the trawlers, two British Blenheims were seen who courageously engaged the Messerschmitts; Lutz and another of his pilots claimed one Blenheim shot down into the sea, following which *1/EGr 210* had another go at the ships.[49] This second, strafing attack was a disappointment, however; three of the four Me 110s armed with the 30 mm cannon experienced jammed weapons. Upon landing, *Lt* Beudel found a number of 0.303-inch calibre hits in one wing,[50] presumably from either a Blenheim or shipborne machine guns. The Blenheim lost in this action may have been from either 235 Squadron, Coastal Command, lost on convoy patrol between 10h30 and 12h00 off the East coast, crew killed, or from 15 Squadron of Bomber Command, time apparently *c.* 14h00, crew survived crash on East coast;[51] but the time of the latter loss does not support it being part of the *EGr 210* action. Between eleven o'clock and lunchtime, the coastguard station at St Margaret's Bay in Kent was bombed and the East Goodwin Lightship was sunk.[52] Clearly, the *Luftwaffe* was targeting convoy navigation aids as well as sea rescue facilities to aid downed RAF fighter pilots in the crucial Dover Straits region, so heavily fought over during July 1940.

18 July 1940: not all bounces succeed

About half an hour after 610 Squadron lost P/O Litchfield and while *1/EGr 210*'s Me 110s were making their way towards the Thames Estuary, in the Western Channel, Yellow Section of 152 Squadron led by F/O Bayles were on convoy patrol in the area off Poole.[53] The section saw about forty German aircraft proceeding west at about 2,000 ft, and Bayles put them into line astern and followed, but they then intercepted a lone Do 215 at *c.* 10h25 and went for this instead.[54] As the subsequent action against Me 109s took place closer to the Isle of Wight[55] this reconnaissance machine was presumably going in the opposite direction; possibly it had spotted a convoy closer to Portland towards which those forty low-level *Luftwaffe* attackers were winging their way. As F/O Bayles opened fire from almost astern on the rather helpless Dornier and Yellow 2 prepared to follow him in, P/O Richard Hogg, Yellow 3, gave a warning of two Me 109s which had flashed past Bayles, one of them hitting his wing.[56] Both Bayles and P/O Warren, Yellow 2 reacted fast and managed to shake off a number of attacking Me 109s after sustaining some hits; meanwhile Hogg was left to his own devices astern of the Dornier, his two colleagues and the German fighters having fortuitously vanished, he rapidly closed on the bomber from astern and fired all his ammunition at it from relatively close range, only to see it turn rather gently away and vanish into cloud.[57] He only claimed it as damaged but the machine, an older model Do 17 M from *Stab/StG 77*, did not get home, its crew being lost as well.[58]

The attacking Me 109s belonged to *2/JG 2* led by *Oblt* Greisert, who appear to have flown a sweep over the Isle of Wight area where Greisert claimed a Spitfire shot down at about 10h20, which was not confirmed by the German claims system.[59] While obviously having achieved complete surprise, he and his *Staffel* did little damage to the rather helpless section of 152 Squadron who never saw them coming, only damaging two Spitfires in a fairly minor way. Greisert thus performed the perfect bounce in faithful alignment with the standard German practice, but obviously he was no expert shot like *Hauptmann* Horst Tietzen. For his part, Yellow Section leader F/O Bayles must have been concentrating too much on his intended Dornier victim. It would appear that 2/JG 2 arriving in the right place at the right time was probably just chance – the sky is a big place for such a rendezvous to have been planned between them and the Dornier; but they fluffed any chance of saving the poor bomber and its crew.

At almost exactly the same time as the 152 Squadron–2/JG 2 action, and far to the north, P/O Berry of 603 Squadron was scrambled from Montrose at 10h21 and as he gained height he saw a single He 111 emerge from the clouds, at the cloud base of *c.* 1,500 ft.[60] With little time to plan his attack he managed to let off two short bursts at about 100 yards range before the German bomber vanished into the clouds again; no claim was made.[61] Apparently, three He 111s of *KG 26* had bombed Montrose airfield at about 10h00,[62] unopposed at the time but one at least thereafter was intercepted by P/O Berry. The casualty file from Montrose noted the death of two RAF men in the bombing, with three more wounded.[63] It is noticeable that three widely dispersed operations took place that morning in the *c.* 10h00-10h30 time slot: the *II/JG 51* sweep towards Dover, the small Montrose raid by *KG 26*, and the 2/JG 2 sweep in the area of the Isle of Wight. It is not known if there was any *Luftwaffe* planning behind this apparent coordination.

18 July 1940: the casualties of war

When the section of three Spitfires of 152 Squadron were on their convoy patrol off Poole, before being intercepted by 2/JG 2, they had sighted about forty German aircraft at the rather low altitude of 2,000 ft sweeping westwards and initially followed them before they were distracted by the single Do 17 they met, apparently proceeding eastwards towards the Isle of Wight, where *JG 2* caught them by surprise. Putting these facts together suggests that a low-level raid on a convoy somewhere in the Portland–Weymouth Bay area or further south in the Channel was attempted by the *Luftwaffe*; this would logically explain the lone reconnaissance Dornier met, and the low-level formation of forty enemy machines flying westwards. These might have been missed by the British radar system due to a low altitude or just confusion resulting from several formations approaching the island from highly divergent directions and origins; in these early days of the Battle, and even later on, not every raid was picked up by Dowding's system. In the event, no recorded convoy attack has been located in documents, but the minesweeping trawler HMT *Rinovia* suffered aerial attack in the Western Channel, losing three crew members. Seaman F. R. Burgess was decorated with the Distinguished Service Medal (DSM) for shooting down one of the German bombers.[64]

Most actions in war, no matter how superficially insignificant they might appear in historical context, bring loss, pain and hardship to the next of kin; one of the three lost ratings on HMT *Rivonia* was Seaman Alexander Maciver, age thirty and the only son and support of his widowed mother.[65] No DSM for him, just interment in the cemetery of his native village of North Tolsta on the Isle of Lewis.

A Ju 88 of *I/KG 54*, along with its crew, was lost on operations this day and may conceivably have been the aircraft claimed shot down by the gallant Seaman Burgess; more likely, perhaps, a 35%-damaged Ju 88 of *II/KG 54* reported in German loss returns was hit by Burgess.[66]

At lunchtime, six Hurricanes of B Flight 145 Squadron were sent aloft and told to patrol below cloud over Bembridge, Isle of Wight; they were then vectored in all directions, first over St Catherine's Point on the southern tip of the island along with a climb to 10,000 ft, then directly southwards and then finally on a course of 90 degrees eastwards.[67] The advantage bestowed by having a full flight rather than just a section to perform the interception and subsequent attack is described by F/Lt Boyd in an excerpt from his combat report, the action timed at *c.* 13h15:[68]

> While on this course Blue 2 sighted a Heinkel 111 beneath us and we dived to attack. The Heinkel twisted and turned to get away. The whole flight attacked in turn, some carrying out F.C. No. 1 attacks. After the leader's attack, the Heinkel jettisoned 5 heavy bombs and the E/A then dived through clouds but was attacked below by Green Section who had anticipated this. E/A dived into sea and broke up during this attack. Two men were flung clear but one sank almost immediately, the other was still swimming. [F.C. = Fighter Command, the No. 1 attack being from below and astern by fighters in line astern]

In view of what 145 Squadron reported, it would appear that the Ju 88 of *I/KG 54* and its crew were actually the victims of this action and not lost to HMT *Rivonia;* another minor combat event, but once more tragedy to several families, this time on the enemy's side. F/Lt Boyd's Hurricane was hit by return fire from the Heinkel and returned to base damaged.[69]

An hour and a half later, A Flight of 609 Squadron was engaged in protecting a convoy off Swanage and were much luckier in terms of casualties; F/Lt Howell leading F/O Edge and Sgt Feary, Red Section, climbed after a lone Ju 88 sighted some 2,000 ft above them, which they intercepted south of Swanage.[70] Each pilot of the section made two attacks on the lone bomber, Edge covering his leader during the first one before diving down himself to put in his first attack between the two of F/Lt Howell; Feary similarly guarded Edge from surprise above, diving down after F/O Edge's first attack to make his initial attack.[71] Howell's two attacks were diving attacks from the beam and above, closing to the quarter, and he pulled away upwards after the first one, which is when he was most likely hit by the rear gunner; by the time of his second attack the Ju 88 was diving steeply seawards and this time Howell pulled away sideways, but it was too late as his cockpit began to fill with glycol fumes and he bailed out into the sea.[72] F/O Edge followed the Junkers' dive, using his boost cut-out to speed up to *c.* 400 mph and catch the bomber; his first attack was from less than 100 ft range and from dead astern as the controls almost froze and he could not manoeuvre at the high speed.[73] His second attack, now at sea level, was a quarter attack changing to dead astern again. Feary also made a diving quarter attack at first, the second also being at sea level as the Ju 88 flew at *c.* 350 mph.[74] The enemy bomber had jettisoned four bombs after the initial attack by Howell, and was last seen by the section as it sped off at sea level, smoke pouring out from the port engine.[75] F/O Edge had also been hit by return fire, he thought from two guns firing directly backwards behind each engine nacelle, and force-landed on Studland Beach not far north of Swanage; ammunition expenditure was *c.* 4,880 rounds for the Section, and the Spitfires carried a standard load of 2400 rounds per machine.[76] F/Lt Howell came down off Bournemouth at about 15h15 and was rescued, none the worse for his swim, by a motorboat; F/O Edge's Spitfire was salvaged from Studland Beach despite being covered by the sea during high tide.[77] F/O Edge would take over 253 Squadron in September 1940 where he became an exponent of the head-on squadron attack against German bomber formations; possibly his experience on 18 July spurred on that evolution in his tactics.

Meanwhile, Yellow Section of 609 Squadron, with F/O Overton leading F/O Newberry and P/O Bisdee, had stayed with the ships after Red Section took after the Ju 88; soon after they noticed anti-aircraft bursts from the convoy they were looking after, and Overton did a steep climbing turn followed by a short burst of fire at another Ju 88 before he almost spun in.[78] Bisdee chased the Junkers seawards, firing and apparently silencing the rear gunner while damaging the port engine, before running out of ammunition.[79] The two claims of 609 Squadron in these actions around the convoy south of Swanage are related to two casualties from *II/LG 1*, one being missing with all its crew including one or two very gallant and skilled rear gunners, and thought to be Red Section's victim. The other, with one man killed, managed to return to base damaged, and was probably the victim of Yellow Section as outlined above.[80]

In the Red Section account of the action, three reports from witnesses at separate gun and searchlight sites in the area of Hengistbury Head claim to have seen a twin-engined machine dive steeply with both engines smoking heavily and hit the sea some 8 miles south of them.[81] What they exactly saw is open to question, but it may have been the Ju 88 pursued by Red Section as it dived to sea level, as the pilots described in their reports, giving the impression to the ground observers, that it went into the drink. This bomber was last seen by the 609 Squadron pilots making off at high speed, one engine smoking and presumably did end up in the sea, but further towards France, out of sight of any observer.

18 July 1940: some inconclusive actions at end of day

A full strength 111 Squadron was ordered off at 15h20 for about an hour and, flying over the Channel, a section led by S/L Thompson met a short-range Hs 126 reconnaissance machine of *2(H)/21*, which they claimed as a probable; however, it made it back to France but crashed at St Sabine where it was further damaged.[82] Sources vary on whether it was only damaged or burnt out, and whether the two crewmen were injured or unhurt.[83]

In the north again, Yellow Section of 603 Squadron was vectored onto a Do 215 about 10 miles off Aberdeen in the early afternoon, which they found flying at 3,000 ft and heading north-west; the section led by P/O Ritchie adopted a wide vic formation and took up the chase.[84] Two of the pilots made port quarter attacks on the bomber at *c.* 14h38 while P/O Morton, Yellow 2, attacked from above on the port beam, where he also collected six bullet holes, discovered after landing.[85] The bomber showed no results except for jettisoning its bombs and giving off a large puff of white smoke from the fuselage.[86] Yellow 1 and 2 put in second quarter attacks, which again seemed to have little effect. P/O Ritchie, his ammunition expended, followed the enemy machine out to sea for another 15 miles during which time it kept a straight course, speed about 210 mph at a height of only 50 ft above the water.[87] Although the Dornier was presumably damaged, no official claim was put in. No Dornier casualty to equate with this action can be found in the German loss returns. The enemy machine kept up a violent evasive action throughout the Spitfires' attacks.[88] Interestingly, P/O Ritchie led his section of 603 Squadron in a wide or open vic formation during pursuit of the Dornier, analogous to that applied by 64 Squadron's S/L MacDonell soon after taking command of that squadron.[89]

Further action in the Aberdeen area followed when 603 Squadron scrambled two Spitfires at 18h55; only one got off timeously and this was vectored onto a lone bomber, finding a He 111 flying north-west some 10-25 miles north-west of Dyce.[90] P/O Gilroy made several astern attacks from 400, 200, 100 yds, in and out of clouds and one from vertically above when he closed in to *c.* 50 yds.[91] The raider escaped, state of damage, if any, unknown, after return fire from its dorsal gun position had hit Gilroy's glycol system; a spray of the fluid in the cockpit and loss of engine forced him down near Old Meldrum, in a field running uphill and with cloud almost down to ground level.[92] He did not have time to get the undercarriage down, damaging the Spitfire in the forced-landing.[93] German loss returns contain no suitable casualty for this action; a Ju 88, 35% damaged of *II/KG 54*, which crashed at its base in France[94] would have been very unlikely to have operated that far north. This damaged Ju 88 may in fact have been hit by a gunner on HMT *Rivonia* as discussed above. The second Spitfire which had trouble getting off the ground was flown by Sgt James Caister; he had some satisfaction later that night, claiming a Ju 88 damaged south of Aberdeen at *c.* 22h30; in fact, a Ju 88 from *I/KG 30* was hit and crash-landed at Aalborg, 50% damaged and with one wounded man aboard.[95]

It is also just possible that the damaged Ju 88 of *II/KG 54* related to a claim for a damaged Junkers made by P/O Saunders of 92 Squadron, at about 11h55 off Cardiff;[96] while the Bristol Channel lay outside the normal operating area of this *Geschwader*, it would have been within its operational range. His own Spitfire being hit by return fire and no oil pressure registering at all, Saunders was lucky to have made it back to base with a damaged machine; the two enemy rear gunners had put only two bullet holes in his Spitfire but one presumably hit an oil pipe.[97] The Ju 88 jettisoned its bombs upon sighting Saunders approaching, and then evaded his attacks with steep turns in and out of cloud, forcing him to expend his ammunition in a series of deflection bursts.[98] He claimed an unconfirmed victory in the IPR. As a caveat to this account, other sources suggest this entire action took place the previous day, 17 July;[99] however, the Intelligence Patrol Report (IPR) is dated 19 July 1940, the day immediately after the indicated date of the action, 18 July, and is likely to have been correct.

Another mission, at *c.* 19h30 and close to dusk, was an attack on invasion targets in Boulogne harbour by Bomber Command Blenheims escorted by Fighter Command Hurricanes; two sources provide different figures, namely nine Blenheims escorted by twenty fighters[100] or eighteen Blenheims accompanied by twenty-four Hurricanes from 111 and

615 Squadrons.[101] A detailed analysis of 615 Squadron records suggests only six Hurricanes from that unit took part.[102] Although there appear to have been no losses to any of these aircraft, it was rather a strange decision by Fighter Command to risk a relatively large number of Hurricanes over enemy territory, with a landing back at base in darkness; the combined dangers from enemy fighters, flak and accidents in landing would appear to run counter to Dowding's and Park's tactics of preserving their assets while causing steady attrition to the *Luftwaffe*.

19 July 1940: early morning actions, and the importance of 'De Wilde' ammunition

The day's aerial action began with an early morning lone reconnaissance Dornier 17 belonging to *4(F)/121*, based at Caen-Carpiquet,[103] which apparently made it through the radar screen along the South coast undetected and penetrated inland to the Croydon area where it was finally reported by the Observer Corps at about 06h40.[104] A section of 145 Squadron, led by S/L Peel, part of a flight of six Hurricanes which were airborne from just after 06h00 until about twenty minutes past seven, intercepted the Dornier, as did a section of 257 Squadron soon after, and the unfortunate Dornier fell into the sea about 20 miles south of Shoreham with the loss of all three aboard.[105] While several standard Battle sources give the credit, or most of it, to 145 Squadron,[106] the 257 Squadron Intelligence Patrol Report (IPR) suggests 145 Squadron's fire was out of range, and that theirs was on target![107]

The 257 Squadron report concluded with the observation that the enemy aircraft was still returning fire and making evasive turns when first attacked by the section leader, F/O Mitchell; in addition, the speed of the Dornier, the lack of observed damage or smoke from the engines before he attacked, and the fact that the enemy turned from a course parallel to and close to the coast to a southward course back over the Channel are mentioned specifically.[108] Together these observations make a reasonable case for the 257 Squadron trio having not only given the *coup de grace* but also having done it some serious damage before. This is not to argue that the 145 Squadron section led by S/L Peel who made the earlier attacks did not also hit the machine and damage it and/or likely wound some of the crew. The victory should in effect be shared between the two units in a fair appraisal.

Most interestingly, the 257 Squadron IPR also gives the different ammunition types carried by each fighter in the section, and the relevant number of rounds fired for each. F/O Mitchell used all his ammunition, totalling 2,650 rounds, like many other units more than the standard

2,400 rounds, or 300 per gun, carried.[109] Mitchell actually fired 1,680 rounds of ball ammunition, 660 armour piercing, 300 De Wilde rounds and ten tracer rounds; his two companions fired fewer rounds but the proportions of each type for each pilot were basically the same: ball = 63-65%, armour piercing = 22-25%, De Wilde = 11-13%, tracer = 0.4%.[110] Although the British had purchased the Belgian-designed De Wilde design in 1938, a tracer-incendiary round which ignited on firing, the bullet was not too stable and was hand-made; Major C. A. Dixon of the Royal Arsenal at Woolwich totally redesigned the projectile, which could be mass-produced, a true incendiary which had no tracer effect but upon hitting its target exploded, giving off a small flash as the incendiary filling ignited.[111] The Dixon projectile kept the De Wilde name for wartime security reasons and became available from the Dunkirk fighting onwards into the Battle of Britain, during which it was in relatively short supply.[112] The RAF loaded the different ammunition types in separate guns rather than mixing them in belts for individual Browning machine guns in the Hurricanes and Spitfires.[113] Applied to the F/O Mitchell figures quoted,[114] this would have meant five guns firing only ball ammunition, two guns only armour piercing rounds, and one gun a very few tracer rounds and all the 'De Wilde' projectiles. The success of this new 'De Wilde' ammunition, also called Type VI, made it very popular amongst Fighter Command pilots.

At *c.* 08h00 four Dorniers bombed the Rolls-Royce engine works in Glasgow at low level, having approached from the west, causing several casualties and quite heavy damage, and got away without any casualties.[115] The bombers may have been from *Küstenfliegergruppe 606*. The unit was based at Brest, Dornier-equipped and initially trained for attack on coastal targets.[116] *Luftflotte 5* based in Norway and Denmark is not known to have included any Do 17 bombers.

19 July 1940: first Me 110 raid on Dover; Defiant massacre

The next combat, involving the Defiants of 141 Squadron and some Hurricanes of 111 Squadron, in action with Me 109s of *III/JG 51*, should really not have happened at all; but in wartime, when realities intrude upon over-stretched people, mistakes are made and judgments can become flawed. There are a relatively large number of accounts of this action and what led to the fighter battle in the end. Shortly after noon on this day, the radar network gave warning of enemy aircraft building up over the Pas de Calais, but for some time thereafter there was no apparent movement of these machines.[117] This was almost standard daily fare across the Straits of Dover anyway. Then at about 12h10 the enemy advanced across the Channel and about five minutes later German dive bombers, mistakenly reported as Ju 87s, were attacking two destroyers in Dover harbour.[118] Only at *c.* 12h20 did the first RAF fighters scramble, followed by 111 Squadron Hurricanes, and 141 Squadron Defiants at about 12h30.[119] In fact, before 111 Squadron even took to the air, two sections of enemy machines had been sighted from the ground at Hawkinge.[120] The radar system and controllers had not seen the German advance across the Channel in time.

Due to this situation, there was no time to think about the wisdom of sending the Defiants of 141 Squadron into combat in such a dangerous area as the Straits of Dover; whatever was available close by, such as 111 and 141 Squadrons at the coastal airfield of Hawkinge, had to be scrambled in great haste. Ordered up at about 12h20, 111 Squadron was vectored north-east towards Deal at 10,000 ft, taking them initially away from the action.[121] The attack on Dover was actually carried out by the two Me 110-equipped and one Me 109-equipped *Staffeln* of *EGr 210*, escorted by *III/JG 51* under their *Kommandeur Hpt* Trautloft, who bombed the two destroyers HMS *Beagle* and HMS *Griffin* off Dover; both were lightly damaged by near misses, returning to duty after, respectively, six and two weeks.[122] *Beagle* was on patrol off Dover while *Griffin* was starting her passage to Devonport at Plymouth when they were attacked.[123] *EGr 210* typically made fast and low attacks on shipping, diving straight into the attack with minimal warning and would have made much faster passage across the Channel than either Stukas or bombers; this provides a plausible explanation why the radar and controllers didn't get their fighters airborne before the bombing was over and the assailants well on their way home. Having seen their charges safely back to the French coast, the escorting Me 109s of *III/JG 51* turned north again on a free chase over the Channel, where they ran into 141 Squadron's Defiants[124] and soon after a few of 111 Squadron's Hurricanes.

As 141 Squadron was scrambled from Hawkinge, two Defiants experienced spluttering engines and another refused to start, so only nine machines got off,[125] led by thirty-seven-year-old Squadron Leader William Richardson, whose gunner aged thirty-five[126] was also a rather grizzled old-timer for Second World War fighter combat. The shock of this, their first action, and the disastrous casualties suffered must have had a considerable impact on their commanding officer. However, he had done his best in tactical terms, as described below in an excerpt from the relevant Intelligence Patrol Report (IPR),[127] bearing in mind the limited abilities of the slow and clumsy Defiant, which the Me 109 could easily out-turn, something it could hardly ever do to a Hurricane or Spitfire.

At 1233 hours 9 a/c. left Hawkinge to patrol 20 miles south of Folkestone and were subsequently vectored to a point off Cap Gris Nez at 5,000 ft and were flying sections astern formation when F/Lt Louden gave warning of e/a. From 12 to 20 Me. 109's dived from 20,000 ft out of sun in line astern and the Defiants went into a steep left hand turn which was maintained during initial attack. Almost immediately two Defiants were seen to dive vertically into the sea. On the second attack the Me. 109's came up from below, attacked from dead astern and broke steeply away. Our A/g's could only bring guns to bear as Me. 109's passed on the beam but frequently enemy a/c. and our a/c. were on opposite turns and A/g's could not fire. The Defiants now went into steep left and right turns, turning each time into Me.109's which proved effective. P/O Halliwell (a/g. to S/Ldr) and Sgt Powell (A/g. to P/O Tamblyn) confirmed one Me. 109 caught in their cross fire and seen to dive in flames into the sea. P/O. Farnes (a/g. to F/Lt Louden) saw his tracers enter Me. 109 but he was unable to follow it down owing to other attacks. P/O. Tamblyn's a/c. was hit in petrol tank but was brought back safely. P/O. MacDougall was hit in engine and went into dive, the A/g. Sgt Wise, being told to bale out (now missing). P/O. MacDougall prepared to do so but engine restarted and a/c. was brought safely to base. F/O. Louden was hit in engine and A/g. [P/O Farnes] ordered to bale out. He was subsequently picked up from the sea uninjured. F/Lt Louden injured on landing. F/Lt Donald crashed on land near Dover and was killed. His A/g., P/O. Hamilton also killed. P/O. Gardner crashed in sea and was picked up injured. His A/g., Sgt Slater, Missing. 3 a/c. must have crashed into the sea during engagement and following are missing, believed killed:-

P/O. Kemp	A/g. Sgt Crosbie
P/O. Howley	A/g. Sgt Curley
P/O. Kidston	A/g. Sgt Atkins

P/O. Kemp was seen to dive vertically into the sea with hood closed. All crews remarked the immensely superior speed of the Me. 109's which passed Defiants on same course at over 100 m.p.h. 111 Sqdn. were engaged by about 50 Me. 109's at 15,000 ft. above 141 Sqdn. They report that about 20 Me. 109's dived to attack 141 and they saw 10 a/c. crash into the sea out of which they claim 3 Me. 109's. Three Defiants went down and it can, therefore, be presumed that a total of 4 Me. 109's were shot down. [A/g. or a/g. = air gunner; S/Ldr = Squadron Leader]

This combat took place at *c.* 12h45 and 141 Squadron claimed one confirmed Me 109 and one unconfirmed, and credited the missing Defiants with two probables; air gunners Halliwell and Powell each fired from a range of 200 yds, the first firing thirty rounds from each gun and the second, fifty rounds each from only two guns.[128] The damage to P/O Tamblyn's Defiant must have been minor as it is not listed as a casualty.[129] Four of the Defiants had been shot down into the sea (flown by Kemp, Howley, Kidston, Gardner), two had crashed on land in the Dover-Hawkinge area (flown by Louden and Donald) and one was damaged (flown by MacDougall), making total losses of six Defiants plus one damaged, from which four pilots and six gunners were lost, with two more pilots wounded. Truly a shattering baptism of fire for the Squadron, but it was no turkey shoot.

The aircrew of 141 Squadron were not surprised by the Me 109s, saw them coming and on S/L Richardson's orders formed essentially a defensive circle but lost two Defiants rapidly. They then seem to have broken up and were attacked a second time by the Messerschmitts from dead astern in a blind spot for the gun turrets.[130] Following this, Richardson ordered them to fly steep left and right turns, also turning into the German attacks, which worked well enough to enable three Defiants to make it back to Hawkinge, flown by Richardson, Tamblyn, McDougall, albeit one of them being badly damaged, while another two in dire distress made the coastline only to crash near Dover-Hawkinge, killing the one crew and wounding the pilot of the other machine.[131] And they shot back at the Germans as best they could. It being a clear day across the Channel, many people in the coastal area around Dover-Folkestone, including members of the press, were able to witness much of 141 Squadron's tragic battle, including seeing F/Lt Donald's flaming aircraft just make it across the coast before crashing to destruction, and observing F/Lt Louden's spluttering machine crash at Hawkinge.[132] P/O Gardner suffered quite an ordeal: shot down in the first German attack, he glided down and as he neared the sea, unwisely undid his straps and opened the hood and as he ditched hit his head hard and sank in the aircraft; he went quite deep before getting out of the aircraft, surfacing and being picked up by a coastguard launch.[133]

The twenty-odd Me 109s of *III/JG 51* that had turned back across the Channel after seeing their *EGr 210* charges safely back to the French coast ran straight into the nine hapless Defiants of 141 Squadron at 13h43 between Folkestone and Cap Gris Nez, just after the RAF machines were vectored to the south.[134] Their *Kommandeur*, *Hpt* Hannes Trautloft, recorded leading his *Stabschwarm* down into the first attack, with *Leutnants* Pichon-Kalau von Hofe and Wehnelt as well as *Oblt* Kath in tow, with two Defiants going down in this first attack, one exploding into a ball of flames and plunging seawards. But the Defiants were not asleep and met this first assault with a hail of machine gun fire, hitting and damaging Trautloft's and Kath's Messerschmitts.[135] Both were lucky to get back to the French coast, where Trautloft managed to force-land with his propeller feathered at St Inglevert forward base, and Kath bellied in a few miles away; both had been hit in their engine cooling systems and both were unhurt.[136] Another German eyewitness was *Oberfeldwebel* Artur Dau of *7/JG 51*, led by *Oblt* Oesau who were tasked as top cover, with *8/JG 51* watching the airspace below the Defiants, when Trautloft led his *Stabschwarm* down.[137] The *9/JG 51* was also present but due to wear and tear of continued operations during July 1940 thus far, the entire *Gruppe* was there in much reduced numbers, of about twenty.

Such an intense fighter versus fighter combat, involving about thirty aircraft, did not really lead to the inevitable over-claiming to be expected in such a situation. *III/JG 51* claimed a total of eleven victories, but only four of them were confirmed, the other seven being categorised by the *Luftwaffe* as probable victories.[138] This equates quite well with four Defiants which fell into the Channel, probably the four confirmed, and likely also involving four probable claims, which might have preceded the *coup de grace* delivered by the confirming pilots; the three other Defiants which made it back to the Hawkinge-Dover precincts only to have two crash and be written off and one land at Hawkinge badly damaged could equate to three more probable German claims. For 141 Squadron, their claims of one confirmed, one unconfirmed and two probable Me 109s do not appear that far-fetched either: *Fw* Heilmann of *9/JG 51* had his Me 109 badly damaged by Defiant gun fire, crashed back at base and died the next day, while, as already discussed, Trautloft and Kath from *Stab III/JG 51* both had their aircraft damaged from Defiant return fire and force-landed just behind Cap Gris Nez.[139] Damage in the end to the two *Stab III/JG 51* Messerschmitts must have been minor. Similarly, P/O Tamblyn's damaged Defiant was not recorded in RAF loss lists, most likely for the same reason, presumably minor damage repairable at squadron level.

The final act in the tragedy that befell 141 Squadron was the advent of 111 Squadron on the scene. Vectored to the Deal area earlier at 10,000 ft, as already described above, Green 2 P/O Copeman spotted a formation of Me 109s off the coast between Dover and Folkestone; having informed his section leader, F/Lt Connors of this, the latter was unable to raise the squadron leader and thus took only his section south-westwards where they observed the Messerschmitts already attacking the Defiants.[140] The three Hurricanes were not able to get down to help the Defiants directly, as they had to take on Me 109s between 10,000 and 15,000 ft flying the top cover in *III/JG 51*.[141] F/Lt Connors made an initial beam and then an astern attack on a Me 109 which burst into flames, and then took on another German fighter but was kept away from it by two more; P/O Copeman closed to 150 yards from a Messerschmitt and gave it 800 rounds before breaking away as they got near the French coast.[142] P/O Simpson, the third member of the section, was attacking a Me 110 from astern when forced to take on three Me 109s that were coming for him; he left the leader enveloped in smoke after expending all his ammunition, and Connors saw this machine fall into the sea.[143] The section claimed two confirmed Me 109s and one damaged;[144] however, none can be recognised in German loss returns.[145]

Analogously, from the German side, *Oblt* Oesau, the *Staffelkapitän* of *7/JG 51* and *Uffz* Mayerl of *8/JG 51* claimed, respectively, a Hurricane and a Spitfire, both confirmed by the German claims system,[146] while none were lost by the 111 Squadron section.[147] While quite a few sources credit the arrival of 111 Squadron as having saved the survivors of 141 Squadron from total annihilation,[148] it is clear from the relevant Intelligence Patrol Report that only a single section of the twelve Hurricanes was engaged, and that against the top cover of *III/JG 51*, where despite claims from both sides, no losses appear to have occurred. What was saved of 141 Squadron's nine Defiants was rather more due to their own efforts and also very likely the twenty-odd attacking Me 109s getting in each other's way.

19 July 1940: second Dover raid, *c.* 15h40-16h15

A second raid was mounted on shipping in Dover harbour. A large build-up was observed over Calais and 11 Group scrambled thirty-five fighters from 32, 64 and 74 Squadrons in response.[149] As with the earlier raid, it was mistakenly thought that Stukas were responsible but in fact the raid was once again made by *EGr 210*, and this time apparently by their *3 Staffel*, which operated Me 109s, and which lifted off from their forward base of St Omer at 15h07, whence they returned again by 16h02.[150] In the harbour, the Admiralty oiler *War Sepoy* was sunk by a direct bomb strike, and a drifter and a tug were damaged.[151] The distance flown by these bomb-carrying Me 109s was recorded as 86 km there and back,[152] and at a cruising speed of about 5 miles per minute they would have reached their target within about nine minutes. This would have given very little time for the controllers to react, as had been the case with the earlier *EGr 210* raid on Dover this day; however, this time they did an excellent job, getting three RAF fighter squadrons airborne in time for two to be able to observe the bombing and one of them to interfere with the Messerschmitts carrying it out. First off was 64 Squadron from Kenley at 15h30 whose nine Spitfires were led by F/Lts Hobson and Henstock on a vector towards Dover.[153] Having the greatest distance, 63 miles to go, they were most likely the last to arrive in the Dover area, preceded by 32 Squadron whose twelve Hurricanes scrambled from nearby Hawkinge at 15h33-15h38, and 74 Squadron whose twelve Spitfires took off from Manston at 15h46.[154]

Sent to patrol Dover at 9,000 ft, 32 Squadron were ordered to keep away from the harbour and town due to the intense anti-aircraft barrage, and as the flak bursts appeared in the sky they clearly saw several dive bombers going for the harbour; as the Hurricanes turned away from the barrage they were attacked by the Me 109 escort to the dive bombers.[155] F/Lt Brothers leading Blue Section saw twelve Messerschmitts diving on them from the starboard quarter and his three machines broke away from the squadron; F/Sgt Turner, flying in the Blue 3 position engaged one of the Me 109s, but another quickly got on his tail and Brothers saw Turner's engine belching smoke, and later observed him coming down by parachute.[156] Turner had indeed bailed out, badly burned, and came down near Dover where he was on the hospital danger list for some time; his Hurricane crashed at Hougham, between Folkestone and Dover.[157] F/Lt Brothers himself went after one of two Me 109s which passed to his left, hit it and as he tried to follow it down as it turned onto its back and dived, another Me 109 came in at him and he had to break away; his supposed victim was seen to hit the sea by one of his fellow pilots, and searchlight sites along the coast reported two enemy machines down in the drink as well.[158] No Messerschmitt was lost in the sea that afternoon.

The experiences of Yellow Section, flying rear-guard for the squadron, were recorded in the relevant combat reports of the three pilots. P/O Smythe, in the lead, while noting anti-aircraft bursts above the harbour, also noticed a section of Me 109s coming up over him to attack Red Section ahead, and pulled his Hurricane up vertically to fire a quick burst as they passed overhead; climbing up he opened fire on the leader of these Messerschmitts, hitting its wings as an engine cowling also became detached.[159] As these three Me 109s passed over Smythe and he attacked them, Yellow 2 P/O Gillman saw them pass into a dive down towards Red Section, and went for the number two enemy machine, observing a piece of this aircraft fall off as it dived seawards apparently out of control.[160] Sgt Henson, Yellow 3 followed P/O Smythe and seeing a Me 109 on his tail, gave it a quick burst at only 40 ft range and turning steeply, it dived away.[161] Henson then saw what he thought to be a Ju 87 diving for Dover harbour, and he followed, cannily waiting for the enemy machine to pull out of its dive and at this most vulnerable instant, opened up with a long burst from *c.* 300 yds, following which it dived steeply away to port with Henson turning inside him and following up with another long burst.[162] The enemy's engine gave off volumes of smoke and it began to glide for the French coast; as the Sergeant closed in to only 50 yds for the *coup de grace*, tracer from behind distracted his attention and seeing his pursuer immediately climbing away, he looked forwards once more, observing a large splash in the sea, which he presumed to be his dive-bomber.[163] He must have pursued and damaged one of *3/EGr 210*'s Me 109 dive-bombers; seeing as this unit did not submit any reports of damaged machines for this mission, it can be assumed that possible damage to any of its aircraft was light and repairable at unit level.

S/L Worrall, leading 32 Squadron as Green 1, also intercepted 'Ju 87s', in reality dive-bombing Me 109s from *3/EGr 210*. That this enemy contact was experienced by a number of the 32 Squadron pilots, but not by the next unit in action, 74 Squadron, who did however see bombing take place, supports the latter unit appearing over the Dover area slightly later than the 32 Squadron Hurricanes. 74 Squadron only had minor action with Me 109s, and appear to have been involved in a skirmish between S/L Worrall and some Me 109s, as is clear from excerpts from the two Intelligence Patrol Reports:[164]

S/Ldr Worrall was leading Green section and the squadron and intercepted 5 Ju. 87's and 12 Me. 109's near Dover. As they were about to attack the Ju's, they were themselves attacked by Me's. He saw 2 of these 2,000 feet above him. Climbing up he got on the tail of one and fired a short burst. One Me. broke away. He fired a second burst at the other and holed his port tank, streams of petrol pouring out and bits flew off the wing near the tank. He continued to close and was about to reopen fire when a Spitfire appeared between him and the Me. The Spitfire then followed the Me. down and S/Ldr Worrall was again engaged so was unable to watch the Me. down. [Excerpt IPR 32 Squadron]

Salvos of bombs were seen to be falling in Dover Harbour, and at the same time a message was received by R/T that the Raid had turned South. The Sqdn climbed in sections line astern towards several groups of fighters sighted above. Red Section broke off towards the left and on to a group of three a/c at 13,000 feet which were identified as 2 Me. 109 and 1 Hurricane in a tight circle. Red 1 attacked one E/A which was trying to turn on to the tail of the Hurricane, closing to 100 yards range, giving one 2 second burst. The Hurricane immediately broke off, and Red 1 applied full starboard bank and turned on to the tail of the E/A. Red 1 got in two more bursts of two seconds each at 75 yards range. E/A emitted black smoke from starboard side and straightened up into a staggering dive. Red 1 then climbed steeply to starboard as the other E/A was turning into his starboard quarter. During his climb Red 1 noticed that Red 3 was pursuing the second E/A at close range. Red 3 got in a deflection shot and E/A dived steeply to the West. Red 3 gave chase closing to 75 yards, giving four bursts of four seconds each. E/A was seen to be damaged, liquid pouring out of port radiator, the oil tank and starboard radiator were also seen to be hit. Red 3 having expended all his ammunition left E/A 15 miles out to sea from FOLKESTONE heading for CALAIS in a 40 degree dive at 4,000 feet, and returned to Base. The remainder of 74 Sqdn were not engaged and after identifying other fighters in the vicinity as friendly returned to Base. 74 Sqdn appeared to have arrived over DOVER as the enemy bombers and fighters were returning to the French coast. [Excerpt IPR 74 Squadron; R/T = radio telephone]

74 Squadron claimed two Me 109s probably destroyed, F/Lt Malan leading the Squadron as Red 1 firing 1,200 rounds and his wingman, Red 2 P/O Stevenson, expended all of his 2,720 rounds.[165] As so often with Fighter Command, 74 Squadron also carried more ammunition, 40 rounds more per gun, than the 'standard' of 300 rounds per gun, or 2,400 in total. Although not fully explicit from the 74 Squadron IPR, it would appear that both pilots in fact attacked the same Me 109; additionally, the damage S/L Worrall of 32 Squadron observed from his attack agrees well with damage seen by P/O Stevenson of 74 Squadron. All three pilots may thus have hit the same enemy machine! Once more, this is how unintended over-claiming occurs easily in the heat and speed of aerial combat. It should be noted that the Me 109s had a single L-shaped petrol tank beneath and behind the pilot's seat,[166] and what Worrall saw could more likely have been cooling fluid from the port radiator, situated beneath the wing. Malan's description of black smoke from the starboard side of the Me 109 he shot at would suggest he hit the oil tank. S/L Worrall's actions were certainly aggressive, taking on two Me 109s well above him, while 'Sailor' Malan's sudden turn away from the rest of his squadron was probably motivated by seeing a British fighter apparently in need. Also of note was Malan's very disciplined fire of short, two-second bursts only. He was well known as a superb shot.[167] 32 Squadron claimed two Me 109s confirmed, one 'Ju 87' unconfirmed, a probable and a damaged Me 109 in total.[168]

As 64 Squadron's reports make no mention of having seen bombing of Dover harbour or activation of its anti-aircraft barrage, nor of having spotted any German dive-bombers, it is reasonable to suggest they were the last of the three squadrons scrambled against the raid to reach the Dover area. As this unit came in towards Dover, Yellow Section at the back appears to have detached itself and climbed towards Hawkinge; it is not known if the balance of the squadron saw any action, but they recorded no claims or losses.[169] F/O Jeffrey, Yellow 1, flew off seemingly alone after two retreating Me 109s and then spotted two aircraft near France and dove after them, finding two He 115 mine-layer floatplanes from *3/Küstenfliegergruppe 906*, one at 200 ft and the other taxying on the water; he shot down the airborne one and fired on the taxying one before shore-based anti-aircraft fire drove him away.[170] The crew of the first He 115 apparently perished.[171] The other two members of Yellow Section, F/O Woodward number two and P/O O'Meara, three, climbed up after Me 109s spotted above them while their leader went across the Channel and when at 13,000 ft saw another small formation of Me 109s below them, three of which climbed up towards them.[172] Both pilots dived on these Messerschmitts, and in a violent melee O'Meara claimed one in flames but was hit himself on the armoured windscreen, which starred and was obscured, with another hit on an aileron; he got away at sea level and made it back to base.[173] Woodward dived on an Me 109, fired from too far away and was himself hit from behind, damaging the cockpit canopy. He then found himself flying head-on at another; opening fire from 500 down to only 50 yards, he saw its engine smoking and in trying to evade a collision at the last moment, struck it with his wingtip.[174] He landed at forward base Hawkinge, had his wing patched up and flew back to Kenley.[175] Each pilot claimed a Me 109 destroyed.[176]

With both 32 and 64 Squadrons claiming two Me 109s destroyed each, and two probables recorded by 74 Squadron, as described above, it becomes difficult to assign German casualties with any certainty. *9/ JG 51* had one Me 109 force-land in France, 60% damaged and thus a write-off with the pilot wounded; another regained its base 40% damaged.[177] While one standard Battle source ascribes the loss of F/Sgt Turner's 32 Squadron Hurricane as well as the two damaged Spitfires of 64 Squadron to *III/JG 51*, and also credits the two damaged Me 109s of this *Gruppe* to 64 Squadron's P/O O'Meara and F/O Woodward,[178] another interpretation may be pertinent. German claims preserved in records have one confirmed and one probable Spitfire over Folkestone by *9/JG 51*, and two more confirmed in the Dover area by *2/JG 51*.[179] The latter two are timed later than the first two claims in that list.

This suggests the possibility that *9/JG 51* were responsible for F/Sgt Turner being shot down thereby accounting for one confirmed claim; the probable claim was likely against another 32 Squadron machine not hit in any meaningful way. It also suggests that the two damaged machines of *9/JG 51* were inflicted by 32 and 74 Squadrons. As already discussed, it appears fairly likely that S/L Worrall, 32 Squadron, and F/Lt Malan and P/O Stevenson of 74 Squadron in fact all hit the same machine, presumably the one written off, and from their combat reporting very visible damage was suffered by at least one Messerschmitt. The less damaged Me 109 (40%) was probably hit by another/other pilots from 32 Squadron, possibly P/Os Smythe and Gillman, who both claimed to have hit a Me 109 which lost a piece of itself as a result.[180] If there is any veracity to this interpretation, then the somewhat later claims of *2/ JG 51* for two Spitfires confirmed over the Dover area would better fit the two damaged Spitfires from 64 Squadron, demonstrably the last to arrive in the combat zone. In that case the claims of 64 Squadron for two Me 109s shot down would fall away, possibly relating to minor damage inflicted which was repairable at base and thus not entered into German loss returns.

19 July 1940: a dogfight off Selsey Bill and Worthing; Heinkel hunt

Twelve Hurricanes of 43 Squadron were sent up from Tangmere at 16h54 to patrol over Selsey Bill, and A Flight led by F/Lt Simpson was detached by the controller to check on an aircraft plotted flying from east to west, in the opposite direction to the Squadron.[181] As A Flight, at 10,000 ft reached a cloud layer just above them, ten to fifteen Me 109s emerged from it with the enemy leaders flying in a vic and the balance in line astern behind them.[182] It looked like they had not spotted A Flight and they appeared to be getting set to bounce B Flight below, which had just been sent on a vector of 270° by the controller; B Flight saw nothing of the enemy or subsequent action, A Flight occupying all the 109s' attention.[183]

P/O Carey, leading Yellow Section, fastened onto the rearmost Messerschmitt, gave it a long 20° deflection burst from below on the port quarter, and saw it turn abruptly from a left-hand turn into a right-hand one as it rolled onto its back and dived vertically into the cloud layer, where Carey lost sight of it.[184] Yellow 1 followed through the cloud and observed a patch of foam and oil on the sea along with pieces of wreckage that appeared to be fabric or wood about 5 miles south of Bognor.[185] Carey climbed back up into the melee and shot several apparently ineffective bursts at enemy machines before seeing a lone Hurricane gliding gently down on its back and then a parachute descending, presumably the pilot.[186] Noticing a Me 109 nosing about the parachutist, Carey finished his ammunition chasing it out to sea from dead astern; flying back to the coast he saw two oil patches approximately half a mile apart and 2 miles offshore.[187]

All three pilots of Red Section became involved with the Me 109s. Red 2, P/O Cruttenden diving down onto one managed one quick burst before his excessive speed made him overshoot.[188] Flying in the number three position in the section, P/O Tony Woods Scawen's role is perhaps best summed up by a short excerpt from the 43 Squadron Intelligence Patrol Report:[189] 'Red 3, P/O. Woods Scawen got two separate bursts in a e/a, the first, a deflection shot, he fears may have missed, but the second from astern was more likely to have gone home but e/a disappeared under control.'

The wry tone adopted by F/O F. J. Cridlan, the Intelligence Officer of 43 Squadron who wrote the report in this short segment stands out against the dry and official style of the rest of a fairly long document. Tony Woods Scawen was one of the major characters on 43 Squadron, well known for his guts and sense of humour, but also for his poor eyesight: he went by the nickname of 'Wombat'.[190] It would appear that his character had an impact on the compiler of the report who let slip a short glimpse of the real human being within a typically staid RAF report. He exhibited courage of a high order, to keep fighting with such a handicap, and 'Wombat' did not survive the Battle.

The Red Section leader, F/Lt Simpson had led his men up into the sun when the Me 109s emerged from the clouds and then ordered his flight to break up, and turned for the enemy out of the sun; in the ensuing dogfight, Simpson got on the tail of a Me 109, damaged it and closed for a second burst, which left it diving out of control and he observed it plunge vertically into the sea.[191] But Simpson was then surprised by another Messerschmitt, hearing bullets hitting the armour behind his seat and damaging wings, glycol system and engine, and one projectile hit his left foot; he bailed out at about 10,000 ft some miles off the coast and was anxious when a Messerschmitt circled him but its pilot then opened a part of his cockpit cover and waved.[192] Fortunately his 'chute drifted over the coast at Worthing where he hit the roof of a house and then fell through a garden fence and into a cucumber frame, being badly bruised and breaking his collar bone.[193]

Ground observers along the coast had seen two parachutists coming down, the first one landing in the sea about a mile off Angmering, who was not found for some time, and the second was F/Lt Simpson.[194] Sgt Buck had bailed out of the empty and apparently undamaged Hurricane observed gliding upside down by P/O Carey, but had been badly wounded in the leg and drowned, his body later being recovered.[195] Carey was mildly critical of Sgt Buck's abandoning an apparently undamaged machine and pointed out that if he had stayed in the Hurricane a bit longer he would have got to land and may not have perished.[196] However, a man *in extremis* may do things that appear illogical to another not experiencing the trauma; Sgt Buck may have been in such pain he feared losing consciousness in the aircraft, or could have been losing too much blood thereby risking passing out or worse. He may have believed that by bailing out he could avoid such dangers and may have pinned his hopes on a quick rescue, close to the coast. Very few RAF fighter pilots of 1940 would easily have abandoned a functional aircraft without good reason. No criticism of Carey is implied here, but perhaps Sgt James Buck deserves a better epitaph than he has received so far.

43 Squadron's opponents in this fight were *III/JG 27*, flying out of Cherbourg West and apparently escorting Stukas, although no Stuka operation in this area is recorded.[197] Within sight of the Isle of Wight, the Me 109s spotted some Hurricanes and *Oblt* Adolph claimed one down in flames near the Isle; the Messerschmitts were then attacked by Hurricanes from behind but claimed four more shot down.[198] Apart from the two Hurricanes already recorded lost to 43 Squadron, flown by Sgt Buck and F/Lt Simpson, another was damaged in this combat, but Sgt Crisp managed to get it back to base.[199] The five victories claimed by *8/JG 27* were all confirmed in the German system, with *Oblt* Adolph, *Fw* Lehmann and *Fw* Blazytko being credited with the three casualties recorded by 43 Squadron, claimed at *c.* 17h25-30.[200] The remaining two confirmed claims were made by *Lt* Graf von Kageneck, who was wounded in the fight against 43 Squadron and his machine damaged, but who managed to get back to Cherbourg West.[201] He was probably hit by either Simpson or Carey.

At about 18h00-18h20 a lone Heinkel of *7/KG 55* fought against two interceptions, each of three Hurricanes, and although eventually succumbing itself, managed to shoot down one and damage another of its tormentors. The often tough encounters with single German bombers and reconnaissance machines during July must have given many an RAF pilot food for thought for what everybody knew was still to come: massed raids by tight German bomber formations on inland targets. This particular saga began when S/L Pemberton led Red 2, F/Lt Mathews and Red 3, P/O Browne of 1 Squadron up from Northolt at 17h30 to intercept the lone raider then flying more than 20 miles north of Brighton.[202] The section was vectored successfully on to the Heinkel but both Pemberton and Mathews lost it soon enough in the very cloudy conditions, while P/O Browne who had become separated from the other two managed to keep the enemy in sight; skilful evasive action within the clouds allowed the Heinkel to escape, smoking from one engine, but Browne's Hurricane had been hit in the glycol tank and smoking heavily, he force-landed it outside Brighton, unhurt and getting away from it as it burnt out.[203]

The German bomber had performed credibly, its evasive action proving effective, and interestingly including a turn and almost head-on dash past the pursuing Hurricane. However, this plucky crew were soon to meet their nemesis in a section of 145 Squadron Hurricanes. F/Lt Dutton, P/O Newling and F/O Ostowicz took off from Tangmere at 17h50 with orders to patrol Brighton at 10,000 ft; they were then vectored westwards at 2,000 ft and following that slightly south to the sea where they spotted the Heinkel flying south – south-east about 10,000 ft above them.[204] While Newling fell back, Dutton and Ostowicz attacked the bomber, firing from *c.* 300 yds and saw smoke issuing from the starboard engine.[205] Ostowicz attacked again and looked back to see Newling turning north and streaming black smoke, while the Heinkel dropped to the right, beginning a glide which ended in a successful ditching in the sea, the Polish pilot seeing four crew members in the water.[206] All five crew members from *7/KG 55* perished when it crashed into the drink some 5 miles off Shoreham, the victim of the combined efforts of the three 145 Squadron Hurricanes and that of Browne of 1 Squadron; P/O Newling of 145 Squadron force-landed wheels-up at Shoreham airfield, slightly wounded.[207]

Other, minor actions this day encompassed a section of 87 Squadron claiming damage to a Ju 88 south of Portland at about 19h00; a He 111 of *2/KG 26* damaged by anti-aircraft fire somewhere in the 13 Group area as well as a Spitifre of 603 Squadron damaged by return fire presumably from a lone bomber or reconnaissance machine; two Me 110s presumably from *EGr 210* strafed anti-submarine motor boats at about 09h50 (Dover harbour?); the loss of HMT *Crestflower* to the south of St Catherine's Point, Isle of Wight, where she suffered a direct hit from a Stuka while in the company of a second mine-sweeping trawler, slightly damaged as well – two *Crestflower* crewmen died.[208]

6

20–23 July 1940: Convoy Attacks in Western Channel and Dover Straits; the RAF Fighter Rear-guard Problem

20 July 1940: lone aircraft interceptions

A set of single aircraft interceptions marked the first half of the day. F/Lt Gracie led P/Os Sutton and Page of 56 Squadron up from North Weald at the ungodly hour of 05h19, detailed to patrol West Mersea; they were then vectored perfectly in cloudy weather onto a lone Ju 88 which came diving out of clouds at about 18,000 ft and which they attacked off Burnham at 05h45.[1] The enemy made only gentle turns left and right as it dived for cloud, probably relying on its speed; the three RAF pilots attacked from several hundred yards away, only one, P/O Sutton closing briefly to 50 yds and none used all their ammunition.[2] However, despite this, their accuracy must have been spot on as the Junkers force-landed, on fire, at St Osyth near Clacton (Illustration 40).[3] The four-man crew from 4(F)/122 was taken prisoner, but the mortally wounded rear-gunner perished.[4]

The full complement of 54 Squadron's twelve Spitfires under S/L Leathart was sent aloft from Manston just after 09h00 to intercept a raid of three aircraft at 8,000 ft; once airborne they were met with solid cloud from about 1,000 ft up to 7,000 ft, as well as rain, and the squadron's formation became split up.[5] Leathart's Blue Section emerged from the muck over the Dover area and turned east, heading approximately for Calais; at 09h08 they sighted an apparent Me 110 flying in the same direction on their port side.[6] Leathart was ahead of his two wingmen and as he manoeuvred to attack, the Me 110 turn towards him, but Leathart got in a beam attack, closing to 100 yds range and firing a short burst that appeared to hit the pilot's cabin; the Me 110 dived into the clouds and disappeared.[7] A Do 17 of III/KG 2 which force-landed at Zuyenkerke, Belgium, and was written off with one crewman killed, one wounded after being damaged in a fighter attack[8] may have been 54 Squadron's victim. Other possible claimants would have been 85 Squadron or 601 Squadron,[9] although the former unit made no official claim.

Two Hurricanes of 85 Squadron up from Martlesham patrolling off Dunwich after 07h00, were successfully vectored onto a lone Do 17 at about 10,000 ft and 15 miles off Lowestoft; S/L Townsend got in a short burst in a break in the clouds before the aircraft vanished again in the murk.[10] On a mission flown between 08h45 and 09h45, three Hurricanes of 601 Squadron intercepted a lone Do 17 about 6 miles south of Horsham and claimed it probably destroyed.[11] Horsham lies north of Worthing an area less often visited by *KG 2*'s Dorniers than East Kent where 54 Squadron had their action. Zuyenkerke lies close to the Belgian coast near Zeebrugge and is slightly north of due east from Dover where 54 Squadron was in action. *Stab/StG 2* lost a reconnaissance Do 17 to enemy action this day, which crashed near Theville in the Cherbourg area, killing one crew member and wounding two;[12] this would perhaps be a more logical victim for the 601 Squadron claim. No times are available for either *KG 2* or *StG 2* loss.

F/Lt Cunningham led F/O Waterston and P/O Stapleton of 603 Squadron who were ordered to orbit at 14,000 ft 30 miles east of Peterhead at about midday; they spotted a lone Do 17 some 6,000 ft below them and heading north, and dived to the attack.[13] The three pilots each made multiple astern and beam attacks on the hapless bomber, now heading east-south-east and watched as it plunged into the sea in flames about 30 miles east of Aberdeen, leaving two survivors struggling in the sea.[14] The 603 Squadron IPR describes the Spitfires' ammunition load as being 2,800 rounds per aircraft, 400 in excess of the 'standard'. The Dornier fits with with a reconnaissance aircraft of *1(F)/120* whose crew of three perished.[15]

A very strange encounter this day was an interception shortly before 13h00 by two members of Blue Section, 66 Squadron, about 20 miles east of Yarmouth, of an unmarked, dirty black short-nosed Blenheim, which was heading persistently to the east to get away from them; after some brief attacks from 200-300 yds range it got away in the clouds and no claim was made by the Squadron.[16]

20 July 1940: convoy attack south of Swanage; the problem of RAF weavers

Blue Section of 238 Squadron were the first unit to take off, led up from Middle Wallop at about noon by F/Lt Walsh and arrived over the convoy *c.* 15 miles south-east of Portland at 12h20.[17] The section later broke up,

Walsh himself investigated several friendly Hurricanes, and soon after *c.* 13h00 was on his way home nearing Swanage and had just switched to his reserve tank, when he saw a formation of fifteen machines flying north at about 12,000 ft, above him.[18] These were very likely the seventeen Me 109s of *I/JG 27* that took off from Plumetot, an airfield on the Normandy coast just north of Caen at 12h46, as cover to nine Ju 87s of *III/StG 2* that flew from Cherbourg-Theville.[19] The limited range of the Me 109 (see Map 2) and the distance from Plumetot to the Swanage area would have meant that *I/JG 27*'s Messerschmitts would have had enough fuel only to fly as far as the northern coast of the Isle of Wight or to approach the coast at Swanage, following which they would have had to turn around and head back to France having only limited time for combat along the way. *I/JG 27* thus planned a sweep ahead of the Stuka *Staffel*, clearing the airspace of British convoy patrols and any further scrambled fighters from Fighter Command between coast and convoy.

There was thus no direct escort of the Ju 87s who were to bomb as the Me 109s retreated homewards. This range factor and resultant limited combat time over Southern England in the Tangmere-Portland region was always a factor over the Western Channel, much broader than that in the Dover Straits. *Luftwaffe* tactics espoused and inspired by *Oberst* Theo Osterkamp over Dover were never going to be as effective in the Western Channel.

The RAF controllers would most likely have seen the two German formations approaching across the Channel, their speed of advance as deduced from radar signals allowing discrimination of bombers and fighter screen ahead. A further section, Red of 238 Squadron led by F/Lt Turner, was thus scrambled from Middle Wallop at 13h03[20] to reinforce F/Lt Walsh's Blue Section and was preceded by B Flight of 152 Squadron. The latter took off from Warmwell at 12h45, Blue Section leading, followed by Green, led by P/O Beaumont, with P/O Williams as his number two, and flying as the lone 'weaver' some 200-300 yards behind and a little above the rest of the section was Green 3, P/O Posener.[21]

Early in the Battle it was fairly common practice for Fighter Command squadrons to have a rear-guard element, comprising either a single machine, as here for 152 Squadron, or a pair flying above and behind the squadron on either flank, or even an entire section of three fighters, above and behind. They were not very effective, as despite providing an element of protection for the rest of the squadron and sometimes a hurried warning call, they were often effectively sacrificial lambs. Some units rather ruthlessly put their less experienced pilots in these positions, but P/O Posener was in fact the first of the three pilots of Green Section, 152 Squadron, to join that unit, some two and a half months before Beaumont and seven and a half months prior to

Williams.[22] This practice was dangerous for the hapless weavers, in an environment already dangerous enough and they were almost always first in line for the favoured *Luftwaffe* bounce tactic and often paid the price for their bravery. While the vic formations favoured earlier in the Battle and for some units, later, exacerbated the vulnerability of RAF Fighter Command's fighters to surprise attack from above and behind, the problem remained for any formation used. (See 17 July 1940.)

Applying standard cruising speeds of Spitfires and Hurricanes and relevant distances from their bases to the convoy, the 152 Squadron formation would have been over the ships several minutes before 13h00 while F/Lt Turner's 238 Squadron section would only have got there some twenty minutes later. The 152 Squadron flight appear to have patrolled the ships at about 10,000 ft for some fifteen to twenty minutes[23] before all hell broke loose above the convoy for both 152 and 238 Squadron detachments. Having lifted off from Plumetot at 12h46 and applying cruise speed for Me 109s, *I/JG 27* would have been nearing the coast at *c.* 13h10, probably on a north-westerly course direct from Plumetot towards Swanage, in view of fuel limits, and probably then turned south off Swanage for the convoy, some 15 miles offshore, arriving there by about 13h15. They would no doubt have seen the flight from 152 Squadron orbiting the convoy and about a few minutes later would have seen F/Lt Turner's Red Section, 238 Squadron, arriving from the north, providing them with two opportunities for surprise attacks from several thousand feet higher than the RAF fighters.

Soon after arriving over the convoy F/Lt Turner saw a Hurricane descending in flames and the pilot bailing out and landing in the sea well ahead of the convoy, which was sailing eastwards; soon after he observed another fighter descending but not on fire, the pilot again bailing out into the sea, quite near the convoy but close astern and to starboard.[24] At that moment Turner saw a Me 109 some 2,000 ft below him, heading back to France, and applying maximum engine boost caught him up, gave a very short burst at 100 yards range and the enemy dived vertically, giving off smoke.[25] However, the Me 109 then flattened out and again made for home, so Turner gave another short burst and it went straight into the sea, giving him an unconfirmed claim, i.e. no witness. Turner's aim was spot on as after landing his armourers found he had only fired thirty-six rounds per gun.[26]

Red 2, P/O Davis, attacked another Me 109 which he believed had accounted for Red 3, Sgt Parkinson, who bailed out and was rescued but died of his wounds the next day.[27] Davis had seen Parkinson's Hurricane catch fire and the pilot exit very fast, but he may have hit the tail of his aircraft; P/O Davis gave the Me 109 he attacked several long bursts and exhausted his ammunition, seeing his victim burning and giving off lots of black smoke, but due to the attentions of two more Messerschmitts did not see it crash, claiming it as a probable.[28] F/Lt Walsh of 238 Squadron's Blue Section, despite by then flying on his reserve tank, had turned back south for the convoy after spotting the formation of aircraft flying north, and 5 miles from the ships observed bombs exploding all round an escorting destroyer.[29] Then, sighting a wide vic of three Me 109s haring south-eastwards back for France about 1,000 ft below him, he dived down and latched onto the left-hand machine, firing from 200 down to 50 yards and seeing black smoke billowing out from under the engine; just like P/O Davis with whom he shared the victory, he was distracted by the attentions of the other two Me 109s from seeing his target actually hit the sea following a vertical dive.[30]

Just as F/Lt Turner did not see his number 3, Sgt Parkinson being shot down, neither did the other two members of Green Section of 152 Squadron, P/Os Beaumont and Williams, notice P/O Posener being shot down; both pilots had last seen Posener before they reached the convoy, when he was doing fairly wide sweeps to either side in his role as weaver.[31] Posener simply disappeared and one word, 'tail' at the end of a garbled radio message from him was heard by P/O Beaumont; P/O Williams was witness to two machines shooting down a third into the sea far away to the south, presumably the two 238 Squadron pilots sharing the Me 109 of I/JG 27 discussed above.[32] Only F/Lt Turner of 238 Squadron had seen P/O Posener bail out and land quite near but astern of the convoy, and he later saw that the other downed pilot, his number 3, Parkinson, had been rescued by a destroyer, while there was no sign of the pilot who landed astern of the convoy.[33] HMS *Acheron* was the destroyer F/Lt Walsh had seen being bombed and which P/O Beaumont of 152 Squadron and F/Lt Turner of 238 Squadron had seen pick up the gravely wounded Sgt Parkinson; she had been bombed about 10 miles south of St Catherine's Point, Isle of Wight, and near-missed by nine bombs. She later put in to Portsmouth for fairly extensive repairs.[34] No doubt this likely played a role in P/O Posener not being rescued.

It is noticeable that in this convoy attack and that off Dover, German bombing concentrated on naval escorts, specifically destroyers. This was common throughout July 1940 and reflects German intentions to invade, where Royal Navy destroyers would represent a major threat to any landings and their associated vessels. In the month there were also several deliberate attacks on smaller naval vessels, particularly trawlers equipped for mine-sweeping and anti-submarine work.

Both RAF fighters lost, the Hurricane of Sgt Parkinson, 238 Squadron, and the Spitfire of P/O Posener, 152 Squadron can be linked to *Oblt* Homuth, *Staffelkapitän 3/JG 27*, who claimed two Spitfires west of Swanage at 13h25 and 13h28.[35] This *Staffel* lost two Me 109s, both pilots

Ofw Beushausen and *Lt* Scherer losing their lives.[36] The latter was seen
to ditch but was listed as missing and is ascribed to F/Lt Turner, while
Beushausen was killed and is credited to P/O David and F/Lt Walsh.[37] For
a Me 109 *Staffel* to lose two of their own men and machines in return for
two confirmed victory claims much better fitted the aims of the battle of
attrition being waged by Park and Dowding, than the five-to-one victory
margin recommended by Channel fighter leader Theo Osterkamp. For a
Hurricane squadron to destroy two Me 109s for the loss of one of their
own reflects well on 238 Squadron, but one should also perhaps bear in
mind the fuel shortage of retreating German fighters over the Western
Channel enhancing their vulnerability.

.Homuth used typical *Luftwaffe* fighter arm bounce tactics, clinically
shooting down the tail-end Charlie of each formation attacked; the
German formation leader had his successes and there was no general
attack by the whole *Staffel*. P/O Williams of 152 Squadron also
remarked that with clear skies and bright sunlight, upward visibility was
very poor;[38] an almost endemic problem to all fighter pilots for much
of the Battle. Height was safety, survival and often the key to success,
as all pilots on both sides learned very soon. However, when defending
convoys, RAF fighters had perforce to be kept at altitudes allowing good
visibility of the ships and close access to Ju 87 dive-bombers, which
tended to bomb below 10,000 ft.

20 July 1940: Me 110s make small raid on Dover

These two raids at opposite ends of the Channel appear to have been
timed to coincide, reflecting a growing overall tactical doctrine for the
Luftwaffe along the Channel. Dover harbour was raided by a small Me
110 force at about 13h30, which was intercepted by three Hurricanes
of the nine which 32 Squadron had sent up from Hawkinge just after
13h00.[39] The Me 109 escort remained at 10,000-15,000 ft[40] but
apparently did not intercede. F/Lt Crossley leading Red Section and P/O
Proctor, his number two, saw three Me 110 Jaguars or fighter-bomber
versions, at about 3,000 ft about to dive-bomb Dover harbour; Crossley
in hot pursuit of one watched it drop a bomb at about 2,000 ft and
then dive to sea level as it turned south for France.[41] He and Proctor
followed, flying at full boost, but not yet having the Rotol propellers
installed on their Hurricanes they could only make just over 300 mph.
After flying about 12 miles out to sea they caught up to a couple of the
Me 110s, both firing at one machine and observing it suddenly pull up to
starboard, upon which both RAF pilots turned port to place themselves
for a follow-up beam attack and also avoid a second Jaguar coming in

from behind.[42] The latter was tackled by P/O Proctor who opened up on it before it could hit Crossley's machine, the latter having seen the first Me 110 go into the sea and the second heading back for France; as Proctor pulled up only 15 ft above the sea he observed Crossley making for home in one direction and the second Me 110 doing likewise in the opposite direction.[43] Crossley and Proctor claimed one Me 110 confirmed destroyed.[44]

Looking at this action from the other side, there is some confusion. No Me 110 losses or damaged machines are reported for 20 July in standard sources.[45] However, there is an account of a Me 110 from *2/EGr 210* flown by *Oblt* Habisch and his gunner *Uffz* Elfner whose machine was 45% damaged on this day, its starboard undercarriage collapsing upon landing and the aircraft having seventy-eight bullet holes.[46] The German account of this action given by the crew closely matches the 32 Squadron IPR; the second Me 110 which fired at Crossley was flown by the commander of *EGr 210*, *Hpt* Rübensdorffer, who put a bullet through a tyre that just missed Crossley's ankle.[47] While the latter source[48] equates this account with a later raid where 32 Squadron was also involved with fighting Me 110s on 20 July, examination of the two Intelligence Patrol Reports for 32 Squadron on the day make it clear that Crossley and Proctor were in this action against the two Me 110s on the earlier raid, *c.* 13h30 against Dover harbour, as described above. The confusion increases when one looks at the *EGr 210* history, which places the entire action on 21 July 1940.[49] The same history, however, does have the Me 109-equipped *Staffel*, *3/EGr 210* of this fighter-bomber unit making two attacks on shipping on 20 July.[50]

Respected aviation author Brian Cull places this action between Red Section of 32 Squadron and two Me 110s of *EGr 210* on 20 July 1940 rather than the next day,[51] in line with the relevant German Quartermaster General Loss Returns; however, a handwritten correction to '13/7' has been added to five losses typed under 20 July 1940 in these 'Returns' including the damaged Me 110 of *EGr 210*.[52] The quoted date of 21 July 1940 in the *EGr 210* history, for this Me 110 being damaged, as given by one of its crew members, must presumably be out by one day. Such challenges in documentary historical research illustrate how difficult it is ever to come up with a definitive number for Battle of Britain losses, for either side. While surviving records and published sources thus leave some uncertainty, there is a case to be made for 32 Squadron having damaged one of the Messerschmitt 110s involved in this action, at about 13h30 on 20 July 1940. The machine was 45% damaged and the crew unhurt. The large number of bullet holes in this Me 110 reflects well on F/Lt Crossley's and P/O Proctor's marksmanship and less so on the effectiveness of the .303 calibre ammunition.

20 July 1940: Stuka raid on Convoy CW 7

Erprobungsgruppe 210 appears to have taken part in the main raid of the day also, an attack by *II/StG 1* on convoy CW 7 off Dover at about 18h00.[53] *II/StG 1* bombed at *c.* 18h07, converging with the *EGr 210* Me 110s on the destroyer HMS *Brazen* and breaking her back with a bomb which exploded beneath her, the vessel finally sinking at *c.* 20h00. A small steamer, *Pulborough* of 860 tons, was also sunk by the Stukas.[54] The convoy was well escorted by four destroyers and a trawler.[55] S/L Worrall flying fortuitously out of the evening sun led nine 32 Squadron Hurricanes from 10,000 ft straight through some lower escorting Me 109s into the Ju 87s which were just starting to dive, and who they proceeded to chase all over the sky while being pursued equally enthusiastically by the escorting Me 109s, from *I and II/JG 51*.[56] There was seldom time for tactical finesse in the July Stuka raids, formation leaders having little choice but to bore in at them as fast as possible. The whirling aerial combat in all its fleeting confusion is well illustrated by a short excerpt from the 32 Squadron Intelligence Patrol Report, uncorrected:

> S/Ldr Worrall was leading green sec. off Dover at 1740 he was later joined by Blue and Red Sections, at 1745 Sappa told him that e/a were approaching the convoy at 10,000′ and 20,000′ from the S.E. At 1755 he spotted the e/a and ordered green sec. line astern and to attack a Ju. 87 as he was starting his dive, although he had throttled back he overtook him after a 2 sec burst, he turned and attacked another but had to break off as he was attacked by a 110. Losing the 110 he saw Ju 87's making off after bombing a destroyer, he attacked the nearest who started to smoke, being attacked by a 109 he had to break off, but then attacked another Ju. 87 he also started to smoke but S/Ldr Worrall was again attacked by a 109 and had to break away, the 109 disappeared so he again attacked a Ju. 87 this also started to smoke, he was just about to finish it off when he saw tracer passing his wings, he broke away and felt bullets hitting the rear armour plating also 2 cannon shells hit his engine and the gravity tank. He turned for home and his engine petered out just too far for him to reach the aerodrome at Hawkinge, he made a crash landing in a field near the aerodrome, almost at once the a/c went up in a slow fire, S/Ldr Worrall had ½ a min. to get out, he was slightly injured in the crash. [Sappa = controller]

Despite all these chaotic experiences, a Fighter Command squadron leader like John Worrall was expected to take care of the running and administration of his unit and to lead it into action again on the next sortie. Leadership of a squadron in 11 Group was no sinecure.

While Green led by S/L Worrall and Red Section of F/Lt Crossley went for the Ju 87s, Blue Section under F/Lt Brothers climbed up and tackled thirty-odd Me 109s of the upper escort. Sub Lt Bulmer, Blue 2, only twenty years old, was lost, last seen descending near North Foreland on his parachute.[57] The Me 110s also attacked 32 Squadron's machines in their dogfight with the Ju 87s.[58] 32 Squadron's losses encompassed Sub Lt Bulmer missing, Green 3 Sgt Higgins' Hurricane damaged and he slightly wounded in the face by splinters from bullets hitting his cockpit hood, and S/L Worrall's machine, he bashed his head against the gunsight when it crash-landed, after which his favourite Hurricane was consumed by flames.[59] 32 Squadron claimed one Ju 87 confirmed, three damaged by S/L Worrall, two Me 109s and three Me 110s all unconfirmed (no witnesses) and a Me 109 damaged.[60]

F/Lt Ellis led nine Spitfires of 610 Squadron up from Hawkinge at 17h45, when 32 Squadron's Hurricanes were already almost over the convoy.[61] 610 Squadron were in time to witness the bombing of the convoy off Folkestone and had several actions with various small groups of Me 109s, making only one claim for a possibly damaged Messerschmitt. F/O Lamb led Red Section inland first, to get altitude, before turning back and attacking three Me 109s near the ships.[62] P/O Keighley of 610 Squadron was hit by a Me 109 which disabled his controls and wounded him with a bullet in the leg and shrapnel in his shoulder, forcing him to bail out, landing without further injury a few miles inland of Dover.[63]

65 Squadron was scrambled from Manston between 18h13 and 18h20 and vectored towards enemy aircraft attacking the convoy at 10,000 ft, but only saw a few Me 109s 15,000 ft above them.[64] Yellow Section on its way to Dover witnessed a Hurricane, presumably Sub Lt Bulmer of 32 Squadron, being shot down from above and behind by a Me 109, losing part of its tail, and the pilot bailing out at 9,000 ft to land in the sea 5 miles north-east of Dover.[65] Yellow 1, F/Lt Olive, chased the Messerschmitt back across the Channel, finally catching it near the French coast where he gave it all his ammunition in a single long burst from about 150 yds range, and saw it crash in the sea in flames about 2 miles west of Cap Gris Nez; claimed as a confirmed Me 109, witnessed by a member of his section.[66] Over the convoy, Red Section was attacked by a single Me 109, which fired ineffectively at one Spitfire and carried on diving across the Channel.[67]

The *Luftwaffe* credited four confirmed victories in the Dover-Folkestone area between 18h15 and 18h20: Hurricanes by *Hpt* Tietzen *5/JG 51*, *Oblt* Priller *6/JG 51*, *Ofw* Illner *4/JG 51* and a Spitfire by *Lt* Sonner *3/JG 51*.[68] These claims equate well with the two Hurricanes of 32 Squadron lost and another damaged, plus the 610 Squadron Spitfire shot down. German casualties encompassed four damaged Stukas of *II/ StG 1*, three 30% and one 60% damaged, and all thus sent away for repair, normally to Germany; these in turn can be equated with the 32 Squadron claims for one shot down and three damaged.[69] However, HMS *Brazen* claimed three of her tormentors shot down before sinking[70] and may have inflicted some of the damage on these four Ju 87s. *1/ JG 51* lost *Ofw* Sicking who bailed out over the French coast but was killed, his machine crashing to destruction at Audinghem; *II/JG 51* also had a Messerschmitt abandoned off Cap Gris Nez, but its pilot was rescued.[71] While the second loss can easily be ascribed to F/Lt Olive of 65 Squadron,[72] the first, *Ofw* Sicking, was almost certainly a victim of 32 Squadron, where F/Lt's Crossley and Brothers each claimed a Me 109 unconfirmed and Sgt Pearce another damaged.[73]

20 July 1940: losses from rescue missions around Western Channel convoy

A number of rescue missions were mounted from the German side to try and locate their lost airmen from the earlier convoy raid south of Swanage; these steadily moved eastwards to positions south of the Isle of Wight and Selsey Bill as the ships steamed on eastwards.[74] The first such mission involved a lone He 59 air-sea rescue floatplane encountered by Green Section, 238 Squadron, some 7 miles south of the convoy, now lying due south of the Needles, Isle of Wight.[75] Pursuing his quarry to within a few miles of the French coast, section leader P/O Urwin-Mann stopped its starboard engine, claiming a damaged enemy.[76] In fact, *Seenotflugkommando 4* lost a He 59 and its crew off Cherbourg about 15h15.[77]

Led by their *Gruppenkommandeur, Major* Riegel, *I/JG 27* launched a number of Me 109s to search for their missing comrades, and some of these met up with elements of a dozen Hurricanes of 501 Squadron which took off from Warmwell just before 16h00 with orders to patrol the convoy 20 miles south of Swanage.[78] The squadron was directed to a new position about 20 miles south of Warmwell, where a destroyer was under bombing attack.[79] Flying at 8,000 ft, S/L Hogan noted seven Messerschmitts heading for France, as well as two Do 17s and a Ju 88 heading in a similar direction at sea level.[80] Three attacks were made on retreating Me 109s about 3,000 ft lower, with claims for one destroyed unconfirmed by S/L Hogan, and two confirmed by F/Lt Cox and Sgt Lacey.[81] Only one Me 109 was lost with *Major* Riegel missing in the waters of the Channel some 30 miles north of the island of Sark, Channel Islands at *c.* 16h15.[82] In return, *Lt* Zirkenbach, *1/JG 27* claimed a confirmed Spitfire north of Cherbourg about five minutes later.[83] The two wingmen in the rearmost, Green Section of 501 Squadron, flying behind as protective weavers, were inadvertently left behind when the rest of the squadron including P/O Sylvester (Green 1, missing) dived down to attack, not having seen their section leader dive until it was too late to follow.[84]

A section of 43 Squadron Hurricanes sent from Tangmere to investigate a He 115 floatplane reported south of the Needles lost F/O Haworth, missing, last seen bailing out at *c.* 18h00 after probably being hit by what was actually a He 59 floatplane.[85] Some Me 109s were also met, one being claimed damaged by Sg. Mills;[86] no applicable Me 109 appears in German records. A few minutes after this action, six Hurricanes of 601 Squadron left Tangmere to patrol the convoy where they found a He 59 air-sea rescue floatplane from *Seenotflugkommando 1* at very low level, flying away to the south; Green Section led by F/O Hubbard shot it down about 25 miles south of Selsey at *c.* 19h20, after they failed to encourage it to fly back to southern England.[87] The crew of four bailed out too low and perished in the attempt.

21 July 1940: convoy attack off Isle of Wight

A Do 17 of *1/Küstenfliegergruppe 606* was shot down by anti-aircraft fire, falling in the sea off the Scottish coast with the loss of its crew.[88] In a rather unusual set of encounters, a Me 110 reconnaissance aircraft of *4(F)/14* penetrated inland some 12 miles north of Southampton where it shot down a Battle trainer, the instructor being injured in the crash-landing and the pupil unhurt. Flying then to the west, over Old Sarum it shot down a Hart trainer, killing the pilot.[89] Retribution was enacted when Red Section of 238 Squadron, F/Lt Turner, P/Os Davis and Wigglesworth, were vectored onto the Me 110 south-west of Middle Wallop and in a running fight in and out of cloud towards the south-east, and with the Me 110 performing prodigies of evasive action, they shot it down, the machine force-landing near Chichester at *c.* 10h25 and the crew made prisoner.[90] Despite using 5,760 rounds, only eight or nine bullets hit the Me 110, one fortuitously disabling an engine; 238 Squadron at this stage of the Battle were using standard ammunition loads of 2,400 rounds per Hurricane.[91]

In a couple of confusing cases for this day, Sgt Bann, 238 Squadron, is reported shot down by Dorniers over a convoy on this date, and 615 Squadron is credited with two victories, two probables and three damaged machines, Me 109s and one Ju 87, off Cap Gris Nez in the early evening.[92] However, other volumes based directly on records from both units do not corroborate these reports.[93]

Convoy CW7 had left Southend at the northern side of the mouth of the Thames Estuary on 20 July (when it was attacked off Dover in the evening, as recorded above), and was intended to reach Falmouth at the western end of the Channel on the 22nd.[94] The westward-sailing Channel convoy was made up of twenty-nine merchant vessels with three escorts.[95] By mid-afternoon on 21 July, the convoy was sailing about 10 miles south of the Needles, Isle of Wight; S/L 'Tubby' Badger was leading six Hurricanes of 43 Squadron on convoy patrol at about 15h30 leading his own Green Section, followed by Blue Section led by F/Lt Tom Dalton-Morgan.[96] Dalton-Morgan gave the Tally-Ho (enemy sighted); Badger sighted them almost simultaneously, about eighty enemy aircraft in all, made up of Dornier 17 bombers, Me 110s and Me 109s coming up on the convoy from behind.[97] The Dorniers were flying in stepped-up waves of eight aircraft, en echelon, with an upper escort of the Me 109s. Ordering Dalton-Morgan to tackle the Me 109s, Badger closed his section up into line astern and made for the Dorniers.[98] An excerpt from Badger's combat report describes the action:

I was leading B Flight on convoy patrol as Green 1, Blue section was behind and above. The convoy was steaming W and we were flying south across its bows when I heard Blue one give Tally Ho. Simultaneously I saw the hostile formations. I closed my section up in line astern. The enemy were in echelon and stepped up so I decided to attack from the inside of the circle of bombers as they swept round to attack. I attacked one Do. 17 and got in a short burst using full deflection. I had to pull away immediately because I was in close line abreast with the succeeding Do. 17. I returned to attack another Do. 17 and had just opened fire when tracer started whipping past me. I took immediate avoiding action but my starboard aileron was badly hit and partially jammed and the A/C was difficult to control. I then returned slowly to base and pancaked. It was impossible to see the results of my fire because of the great number of E/A diving on convoy. [W = West; pancaked = landed]

Dalton-Morgan meanwhile had found himself at 13,000 ft, above and behind the Dorniers, and led his three lonely fighters against the Me 109 escort; he attacked two of the Messerschmitts, claiming one down in the sea and the other damaged, himself suffering one hit in the port wing headlight.[99] Freeing himself from the attentions of the Me 109s, F/Lt Dalton-Morgan dived for a Dornier trying to join a circle of about ten others, and as he came in his windscreen suddenly became covered with oil and he had to break away and head home, his aircraft slightly damaged.[100] In the wild dogfight with the Me 109s, which were from *III/*

JG 27, P/O de Mancha of 43 Squadron collided with *Lt* Kroker of 7/JG 27, both pilots being lost.[101] *Oblt* Gerlitz, 7/JG 27, claimed a Hurricane[102] and may have been the one who damaged Badger's machine. The majority of the dive bombers appear to have been successful in launching their missiles; there is only so much that a mere three Hurricanes can do, and three ships were in fact hit.[103] The SS *Terlings* of 2,318 grt was sunk on the first attack, 10 miles south-west of St Catherine's Point, losing ten crew members; the eighteen survivors reported that they had been attacked by thirty-six escorted Do 17s and with Me 110s also attacking the ship.[104]

Three Hurricanes of Blue Section, 238 Squadron, had taken off at 15h15 and were initially vectored towards Portland but then diverted to the convoy being attacked off the Needles by fifteen Me 110s coming in from the northern side, flying in an echelon right formation, also described as wide line astern.[105] F/Lt Walch leading the section ordered his small force into line astern and to make independent attacks; Walch himself dived from 12,000 ft to 8,000 ft to attack Me 110s flying line astern and which were pulling out of a dive after bombing the ships and heading south-east to France.[106] The Messerschmitts didn't see him until he was within 500 yds and then rapidly turned right, still flying line astern; Walch opened fire at 250 yds, closing to five yards and saw the Me 110 he attacked steepen its turn and dive seawards giving out black and white smoke.[107] Soon after, Walch observed a Me 110 which flew straight at sea level for about a mile and then dived into the sea, but was unsure whether this was his or P/O Considine's victim; his number two had attacked an Me 110 behind Walch with a three-second full deflection burst as the Me 110s went into a right turn and saw his starboard engine on fire.[108] Blue 3 was attacked by the leading Me 110s from his starboard side and then skirmished with several Me 110s and a Me 109.[109] Walch also saw some Me 109s approaching but they left him alone.[110]

It would appear likely that the Dorniers described by 43 Squadron were in fact Me 110s armed with bombs, of about *Gruppe* strength. *Luftflotte 3* had only one unit which operated Do 17s, namely *Küstenfliegergruppe 606*, based at Brest, but this flew sorties mainly over the northern parts of the British Isles rather than over the Channel.[111] The tactics applied by the Dorniers, coming in with a circular approach and then diving in turn from the half circle onto the ships, as described by 43 Squadron above, would far better fit Me 110 tactics; in addition, Dorniers were not stressed for dive bombing and had no dive brakes either. Survivors from the SS *Terlings* recalled being attacked by a *Gruppe* of Do 17s and also by Me 110s, and 238 Squadron's section saw only Me 110s bombing the convoy. It would by no means be the first time that Dornier 17s and Me 110s has been confused in the heat of combat by British interceptors, and this error was a frequent occurrence throughout the Battle. This raises the question of who then did carry out the attack on convoy CW7? The escorting Me 109s were certainly from *JG 27*, with *III Gruppe* being identified in losses and claims.[112]

V/LG 1 was also on this mission, and several sources name them as being the Me 110 dive-bombers witnessed from the air and the ships of the convoy.[113] However, the unit history states clearly that this *Gruppe* escorted Stukas, a generic German term for dive-bombers, whether Ju 87s, Ju 88s or Me 110s, but also applied often and specifically to the Ju 87, attacking the convoy.[114] There is an account of a circle to the south of the convoy made up of escort Me 110s;[115] this would logically have been from *V/LG 1*. *15/LG 1* returning to Cherbourg catching up with a lone straggler from *14 Staffel*, whose crew reported over the radio having been in action and having suffered fairly significant damage; this Me 110 unwisely attempted a wheels-down landing at Theville at *c*. 15h50 despite suspected undercarriage damage, flipped over onto its back and was written off, and the machine crushed its crew before they could be saved.[116]

15 Staffel could also equate well with the fifteen Me 110s reported attacking the convoy at the end of the action by 238 Squadron, and presumably *14 Staffel* were in action earlier on, probably against 43 Squadron where S/L Badger claimed a damaged Do 17;[117] however, both *Staffeln* may have been in action against both British squadrons and the *14 Staffel* machine may equally have been the victim of 238 Squadron, who claimed one Me 110 confirmed by F/Lt Walch and a probable by P/O Considine.[118] With no reports of bombing from the *V/LG 1* unit history and a description of their escorting 'Stukas' to attack a convoy off the Isle of Wight at *c*. 15h50,[119] it can be speculated that other Me 110s from *Luftflotte 3* made up the dive-bombing force reported as 'Dorniers'; a Me 110 *Gruppe* from either *ZG 2* or *II* and *III/ZG 76* can be suggested in this regard. *Erprobungsgruppe 210* was part of *Luftflotte 2* and based in the Pas de Calais, and its unit history reports no such convoy bombing on 21 July 1940 but does detail operations over the Straits of Dover.[120]

F/L Walch leading the 238 Squadron section described diving from 12,000 ft to 8,000 ft to attack the Me 110s as they pulled out of a dive over the convoy.[121] *EGr 210*, the experts and standard setters of Me 110 fighter-bombers, started their dives typically at 13,000 ft, levelling off only at 1,500 ft and applying a 45° dive angle.[122] This suggests that the dive-bombing described by 238 Squadron's pilots, possibly carried out by *15 Staffel*, *V/LG 1*, was either just a gesture or that this unit, with no experience of such bombing rather botched their attack method. In addition to the SS *Terlings* sunk from this convoy, the German raid also hit a large Norwegian tanker, *Kollskegg* of 9,858 tons, with the crew reporting several attacks with twelve out of the estimated total of eighty or so German raiders bombing this ship; they hit her with five bombs, of which three went through her bottom without exploding, but the remaining two damaged her severely, setting the ship on fire. A second tanker was less badly damaged as well.[123]

Overall, in this large convoy raid the nine RAF fighters sent achieved little but at small cost. These fighters did not in any significant way hinder the dive-bombing, apparently by a Me 110 *Gruppe* which sank one vessel, seriously damaged a large tanker and also hit another. S/L Badger, leading the 43 Squadron flight tried to turn into the Me 110s as they circled just before diving, while F/Lt Walch led his three 238 Squadron Hurricanes into diving attacks from the rear on the retreating last group of Me 110s. Badger also split his six Hurricanes, deploying three against a much larger Me 109 escort while his section tackled the bomb carriers; a brave and surprisingly often successful tactic that would be applied often enough in the future. However, in the end, there were just too few RAF fighters to successfully take on a raid estimated at eighty enemy aircraft. Six more Spitfires from 609 Squadron had actually been sent up soon after the section from 238 Squadron took off and were directed towards the convoy but never made contact; A Flight of five Hurricanes, 238 Squadron, in addition to F/Lt Walsh's section had been in the air about half an hour before the convoy was first attacked but was only directed towards the convoy once the attack had begun[124] and did not reach it in time. The fault thus most likely lay in the vectoring of squadrons at sector level and not in allocation of resources at group level; another dozen RAF fighters could have made a big difference.

In fact, A Flight of 238 Squadron, led by F/Lt Turner with S/L Fenton flying as Yellow 1, was vectored to within a mile of a lone reconnaissance Do 17 of *4(F)/14* at *c.* 18,000 ft over Blandford; there, repeated attacks by all five Hurricanes from astern and abeam expended a total of 4,196 rounds to bring it down in flames, and the three wounded crew members survived as prisoners.[125] F/O Davis's Hurricane was hit by return fire and damaged.[126]

22 July 1940: single aircraft actions

No daylight bombing raids were undertaken by the *Luftwaffe*, except for lone aircraft. Blue Section of 46 Squadron took off very early from their 12 Group base at Digby to cover a convoy at sea some 39 miles east-north-east of Skegness; over the ships, anti-aircraft fire helped guide them to a lone Do 17 at 3,500 ft at 05h17.[127] Despite firing a total of

6,685 rounds and claiming an unconfirmed victory, no lost or seriously damaged machine can be identified in German loss records. 46 Squadron reported firing from 300 to 200 yards range but felt no slipstream from their intended victim despite several rear-quarter attacks.[128] The Dornier first climbed into cloud, then dived almost vertically to sea level[129] and appears to have got away unscathed or only lightly damaged. A Do 17 of *2/Küstenfliegergruppe 606* did report attacking a convoy in this area, and then being chased by three Spitfires ('Spitfire snobbery'), suffering fifty bullet strikes, lightly wounding a crew member.[130] 46 Squadron had been largely destroyed over Norway and it is likely its inexperienced replacement pilots opened fire too far away. Like quite a few other squadrons, 46's Hurricanes had ammunition loads well in excess of the 'standard' 2,400 rounds, one pilot firing 2,584 rounds in this action.[131]

Soon after this, S/L Leigh led six Spitfires of 66 Squadron over another convoy near the Cross Sands Lightship off Norfolk, where they found a single Do 17 at about 8,000 ft at 05h37.[132] The German aircraft hid very effectively in clouds and only one pilot got in a short squirt from about 350 yards and no claim was made.[133] A little later on that morning, at about 07h30, a Do 17P reconnaissance aircraft from *4(F)/121* was intercepted by a flight of Hurricanes of 145 Squadron led by F/Lt Boyd and shot down into the sea about 20 miles south of Selsey by three of them, Boyd and P/Os Dunning-White and Weir; only the pilot of the three crew members survived and was lucky to be rescued by a Royal Navy MTB.[134]

A meeting was held at the Karinhall estate this day between Göring, the host, his deputy Field Marshal Milch, and the three *Luftflotten* commanders and their key staff, to issue detailed instructions for aerial operations as a pre-requisite for the invasion.[135] The naval staff, while still unsatisfied that convoys continued to traverse the Channel, requested that naval targets within the ports of Dover, Portsmouth, Portland and Plymouth be emphasised, leaving the other ports alone as they would be required by the invading German forces.[136] Göring also stressed avoiding tying the Me 109s too closely to bomber formations and suggested the latter need rely more on good formation flying and defensive return fire; *Kanalkampfführer Oberst* Fink and his fighter commander, *Oberst* Theo Osterkamp held that the Me 110s should perform the close escort duty, thereby agreeing with freeing up the Me 109s for roving free chase type missions.[137]

23 July 1940: more single aircraft actions

Another day without bombing raids during daylight. A Do 17 of *2/KG 3* is thought to have fallen into the sea south of Brighton close to midnight on the night of 22-23 July 1940.[138] One of the crew is described as having ditched in the Channel south of Brighton after having been attacked by a Blenheim on the night of 22-23 July, the crew being rescued later by a He 59 in daylight.[139] This was the first onboard radar-guided interception and victory for the RAF and thus a highly significant event; the Dornier went down close to midnight.[140]

Blue Section of 603 Squadron had intercepted a Do 17 bombing a trawler, apparently without success, east of Peterhead in mid-afternoon on 23 July, and subjected it to multiple attacks from rear, quarter astern and beam, expending 7,425 rounds; their Spitfires carried *c.* 2,800 rounds, some 400 more than the official ammunition load.[141] Finally, with the Dornier giving off thick black smoke it vanished in cloud again, and thereafter two of the pilots saw wreckage in the sea giving off black smoke, which lasted for some time and was still visible on the return trip to base, including a large red object on fire, interpreted as a rubber boat; no survivors were seen.[142] *Küstenfliegergruppe 606* based in Kiel lost one of seven Dorniers dispatched on reconnaissance over the North Sea that afternoon, headed for the Scottish east coast, a *1 Staffel* machine and her crew of four, and this was the logical victim of 603 Squadron.[143] Return fire lightly damaged two Spitfires.[144]

A Ju 88 of *4(F)/122*, crew killed, went into the sea in the vicinity of Dover,[145] reported shot down south-east of Yarmouth.[146] It is generally credited to F/Lt Powell-Sheddon of 242 Squadron.[147] Yarmouth is some 125 miles north of Dover, but assuming the Ju 88 was not initially mortally hit, it may have flown that far, heading for its base just outside Brussels,[148] which course would have taken it to the east of Dover. Indeed, Powell-Sheddon reported no visible damage from his repeated attacks, from astern, rear-quarter and a frontal one except for a thin stream of smoke from the port engine, and he made no claim upon landing.[149] Powell-Sheddon's Hurricane carried the 'official' ammunition load, firing off 2,390 rounds with only one stoppage.[150]

7

24–26 July 1940: Multiple Convoy Attacks in Eastern Channel and East Coast; Limited Action in Western Channel

24 July 1940: early actions and two complex convoy attacks

Early morning activity included Red Section of 92 Squadron led by F/ Lt Kingcome being vectored onto a lone Ju 88 over the Bristol Channel, which they found at 11,000 ft near Porthcawl on the northern side of the channel. Pursued by all three Spitfires who made a series of astern and beam attacks as the Junkers dived for cloud, it crashed near Lynton, on the southern side of the Bristol Channel.[1] This was a machine from *3/LG 1* whose crew became prisoners, one being wounded; the Ju 88 was also attacked by P/O Beamont of 87 Squadron.[2] Not long after, off Northern Scotland, P/O Gilroy led Red Section of 603 Squadron to intercept a Heinkel 111 over the sea off Aberdeen; they pursued it further to the north-east and made a large number of attacks from astern, quarter astern, beam and even a single head-on attack from above by Gilroy, in and out of cloud, putting the port engine out of action.[3] Despite several attacks closing in to 100-50 yards range the Heinkel disappeared in cloud north-east of Peterhead, last seen circling. P/O Gilroy used all his considerable ammunition supply, 2,800 rounds, 400 above the norm.[4] This was a Heinkel from *3/KG 26* and 603 Squadron wounded three of the crew, the machine getting back to base 25% damaged.[5]

The Germans completed installing a Freya radar set at Cap Blanc Nez on 24 July,[6] close to the headquarters of *Obersten* Fink and Osterkamp. This provided the means to detect British convoys early as they moved through the Straits of Dover and the adjacent Channel areas, at all times and in all weather, and supported an increase in intensity of the convoy attacks that had been taking place since the beginning of the month; some Germans put the beginning of the Battle of Britain at 24 July as a consequence.[7] Along the Channel, the CE, Channel East or sailing eastwards, and CW, sailing westwards, convoys made regular trips between St Helens Roads off the north-east of the Isle of Wight and Southend at the northern side of the entrance to the Thames Estuary.[8]

CE 7 left The Isle of Wight on 22 July, arriving at Southend on 24 July and this convoy of fifteen ships, without escorts,[9] would thus have passed through the Dover Straits on 24 July and may well have been the convoy targeted in both raids described in RAF and *Luftwaffe* sources. In any case, Southend was a major convoy base for both Channel and East coast convoys arriving and departing regularly. These convoys provided many merchant vessel targets for the *Luftwaffe* to attack, which were still in open waters at the entrance to the Thames Estuary. A convoy emerging from the Medway into the Thames Estuary has been linked to the second German convoy bombing attack,[10] but it is perhaps more likely to have been naval units, as Chatham Dockyards on the Medway River was a major naval base, and with each convoy minesweeping and anti-submarine trawlers would have been sent out from their various bases to clear passages for these convoys. Dover and Harwich were other ports where naval trawlers were based, including those attacked on this day.

There is some confusion in the relevant literature, as each shipping raid in the south-east this day appears to have had two coordinated parts, and these are related to separate convoys off Dover and in the Thames Estuary by some.[11] *EGr 210* was certainly involved in attacking ships on 24 July, but the unit history is somewhat vague on details, merely referring to being in action over the Channel and south-east coast of England, claiming five vessels sunk for a 20,000-ton bag of shipping.[12] While their tonnage claim was vastly overstated as will be seen later, the vague indication of two separate convoy raids, in the Channel and off south-east England, is borne out by the German naval war diary.[13] The diary records that 2 *Staffel* of *EGr 210* sank four steamers from a convoy comprising six merchant ships while setting another afire, and in the afternoon made a second convoy attack between Harwich and Orfordness during which they claimed another merchant vessel sunk.

24 July 1940: first raid on convoy off Dover, a double attack

Two *Staffeln* of Dornier 17s from *II/KG 2* made an attack on a convoy in the Straits of Dover at *c.* 08h40.[14] Six Spitfires of B Flight, 54 Squadron, were scrambled at 08h12 from Rochford and intercepted the bombers as they approached the convoy; they put at least some of them off their aim but made no claims.[15] The 54 Squadron pilots noted twelve Dorniers in two waves, the first reaching the ships and bombing before they could hinder them, but all bombs missed.[16] In contrast, the second wave was subjected to a fierce attack led by P/O Gribble, despite coordinated crossfire from the rear gunners and somewhat bizarrely, long coils of wire thrown out of the bombers. The Dorniers jettisoned their loads and turned tail for France.[17] Although the controller dispatched A Flight as a reinforcement, they failed to make contact.[18] The bomber crews on their return to base claimed three Spitfires shot down.[19] Two Spitfires were in fact damaged, one force-landing at a farm near Mayfield, but the pilot later managed to fly it out and back to base in its damaged state.[20] *III/JG 52* flew protective patrols near Calais for any returning German aircraft under attack and pursuit, but saw no action.[21]

While it would appear that the *II/KG 2* raid on the convoy off Dover inflicted no losses, a number of small naval auxiliary vessels, converted trawlers performing mine-sweeping and anti-submarine services, were not so lucky: HMTs *Kingston Galena* and *Rodino* were sunk in an air attack off Dover on 24 July 1940, while the Trinity House Vessel *Alert*, 793 tons, was damaged near the South Goodwin Light Vessel not far from Dover.[22] Trinity House vessels (THV) included lightships, vessels servicing them, and the organisation was responsible for buoys and marking wrecks and their ships made rapid interventions in cases of need. The naval trawler *Orofino* was also reported as lost to air attack off Dover.[23] These three small sunken trawlers and the slightly larger and damaged THV *Alert* provide the only known shipping casualties from air attack to balance against *EGr 210*'s claim of four steamers sunk and a fifth set on fire from a convoy of six vessels,[24] nowhere near 20,000 tons total tonnage as claimed.

Three Spitfires from 64 Squadron were scrambled at 08h50 from Hawkinge and directed against these early shipping raids, but only that indefatigable pilot Sub Lt Dawson-Paul made contact, off the Goodwin Sands where he made a beam attack on one of six Dorniers, flying in two vics of three; one Dornier was hit and spun away which he claimed as destroyed, unconfirmed and his own petrol tank was hit by return fire.[25] Dawson-Paul observed the Dorniers attack the convoy without obtaining any hits.[26] In view of the location of this aerial action, it may rather have been against an Me 110 from *EGr 210* attacking the naval auxiliaries supporting passage of the convoy through the Dover Straits. The fact that the twin-engined machine which Dawson-Paul fired at spun away is also more compatible with a Me 110 than a Dornier, bearing in mind no aircraft of either type was lost or seriously damaged. The 64 Squadron tyro may have lightly damaged a Me 110 which was repairable at unit level and thus not reported at higher echelons. However, there are some similarities between the reports of both 54 and 64 Squadrons.

While these actions were taking place over the Dover Straits, far to the north, East of Wick, F/Lt Rook led Red Section of 504 Squadron who were expertly vectored onto a lone He 111 flying in and out of dense cloud layers, and they made repeated Fighter Command No 1 attacks – line astern from behind and below – and some quarter astern attacks.[27] While thus apparently following Fighter Command orthodoxy in attack method, they also carried the 'official' ammunition load of 2,400 rounds per Hurricane, but all three aircraft suffered gun stoppages.[28] A brief excerpt from the Intelligence Patrol Report carried some wisdom, as no such damaged machine is listed in the German loss returns, and 504 Squadron made no claims: 'Before entering cloud e/a emitted black smoke from both engines for about 2 minutes but pilots considered this due to over boosting.' Many other units with greater recent experience would likely have made something more of this smoking engines observation.

24 July 1940: second raid on convoys off the Medway and Harwich; again, a double attack

The second major raid on a convoy in the south-east at about midday on 24 July was preceded by a sweep launched ahead of the main formations, from *II/JG 26*; just recently arrived at the Channel coast and not yet fully operational, the *Gruppe Kommandeur Hauptmann* Erich Noack led a force of only ten Me 109s on this mission.[29] Noack has been the subject of some doubt in some relevant literature.[30] A thirty-year-old man of ten years' military experience, at least six years of which as a fighter pilot, he had been *Staffelkapitän* in three different units before promotion to *Hauptmann* and command of *II/JG 26* on 1 June 1940.[31] By 24 July he had as yet no known victories to his credit and from post-war reminiscences enjoyed little credibility as either leader or fighter pilot.[32] On this sweep on 24 July he is said to have led his small band of Me 109s towards Dover when he saw about thirty Spitfires above them, panicked, immediately aborted the mission and turned back, crashing at his base of Marquise-East in France at *c.* 12h00 British time, and being killed after an aborted high approach.[33] However, in the post-war *JG 26* history co-authored by a highly respected former *Kommodore* and ace, Josef Priller, he is described as dashing and as having been killed as a result of aerial combat on 24 July 1940;[34] his loss is ascribed to severe wounds inflicted in combat over the French coast prior to his fatal crash at Marquise.[35] This crash was related to a wing stall following combat with 610 Squadron.[36]

610 Squadron records certainly support air combat having taken place. Nine Spitfires of this squadron took off from Hawkinge at *c.* 11h12 with orders to patrol Dover at 12,000 ft.[37] F/Lt John Ellis was leading and

observed three Me 109s flying westwards about 3,000 ft above them; turning his machines about and climbing steeply, he led his men against them and the Me 109s broke formation; Ellis latched onto one of them, which performed a strange manoeuvre four times: a steep dive followed by a vertical climb, when Ellis each time managed to get in a good burst.[38] The 610 Squadron IPR further details how on the fourth repeat, Ellis's fire was on target and the Me 109 was last seen spiralling vertically down into cloud at about 3,000 ft, shovelling out black and white smoke and apparently out of control, as also witnessed by two other pilots of the squadron.[39]

One more Me 109 was claimed shot down by F/Lt E. B. B. Smith of 610 Squadron, also last seen descending vertically into cloud, smoking heavily and out of control.[40] Irrespective of who the victor may have been, perhaps both 610 pilots, it would appear to support that *Hpt* Noack of *II/JG 26* was involved in a combat which must have left his aircraft damaged and very likely himself wounded. The repeated steep dives and subsequent climbs he made upon being attacked are more indicative of a seriously wounded pilot trying to control his powerful machine rather than being dogfighting manoeuvres. This would provide an 'honourable' reason for Noack's subsequent fatal crash at his home base in France, rather than an ignominious crash for an experienced pilot. What might have been behind the views on him from former *JG 26* veterans remains unknown.[41] Dead men tell no tales but can equally not defend their reputations either.

Despite having essentially disposed of the *Gruppenkommandeur* of *II/JG 26* so summarily, 610 Squadron appear to have put up a rather large black when several pilots intercepted three unidentified aircraft which they thought were ex-French Chance Vought-156s now in *Luftwaffe* employ in the same vicinity as the Me 109s, and promptly shot one down and damaged another.[42] Although there are some doubts as to their identity,[43] they were very likely hapless Skuas from RNAS Worthy Down, and one appears to have crash-landed with a wounded pilot and another possibly force-landed or was only damaged.[44] What three such defenceless Fleet Air Arm aircraft were doing almost flying through the middle of a Battle of Britain dogfight over the Dover area, in broad daylight, begs several questions.

The second complex convoy raid, again on two separate targets, was made at about midday, one objective apparently being a convoy just debouching from the Medway river into the Thames Estuary,[45] and the other objective a convoy off Harwich.[46] Fifteen Dorniers of *I/KG 2* had a close escort of *III/JG 52* flying at reduced speed thereby being more vulnerable, and a luckier remote escort of *III/JG 26* flying some 6,000 to 9,000 ft higher and able to maintain a better fighting speed.[47] First-hand reports from the two intercepting RAF squadrons both give the number of Dorniers as eighteen.[48] *EGr 210* provided the Me 110s for the Harwich convoy attack,[49] with this much faster attack unit flying in together with, or perhaps close behind the heavier Dorniers and their two-part fighter escort, and then breaking away for their own attack. These were typical tactics as employed through much of the Battle by Kesselring's *Luftflotte 2*. The build-up of these attacking forces behind Calais was detected by British radar well before they were observed on the radar to be coming in shortly before noon.[50] Routing of the German force would have avoided flying over Kent to get to targets in the Estuary and off Harwich, instead flying north over the sea roughly parallel to the eastern Kent coast. In the vicinity offshore of Margate, the Dorniers and their direct escort would have turned west along the south of the Estuary towards their Medway convoy; *EGr 210* meanwhile continued on northwards past Margate and made for their target off Harwich, unnoticed by all except a few.

11 Group had put up 54 Squadron from Rochford, at *c.* 11h25 to patrol Deal at 7,000 ft, as the German build-up became apparent on radar. While this height might seem rather low, the weather was poor, 54 Squadron reported 10/10 cloud at 8,000 ft and 3/10 cloud at 5,000 ft.[51] Bombing by either Dorniers or Me 110s would have been impractical at higher altitudes and much of the subsequent action took place below 10,000 ft. The Germans also noted the cloudy and rainy weather,[52] which was to hamper both sides. This mission was to be the first along the Channel coast for the newly arrived *III/JG 52* and *III/ JG 26*.[53] When F/Lt Deere leading 54 Squadron sighted the enemy, he immediately asked for reinforcements to be sent up, resulting in six Spitfires of 65 Squadron being scrambled from Manston at 12h04.[54]

54 Squadron was the first to meet the German raiders, and having been warned that these were approaching Manston soon saw eighteen Dorniers at about 5,000 ft, flying in stepped-up vics of three and heading for a convoy in the Thames Estuary just off the North Foreland; as the twelve Spitfires headed north for the enemy from Deal they found themselves approaching from the beam and also saw Me 109 escorts above and behind the bombers in the murky weather.[55] F/Lt Deere split the squadron into sections line astern, which attacked individually, but they were outnumbered and a series of dogfights soon developed; the German fighters fought it out in vics of three and five aircraft but didn't really trouble 54 Squadron overmuch.[56] In the conditions, damaged aircraft could not be followed to their possible demise in the sea, but the Spitfires found that they could easily outpace the Me 109s at *c.* 5,000 ft by using twelve boost on their Merlin engines; short steep dives and deflection shots characterised the confused dogfighting, but the German fighters kept the squadron from getting anywhere near the Dorniers.[57]

In any case, the latter were seen to drop a single salvo of bombs near the convoy before heading straight back home to France.[58] The leader of 54 Squadron in this action, F/Lt Alan Deere as Red 1, managed to keep his sense of humour despite the intensity of the fighting, as is evident from this excerpt from the Intelligence Patrol Report obviously based on his description as given to the intelligence officer who wrote it:[59]

> Me 109 tactics and manoeuvres appeared clumsy to our pilots; Red Section which alone saw the He. 113's (sic, Me 109s) had no difficulty in overtaking them at 5,000 ft when using 12 boost. The He. 113's first appeared on the tails of Red Section which mistook them for friendly fighters coming to their assistance. Red leader reported that these A/C. appeared to have strips painted on the tail unit, but was never near enough to be more positive than this. A burst of machine gun fire from astern by the He. 113's soon convinced Red Section that these A/C. were far from friendly.

Me 109s were quite often erroneously reported as He 113s during the Battle. Use of maximum engine boost for short periods by both Hurricanes and Spitfires of Fighter Command, as reported above by 54 Squadron, make oft-repeated comparisons of top speeds of fighters somewhat irrelevant. Engine hours and engine condition also affected speeds significantly. *III/JG 52*, unusually amongst *Jagdgeschwader* in the Battle of Britain, still made use of the *III Gruppe* symbol on the rear fuselage[60] and this may be what F/Lt Deere fleetingly saw during combat as tail strips.

Despite by now having accumulated a lot of combat experience over Dunkirk and during July 1940, 54 Squadron was still flying in the standard Fighter Command sections of three aircraft, with one section being the rear-guard, flying behind and above their comrades. Almost inevitably, they appear to have suffered the first blow in the fighting, their experienced and successful section leader P/O Allen being killed, and one wingman having his cockpit canopy shattered; he survived slightly wounded and saved his machine.[61] The other wingman claimed to have dispatched Allen's attacker and despite thus having run out of ammunition then chased a Me 109 far to the north of the Margate area where the fighting was taking place, to Orfordness; as his fuel gave out he force-landed in a field at Sizewell writing off his Spitfire against a dyke and injuring himself.[62] He may well have been chasing an Me 109 from *EGr 210*, which unit attacked ships off Harwich[63] not far south of Orfordness. P/O Allen was very unlucky, having been hit off Margate and seen to come down with his engine stopped; as he came down over the town it picked up again and he turned towards Manston to save the aircraft, but then it cut again and he no longer had height or speed to avoid a stall and was killed in the crash.[64]

It would seem that 54 Squadron attacked the direct Dornier escort of *III/JG 52* and essentially simultaneously was itself surprised by some of the indirect escort of *III/JG 26*.[65] *Major* Adolf Galland leading *III/JG 26* surprised Spitfires above the convoy and attacked one on the left flank of a small formation which he saw descending vertically, with the pilot bailing out but his parachute failing as he and his Spitfire crashed into the sea.[66] This occurred at about 12h35 – all times are British time in this book – about 20 miles north of Margate between *c.* 6,000 and 9,000 ft.[67] A few minutes earlier *Fw* Straub, 7/*JG 26*, claimed a Spitfire near Margate.[68] Galland's observation of a pilot bailing out of a stricken fighter, his 'chute not opening and the unfortunate pilot being killed as he hit the sea, does not fit P/O Allen's loss, the only RAF fatality in this action; Galland could only have seen his colleague, Lt Schauf, who did indeed suffer just such a fate.[69] In the rapidity and confusion of aerial combat, events seen only fleetingly easily became linked with each other into what later became a single coherent memory. *III/JG 26* lost a second pilot, *Oblt* Bartels, the Technical Officer of the *Gruppe* who force-landed in a park in Margate at *c.* 12h00, his brand-new aircraft with only ten hours flying on it being almost intact, unlike its unfortunate pilot who was seriously wounded.[70] Despite his condition, Bartels was able to tell his captors how he had been caught beautifully by a near-perfect deflection shot.[71]

Within the murky weather around Margate and the North Foreland, 54 Squadron must have had a very intense aerial battle, ten of its twelve pilots making claims for a squadron total of two confirmed and four unconfirmed Me 109s, with another eight probables and two damaged.[72] Most of these probably came from *III/JG 52*, much less experienced in battle than *III/JG 26*, the former losing four pilots and aircraft, including *Gruppenkommandeur Hauptmann* Freiherr von Houwald, *Gefr* Frank, as well as the *Staffelkapitäne* of both 7 and 8 *Staffeln*, *Oblt* Fermer and *Oblt* Ehrlich; all disappeared in the sea off Marget at *c.* 12h30.[73] In return, *III/JG 52* claimed two Spitfires north-east of Margate at 13h26 but only one was confirmed by the *Gruppe*.[74]

65 Squadron who were also involved in the fighting around Margate and surrounds made claims for one probable and three damaged Me 109s;[75] the claims of the two RAF squadrons of course need to be compared with six Me 109s shot down, including two from *III/JG 26*. As a rule of thumb, many historians of the Battle, and indeed World War Two aerial combat in general, tend to disregard probable and damaged claims, which leaves two confirmed (witnessed) and four

unconfirmed (no witness) Me 109 claims for the six Messerschmitts actually lost, all put forward by 54 Squadron. However, there were apparently two more claims, by 610 Squadron, for a confirmed and a probable Me 109.[76]

Nine Spitfires of 610 Squadron under F/Lt John Ellis were scrambled a mere fifteen or so minutes after landing from their first action against the *II/JG 26* sweep ahead of the raid.[77] As 610 Squadron's Spitfires climbed following take-off from Hawkinge with cloud at about 400 ft, and emerged from the cloud which was about 3,000 ft thick near Margate,[78] they were attacked from above by a few Me 109s. These made for Green Section but Ellis saw them coming and instructed the section to turn as tightly as they could to starboard, thereby avoiding the Messerschmitts; the latter were immediately set upon by Ellis and his Blue Section, the section leader managing to shoot one down as it tried to climb away and the section watched as it dived down into the sea giving off profuse black and white smoke, some miles north-east of Margate.[79] The relevant 610 Squadron IPR for the action is a confusing document, being dated 25 July 1940, and giving 615 Squadron in the heading, although the text clearly refers to 610 Squadron pilots, and the details correlate with those given in other squadron documents for 24 July and in the Squadron history as well.[80] F/Lt Smith claimed a second Me 109 as a probable, as well as a probable Chance Vought 156.[81] The odds of meeting another presumed RN Skua must have been small, but perhaps this might have been a straggler left over from the earlier action, as 610 Squadron's two sorties were close to each other in time.

S/L Sawyer led A Flight of 65 Squadron up from Manston at 12h04; they were vectored to a convoy in the Medway and were at 9,000 ft when warned of enemy aircraft approaching from the east at *c.* 8,000 ft.[82] They saw the eighteen Dorniers coming in and as the squadron approached, they held back waiting to see the expected escort first before going in for an attack. The bombers meanwhile flew in their vics of three in a large circle, and jettisoned their bombs, then headed for the coast again, a hesitant 65 Squadron flight still in attendance just out of range.[83] Seeing approaching Me 109s at last, at about 10,000 ft, and that 54 Squadron had taken them on, leaving the Dorniers to their fate, the 65 Squadron flight finally fired some bursts at the bombers claiming slight damage to four of them, but did not close in due to the close formation and heavy cross-fire maintained by *I/KG 2*.[84] One Dornier from *2/KG 2* was in fact damaged, and two crew members including the pilot wounded, but it got home.[85] As the bombers made for France, the 65 Squadron pilots became involved with some of the escorting Me 109s, claiming one probable and three damaged, all by S/L Sawyer who used all his ammunition, 2,800 rounds, 400 over the normal load. All six Spitfires returned safely to Manston just after 13h00.[86]

As the fighter battle around Margate developed and the Do 17s of *I/KG 2* went for the convoy in the Thames Estuary, *EGr 210* who had accompanied the bombers and their two-*Gruppe* escort on the way in, broke off to the north of Margate and the North Foreland, making for their target, another convoy approximately 20 miles off Harwich.[87] It is not certain which convoy they attacked, but Convoy FN 231 left Southend on 24 July bound for the Tyne; while it had only three ships and no escort vessels, at least three minesweeping trawlers of the 4th Minesweeping Group were active in their duties nearby in the Thames Estuary, and sailors on two of them counted four attacking German aircraft.[88] HMT *Fleming* of 350 tons was sunk in the attack with the loss 19 out of 22 crew members; HMT *Berberis* claimed to have shot one of the attackers down with possible damage to a second.[89] This was no idle claim, *EGr 210* suffering their first loss of the Battle when a Me 110 of *2 Staffel* caught a direct hit and exploded in the air killing both crew members instantly.[90] HMT *Fleming* sank about 30 miles off Clacton along the Essex coast.[91] The German naval war diary recorded *EGr 210* having attacked a convoy between Harwich and Orfordness, sinking a steamer.[92]

24 July 1940: tactics

The day's operations were brought to a close by A Flight of 74 Squadron, which P/O Freeborn led up from Manston and at about 17h25. They were vectored on to three 'Do 215s' – perhaps Me 110s? – heading east across the Straits of Dover.[93] The IPR details three Spitfires making astern attacks from *c.* 300 yards range, all using up their ammunition load of 2,700 rounds per machine and seeing one engine of a Do 215 trailing some black smoke, they claimed one damaged. No such aircraft nor any relevant Me 110 can be identified damaged in *Luftwaffe* losses.

Without getting involved in the complexities and nuances of a wide spectrum of views on the relative merits of the Hurricane and Spitfire, most would agree that Spitfires with their higher performance levels were better aircraft to vector against Me 109 escorts at often higher altitudes. Equally, Hurricanes were better suited to lower altitudes and being a more rugged aircraft able to absorb more punishment, were better suited for tackling bomber formations. The Hurricane with its much thicker wing and also with the four machine guns per wing grouped together, made a steadier gun platform with better gun harmonisation characteristics, as compared to the very thin wings of the Spitfires with its four guns per wing spread out as a consequence.

By this stage, the Spitfire squadrons involved on 24 July had garnered much experience at both Dunkirk and over the Channel and south-eastern England, most against Me 109s rather than bomber formations. This would provide a logical explanation for the rather ineffective attack on the Do 17s in the first convoy raid by 54 Squadron, although the section led by P/O George Gribble dissuaded the bombers from making an effective attack on the convoy. As was typical for their *Geschwader*, the Dorniers of *II/KG 2* held formation and used disciplined cross-fire to keep the Spitfires at a distance. In the second convoy attack at about noon, *I/KG 2* performed equally well, 54 Squadron were kept off by the large escort and 65 Squadron attacked the bombers only in a half-hearted fashion. Once again, no bombers were lost but the bombing by the Dorniers was poor and no ships were lost.

For both convoy attacks, much more effective ship attacks were carried out by *EGr 210*, which sneaked in under cover of the Do 17 raids each time, accounting in the end for four naval trawlers. In the second convoy attack, with a total of twenty-seven Spitfires pitched against around seventy Me 109 escorts of *III/JG 52* and *III/JG 26*, they did exceptionally well: six Messerschmitts were lost with their pilots, five dead and one POW; some of the slaughter was down to 54 Squadron, which lost two Spitfires and P/O Allen killed, and some to 610 Squadron. With murky weather conditions, cloud layers and rain squalls, the Me 109s were unable to make use of their favourite dive and zoom bounce tactics and the confused close-in fighting greatly favoured the RAF Spitfire squadrons, which were much better at dogfighting, both aircraft and pilots. In addition, with both *Luftwaffe* fighter *Gruppen* experiencing their first mission over England against experienced Spitfire squadrons who had already been fighting over the Channel for seven weeks, the results were not surprising.

One more tactical truth was in evidence on 24 July 1940: the use of rear-guard sections by Fighter Command squadrons, flying above and behind their squadron, placed them very much in harm's way to protect their colleagues. Predictably, the higher flying Me 109s of *III/JG 26* easily bounced Yellow Section of 54 Squadron, killing its experienced leader, P/O John Allen, damaging his one wingman's machine and driving off the other. For 54 Squadron, a unit of very brave and effective men, with normally excellent leadership provided by S/L 'Prof' Leathart and on occasion F/Lt Alan Deere, F/Lt 'Wonky' Way and after his demise, by P/O George Gribble,[94] it was a somewhat inexcusable practice.

Above left: 1. Air Chief Marshal Lord Dowding, after the Battle of Britain. The sure guiding hand of Fighter Command. (Crown Copyright, Admiralty)

Above right: 2. Air Vice-Marshal Sir Quintin Brand, commander of 10 Group, who loyally supported AV-M Park in 11 Group throughout the Battle. (www.raf. mod.uk/bob1940/images/brand.jpg)

3. At the other end of the Fighter Command hierarchy: Hurricanes of 17 Squadron at an active Debden sector station, July 1940. (Crown Copyright, IWM HU54414)

4. *Generalmajor* Theo Osterkamp (right), fighter leader in the Pas de Calais during July 1940, commander of *JG 51* before being promoted to *Jagdfliegerführer Luftflotte 2* towards the end of the month; on the occasion of his forty-ninth birthday, 15 April 1941. In the middle, Werner Mölders describes his latest claim, with both Adolf Galland (left) and Osterkamp looking somewhat sceptical. *Major* Mölders succeeded Osterkamp in command of *JG 51* in late July 1940 while *Major* Galland led *III/JG 26* at that stage. (Bundesarchiv, 183-B-12019)

5. The RAF aircraft: looking business-like and tough, a Hurricane Mk 1 is taxied out by Sgt 'Sammy' Allard of 85 Squadron, July 1940. (Crown Copyright, IWM HU104491)

6. The RAF aircraft: fine profile image of another 85 Squadron Hurricane, flown by Pilot Officer A. G. Lewis, landing at Castle Camps, Debden sector, July 1940. (Crown Copyright, IWM HU54416)

Above: 7. The RAF aircraft: the beautiful lines of Spitfire Mk 1s of 609 Squadron at Drem, 13 Group, Scotland in February/ March 1940. More deadly than the Hurricane, but less rugged. (Crown Copyright, IWM HU104509)

Right: 8. The RAF aircraft: Defiant of 264 Squadron being refuelled, July 1940. Too slow, too clumsy, too heavy, a failed concept harking back to the Bristol Fighters of World War 1. (Crown Copyright, IWM NU104453)

Below right: 9. The RAF aircraft: air gunner in turret of a Defiant of 264 Squadron at Kirton-in-Lindsey, 12 Group. The cramped turret with its four 0.303 machine guns is obvious, and was its only armament. The gunner could only exit in emergency by turning the turret to the side and escaping via the small rear turret doors. If the hydraulics had been hit, there was no escape. (Crown Copyright, IWM CH879)

10. The *Luftwaffe* aircraft: Heinkel He 111, reliable but slow. The fully glazed nose must have distressed crews faced by head-on attacks (Bundesarchiv, 101I-647-5211-33)

11. A captured reconnaissance Messerschmitt Me 110 C-5 of *4(F)/14*, shot down by 238 Squadron on 21 July 1940 at Goodwood. Repaired at the Royal Aircraft Establishment at Farnborough with parts from another Me 110, of *9/ZG 76* shot down over Wareham on 11 July 1940. (Crown Copyright, IWM MH4193)

12. Some faces of the Few: pilots of 43 Squadron RAF at Wick, Caithness in April 1940. Left to right: Sgt J. Arbuthnot, Sgt R. Plenderleith (both served in the Battle with other squadrons), Sgt H. J. L. Hallowes, F/O J. W. Simpson, F/Lt P. W. Townsend, P/O H. C. Upton. (Crown Copyright, IWM CH83)

13. Some faces of the Few: pilots decorated on 27 June 1940 at Hornchurch, cheer King George VI. Left to right: F/O J. L. Allen (54 Squ.), F/Lt R. R. Stanford Tuck (92 Squ.), F/Lt A. C. Deere (54 Squ.), F/Lt A. G. Malan (74 Squ.), S/L J. A. Leathart (54 Squ.) and a bugler. (Crown Copyright, IWM CH432)

14. Some faces of the Few: pilots of 32 Squadron relax on the grass at forward base Hawkinge, July 1940. Left to right: P/Os R. F. Smythe, K. R. Gillman and J. E. Proctor, F/Lt P. M. Brothers, P/Os D. H. Grice, P. M. Gardner and A. F. Eckford. (Crown Copyright, IWM HU54418)

15. Some faces of the Few: pictured at Abbeville, France before the Battle, 615 Squadron pilots: sitting, left to right, F/Os B. F. Young and R. Gayner, P/O T. C. Jackson and F/O L. E. Fredman; standing left to right, unknown, F/O P. Collard and F/Lt J. G. Sanders. Only Sanders, Collard and Gayner returned from France and fought in the Battle; Young was seriously wounded in France, Jackson taken prisoner and Fredman was killed there. (Crown Copyright, IWM C1609)

16. Member of the ground crew of an 85 Squadron Hurricane, with the battery cart plugged in ready for a scramble at short notice. Only the best and most experienced servicemen know that you must relax whenever opportunity offers, July 1940. (Crown Copyright, IWM HU 104451)

17. The two members who typically manned an Observer Corps post plot aircraft positions and height in their sector, 29 February 1940; the often unsung heroes who put in long hours in all-weather at open sites, provided the only information on enemy aircraft inland from the coastal areas, covered by radar. (Crown Copyright, IWM HU104541)

18. Some faces of the *Luftwaffe*: *Major* Johann Schalk, C/O of *III/ZG 26* (middle) in animated discussion on a recent combat, with *Oberleutnant* Theodor Rossiwal (right), recently moved from *III Gruppe* to become *Staffelkapitän 5/ZG 26*, 21 June 1940 in France. (Bundesarchiv, 101I-341-0496-31)

19. *Oberleutnant* Theodor Rossiwall, *Staffelkapitän 5/ ZG 26*, about to clamber into the cockpit of his Me 110, France on 21 June 1940. (Bundesarchiv, 101I-341-0496-33)

20. View of an East Coast convoy from one of the escorts, HMT *Sapphire*. Trawlers filled in where destroyers and corvettes were in perennial short supply. (Crown Copyright, IWM A17494)

21. British convoy under attack by Ju 87 dive-bombers off Dover, 14 July 1940. (Crown Copyright, Air Historical Branch)

22. Three pilots of 85 Squadron run for their Hurricanes, already being started by the ground crew, just outside the dispersal hut at Castle Camps satellite airfield, July 1940. P/O Albert Lewis is on the left, running towards the nearest fighter. (Crown Copyright, IWM HU 104483)

23. As a mechanic warms up the Hurricane's engine, P/O Albert Lewis, 85 Squadron hastily dons his parachute and flying helmet from the tail plane of his aircraft, Castle Camps, July 1940. (Crown Copyright, IWM HU104484)

24. S/L Peter Townsend, commanding officer of 85 Squadron taxis his Hurricane out fast, past ground crew with a battery cart used in the start; Castle Camps, July 1940. (Crown Copyright, IWM HU104488)

25. P/O Rupert Smythe taxis his Hurricane of 32 Squadron out for take-off at Hawkinge forward base near Dover, 29 July 1940. (Crown Copyright, IWM HU54417)

26. 29 July 1940, at Hawkinge forward airfield; a section of 32 Squadron Hurricanes from Biggin Hill prepares to taxi out for take-off. (Crown Copyright, IWM HU69116)

27. Spitfires from 610 Squadron, Biggin Hill, on 24 July 1940, flying in the vic formations of three aircraft typical for many Battle of Britain squadrons. However, squadron leaders often broadened the tight vics to much wider sections or, as in the background of this photo, spread the individual sections far apart, as they took up a stepped down line astern formation prior to action. (Crown Copyright, IWM CH740)

28. A section of Hurricanes, undercarriages and flaps down, cockpit hoods open, comes in to land over the perimeter fence at Martlesham Heath. (Crown Copyright, IWM CH1673)

Top left: 29. Fine air-to-air shot of a He 111 bomber in flight. Note dorsal and ventral rear gun positions and lack of any additional side guns in a photograph taken in September 1939 before combat reality necessitated additional armament. (Bundesarchiv, 101I-317-0045-11A)

Middle left: 30. A vic of three He 111 bombers taxis out for take-off at a French base, 21 June 1940. Note the observer in the foremost machine standing up with his head out of the hatch helping the pilot steer on the ground when forward vision was limited. Note also extra MG 15 machine gun in front of and above pilot's position. Such relatively rough field bases with mowed grass runways limited bombloads that could be safely carried during bumpy take-offs. (Bundesarchiv, 101l-401-0240-20)

Below left: 31. A Spitfire flies over a damaged Me 109 with port undercarriage lowered and seemingly about to ditch at the Kent coast. (Crown Copyright; Royal Air Force Battle of Britain campaign diaries)

Above left: 32. Some Fighter Command personalities: Pilot Officer Geoffrey Page, a pilot in 56 Squadron, who was the first to fly around inside a Me 110 circle 'against the flow', on 10 July 1940. Photo taken on 1 June 1940 following an aircraft crash. The pre-war white flying overalls were coveted gear. (Crown Copyright, RAF official photograph originally)

Above right: 33. Some Fighter Command personalities: Group Captain A. G. 'Sailor' Malan taken later in the war; in 1940 he was a flight lieutenant in and then led 74 Squadron, the famous 'Tigers'. One of the significant tacticians and innovators of Fighter Command. (Crown Copyright, IWM CH12661)

34. Some Fighter Command personalities: Squadron Leader E. M. 'Teddy' Donaldson who led the salty pilots of 151 Squadron until 5 August 1940, at left, with Wing Commander Victor Beamish, right, the inspirational Station Commander of North Weald sector, who flew regular sorties through the Battle, although not required to fly in action. Photograph taken on 30 June 1940 after a successful mission over France. (Crown Copyright, IWM CH490)

35. Some Fighter Command personalities: Wing Commander Alan Deere, right, with Squadron Leader Dennis Crowley-Milling later in the war. During the Battle 'Al' Deere was the senior flight commander in 54 Squadron, and Crowley-Milling flew as a Pilot Officer in Douglas Bader's 242 Squadron. (Crown Copyright, IWM CH9455)

36. Some Fighter Command personalities: another inspirational leader and tactician, John Dewar, leader of 87 Squadron till 12 July 1940, thereafter station commander at Exeter, in 10 Group; at readiness at Exeter airfield during the Battle. He was killed in action on 11 September 1940, and like so many disappeared into the Channel, his body washing up weeks later in Sussex (Photo taken by F/O R. F. Watson, 87 Squadron, part of the Watson family photo collection; provided by another ex-87 Squadron pilot, Sgt Laurence Thorogood).

37. The wreck of a Ju 88 A of *5/KG 51* at Oakridge near Stroud, attracts a considerable crowd. While attempting to bomb the Gloster plant at Hucclecote, it was shot down by an instructor from 5 OTU after initial attack by a Hurricane of the Hamble airfield defence flight, 25 July 1940. (Crown Copyright, IWM HU69164)

38. A Heinkel 111 of *Stab/KG 55* lies in a field at Hipley in Hampshire on 12 July 1940, after having been shot down by Hurricanes of 43 Squadron over Southampton Water. (Crown Copyright, IWM HU90819)

39. RAF men busy camouflaging the 'Hipley Heinkel' from *Stab/KG 55*, 12 July 1940, to avoid the *Luftwaffe* trying to destroy the remains. Note extra side-mounted MG 15 machine gun on the starboard side, halfway down the fuselage, directly below dorsal radio mast. (Crown Copyright, IWM HU72438)

40. RAF technical personnel inspecting the burnt-out remains of a Ju 88 reconnaissance aircraft of *4(F)/122* at St Osyth near Clacton-on-Sea. Only the engines remain reasonably intact. The machine was dispatched by 56 Squadron on 20 July 1940. (Crown Copyright, IWM HU89068)

41. This He 111 of *2/KG 55* was badly damaged by 601 Squadron and given the coup de grace by P/O Wakeham and P/O Lord Kay-Shuttleworth of No. 145 Squadron on 11 July 1940. The burnt-out wreck lies on East Beach, Selsey in Sussex. (Crown Copyright, IWM HU72441)

42. It often took many hits from Fighter Command's .303 calibre machine guns mounted in the Hurricane and Spitfire, to bring a German bomber down, as witness this well-riddled Dornier Do 17 which came down in a hop field in Kent, July 1940. (Crown Copyright, IWM HU104717)

43. Two senior RAF officers study the wreckage of a Heinkel He 111 which came down at Clacton, 1 May 1940 before the Battle. Depending on the level of destruction and commonly deep burial of heavy objects like engines, oleo legs, armour plating and guns, determining the armament and ammunition carried by German aircraft was often a challenging task. (Crown Copyright, IWM HU73395)

44. Heavy, 9.2-inch coastal defence gun on 29 August 1940, overflown by a Coastal Command Sunderland flying boat. The flash from such large guns may on occasion have been confused with crashing aircraft inferred from the air during the rapid evolutions of air combat. (Crown Copyright, IWM H3522)

25 July 1940: multiple attacks on convoy CW 8; shipping off Portland

A day of confused fighting, a lot of the action being repeated attacks against a single convoy throughout much of the day. Convoy CW 8 was made up of twenty-one small ships between 351 and 1,332 tons and two escorts, assembled in the Thames Estuary.[95] It passed through the Straits of Dover from *c.* 12h00 to 18h00, escorted by small RAF fighter formations mostly of section or flight strength. At least four attacks were made on the convoy, at about 11h50, 14h50, 16h30 and 18h40.[96] During most of the day German fighter patrols were flown over the Straits and from them sorties were made against convoy and adjacent coast; some of these sorties were fighters only, while others had bombers with the fighters, which could not be discriminated readily by radar.[97]

Initial small actions this day occurred north of 11 Group. Very early, Red Section of 222 Squadron from Kirton-in-Lindsey, 12 Group, was sent to cover a convoy some 35 miles off Mablethorpe at 10,000 ft, and after about forty minutes, saw two He 111s *c.* 3,000 ft below them, which immediately dived eastwards to sea level.[98] P/O Vigors, Red Leader, attacked from astern and was hit by return fire, but his further attacks from the beam silenced the rear gunner and damaged the Heinkel; more attacks from astern and beam by Red 3, and briefly by Red 2 at *c.* 07h00, resulted in the starboard engine almost stopping.[99] Red 2 than attacked the second Heinkel, also from astern and abeam, silencing the rear gunner and seeing the undercarriage drop before fuel shortage forced him to break away; P/O Cutts, out of fuel, skilfully put his Spitfire down, undamaged, in a field close to base.[100] The section claimed two inconclusive He 111s. While there is no obvious casualty in the German loss returns, *III/KG 53* had a Heinkel 40% damaged when it belly-landed at 'Kotwijk' airfield due to engine failure, crew unhurt.[101] Perhaps Kortrijk airfield in Belgium was meant, also known as Wevelgem, an established *Luftwaffe* base close to Lille-Mouvaux where *III/KG 53* was based.[102] Engine failure would match 222 Squadron's observation of an engine almost stopped in the combat.

Perhaps only one He 111 was in fact attacked by all the pilots, rather than two, the second escaping unscathed. Soon after this combat, two Hurricanes of 3 Squadron, F/O Jones and P/O Lonsdale, were scrambled from Wick to intercept a lone intruder over the Orkney Islands off the far north-east of Scotland and intercepted a Heinkel 111 over Scapa Flow at about 07h35; using several attacks, mainly astern and one from quarter astern, they disabled its starboard engine, killed the rear gunner and saw its undercarriage drop.[103] The Heinkel, a weather reconnaissance machine from *Wekusta 1*, came down off Rora Head, one crew member in a dinghy being rescued by a destroyer 12 miles out to sea.[104]

25 July 1940: midday raid on Dover

The first raid appears to have been on Dover harbour, possibly to disrupt naval response to attacks on the convoy to follow later. Radar signals indicated a fifty-plus raid approaching Dover from the direction of Calais, with a following formation of forty-plus, which was most likely its escort.[105] Accounts and sources differ greatly after this: one finds that Me 109s came in at sea level while Ju 87s from *I/StG 1* bombed the convoy;[106] another two state that Do 17s of *KG 3* raided the harbour, escorted by *III/JG 52* who took off about noon;[107] a fourth source finds that *III/JG 52* were close escort to a Ju 87 *Gruppe* and managed to hold off the first RAF fighters to intercept – 65 Squadron – so that the Stukas could bomb.[108] This is confusing enough but the lack of any accounts of Dover harbour being bombed this day compounds that; the Dover guns did claim three Ju 87s during the course of the day.[109] The only common string to the various reports would appear to be two of the accounts mentioning a low-level incursion over Dover of Me 109s coming in at sea level.[110] A local resident reported a large fighter sweep with little gunfire heard.[111] There is one Luftwaffe unit which could logically explain Me 109s attacking a harbour at low level, namely *3 Staffel* of *EGr 210*, which operated fighter-bomber Me 109s, who were in fact in action three times on this day.[112] In view of two reports of Me 109s at low level over Dover harbour, it would be logical to postulate that this raid was indeed made by them, only dropping relatively few smaller bombs, and if little or no damage ensued, this could explain the lack of reports of any raid on that port from local authorities.

From the RAF side, the first to arrive on the scene were twelve Spitfires of 65 Squadron, ordered up from Manston at 12h10 and vectored towards Dover to intercept approaching enemy aircraft.[113] A brief excerpt from the relevant IPR makes 65 Squadron's tactics clear:[114] '12 Aircraft took off, arrived over the Coast at 14,000 feet and observed A.A. fire to the East of them. Then 5 Me. 109 in vic were seen at about 20,000 feet and fearing an attack from above, the squadron broke up and climbed to the attack individually.'

The Me 109s broke themselves and dove for the French coast, one being chased by a Spitfire who reported being attacked from behind as the chase neared sea level; evading this new danger, F/Sgt Franklin claimed to have seen his pursuer dive straight into the sea.[115] There is no German loss to match this scenario, the only Me 109 loss and that not confirmed in all reports, fell on land west of Deal. One has to wonder at the 65 Squadron leadership, breaking up the unit and climbing for individual attacks on a smaller enemy formation, instead of keeping together to enable a more effective attack. The squadron saw no enemy bombers, and no one else apart from Franklin made contact with the enemy. In view of the height at which the enemy were first seen, 65 Squadron's opponents must have been from either *III/JG 52* or some other supporting/escorting Me 109s, and not from *3/EGr 210* at low level.

Next to arrive in the general Dover area were nine Hurricanes from 32 Squadron, which took off from Biggin Hill at 12h00, and soon after eleven Hurricanes of 615 Squadron who were ordered to patrol Hawkinge.[116] 32 Squadron duly arrived over Dover at *c.* 22,000 ft only to see many Me 109s vanishing rapidly in the distance in the direction of Boulogne;[117] *II/JG 51* were based close to Boulogne and were active over the Straits this day,[118] but they may also have been from *III/JG 52*. Sometime later, at 12h46 at 22,000 ft and 2 miles south of Dover, 32 Squadron intercepted a *Staffel* of eight Me 109s coming in from the south; Mike Crossley in the lead had to endure head-on cannon fire before his machine guns could become effective as the range shortened, detailed in an excerpt from the Intelligence Patrol Report:[119]

> F/Lt Crossley D.F.C. who was leading "A" Flight, wheeled round and engaged them. Their leader opened fire with cannon out of m/g range and head on; when about 400 yards away F/Lt Crossley opened fire and saw white plumes of glycol and petrol pouring from both wings of the e/a near the fuselage. P/O. Gillman who was flying Yellow 3 confirms seeing these two streams of smoke. The e/a yawed away to starboard and dived steeply. Neither saw it crash. [m/g = machine gun]

P/O Daw of 32 Squadron became separated in the fighting and about 6 miles east of Dungeness rather unwisely took on six Me 109s, was hit and wounded in the leg by two bullets, force-landing in a field near Dover, his aircraft badly damaged. Despite his wounds he was back at Biggin Hill that evening.[120] The squadron also observed two groups of six E-boats each, sailing fast north-west of Cap Gris Nez.[121] 615 Squadron, up from Kenley at 12h03, had been sent to patrol Hawkinge, and once there Red Section was attacked by a *Schwarm* of Me 109s, which they evaded by steep turns, and then themselves attacked the Germans at 3,000 ft, F/Lt Gaunce and P/O Hugo each claiming one, the first seen to dive into the sea and the other to give off lots of smoke and with the engine seeming to have stopped. Red 3 and Yellow 2 also had brief engagements, with no results.[122]

In the various actions against small Me 109 formations met in the general Dover-Folkestone area, 65 Squadron claimed one that dived into the sea, 615 Squadron two in the Hawkinge-Folkestone area, one crashed into the sea, the other with an apparently stopped engine, with 32 Squadron claiming only a probable Me 109 south of Dover. There is one possible Me 109 victim to fit any of these claims, which fell north of Dover and West of Deal at Elvington Court, with both pilot and machine in relatively good shape.[123] This might best fit the claim of F/Lt Crossley of 32 Squadron who met his opponent coming in from the south head-on, about 2 miles off Dover; If he damaged this Me 109, which was seen to dive steeply away from *c.* 22,000 ft streaming fuel or glycol, it could fit the one that crashed at Elvington, about 4 miles north of Dover.[124] However, there is similar confusion in the sources relevant to the single German fighter which might have been shot down on this raid. In action with RAF fighters, *Uffz* Reiss of *8/JG 52* was shot down and force-landed at Elvington Court, west of Deal at 12h45, and was taken prisoner unwounded.[125] The RAF intelligence report, or 'K report' on this Me 109 gives a time for the forced-landing of 20h00, which is later than the final combats of the day; it also states that the pilot was surprised by Spitfires coming out of the clouds, hitting his radiator, that the pilot was unwounded and his aircraft in good condition.[126] There is thus some uncertainty on the time of this loss.

III/JG 52 lost four Me 109s during the day, and basic sources list all four as being lost at *c.* 18h40 in the evening.[127] In contrast, the unit history lists one lost at 12h45, *Uffz* Reiss, another on a raid on the convoy at about 15h40, *Oblt* Bielefeld, *Staffelkapitän 7/JG 52*, and two lost on the last convoy raid in the evening, at *c.* 17h45, *Gruppenadjutant Lt* Schmidt and new *Staffelkapitän 7/JG 52 Oblt* Keidel.[128] Consultation of the German Quartermaster General Loss Returns, while not giving times of losses, does show Bielefeld and Keidel both flying as *Staffelkapitän 7/JG 52*; the fact that Keidel succeeded Bielefeld to this post after the latter's loss strongly suggests they were not lost on the same mission.[129] This in turn provides support for the loss times as given in the *III/JG 52* unit history, thereby also supporting Reiss of *8/JG 52* being lost in the first, approximately noontime raid. However, no realistic and logical decision is possible here, despite the claim of Crossley looking not unreasonable.

Equally, among German claims for the day, none is timed to equate with P/O Daw of 32 Squadron being shot down, apparently some miles south of Dover and east of Dungeness and force-landing near Dover;[130] two of the German claims by *5/JG 51* lack times but are shown as having been south of Dover,[131] exactly where Daw was when attacked. A third claim by this *Staffel* in the same location is given as having been made at 15h52.[132] *5/JG 51* lost an Me 109 that suffered damage in air combat over the Channel and was written off in a forced-landing in the Pas de Calais, pilot *Uffz* Obst being wounded;[133] Obst was one of the *5/JG 51* claimants, and although no time is given for his being shot down, he may have fallen to 65, 615 or 32 Squadrons, according to their various claims discussed above.

A rather unusual set of encounters intervened before the next convoy raid. A lone Ju 88 of *5/KG 51* on a sortie to bomb the Gloster Works located at Hucclecote in the outskirts of Gloucester, at about 14h15 was intercepted south-east of Stroud by two Hurricanes of the Hamble airfield defence flight.[134] Hamble, an Avro airfield on Southampton Water not far south of the main Supermarine Works at Woolston, was then largely engaged in aircraft repair, including Spitfires.[135] Presumably the Ju 88 flew in close to Hamble when it began its planned penetration inland to Hucclecote. The leading Hurricane got very close before firing, then appeared to stall and spin down out of control, killing P/O Bird, who fell in the Oakridge area a few kilometres south-east of Stroud.[136] F/Lt Prosser Hanks had been leading two pupils from the nearby 5 OTU in dogfighting practice when he saw the enemy aircraft passing high overhead, and left his charges and climbed to attack.[137] He was a witness to P/O Bird's attack and subsequent fatal spin, following which he gave the Junkers a good burst, causing it to enter a flat spin and the crew to bail out.[138] One German's parachute failed but the other three survived to become POWs; the Ju 88 crashed at Oakridge (Illustration 37), at about 14h25.[139]

25 July 1940: big attack on convoy CW 8

The next major action over the convoy began at *c.* 14h55 as reported by the Commodore, by which time CW 8 was past Dover and off Abbott's Cliff, about halfway between Dover and Folkestone.[140] *Oberst* Fink was the man running the whole show and he planned this first, big Stuka attack to hit the convoy in the narrow waters between the treacherous Goodwin Sands and the shore, using three waves of Ju 87s.[141] Radar had picked up the large dive bomber formation and escorts early enough and the Fighter Command controller reported the enemy as coming in from Cap Gris Nez; the light air escort for the convoy encompassed five Spitfires from 54 Squadron led by F/Lt Way who were patrolling Dover as the first wave approached, but they were soon overwhelmed.[142]

Exactly which Stuka units were involved in this attack on the convoy is a question fraught with uncertainty. While a majority of sources mention three waves or formations of Stukas,[143] the convoy itself appears to have reported four waves and an attacking force of *c.* 100 machines.[144] The convoy Commodore was much more conservative in his estimate of the attackers, judging them as *c.* 40 aircraft.[145] F/Lt Way, leading the pitifully small force of five Spitfires of 54 Squadron flying cover over the convoy as this armada approached, reported a force of about 120 aircraft.[146] Thus a large force of Stukas can be inferred. *II/StG 1* and *IV/LG 1*, the two Stuka *Gruppen* attached to *Luftflotte 2* are mentioned as participants by name,[147] but at least two sources specifically mention *Hauptmann* Hozzel, *Gruppenkommandeur* of *I/StG 1*, part of *Luftflotte 3*, as leading this unit in the convoy attack.[148] While inclusion of the two *Luftlotte 2 Gruppen* is entirely logical, *I/StG 1* stationed in the Evreux-Beauvais area[149] could have been staged forwards to the Pas de Calais without much trouble. Also, at this stage of the Battle, tactical leadership of the Channel *Luftwaffe* aerial campaign lay in the hands of *Kanalkampfführer Oberst* Fink and the domains of the two *Luftflotten* in northern France were as yet not fully established. Fink did in fact have use of Ju 87 units based in the Pas de Calais and general Caen areas.[150] Presumably, this usage would also have included *I/StG 1* lying further to the west, north and north-west of Paris, as well as *III/StG1*, based at Falaise, south-south-east of Caen.[151]

The fighter escort provided was large, including *II and III/JG 26, I and II/JG 51* and *III/JG 52*;[152] German fighter claims lists show *III/JG 51* also being involved in this raid.[153] An escort of six *Jagdgruppen* would support a dive bomber force numbering three *Gruppen*. There are also several reports of Ju 88s from *III/KG 4* attacking the convoy, two of them claiming that 64 Squadron attacked them head-on;[154] there is no mention of any such attack nor of Ju 88s being met in 64 Squadron documentation, or the published autobiography of its commander.[155] Similarly, 111 Squadron is said to have made a head-on attack on the Ju 88s, but again, squadron documents do not mention this.[156]

The *JG 26* unit history finds that *III/JG 26* was close escort to the first of the three Stuka waves with *II/JG 26* flying top cover in the form of a sweep, presumably ahead as they made no contact with the RAF defence; the history furthermore states that the Ju 87s, presumably the first wave, found the convoy unprotected by any RAF fighters and made a successful attack.[157] The *JG 26* history goes on to detail arrival of the five Spitfires of 54 Squadron (F/Lt Way) and their being kept off by *Stab III/JG 26* who claimed a Spitfire shot down. Soon after the balance of 54 Squadron as well as 64 Squadron arrived, in time to attack Ju 87s pulling up from their dive on the convoy, but Me 109s of *Oblt* Beyer's 7 *Staffel JG 26* had dived in formation with the Stukas and surprised the Spitfires, getting four of them.[158] If the first Stuka formation made a successful attack in the absence of RAF fighters as stated above, and it appears that the first attack on the convoy was indeed met only by ship's anti-aircraft defences,[159] then the action of Beyer's 7 *Staffel* of *III/JG 26* could only have been against attackers of the second Ju 87 wave.

Where do the first five Spitfires from 54 Squadron fit into all this? They were already patrolling over Dover as the German raid first came in[160] and thus also do not fit well with action against *III/JG 26*. This suggests that F/Lt Way's five Spitfires may instead have met the other major fighter escort unit involved in this convoy attack, namely elements from all three Gruppen of *JG 51*. Examination of the German fighter claims for the day shows that *Fw* Schmid of *1/JG 51* claimed a Spitfire over Dover at 15h04 British time (German time was one hour later) while *Hpt* Oesau of *7/JG 51* claimed another 5 km south of Dover even earlier, at 14h52.[161] The claims lists also show clearly that *III/JG 26*'s claims comprised one by *Gruppenkommandeur* Galland at 15h17 over Dover harbour with 7/ *JG 26*'s four claims being made between 15h30 and 15h40 over Dover and south thereof. The claims times thus do support an earlier action by *JG 51*, which logically would fit the five Spitfires of 54 Squadron led by F/Lt Way. The latter small Spitfire formation was also not surprised by German fighters, as implied in the *JG 26* accounts. F/Lt 'Wonky' Way did not hesitate at the odds when they saw the approaching enemy and led his men straight in amongst a mass of Me 109s.[162] Way was seen to shoot down a Me 109, no obvious victim in *Luftwaffe* losses, but was then immediately shot down himself by another Messerschmitt and crashed into the waters of the Channel, his body later washing up at Oost-Dunkerke, Belgium.[163]

Another Spitfire was also lost, P/O Turley-George recalling having been attacked by Me 109s while the Spitfires were still climbing, and he was downed by a perfect deflection shot, crash-landing unhurt near Dover writing off his machine.[164] He also recalled seeing his flight commander being hit, his Spitfire falling away before he was himself forced down.[165] F/Lt Way had called for help on first sighting the enemy, and Red Section led by S/L Leathart was sent to assist them and although they did not manage to join up, they did claim damage to one Me 109 by the commander; P/O Gray of Way's formation also claimed a probable Me 109.[166] F/Lt Alan Deere led another section of 54 Squadron over the convoy at higher altitude, and heard F/O George Gribble, flying in Way's section, calling for his leader to break and then lamenting that Way had been shot down; Deere was refused permission to join the fight and ordered to maintain his height.[167]

Eleven Spitfires of 64 Squadron led by S/L MacDonell were scrambled from Hawkinge as the raid approached at 14h50 and were ordered to climb to 10,000 ft.[168] MacDonell recalled arriving over the convoy to see it under heavy attack by Stukas escorted by a reasonable number of Me 109s; he saw bombs bursting on the convoy as well as two ships in a sinking condition, and then noticed about a dozen more Stukas attacking while bursts of anti-aircraft fire from the convoy continued at low level.[169] Clearly thus, 64 Squadron's arrival was just after an initial wave of Ju 87s began to bomb the convoy, and they then observed a second wave of bombers starting their attack from 10,000 ft as they began their dives. The wily MacDonell brought in his squadron from 12,000 ft and up-sun and attacked the Ju 87s just as they began their dives; not only did he place his squadron in a perfect position to attack the dive bombers, but he also avoided the escort's immediate attention – superb leadership and tactics.[170] As MacDonell and his two wingmen of Yellow Section rolled over, they cut power and dived after the Ju 87s, and as they plunged down could do no more than fire a brief and unsuccessful burst as they dived past the descending Junkers; unbeknownst to MacDonell the remaining eight Spitfires did not dive down with him but instead climbed to attack some of the Me 109s, with just one pilot claiming damage to one of them.[171]

At the time and as a relatively newly arrived squadron leader, MacDonell was still experiencing ill-discipline in his unit and struggling sometimes to maintain cohesion in action as he described in his autobiography, as in this instance. As Yellow Section pulled out of their dives at about 3,000 ft and circled the convoy, MacDonell saw a gaggle of Ju 87s wallowing back to the French coast and pursued three of them, taking the middle one, which fired furiously at him as he closed in, hitting his aircraft before turning turtle and plunging into the sea.[172] Yellow 2, F/O Jeffrey had disappeared from view from the start of the engagement and didn't return, and a parachute seen by MacDonell near the French coast could have been his; Yellow Three had dropped too far behind to catch a Stuka.[173]

The squadron leader called his unit ordering them back over the convoy where further dive bombing was taking place, not realising that most of them were still up at altitude, and as he got there the escorting Messerschmitts now joined in and a dogfight began; MacDonell was hit in the cooling system, smelling burning succeeded by fumes in the cockpit, and as the oil and glycol temperature gauges went off the clock he throttled back, making for Hawkinge and passing low over Dover the anti-aircraft fire from which fortunately missed.[174] On his approach his tortured engine gave in and despite a very hot cockpit full of fumes he managed to put the Spitfire down and came to rest only fifty yards from the far boundary; his canopy jammed and fighting panic, he was a witness to the fatal crash nearby of S/L A. T. Smith of 610 Squadron.[175] After about ten minutes ground crew came to his rescue and released MacDonell from his predicament.[176] The actions described for 64 Squadron better fit the narrative of the *JG 26* history than do those of 54 Squadron, as already discussed above.[177] It is thus likely that 64 Squadron was attacked by elements of *III/JG 26*, including the 7 *Staffel* which, as already related, dived down supposedly with the Stukas, and then pounced on the British fighters (Yellow Section) attacking the descending Stukas. However, this *Staffel* would almost certainly not have been able to maintain their dive in formation with the Ju 87s, as described in the *JG 26* history, as they dived even faster than Spitfires, and 64 Squadron's Spitfires were unable to stay with the Stukas in their dives.[178]

F/Lt Ellis led nine Spitfires of 610 Squadron, including the C/O, S/L A. T. Smith, up from Hawkinge at 14h58 to reinforce the convoy's defences, and arrived off the coast between Dover and Folkestone in time to observe twenty Ju 87s dive-bombing the ships, covered by fifteen Me 109s at 12,000 ft.[179] Ellis met the Messerschmitts head-on and both fighter formations then lost cohesion as dogfights ensued; Ellis attacked what appeared to be the leading Me 109 and fought him for about five minutes, a long time in WWII aerial combat.[180] Then he managed to get in several short bursts at close range, and with his ammunition now finished saw smoke and flames erupting from its engine; his victim was confirmed by both his section wingmen.[181] Three other pilots claimed probables, but S/L Smith's machine was badly damaged and crashed at Hawkinge on his return.[182] F/Lt Ellis had the sad duty of writing the Flying Battle Casualty Report on Tom Smith's loss:[183] after having been seen entering the general dogfight with the Me 109s, S/L Smith was seen approaching Hawkinge in obvious difficulties about half an hour later, his engine smoking and it probably cut out. He crashed into a disused engine testing shed housing some vehicles and the machine burnt out. A Cambridge graduate, he was just two months shy of his 34th birthday, old for the strenuous life of a fighter pilot.[184]

F/O Gardiner was more fortunate, claiming one of the probables in the fighting and being grazed on the arm by a bullet which entered his cockpit from below, and landed his damaged machine safely at Hawkinge.[185] 610 Sqaudron's likely opponents in the combat were *III/JG 52*, which had taken off from their Pas de Calais base at 14h40 to escort Stukas due to attack the convoy; in view of their losing the *Staffelkapitän* of 7/JG 52 in the Dover area, supposedly to a Hurricane, at *c.* 15h40,[186] it would be logical that they escorted the third and final wave of Stukas. F/L Ellis did report attacking the leading Me 109 of a formation and his claim for the destruction of a Me 109 was witnessed by two of his comrades, as described above.

111 Squadron scrambled a full complement of twelve Hurricanes from Croydon soon after 15h00 to come to the assistance of the hard-pressed 54 Squadron, but by the time they arrived, the Ju 87s were gone and they tackled a number of small Me 109 formations largely with head-on attacks, claiming one confirmed, one unconfirmed and two damaged.[187] Major Galland, *Gruppenkommandeur* of III/JG 26, reported a brief skirmish with Hurricanes, thus indirectly supporting having been escort to the second rather than the first Stuka wave and previously fighting against 64 rather than 54 Squadron.[188] Galland describes having seen four fighters fall into the Channel as well as a parachute descending.[189] While he may have seen F/Lt Way of 54 Squadron shot down as he came in with his Ju 87 second wave and may also have seen F/O Jeffrey's 64 Squadron machine dive into the sea, the other RAF casualties fell on land, so Galland may have seen two German fighters fall also; logically, one of these could have been that of the unfortunate *Staffelkapitän* of 7/JG 52. The fourth machine Galland saw falling into the sea may possibly have been the Ju 87 dispatched by S/L MacDonell of 64 Squadron. One further RAF contingent making an appearance over the Channel during this Stuka raid was made up of a flight of six Spitfires of 74 Squadron, led by F/Lt Malan, who claimed to have damaged an Me 109.[190]

With the presumed three Stuka waves having attacked it, the convoy became scattered, but being confined between the coast and the treacherous Goodwin Sands, as in *Oberst* Fink's plan, there was no place to hide; the *Leo* was sunk; *Tamworth* and *Gronland* (Commodore's ship) were badly damaged and towed by tugs into Dover; *Summity* was also seriously damaged, her captain managing to beach the vessel under Shakespeare Cliff near Dover, it later being salvaged.[191] The anti-aircraft gunners on the ships had some revenge when they hit one of the Ju 87s, which exploded.[192] Logically, this Stuka and that claimed by S/L MacDonell of 64 Squadron were two reported lost over the Channel by II/StG 1, time unknown.[193] A Ju 87 of IV/LG 1 was damaged in action, time unknown, and was described in *Luftwaffe* loss lists as having been damaged by fighters off Folkestone;[194] possibly, this was due to the missing F/O Jeffrey of 64 Squadron.

Following this dive-bombing attack on the convoy, as the opponents withdrew to their bases three sweeps of low-level Me 109s passed over the ships, causing little damage, but keeping anxiety levels high; being at low level and fast, they were not spotted by radar.[195] The massive *Luftwaffe* escort of six fighter *Gruppen* escorting the Stukas, equating to something like 150-180 Me 109s, was just too large for the forty six British fighters sent in. Some combination of force of circumstances and choice by RAF unit leaders led almost all formations to go for the

Me 109s under disadvantageous conditions, with only S/L MacDonell performing a superb attack, only by his section, on the Stukas as they dived and pulled up over the Channel waters.

25 July 1940: second attack on convoy CW 8, *c.* 16h15

After the previous large, three-wave Stuka attack on the convoy, there was a lull during which the convoy reassembled.[196] By 16h15 the convoy was sailing off Sandgate, the western part of Folkestone, when an estimated 20-60 Stukas returned, diving out of the afternoon sun and executing their mission well by sinking another four ships, *Henry Moon*, *Corhaven*, *Polgrange* and *Portslade*, and damaging another two, which perforce put into Dover.[197] In total, the convoy lost five ships sunk and another five damaged, one of which was beached and later salvaged.[198] Not long before this second Stuka attack, German E-boats had been reported heading out across the Channel, and making in the general direction of the convoy.[199] Exactly which Stukas were involved in this attack is not known, but they may, logically have been from *II/StG 1*, stationed in the Pas de Calais,[200] as the other Ju 87 unit in that area and thus close to the action, *IV/LG 1* was involved in the next attack on the convoy.[201]

According to their unit history, *JG 26* put up a series of small patrols over the Channel in support of continuing dive bomber attacks, after the first, three-wave assault discussed above, and on one of these lost *Fw* Eberz, 9/*JG 26* shot down and killed south of Dover at *c.* 16h30, supposedly by a Hurricane.[202] Elements of *JG 51* were also involved in covering this raid, with *Hpt* Tietzen, *Staffelkapitän* of 5/*JG 51* claiming a Spitfire over Dover early on at *c.* 16h10.[203] Three Fighter Command squadrons are known to have been put up to intercept this raid, 32, 54 and 64 Squadrons. The first-named unit scrambled at 16h20 with orders to intercept a raid near Folkestone, were redirected onto another incursion but met neither enemy formation.[204] 54 Squadron, scrambled one minute later, also met no enemy but reported a number of E-boats off Calais.[205]

It was only eight Spitfires of 64 Squadron led off from Hawkinge at 16h30 by F/Lt Henstock who saw action during this raid.[206] When they were 3 miles offshore south of Hawkinge at 10,000 ft, the leading four Spitfires observed a *Staffel* of about ten Me 109s in loose formation about 1,000 ft lower; Henstock led the two other members of his Blue Section into a quarter attack, seeing his victim diving away apparently damaged, with F/O Wainwright also firing but seeing no result.[207] F/O Woodward would crash-land at Kenley, while Henstock force-landed at Lympne at 17h00 with an overheating engine from the combat.[208] The gallant Sub Lt Dawson-Paul of Blue Section, one of the Royal Navy pilots seconded to Fighter Command to enhance their numbers and who had enjoyed success during July, was last seen attacking one of the Me 109s and being counter-attacked by several more.[209] He must have survived this initial combat as he was reported shot down much later, at about 17h45, being very badly wounded and landing in the sea where he was most fortuitously rescued by a German S-boat, or MTB equivalent; despite them rushing him to hospital in Hardinghen, north-east of Boulogne, he died of his wounds five days later.[210]

Presumably either he or F/Lt Henstock had accounted for the *9/JG 26* Me 109 lost. Dawson-Paul himself was probably a victim of *JG 51*; in addition to the *5/JG 51* claim noted above, this *Staffel* made two more claims this day, but at times unknown.[211] These three claims could equate to the one lost and two damaged Spitfires of 64 Squadron.

25 July 1940: Royal Navy destroyers attacked in Dover Straits

German E-boats from Calais had been reported off Cap Gris Nez as early as 13h30, and had been tracked westwards up till 16h45 when it was assumed that they were definitely making for the convoy.[212] The difficult yet desired aim of coordinating airborne and seaborne attacks on the ships appears to have been achieved: while one source has the attacks in fact overlapping in time just before 18h00, another has the E-boats arriving just after the bombers had departed, to pick off the stragglers.[213] *Oberst* Fink in his command post at Cap Blanc Nez also reported seeing the E-boats arriving to finish off the scattered ships of the convoy.[214] The Stukas attacking the convoy appear to have arrived at a fortuitous moment between RAF fighter patrols and bombed at their leisure,[215] closely followed up by the E-boats. Two Royal Navy destroyers, HMS *Boreas* and *Brilliant* escorted by a few British MTBs thus sortied from Dover to counter the German naval threat, opening up on the E-boats, breaking their attack and seeing them turn away under cover of smoke.[216] *Oberst* Fink sitting securely, supposedly, in his cliff top command post was somewhat shaken to experience several shells from the destroyers exploding around his headquarters and ordered up a further twenty-four Stukas to drive them away.[217] Unfortunately, the destroyers had approached too close to the French coast, and while avoiding return fire from German shore batteries[218] were vulnerable to the Ju 87s, who could get to them well before they could reach the safety of the British coast and their home port of Dover.

It appears, however, that the Me 110s of *EGr 210* got to the retreating destroyers first; the captain of HMS *Boreas* noted an attack by eight Me 110 dive bombers carried out from ahead at 18h08.[219] He ordered the ship to turn as the first Me 110 began its turn into the attack dive so that his guns could be brought to bear, and although both sides failed to hit their respective targets a number of near misses from the bombs did do significant damage to the ship, which was stopped for a short period.[220] A few minutes later it was the turn of the Stukas to bomb, also from ahead and thus coming out of the afternoon sun, and changing from a loose formation to a line-ahead formation just before committing themselves to the dive; the dive was made at *c.* fifty degrees, an angle steeper than the maximum elevation of the destroyers' main armament, and after dropping their ordinance the Ju 87s made off at low altitude in their usual way.[221] *Boreas* was seriously damaged by a direct hit that exploded deep within the ship in the galley flat, with fifteen fatalities and twenty-nine men wounded; her sister ship HMS *Brilliant* was more fortunate, although hit twice through her stern there were no casualties to her crew.[222] Both vessels required a tow back to the safety of Dover harbour.[223] Anti-aircraft gunners on the two destroyers made claims for two Stukas brought down, with another three claims from Dover's barrage.[224]

Which Stuka unit was involved in this action is uncertain. According to a couple of sources, the Ju 87s which attacked the two destroyers had taken off from Tramecourt and belonged to *StG 1*.[225] Tramecourt was the base of *IV/LG 1* during July 1940.[226] *IV/LG 1* may also have been part of the attacking Stukas.[227] *III/StG 1*, based at Falaise[228] may possibly have moved temporarily to the Pas de Calais for this mission. The unit lost one Ju 87 shot down, one killed, one wounded, as well as two damaged machines in one of which a crewman was wounded; the loss is reported as having occurred over the Channel off Cherbourg, while the two damaged aircraft were hit in locations vaguely stated as over the Channel.[229] All three aircraft casualties are ascribed to attack by 152 Squadron Spitfires off Portland/north of Cherbourg at *c.* 11h15.[230] However, the *Gruppenkommandeur III/StG 1* in his published memoirs describes this westerly mission, which he led, and in his text and in the detailed appendix of casualties to his *Gruppe*, notes only the two damaged Ju 87s, with one gunner wounded, the other bailed out over the Channel and missing.[231] This leaves open the possibility that *III/StG 1* may have flown another mission from Tramecourt in the Pas de Calais area in the evening, without its leader having been involved. The Ju 87 lost by the *Gruppe* may then possibly have occurred over the Straits of Dover.

Direct escort for the Stukas was provided by *III/JG 52*, which took off at *c.* 18h20-18h32 and found themselves in combat already within a few minutes of lifting off.[232] The unit history of *III/JG 52* records the loss of three Ju 87s that day, and with the two lost by II/StG 1 already recorded above in an earlier raid, supports the idea that *III/StG 1* suffered the third one lost, as no other Stukas were lost by the *Luftwaffe* that day.[233] Elements of *JG 51* were also over the Channel at about this time, *Hpt* Wiggers of 2 *Staffel* claiming a Spitfire in the Dover area at 18h20.[234] This suggests they were up before *III/JG 52* and would thus logically have been the top cover for *EGr 210's* Me 110 fighter-bombers.

Three RAF squadrons were launched against the German units attacking the two destroyers, 54, 56 and 610 Squadrons. Precisely which was on the scene first was the subject of some acrimonious debate in some of the relevant official Fighter Command records, 54 and 56 Squadrons being the disputants.[235] 54 Squadron's IPR stated that their ten Spitfires were first on the scene and that they only saw other RAF fighters as they returned home. This squadron claimed to have seen Ju 88s, Ju 87s and Me 109s and apparently dispersed the German fighters enabling other RAF fighters to get at the bombers, such as 56 Squadron.[236] Ten Spitfires had taken off from Manston at 18h00 and were directed to enemy aircraft attacking ships in mid-Channel, i.e. the two destroyers; with Red Section in front, Yellow following, and Blue behind and above as rear-guard section, they were initially forced down from *c.* 10,000 ft to 8,000 ft by clouds and rainstorms in mid-Channel but managed to regain height to 11,000 ft, whereupon they saw four Ju 88s at 12,000 ft that were bombing two destroyers.[237] They also saw a large Ju 87 formation coming in from the Calais direction at 5,000 ft, with several layers of escorting Me 109s, both above the Ju 88s and nearer the French coast, presumably the Stukas' top cover.[238]

Red Leader put his section into echelon port, with Yellow Section sliding above them to act as a guard and with Blue Section even higher; Yellow 1 then warned of Me 109s breaking away from their formation and told everyone to break formation, which they did, all 54 Squadron pilots avoiding the attack with the exception of P/O Finnie who was shot down and killed over the Channel, crashing at Kingsdown, south of Deal at *c.* 18h10,[239] very possibly the victim of 2/JG 51. As was tragically so often the case, Archie Finnie was one of the neophytes who only joined the squadron on 8 July 1940,[240] and with the intense action over the Channel for units like 54 Squadron there was no time for him to be adequately prepared for battle. However, the formation leader (unidentified in IPR) on this occasion had prepared his unit well for imminent attack by 109s from above. 54 Squadron were unable to make any claims in the ensuing fighting and the Messerschmitts kept them off the supposed Ju 88s.[241] The only twin-engined aircraft known to have attacked the convoy, and that before the Ju 87s arrived soon after, were the Me 110s of *EGr 210*, and were likely the aircraft reported as Ju 88s by 54 Squadron. 56 Squadron appears to have been in action very soon after 54 Squadron, as discussed below.

Nine Hurricanes of 56 Squadron from North Weald had first put down at Hornchurch from where they took off at 17h31 to fly a patrol line between Dover and Dungeness at 10,000 ft, just below the cloud base; as the Stuka raid was detected coming in by radar, the controller ordered them to wheel outwards from the patrol line, to the south. Once on the way they spotted the Ju 87s with their strong Me 109 escort above coming in from the south and it appeared defenders and attackers would both arrive above the ships simultaneously.[242] S/L Manton was first to spot the enemy and sent two of his sections down, the first led by F/Lt Coghlan, the second by F/Lt Gracie, to attack the Stukas while his own took on the escort;[243] S/L Manton got his timings right and was successful in getting his two sections amongst the Stukas before the escort could come down.[244] F/Lt Gracie led P/Os Page and Sutton down, managing to tangle with the last few Ju 87s as they began their dives from *c.* 4,000 ft and thereby distracting them somewhat from their bombing, and mostly then contacting the majority of the dive bombers as they pulled out from their dives low over the sea and zigzagged homewards as fast as they could go.[245]

The six Hurricanes of 56 Squadron claimed three Ju 87s confirmed and another unconfirmed, Page and Sutton each claiming one confirmed and Gracie, their section leader, the unconfirmed one.[246] P/O Mounsdon claimed the third confirmed Stuka, and all four claimants saw their victims crash into the Channel.[247] However, as already discussed, it is possible that *III/StG 1* lost a single Stuka with one killed, one crewman wounded[248] on this raid, and thus all four RAF pilots probably saw the same aircraft crash into the water, and some or all of them may have attacked the same machine, an occurrence by no means uncommon in fast and intense air combats. *IV/LG 1* may also have been involved and during the day had a Ju 87 damaged and gunner wounded,[249] possibly also in this action. The lead section of 56 Squadron meanwhile had an approximately ten minute set of dogfights with small numbers of Me 109s, claiming one damaged. S/L Manton's Hurricane was damaged and he was slightly wounded in the combat.[250] *III/JG 52* made only one claim against a British fighter on this raid, a Spitfire claimed east of Margate at 18h50 by *Lt* Decker[251] and may have been responsible. However, it would appear that *III/JG 52*'s main opponent on this raid was 610 Squadron.

III/JG 52 had taken off at *c.* 18h20-18h32 as direct escort for *StG 1* in the Dover area where they lost two Me 109s to Spitfires, that of newly appointed *Staffelkapitän 7/JG 52*, *Oblt* Keidel who was killed, and the other was flown by *Gruppenadjutant Lt* Schmidt, posted missing.[252] Keidel was last seen with two white vapour streams trailing behind his fighter after a Spitfire had attacked him, and his body was later washed up on the German-held coast.[253] F/Lt John Ellis had led off seven Spitfires from Hawkinge at 18h27 and saw the Stukas bombing the destroyers in mid-Channel, then shortly after tackling about twenty-four Me 109s at 10,000 ft over the Channel; while they claimed five confirmed and three unconfirmed Messerschmitts shot down in an attack apparently launched from superior altitude, only two victims were in fact dispatched as discussed above for *III/JG 52*, who claimed a single Spitfire, presumably either from 54 Squadron or in this action with 610 Squadron.[254]

The inevitable over-claiming is once again apparent, but 610 Squadron's attack was flawless and they suffered no damage at all. It is possible that *III/JG 52* were themselves distracted by the attack of 56 Squadron on their Ju 87 charges and some of their own machines. If so, this demonstrates the advantage of 11 Group's tactics of launching several squadron-strength formations of fighters against each raid. Several discrete attacks, often from different directions and altitudes, would often cause confusion for German escorts. Overall, a total of twenty-six RAF fighters had taken on a *Gruppe* of Stukas and two escorting Messerschmitt *Gruppen*, tough odds. Losing one Spitfire and pilot and a damaged Hurricane and with another slightly wounded pilot, accounting for two Me 109s and their pilots as well as one Stuka was a fine performance. The final act in this convoy saga took place early the next morning, 26 July 1940, when E-boats attacked once more and sunk three more ships and damaged another four bringing total losses for the convoy to eight sunk and nine damaged.[255]

25 July 1940: shipping raid off Portland, Western Channel

All of the action related directly and indirectly to Convoy CW 8 throughout much of this day had taken place in the Straits of Dover area. There was one other raid this day to the west, which slightly preceded the first assault upon Dover at *c.* 11h50 related to CW 8. *Hauptmann* Helmut Mahlke, *Gruppenkommandeur* of *III/StG 1* had led his unit up from Theville at 11h03, where they had previously landed to refuel after leaving their base at Falaise earlier in the day, their objective to attack Channel shipping off Portland.[256] This raid and its escort of *III/JG 27*,[257] initially reported by radar as an estimated thirty aircraft and another formation of twelve-plus, first approached Portsmouth, then turned westwards near the Needles and proceeded towards Portland.[258] One pilot of *8/StG 1* reported having seen RAF fighters high above before they dived on the ships off the harbour.[259] Undeterred, the Stukas began their dives, dropped their bombs and were caught by Spitfires at that very vulnerable point of pulling out and before they could join up in formation again. A wild combat began.[260] *Hauptmann* Mahlke reported all his Stukas as damaged, and though this might be something of an exaggeration, two were damaged significantly enough that one gunner from *8 Staffel* was killed and another from the 7th was wounded.[261]

Ten Spitfires of 152 Squadron were led up from Warmwell by S/L Devitt at 10h50, with orders to patrol Portland, and spotted enemy aircraft at about 11h15, which they estimated as eighteen Ju 87s, twelve Me 109s and a single Do17, about 20 miles south of Portland, flying at 10,000-11,000 ft.[262] 152 Squadron, innovatively, had A Flight operating as three pairs, Red, Yellow and White sections,[263] and on this occasion B Flight had only two pairs, Green and Black Sections; they were unusual at this early stage in the Battle flying in pairs rather than vics of three. However, when flying as a squadron, they tended to adopt a formation wherein the three pairs of a flight formed a large six-aircraft vic, with A Flight's vic flying in front of that of B Flight[264] thereby losing much of the advantage potentially offered by using pairs and showing some loyalty to the Fighter Command fixation with the vic formation. Red 1, S/L Devitt's plan of attack did not quite work out, as shown in excerpts from the Intelligence Patrol Report:[265]

> The aircraft of the squadron operated in pairs. When getting within range, 'B' Flight attacked the formation of Me. 109's which was above and acting as a rear-guard to the bombers. A Flight intended to attack the bombers but were immediately attacked by the Me. 109's. A dogfight ensued. S/Ldr Devitt attacked a Me. 109, but he himself was attacked from the rear and tail of his a/c. was hit by cannon. He turned sharply to the right and was unable to see whether or not the Me. 109 went down out of control.

P/O Innes, Red 2 attacked a Messerschmitt from quarter and above, saw his rounds entering its fuselage and then climbed after his opponent for 2,000 ft before firing at it again from 100 yards, whereupon it dived vertically.[266] Innes had to take avoiding action from two more on his tail;[267] neither British pilot thus saw what happened to their foes. It is possible that there were more *III/JG 27* Messerschmitts stacked higher up, as was the German wont, and that some of these came down when S/L Devitt went for the bombers. The only claim made by *III/JG 27* was that of its *Gruppenkommandeur*, *Hauptmann* Schlichting for a Spitfire shot down south of Portland at

12h20;[268] as leader of the unit it is less likely that he would have flown the close escort, seen initially by 152 Squadron, and was probably placed at higher altitude where the chances for a successful bounce were much better. It is thus probable that Schlichting was the pilot who hit and damaged S/L Devitt's Spitfire.[269] One of B Flight's Spitfires also saw action against a couple of the Me 109s, Sgt Sheppard, Green 2, spinning out from an initial attack on himself, on recovery closed on another which streamed smoke, dived steeply and apparently crashed into the sea.[270] However, there is no loss in German records to support this claim.

Out of sight of Red Section, F/O Deansley led his own Yellow Section and the following White Section to attack a lone Do 17 of *Stab/StG 1* flying reconnaissance with this Stuka raid, directly from behind; the hapless Dornier took no evasive action and returned fire from its rear gun, reported as a cannon.[271] Both Deansley and his number 2, P/O Richard Hogg made single rear attacks on the bomber and then shifted their attentions to the Ju 87s.[272] Sgt Wolton, White 1 and P/O Holmes flying his wing both fired at the Dornier, which came down in flames, crashing at East Fleet Farm, within a few hundred yards of the lagoon behind the beach at East Fleet, near Portland at 12h00, with one crewman killed and two taken prisoner, one wounded.[273] As Deansley pulled away from his pass at the reconnaissance Dornier, he saw a mass of Ju 87s attacking ships below and as he dived and shot at a couple of Stukas on the way down, he could see bombs being released around him; flattening out he was able to catch the dive-bombers at their most vulnerable point as they pulled out of their dives, giving one a long burst which finished his ammunition.[274] He also saw the Ju 87's rear gunner returning fire with his single machine gun who was lucky enough to hit his glycol tank, and the Spitfire's cockpit filled with smoke; Deansley immediately headed north for the coast, climbing to be able to report his position to control.[275]

He adopted a unique system for ditching: loosened his straps, crouched with his feet on the Spitfire's seat and as the aircraft touched the sea, he pulled back on the control column and simultaneously kicked clear, finding himself safely in the sea.[276] He was lucky to get away with this method without serious injury. F/O 'Jumbo' Deansley was rapidly picked up by one of the ships he had been trying to protect, the SS *Empire Henchman*, and soon after transferred to an RAF launch that landed him at Lyme Regis, where he was dispatched to the local hospital, slightly wounded.[277]

Richard Hogg, on breaking away from the Dornier, did a brief beam attack on a Ju 87 without apparent result, then followed several diving Stukas down and expended his ammunition on one he found flying south to escape low over the water.[278] Sgt Wolton, White 1, shared this claim with Hogg, firing his remaining rounds into the Ju 87 at *c*. 100 yards and seeing it dive steeply towards the Channel giving off black smoke.[279] Their claim was confirmed based on a report from one of Portland's searchlight batteries, which stated a Stuka crashed into the sea west of Portland Bill at this time.[280] Official claims made by 152 Squadron totalled a Do 17, Me 109 and Ju 87 all confirmed, one unconfirmed Messerschmitt and another damaged, but only the Dornier was in fact shot down and two Stukas damaged without any Me 109s lost or even damaged.[281]

Once more, although the squadron leader's timing did not permit an attack on the Stukas before the escort could intervene, three of ten Spitfires got to the Stukas at their vulnerable moment some minutes later. It is possible this raid was designed to draw RAF fighters to the west before the attacks started in earnest over the Straits of Dover; if so, then the *Luftwaffe* had little understanding of Fighter Command organisation and methodology. 152 Squadron was another using larger ammunition loads than normal, with 2430 and 2750 rounds per Spitfire recorded in their documents.[282]

F/Lt Gleed led seven Hurricanes of 87 Squadron from Exeter to a position about 20 miles south-east of Portland at 15,000 ft, where they saw a small ship being bombed; Gleed divided his flight, leading three down towards the bombers, three were detailed to remain at 15,000 ft as cover, and the seventh Hurricane was ordered to 17,000 ft just into the cloud base to see what might be there.[283] Only this latter machine, flown by F/O Rayner, met enemy aircraft, suddenly seeing three Me 110s flying at right angles to his course on his port side; he had no time to do more than give one short burst at full deflection, seeing the starboard engine of one Me 110 on fire, the Messerschmitt leader half-rolled and disappeared downwards, soon followed by the second after a short burst from its rear gunner.[284] While Rayner did not see his enemy crash he claimed an unconfirmed Me 110.[285] This apparently small group of Me 110s may well have been a top cover for the Stuka raid and its Me 109 more direct escort, or may perhaps have been detailed to look after the lone reconnaissance Dornier shot down by 152 Squadron. That squadron's combats were at a lower level than the Me 110s met by Rayner of 87 Squadron.[286] There is no damaged or lost Me 110 in German losses to fit this episode. Perhaps one was damaged but only lightly and thus not entered into the *Luftwaffe* Quartermaster General Loss Returns. Alternatively, it is feasible that Rayner's targeted Me 110 merely opened his throttles fully, and the engines thus gave off black smoke with F/O Rayner only seeing one of the engines smoking.

Following this morning raid on Portland, and with shipping still vulnerable outside the harbour, Fighter Command flew protective patrols over the area thereafter. As on the eastern end of the Channel where the

Luftwaffe maintained fighter pressure of their own over the Straits of Dover, so too in the west, German fighter patrols were maintained. One of these involved an observed six Me 109s of *III/JG 27* which attacked a section of 1 Squadron, F/Lt Hillcoat, F/O Salmon and P/O Goodman, south of the Needles, Isle of Wight at *c.* 15h20. Salmon claimed a probable Messerschmitt which was seen to spin down and assessed as out of control. Goodman suffered a beam attack by another Me 109, but it appeared to turn away too tightly, flicked and spun into the sea.[287] The two British pilots might well have observed the same aircraft out of control. The unfortunate Messerschmitt pilot was *Oberleutnant* Kirstein of *Stab III/JG 27*, who was lost in the cold, indifferent waters of the Channel.[288]

Further west a little later, Blue Section of 92 Squadron arrived on patrol over Tenby-Pembroke at about 11,000 ft, saw a lone aircraft about 10,000 ft higher and climbed; led by F/Lt Tuck they intercepted a Ju 88 heading north-east at *c.* 16h20, which then turned around and used turning, climbing and diving evasive action in and out of the clouds.[289] The IPR details a set of attacks by all three pilots, mainly from the beam, and less from astern/quarter-astern, closing in to short range; the enemy machine was seen to give off dense black smoke from the starboard engine, and was lost in cloud about 15 miles out to sea off Fishguard. The section claimed one Ju 88 unconfirmed,[290] but no damaged or lost Ju 88 to fit this claim shows up in German records. Blue 2 fired off 2450 rounds, the most of all three pilots, showing this squadron also used more than the standard ammunition load.

26 July 1940; spasmodic shipping attacks, Western Channel

Poor weather prevented most operations this day but *VIII Fliegerkorps* made use of cloudy conditions to attack ships in the general area south of the Isle of Wight.[291] Here spasmodic shipping attacks were made by the Stukas of this *Fliegerkorps*, and Fighter Command ordered Tangmere sector to send up a flight to intercept. Six Hurricanes of 601 Squadron were dispatched; the squadron lost one machine in the Channel with another damaged flown by F/O J. H. Riddle.[292] The 601 Squadron flight was bounced by a free chase, with P/O Chaloner Lindsey's aircraft falling into the sea 2 miles off St Catherine's Point, Isle of Wight, at 10h00.[293] His body was later washed up on the French coast and buried there.[294] The only German claim made was by *Oberleutnant* Max Dobislav, 9/ JG 27 for a Hurricane about 9 miles south of the Isle of Wight at 10h05,[295] and this can thus be accepted readily. F/O Riddle is reported as having returned to base earlier, at about 09h40, due to engine trouble, his machine being assessed there as undamaged;[296] If this is true, his absence may have contributed to the flight being bounced successfully by Me 109s. In return 601 Squadron claimed a probable Me 110 and a damaged Me 109, which are not supported by German loss reports. The Me 110 may have been a reconnaissance aircraft, as *V/LG 1*, the only Me 110 unit attached to *VIII Fliegerkorps*, did not fly any operations until the afternoon.[297]

Around midday there were further *Luftwaffe* incursions, the twelve Hurricanes of 238 Squadron being sent aloft to patrol Swanage at 10,000 ft, subsequently being informed that the enemy was south-west of Portland at 12,000 ft.[298] F/Lt Walch leading Blue Section put his three aircraft into line astern and climbed after three Me 109s he had spotted at 14,000 ft, heading back across the Channel.[299] The three Messerschmitts maintained a ragged formation of a staggered pair, or standard *Rotte* formation, and a lone wingman to the right, at which Walch gave a one-second burst from the quarter as the French coast neared; the enemy machine half-rolled, dived vertically down and went into a spin, the wings breaking off and the remnants going into the Channel.[300] Walch may have hit the pilot for such a violent result from a very short burst. *Fw* Boer of *2/JG 27* failed to return to his base after this combat, which took place 25 miles south of Portland at *c.* 12h00.[301]

Other members of 238 Squadron briefly duelled with Me 109s, presumably also from *JG 27*, Sgt Little's Hurricane being damaged in a head-on attack on some Me 109s off Swanage at about the same time.[302] *V/LG 1*'s Me 110s reported two escort missions over the Isle of Wight area in the afternoon, the first at 14h35-15h25, perhaps escorting a reconnaissance mission? The second was protecting Ju 87s at 18h40-19h50, but neither incursion met any RAF fighters.[303]

Two other actions this day related to reconnaissance aircraft. In the Dover region, British radar tracked six enemy aircraft flying inland from Dover towards Ashford, whence they turned back towards Folkestone; twelve Spitfires of 65 Squadron were scrambled at 16h29 and saw a Do 17, which promptly disappeared again in the thick clouds.[304] Red Section having thus lost the enemy, Blue Section then spotted what they identified as a Ju 88 at about 7,000 ft and the indefatigable F/Sgt Franklin held on in pursuit in and out of the clouds as it fled towards France, and as he climbed and got close, was suddenly attacked by a diving Me 109, which he promptly avoided and then attacked himself from astern; he claimed he damaged it vitally and watched it crash into the sea off Folkestone.[305] *5(F)/122* reported a Do 17 slightly damaged in combat,[306] and this was most likely the reconnaissance machine tackled by Franklin, but no Me 109 appears in *Luftwaffe* loss lists for the Dover area or adjacent France for the day.

Soon after 16h00 a section of 92 Squadron Spitfires intercepted a lone Ju 88 in rain clouds south of Pembroke far to the West, and while they attacked it from close range and observed heavy smoke from one engine, again no potential casualty can be identified in *Luftwaffe* loss lists.[307] A Do 17 from *3/KG 76* went missing with its crew from a mission to Rochford airfield, off Portishead Point in Essex, time unknown;[308] it does not appear to fit either action by 65 or 92 Squadrons. The RAF noticed that on three occasions on this day in the Isle of Wight–Portland area, German raids did not fly closer than 5 miles from the coastline, and that as soon as any RAF fighters were sighted, they set course back to France.[309]

8

27–29 July 1940: Repeated Attacks on Harbour and Naval Vessels at Dover; Limited Attacks on Convoys and Naval Vessels off Harwich and in Western Channel

27 July 1940: convoy attacked off Portland; 09h20

This day was to be marked, once more, with attacks on convoys along with bombing of naval targets in Dover harbour and off Harwich. Stopping Channel shipping movements and clearing naval forces before the planned invasion, Operation Sealion, remained the German agenda during July 1940. A large British convoy codenamed 'Bacon' was steaming off Portland early this morning when it was found by *Luftwaffe* reconnaissance aircraft; as a result, soon after 08h00 the Germans dispatched an armed reconnaissance force, supposedly composed of thirty Ju 87s of *I/StG 77* escorted by Me 109s from *JG 27*, to make the initial attack.[1] However, there is some confusion in accounts of the attack(s) on convoy Bacon: an earlier attack is proposed, supposedly met by a section of 238 Squadron which shot down a Ju 87 from *I/StG 77*, followed by a second, later attack involving 609 and 145 Squadrons from the RAF, and *I/StG 1*.[2] From RAF records there is firm evidence for only one action by the British fighters, involving machines from 238, 145 and 609 Squadrons, during which a Ju 87, which could only have been from *I/StG 77*, was dispatched while escorts from *JG 27* shot down a 609 Squadron Spitfire.[3] So there seems little doubt that the later attack was by *I/StG 77*'s Ju 87s, escorted by elements of *JG 27*, and that the earlier German mission, described as an armed reconnaissance, did not result in combat. Whether *I/StG 1* formed part of this reconnaissance force or was perhaps a second wave behind *I/ StG 77*, as explicitly stated by one source,[4] is unknown.

10 Group of Fighter Command had kept a section of three Hurricanes from 238 Squadron on convoy patrol over 'Bacon' since about 08h40

and only at the end of their patrol about an hour later did these machines become involved in combat, along with members of 609 Squadron.[5] At 09h20 after detection of a one-plus radar plot between the Needles and Swanage, 11 Group put up Blue Section of 145 Squadron from Tangmere to intercept, while 10 Group scrambled Red Section of 609 Squadron a quarter of an hour later after the same target.[6] Was this German incursion possibly the armed reconnaissance, or a fighter sweep ahead of the main raid?

At 09h42, British radar plotted an incoming raid of twenty-plus about 20 miles directly south of Portland and 10 and 11 Groups responded with significant reinforcements: 11 Group scrambled the remaining three sections of 145 Squadron and vectored them to 20,000 ft over St Catherine's Point on the Isle of Wight, simultaneously ordering Blue Section, already airborne, to join up with them; 10 Group sent up the remaining three sections of 609 Squadron to patrol at 15,000 ft over the convoy, then in Weymouth Bay, while instructing Red Section of the squadron to join up with them there.[7] The lone section over the convoy, Red of 238 Squadron, was then coming to the end of its patrol and was about to be replaced by Green Section, and 10 Group ordered the whole squadron of twelve Hurricanes to assemble above 'Bacon'.[8] However none of the three reinforcing sections of 238 Squadron made it in time as Middle Wallop was just that much too far away from the forthcoming action.[9]

609 Squadron actually managed to rendezvous over the convoy, and leaving Red and Yellow Sections over the ships, B Flight flew about 10 miles to the south, meeting a formation of Stukas at 17,000 ft arranged in three parallel lines astern with an outlying Ju 87 on both sides, escorted by a large formation of Me 109s flying about 3,000 ft higher.[10] Two of their Spitfires climbed and skirmished with the Me 109s, while P/O Buchanan, Green 1, took off southwards, soon being lost to view by his section;[11] his two wingmen, P/Os David Crook and Johnny Curchin, had turned away for a good look behind and as they turned back round again their leader had disappeared.[12] The original convoy escort of Red Section, 238 Squadron, led by S/L Fenton, had seen the three reinforcing sections of 609 Squadron climb out of nearby Warmwell and followed their one flight as it went southwards.[13] Fenton's radio had failed and he handed over to Red 2, seeing his two wingmen follow the 609 Squadron Spitfires to take on the Ju 87s while he climbed to tackle some Me 109s above them, chasing one, which came down to attack Red 3, to within 5 miles of the French coast.[14]

S/L Fenton was also witness to a Spitfire being shot down, which can only have been P/O Buchanan of 609 Squadron, and to his wingman P/O Davis (Red 2) dispatching one of the Stukas, a machine from *I/StG 77* that plunged into the waters of the Channel with its crew, south-east of the Shambles lighthouse.[15] *Oberleutnant* Framm from *I/JG 27* claimed a Spitfire shot down during combat off Weymouth, at about 10h20[16] and was almost certainly responsible for the loss of P/O Buchanan. 145 Squadron after successfully rendezvousing as instructed, met the same Ju 87/Me 109 raid about 20 miles off the coast just after 10h00 between the Needles and Swanage, where they claimed a Messerschmitt shot down, apparently witnessed by a Spitfire (Buchanan prior to his own demise?) though nobody from 609 Squadron acknowledged this.[17]

27 July 1940: naval assets in Dover attacked twice

Further attacks on convoy Bacon were prevented by bad weather, including severe thunderstorms, and nothing of note happened until the ships passed the western coastal boundary of the Biggin Hill sector of Fighter Command, just east of Beachy Head in the early evening.[18] Air Vice Marshal Park dispatched three squadrons of 11 Group to forward bases at Hawkinge (501 and 615 Squadrons) and Manston (41 Squadron).[19] It was a prescient move, all three units seeing action. It was not the convoy that was attacked but rather naval assets in Dover harbour. There were two attacks, one by the Me 109-equipped fighter bombers of *3/EGr 210*, six machines using the cover provided by the bad weather to sneak in at *c.* 14h30, dropping four light bombs on the harbour that damaged the destroyer *HMS Walpole* and another five projectiles on the barracks there.[20] As always employing innovative tactics, *3/EGr 210* came in at low level, high speed and from the landward side, several near-misses damaging the destroyer.[21]

The second Me 109 attack on Dover, shortly before 18h00 was to have much more serious results. Again, a small formation of *3/EGr 210* Me 109s were the aggressors, and this time were observed coming in from the Folkestone side at *c.* 7,000 ft and then dive-bombing ships in the harbour, releasing their bombs and escaping at low level, only about 50 ft above the water.[22] The few bombs scored at least one more near-miss, on the destroyer *HMS Codrington* moored alongside a depot vessel, HMS *Sandhurst*; the destroyer broke her back and sank at her moorings while *Sandhurst* suffered damage.[23] The twelve Hurricanes of 501 Squadron were sent up at 17h36 with orders to patrol Dover–Deal at 5,000 ft, and as the raiders came in they were seen bombing the ships in harbour with others just entering their dives; the squadron's efforts to interfere were spoiled by the Dover anti-aircraft barrage opening up, splitting the squadron.[24] Two of the Hurricanes managed to close enough with some Me 109s to open fire, but with little if any effect, and the leader of the formation, F/Lt P. A. N. Cox, was not seen again after the anti-aircraft guns opened up and was presumed to have fallen victim to friendly fire.[25]

S/L Hood had led B Flight of 41 Squadron, soon reduced to five machines by an early returnee, at 17h20 to patrol the area and was vectored onto the incoming Me 109s; F/Lt Webster broke formation and attacked one at low level as it pulled out of its dive and claimed to have seen it dive into the Channel off Dover, and skirmished with another two before returning to Manston.[26] As *3/EGr 210* returned over the Channel in the Calais direction, the Me 109 at the back was attacked by a single Hurricane. The entire *Staffel* turned back and three pilots attacked it as the Hurricane in turn veered away, *Lt* Marx causing the fatal damage and being credited with the victory; the three German pilots saw what can only have been F/Lt Cox's Hurricane dive into the Channel outside of Dover from about 1,000 ft, on fire.[27] One source ascribes this lost Hurricane to a pilot of *III/JG 52*, but the *Gruppe*'s unit history records that no operations were flown on this day.[28]

Twelve Hurricanes of 615 Squadron, sent forward towards Hawkinge from Kenley, were flying in pairs, three sections, Green, Yellow and Red, each of two machines making up A Flight; just before arriving there, they were vectored onto a He 59 air-sea rescue seaplane north-east of Dover, which they rapidly dispatched into the Channel on fire, only one wounded crew member being rescued, with S/L Kayll apparently doing much of the damage.[29] On this day, the loss of two destroyers to the *Luftwaffe*, a second being sunk off Aldeburgh, as described below, and reconnaissance data showing the Germans setting up a battery of long range, heavy guns in the Calais area, ranged on Dover, led the Royal Navy to relinquish Dover as an anti-invasion base, withdrawing the vulnerable and precious destroyers to Harwich and Sheerness.[30] However, they remained a potent defensive weapon close to hand, with four flotillas deployed between the Humber estuary and Portsmouth.[31]

That busy *Gruppe*, *EGr 210*, launched their Me 110s against a naval group off the East coast not long before their Me 109 *Staffel* attacked Dover for the second time, at *c.* 18h00 as described above. At 17h06 while two Royal Navy destroyers were providing anti-aircraft protection for a flotilla of six minesweeping trawlers, they were attacked off Aldeburgh; the assault was variously reported, as having been carried out by fifteen Ju 87 dive bombers or by He 111s of *KG 53*.[32] HMS *Wren* suffered several near misses from dive bombers, leading to her being holed below the waterline and was sunk,[33] while the second destroyer, HMS *Montrose* was damaged. While Heinkel 111s are reported to have made an attack on this small naval force and an aircraft and its crew were reported missing this day from *4/KG 53*, it is unknown what damage they may have inflicted.[34] The dive bombers reported by the ships were in fact Me 110s from *EGr 210*, which entered a claim for two cruisers sunk and one of their own machines and its crew of *2 Staffel* blown to pieces by a direct anti-aircraft hit just before it could release its bombs on one of the destroyers.[35] Apparently both destroyers were hit in the same attack *c.* 20 nautical miles off Aldeburgh,[36] most likely from the Me 110s. Exactly what target elements from *KG 53* may have attacked remains unclear. With the regular arrival and departure of convoys from the Thames Estuary northwards up the East coast, regular minesweeping operations were essential, and this attack once again was aimed at disrupting British coastal traffic. The successes scored by *EGr 210* this day were significant: two destroyers sunk, two damaged for the loss of only one of their aircraft. These fast fighter-bomber raids on coastal harbours or convoys at sea were very difficult to intercept.

In a minor action, three Spitfires of 234 Squadron led by F/Lt Hughes intercepted a lone Ju 88 reconnaissance aircraft of *3(F)/121* about 25 miles south-west of Land's End soon after 15h00.[37] The Ju 88 made a desperate dive almost to sea level to try and escape but was fired at by all three pilots who expended all their ammunition, silencing both rear gunners, with one being seen to fall from the damaged Ju 88 at a height of only *c.* 150-160 ft above the sea; while the three RAF pilots claimed an unconfirmed victory, the Ju 88 got away damaged and made a successful belly-landing at base minus the unfortunate missing gunner, *Gefreiter* Schmidt.[38]

As is clear from the relevant IPR, the 234 Squadron pilots fired from ranges estimated at 200 and 300 yards, which with the relatively light calibre 0.303 inch machine gun rounds was just not close enough for a lethal result. This lesson was learnt rapidly by the section leader, F/Lt 'Pat' Hughes, who became the leading scourge of his unit, building up a very respectable score before losing his life in an attack on a bomber which appeared to have been from too close a range, on 7 September 1940.[39] This was the essence of tactical engagements in the Battle for the RAF machine gun-armed fighters: for real success a close-range attack was essential with inherent risk to the attacking pilot each time. Many paid the price for this reality, despite their often superior experience and abilities and proven success, in contrast to others who fired from further away and were often wrongly convinced of their success.

28 July 1940: F/Lt Hughes strikes again; deception over Dover

Early in the morning, at 05h25, three Spitfires of Blue Section, 234 Squadron, lifted off from St Eval, being ordered to Plymouth; once there, plentiful anti-aircraft fire drew their attention to a single Ju 88 diving steeply at a target on the ground.[40] Leader F/Lt Hughes cannily waited for the Ju 88 to pull up from its dive when it was at its most vulnerable and closing in from 100 to 50 yards, much closer than on the previous day, hit the starboard engine, which issued volumes of yellow-grey smoke.[41] The two wingmen followed in and after the third attack the starboard engine was in flames and the machine plunged into the water, disappearing within a few seconds, no survivors being seen.[42] The aircraft was from *II/LG 1* and only one wounded crew member was rescued from the sea.[43]

Over the Dover Straits subterfuge was the order of the day, no doubt due to the influence of the newly appointed German fighter boss, or *Jagdfliegerführer (Jafü)* of *Luftflotte 2, Generalmajor* Theo Osterkamp. At about 12h00 British radar stations at Dover, Rye and Pevensey tracked two large German formations either side of Calais making for Dover, but halfway across the Channel they turned back and dispersed.[44] About ninety minutes later a second raid was picked up coming in, and as they neared the coast, the Observer Corps counted more than sixty He 111s and about forty Me 109s.[45] Once again, the bombers retired before crossing the coast but the German fighters carried on.

The main action on this day then took place in the Dover area with four Fighter Command squadrons involved, numbers 74, 257, 111 and 41, against four *Staffeln* of I and II/JG 51 as well as III/JG 26. A point of interest in this action has long been how the leading German ace, *Major* Werner Mölders, just appointed to lead *JG 51* and first fighter pilot to hold the coveted Knights Cross, came to be shot up and wounded, only just making it back to France. There has been considerable debate whether Spitfires of 74 or from 41 Squadron were the victors, and on the merits of various aces' claims, such as the famous F/Lt 'Sailor' Malan of 74 or F/Lt John Webster from 41 Squadron.

The IPR for 74 Squadron clearly describes how they observed between six and nine Me 109s in a vic formation approaching Dover from the direction of the sun (essentially from the west) at about 18,000 ft, to attack some Hurricanes, presumably at a lower level. F/Lt Malan leading the squadron as Red 1 coming in from approximately north-east of Dover – they had taken off from Manston, north-east of the town – and slightly above the Messerschmitts, shrewdly turned port at exactly the right moment and dived, placing the Spitfires of Red and Blue sections perfectly behind the Me 109s and unseen.[46] Malan fired at one of the Me 109s, using five two-second bursts as he closed from 250 to 100 yards, the enemy fighter making only gentle right-hand turns and slowing down as Malan closed in, leading him to conclude its controls had been hit.[47] Anyone under fire and their aircraft being hit would normally have reacted rather more violently. P/O Stevenson, number two in Malan's section, fired briefly on a second Me 109 flying next to Malan's target from a range of *c*. 250 yards and it dived for the French coast.[48] Both British pilots then fired brief deflection shots at Messerschmitts passing across their noses, with P/O Stevenson then moving on to a third enemy fighter diving away for France, giving it a long burst from dead astern and leaving him with the impression it was badly damaged.[49] Stevenson's engine then seized but as he was by then at 20,000 ft he managed to glide his Spitfire to a successful landing at Manston.[50]

Apparently, Red Section had badly damaged two Me 109s, but seeing as the relevant claims were made sequentially it is possible they may have been against the same aircraft, Stevenson catching up to Malan's already damaged victim diving hard for home and safety. From the original documents detailed in the notes, Red Section had attacked various aircraft from the originally sighted vic formation of six-nine Me 109s, thus likely from a single German *Staffel*.

Flight Lieutenant Kelly, leading Blue Section of 74 Squadron some 300 yards astern and to port of Malan's section, had just turned in behind the first vic of Me 109s when he saw three other Messerschmitts cutting across in front of him at *c*. 300 yards range, and managed a snap shot at them with no apparent effect; he then saw a further three Me 109s on his left and diving rapidly.[51] Kelly used the Merlin engine boost cut-out to catch one of these diving Germans and fire at him with a slight deflection from 250 yards, noting flames appearing on its port side as it dived away; Blue 2 confirmed this enemy aircraft was giving off smoke and glycol, after which Kelly observed it diving into the sea, still burning.[52] P/O Stephen, Blue 2, attacked one of these Me 109s seeing some hits in its tail and rudder.[53] P/O John Freeborn, leading Yellow Section, had watched Malan make his attack and then, noticing some thirty more Me 109s above and behind, climbed and attacked a Messerschmitt from the rear, firing at some 200 yards range and seeing it burst into flames; he was himself then attacked by more Me 109s, slightly wounded and his Spitfire damaged, but he got away and nursed his aircraft back to Hornchurch.[54] As only one Me 109 was lost in the Dover area that day, again it is possible that Freeborn and Kelly had fired at the same victim.

P/O St John, flying number three position in Freeborn's section, noted a group of eight Me 109s – again, what must have been a whole *Staffel* – fired at one which broke away and he saw some hits, but on looking behind his Spitfire and seeing four Me 109s on his tail, dived rapidly through a cloud, coming out and passing straight through a Hurricane squadron, no doubt to each party's surprise, then pulled out of his headlong dive and finding himself alone, went back to his base.[55] There thus appear to have been three *Staffeln* of Me 109s involved from the various reports emanating from 74 Squadron: the vic of six-nine attacked initially by Malan and his Red Section; at least two sets of vics of three each noted by F/Lt Kelly; and finally the eight reported by P/O St John. On the German side, three distinct *Staffeln* reported combat in this battle.

Firstly, *1/JG 51* claimed a Spitfire over Dover at *c.* 15h15 by *Ofw* Karl Schmid while the Me 109 flown by *Uffz* Erwin Fleig was damaged 20% and belly-landed at Wissant.[56] Schmid's victory likely was the Spitfire of Sgt Mould, hit and wounded in the left leg over Dover, who bailed out, his flaming aircraft coming down in the northern part of the town itself at *c.* 14h30.[57]

Secondly, *2/JG 51* suffered the loss of *Gefr* Martin Gebhardt shot down into the sea off Dover; although a claim by him for a Spitfire over Dover at *c.* 14h35 is shown in a *JG 51* claims list, it does not figure in Tony Wood's confirmed claims list.[58] Thus Gebhardt's claim was not confirmed. The fact that he was able to make a verbal claim over the radio before himself being shot down and lost, suggests strongly that 2/JG 51 was the second *Staffel* or group of Me 109s, that noted by F/Lt Kelly of Blue Section 74 Squadron, diving down on Red Section under Malan as they attacked another *Staffel*. This latter would logically then have been *1/JG 51* with *Uffz* Fleig most likely being the Me 109 attacked by both Malan and Stephenson. Gebhardt of *2/JG 51* was probably dispatched by the combined efforts of Kelly and Freeborn of 74 Squadron who saw a flaming Me 109 diving down into the sea.

Thirdly, the Me 109 *Staffel* noted by Yellow 3, P/O St John, must then have been *3/JG 51*; *Oblt* Leppla, its *Staffelkapitän*, claimed a Spitfire shot down at *c.* 14h40.[59] This victory by Leppla has often been described as his having shot a Spitfire off the tail of *JG 51 Kommodore* Werner Mölders, as the latter nursed his badly damaged Me 109 back across the Channel, discussed in more detail below. However, Mölders' wingman who was a direct eyewitness to much of what happened to his commander that day, clearly states that he and his boss saw their action after all the rest of *JG 51* had been ordered back to France.[60] Mölders himself was wounded, frightened and struggling to reach the French coast in a dying aircraft and would not have been able to make detailed observations of what was going on around him.

There is another possible Spitfire which might have fallen to Leppla. P/O Young of 74 Squadron is thought to have plunged into the Channel off Dover, close to the coast, as described in the relevant casualty file.[61] The Spitfire which some 74 Squadron pilots thought they saw going down in flames near the Kent coast could alternatively have been *Gefr* Gebhardt's Me 109. While James Young's aircraft was also reported as down in the sea near the Goodwin Sands with its pilot missing,[62] this officer was in the end not missing. As described in his RAF casualty file, his Spitfire crashed into the sea just off the coast at Escalles, France, where his body was also found, on the beach, and he was buried the same day by the Germans alongside the road to the seashore from the nearby village of Escalles; the grave was discovered after the war, his one dogtag still nailed to the wooden cross, and he was later reburied in Pihen les Guines, the recognised British war cemetery in that part of France.[63]

Coincidentally, just a few miles up the coast towards Calais, was *Stab/JG 51*'s base at Cap Blanc Nez, whence Mölders had taken off that morning for the mission. Young was presumably chasing after a Me 109 right across to the French coast and was possibly surprised by *Oblt* Leppla returning home himself, to shoot a Spitfire off the tail of a comrade he assumed to be the wounded *Kommodore* in his failing Messerschmitt; it might even have been *Uffz* Fleig's damaged Me 109 that Leppla saved. Stevenson's Spitfire has been interpreted as Leppla's victim quite often,[64] and quite logically so, it having suffered a seized engine supposedly near the French coast. However, there is nothing in the 74 Squadron IPR that says Stevenson's aircraft was in fact hit over the French coast before he managed to glide back across the Channel to Manston. Such a long glide from the French coast to Manston would anyway almost certainly not have been possible, even from high altitude. It did not take too much use of boost cut-out, which many RAF fighter pilots applied when they felt it was warranted, to make even a Merlin engine seize up.

Major Mölders had led up four *Staffeln* from I and II/JG 51 to escort a convoy raid, with *III/JG 26* as top cover.[65] When the He 111s making up the bomber force turned back short of the coast and made for France, the two sets of Me 109s carried on and flew over south-east Kent; it is uncertain whether the bombers turned back due to RAF fighter reaction or whether their presence was a planned decoy. In view of the ideas of the recently appointed *Jafü*, *Generalmajor* Theo Osterkamp, the latter is more likely.[66] The He 111s possibly belonged to *KG 53*, based in the Lille and Vitry-en-Artois areas,[67] which lay inland of Calais, and on a line passing through both Calais and Dover. They were operational, suffering losses also, both on the day preceding and the one after 28 July 1940.[68] When the escort leader Mölders saw a Hurricane squadron over the Dover area at a lower altitude, he would logically have used his I/JG 51 Me 109s to bounce them and cause likely heavy casualties; it was German fighter policy always to try and use superior numbers from a favourable tactical situation. As already argued above, 1 *Staffel*, followed by the 2nd and 3rd, in that order, were just coming in to start their attack on the Hurricane squadron when F/Lt Malan brought 74 Squadron into the picture and spoiled their plans. Through judicious manoeuvring he managed to insert his twelve Spitfires onto the tails of the leading *Staffel*, 1/JG 51, and he was obviously also aware of 2/JG 51 coming up from behind.[69] Despite this possibly unfavourable situation, Malan's timing was good enough that his first two sections were able to make a successful surprise attack on *1/JG 51* unhindered before *2/JG 51* was upon the rear two sections of 74 Squadron, following which the usual rather chaotic dogfight began.

This cost *I/JG 51* one Me 109 seriously damaged, which belly-landed on the French coast, and another destroyed, its pilot dead; in exchange *I/JG 51* dispatched the Spitfire of Sgt Mould, its wounded pilot bailing out successfully. P/O James Young of 74 Squadron seems to have become involved in a chase made by several of the Spitfires of the first two *Staffeln* back across the Channel. Behind were the Me 109s of *3/JG 51* who shot Young down over the French coast. Malan thus saved the Hurricane squadron from a possibly nasty and costly bounce, gained the initiative and caused casualties to *I/JG 51* while paying the price of being outnumbered in his two lost Spitfires, one pilot killed, another wounded, and two more damaged.[70] Malan's acceptance of the inherent risks in such tactics can be read from the relevant Intelligence Patrol Report excerpt:[71]

At 1350 hours twelve aircraft 74 Squadron were ordered to intercept enemy raiders over Dover. Visibility was good with 2/10 cloud at 6,000 ft. Orders were received by R/T to attack enemy fighters, and leave bombers to Hurricanes. Climbing to 18,000 ft. a Vic formation of 6 or 9 ME. 109's were sighted at 18,000 ft. coming from the sun towards Dover to attack some Hurricanes. Red Section turned onto the tails of the enemy aircraft and Red 1 led Section to attack. [R/T radio-telephone; Red 1 = Malan]

74 Squadron's total claims were four unconfirmed Messerschmitts, with another probable and five damaged; while greatly exaggerated, these optimistic claims in the IPR point to the generally favourable tactical leadership they had enjoyed. *I/JG 51* made three claims in all, two of which were confirmed.[72]

The Hurricane squadron at lower altitude saved from being bounced through Malan's attack could have been 257 Squadron, scrambled from Hawkinge at 13h32, eighteen minutes before 74 Squadron was launched from Manston, and which had orders to tackle the bombers while Spitfires took on the Me 109 escorts.[73] However, 111 Squadron makes a more likely candidate. Above, P/O St John described diving headlong away from pursuers, and on passing out of clouds then through a Hurricane squadron without any warning.[74] Logically, this would have broken up the Hurricane formation. 111 Squadron itself reported attacking two He 59 seaplanes *c.* 10 miles west of Boulogne later on, each attack being carried out by two separate pairs of Hurricanes, indicating a somewhat scattered squadron formation by then.[75]

The other Hurricane squadron flying in the general area at the same approximate time as 74 Squadron, 257 Squadron, was attacked north-east of Dover and lost a Hurricane to German fighters.[76] At the time Red and Green Sections were ahead and still together, with Blue Section having fallen a bit behind, and the squadron leader saw Blue 3 being hit; Yellow Section was to the right of Blue, and below.[77] The fact that the squadron leader saw Blue 3 being shot down supports that a relatively coherent squadron formation was thus maintained, which argues against the surprise of a Spitfire of 74 Squadron suddenly emerging from clouds and diving straight through it. Blue 3, Sgt Forward, at the moment of attack was with the rest of his section, at 5,000 ft, changing from a line astern to a vic formation.[78] He was therefore the perfect victim for a typical German bounce attack from above and astern – logically he would have been the rear machine for descending attackers, Yellow Section being lower down. Despite being covered in petrol in a cockpit now also full of fumes, Sgt Forward bravely kept his head despite petrol up to his knees, opening the hood, gliding down in a Hurricane still controllable and not using the engine due to the obvious fire hazard.[79] Remarkably, he managed a successful crash-landing at Laughton Abbey, West Langdon, despite a single oleo leg down and the other up, also no flaps, suffering only from petrol and oil in his eyes.[80] The Hurricane, though was a write-off.[81]

Several ground observers reported two aircraft nipping out of cloud and firing on Forward's aircraft, which then fell away,[82] then promptly pulling back up into the cloud. They could only have been from *III/JG 26*, who were flying top cover to *JG 51*;[83] *Major* Adolf Galland and his wingman, *Oblt* Müncheberg of *Stab III/JG 26* both claimed a Hurricane within a minute of each other at 15h14-15, some 10-15 km north-east of Dover.[84] However only the claim of Müncheberg was confirmed.[85] It was common practice for a *Gruppenkommandeur* flying with his Staff *Rotte* or *Schwarm* at the head of his unit to bounce likely isolated or vulnerable victims, his wingman or men in attendance, and under the protective umbrella of the entire *Gruppe* at altitude, who could intervene if danger threatened. *Fw* Carl of *9/JG 26* made a claim for a Spitfire some ten minutes later, also north-east of Dover,[86] but this may well have related to 41 Squadron, whose role is discussed below.

Much attention in Battle of Britain literature has been given to trying to link a specific RAF pilot, generally a known ace, to the wounding of *Major* Werner Mölders, the newly appointed *Kommodore* of *JG 51*. Mostly it has come down to promoting either F/Lt Malan of 74 Squadron or F/Lt Webster of 41 Squadron. The two German pilots involved in this action, Mölders himself and his wingman, *Geschwader* adjutant *Oblt* Erich Kircheiss, both left accounts of the combat and each states that they first attacked a few Spitfires, with more seen to be coming behind, which then attacked them.[87] As already discussed, 74 Squadron Spitfires surprised a *Staffel*-sized Me 109 formation before becoming involved with other Messerschmitts. 41 Squadron records equally clearly show that their leading section of Spitfires was attacked by two Me 109s[88] before further Spitfires joined in. Kircheiss's description of the combat also confirms that he and Mölders attacked the Spitfires after the rest of *JG 51*'s fighters had already left the scene, and 41 Squadron was the last RAF unit to take off and see combat in this set of actions over south-east Kent. The facts thus favour 41 Squadron having met Mölders.

Mölders himself described how he and Kircheiss spotted a vic formation of three Spitfires below, to the north of Dover, with others visible in haze behind them, Mölders sending one of the vic down in flames after which he was assailed by eight to ten other Spitfires who initially got in each other's way.[89] Inevitably, however, he was soon hit with serious damage to radiator and fuel tank and he was forced to dive away for the Channel, followed by vengeful Spitfires, but *Oblt* Leppla shot down his nearest pursuer.[90] He was lucky to make the French coast with a fading engine, where he belly-landed at Wissant and only on getting out did he find he was wounded, with five splinters in his legs.[91] His Me 109 was a write-off.[92] Kircheiss's account adds some context to Mölders' story.[93] Kircheiss was shot down and made a PoW on 28 August 1940, thereby surviving the war and being able to tell his side of the story. Having ordered the rest of the *JG 51* fighters home, presumably by then only *6/JG 51*, Mölders and his wingman stayed up high at about 25,000 ft and looked for some trade, then turned for home before spotting the vic of Spitfires *c.* 5,000 ft beneath them.[94] Once the Spitfires retaliated after Mölders' victory, the two German pilots dived away separately, Kircheiss diving and turning frantically to get rid of his pursuers; he made it and landed at Wissant where he discovered two hits to his engine.[95]

41 Squadron were over Dover at 20,000 ft, flying in sections line astern and stepped down, sections 200 yards apart, Blue Section led by S/L Hood in front, followed by Green with F/Lt Webster leading, then Red with F/Lt Ryder in front, and Yellow Section led by P/O Bennions, when attacked by two Me 109s.[96] The squadron had flown out over the Channel in order to approach Dover from the south and thus intercept any outgoing Me 109s, and were in a spiral climb when attacked.[97] The two Me 109s were seen already when 2,000 ft higher, as they came in at the rear of Blue Section, first by Green 1 who gave a warning to S/L Hood,

and then also by Red and Yellow sections who similarly warned their leader; only once attacked did Blue Section react.[98] This stepped-down formation used by S/L Hood for 41 Squadron was not very effective as he and his section, in the lead and at the highest relative altitude, saw nothing of their attackers as they came in. While the lower sections did spot the attackers and try to warn their squadron leader, the initiative had been lost to the Germans.

The German leaders almost always flew in stepped-up fighter formations, the leader in front and lower, and thus well protected and able to lead effectively. F/O Wallens, Green 2, had been placed 1,000 ft below his section to prevent attack from below – probably a rather unlikely event – and was thus out of the forthcoming fight before it started; he, too, witnessed the incoming attackers.[99] Altogether it was a rather strange formation used by 41 Squadron in this action. As the two Me 109s attacked Blue Section, they finally reacted by turning to port, but their assailants merely followed them around closing in from dead astern on S/L Hood and Blue 2, F/O Lovell.[100] F/Lt Webster, Green 1, pulled up and opened fire at one of the Me 109s, but was not successful in saving Lovell from being hit at *c.* 14h35 and his Spitfire fell behind, its pilot slightly wounded (Margate Hospital; non-operational for a week) and petrol sloshing about in his cockpit due to a cut fuel line. Courageously Lovell flew back to Manston where he crashed, further damaging the Spitfire.[101] Green 3, P/O Shipman, had followed Webster as ordered but was behind him initially and observed Webster's attack on the one Me 109, seeing it half-roll and dive away.[102] Shipman made a brief attack on the other Me 109 but Yellow 1, P/O Bennions, flew between him and the enemy, effectively cutting off his attack.[103] An excerpt from the squadron Intelligence Patrol Report describes what Bennions did next:[104]

> Using emergency boost, he closed in full deflection 200-100 yards. The enemy turned over on its side, and went almost vertically down, he followed, full boost, and gave two more bursts of 4 seconds each. Whole of enemy aircraft was now enveloped in black smoke. Yellow 1 pulled out at 3000 and found two E/A on his tail. Returned to base from 15 miles south of Dover.

From his position below the rest of the squadron, Green 2, P/O Wallens, was able to confirm that Bennions' victim turned over, then dived vertically for some thousands of feet giving off thick blue smoke, but he did not see a crash.[105] Bennions' Spitfire suffered minor damage, the flaps being unserviceable and the machine hit by several bullets.[106] F/Lt Webster skirmished with a few outgoing Me 109s, diving down to sea level before extricating himself and getting home at full boost.[107]

From the accounts of both Webster and Bennions there were several additional Me 109s on their way home over the Channel that got involved with some of the 41 Squadron pilots after the two lone Me 109s had first attacked Blue Section of 41 Squadron, shooting up F/O Lovell's Spitfire. Logically, these two Messerschmitts were those flown by Mölders and his wingman Kircheiss, who made just such a lone attack after departure of the balance of *JG 51*. Some of the latter probably hung around over the Channel, chasing a few of the 41 Squadron Spitfires pursuing Mölders back across the Channel. The *JG 51 Kommodore* made a claim for a Spitfire over Dover at *c*. 14h35 and *Fw* Haase of 6/*JG 51* also claimed one,[108] probably in action against 41 Squadron machines further out over the Channel. Mölders' claim was confirmed, but not that of Haase.[109] *Fw* Carl of 9/*JG 26* could also have become involved with a 41 Squadron Spitfire if he was a bit behind his *III/JG 26* comrades in crossing back over the Channel. As to who shot down Germany's then leading ace, *Major* Werner Mölders, it would appear that P/O Bennions was most likely the successful pilot, possibly assisted by P/O Shipman's brief attack.

As this set of actions between *JG 51*, *JG 26* and the defending RAF fighters petered out, the Germans sent a number of air sea rescue He 59 floatplanes out to retrieve their (and enemy) airmen who had come down in the Channel.[110] 111 Squadron initially sent up to intercept the German raid, specifically the bombers, was later diverted to mid-Channel; P/O Wilson spotted one of them over some ships *c*. 10 miles west of Boulogne at about 15h15, and while Wilson refrained from firing due to the red cross markings on the enemy machine, Sgt Robinson bored in and shot it down, the floatplane bursting into flames and crashing into the water, sending up a large column of smoke.[111] Five minutes later, another pair of pilots from the squadron found a second He 59 which had alighted on the water to aid the first crew, and F/O Ferriss and P/O Basil Fisher strafed it, the latter holding his fire after a short burst, again due to the red crosses, but Ferriss gave it the works, claiming an unconfirmed victory, the floatplane in fact being a write-off at 60% damage.[112] This second machine was from *Seenotflugkommando 1* and suffered two wounded crew members, and that shot down by Robinson, from *Seenotflugkommando 3*, had two crewmen killed and the other three wounded.[113] A third He 59 , also from *Seenotflugkommando 3*, was lost in the evening off Denmark, after an attack by a Hudson of 220 Squadron who saw their rounds hitting home; only one of the five crew members was rescued, wounded.[114]

The 1,563 grt freighter *Orlock Head*, sailing as part of Convoy OA190 from London to Liverpool, was lagging behind the convoy when bombed by a German aircraft and set on fire north-west of Thurso in Northern Scotland; four crewmen were killed and three seriously wounded, of whom two later succumbed to their wounds.[115] The time of the attack is not known. They must have fought back some as four of the crew were later awarded Commendations.[116] A He 115 floatplane of *3/KüFlGr 506* went missing on this day and may have been the aircraft involved, all three crew members being killed by ship's anti-aircraft fire.[117] This *Staffel* was based at Stavanger, Norway,[118] just over 300 miles almost exactly due east of where the attack on the vessel took place. In the evening, a Spitfire of 19 Squadron was damaged in a crash-landing at its base, Duxford, after having attacked a Ju 88 at about 18h00; the pilot, Sgt Roden was unhurt.[119]

29 July 1940: major Stuka raid on Dover

RAF radar clearly saw a German build-up behind Calais at about 07h00 but British fighter controllers delayed sending up and vectoring fighters because of two fairly big convoys off the coastline of the 11 Group area, until it could be inferred where the German aircraft were likely heading for.[120] After about a quarter of an hour, what had originally been interpreted as four formations amalgamated into a single eighty-plus formation, apparently making for Dover, identified as the target by *c.* 07h20, local sirens going off at that time.[121] As the German aircraft neared the coast, the Observer Corps identified them visually as thirty-plus Ju 87s and fifty-plus Me 109 escorts.[122] In fact there were forty-eight dive bombers from *IV/LG 1* and *II/StG 1*,[123] representing Kesselring's full complement of these aircraft from his *Luftflotte 2*. The approximately eighty Me 109s were from *I* and *II/JG 51*, *III/JG 52* and *III/JG 26*.[124] *III/JG 52* flew a free chase mission,[125] while *III/JG 26*, which worked together with *JG 51* on the escort, did not intercept any British fighters[126] and thus presumably flew the top cover. Both *JG 51* and *JG 52* saw action but against Fighter Command machines relatively low down, *c.* 12,000 ft and lower. The main action fell to the two *Gruppen* of *JG 51*.

The 11 Group controller ordered off two squadrons to patrol Dover at *c.* 07h10, comprising eight Hurricanes of 56 Squadron from Rochford and eight Spitfires of 64 Squadron from Hawkinge; as it became clear that Dover was indeed the target of the German raid, eleven more Spitfires from 41 Squadron were scrambled at 07h22, initially orbiting their forward base at Manston before being ordered forward to the Dover area.[127] Although official squadron records for 501 Squadron have their eleven Hurricanes as being scrambled only at 07h45, the same document clearly states that this squadron took off immediately after the departure of 64 Squadron from the same forward base of Hawkinge.[128] This is corroborated by reported interaction between the two squadrons once in action: the damaged Spitfire of Sgt Binham, 64 Squadron, was escorted from the Channel back to land by a 501 Squadron Hurricane, Binham force-landing near St Margaret's Bay.[129] All four RAF squadrons, numbers 56, 64, 41 and 501, fought the German aircraft during and shortly after the dive-bombing of Dover harbour in the region of the port.

The two Stuka *Gruppen*, *IV/LG 1* and *II/StG 1* approached the coast of Kent just to the east of Dover and then turned in behind Dover Castle, which lies just to the north-east of the town and harbour, so as to be able to dive down on the shipping in the harbour from out of the early morning sun in the east; they were observed manoeuvring in this way and then diving steeply from *c.* 2,000 ft by firefighters in the port.[130] With the same logic in mind, the German escort was placed to the right of the incoming Ju 87s, i.e. to the east and up-sun of them[131] and also of any attacking British fighters.

The first Fighter Command squadron to meet the *Luftwaffe* attack appears to have been 41 Squadron[132] and they were flying at *c.* 12,000 ft.[133] The pilots of 41 Squadron, who were flying towards Dover from the north-north-east from Manston could see the German raid approaching from the Channel as they neared Dover, firstly about a dozen Me 109s to their starboard and about 1,000 ft lower, and soon afterwards they observed another formation of these fighters to their port and 1,000 ft higher than them, plus more Me 109s above that.[134] The greatest danger for the RAF fighters in this scenario lay in the second group of Me 109s, those flying about one thousand feet higher, which the 41 Squadron pilots saw wheeling across the sun in line astern to attack them from behind.[135] They did indeed launch an effective attack on 41 Squadron, causing casualties and disrupting any effective attack on the Ju 87s below, who were already bombing the port.[136]

Claims made by *I/JG 51* pilots were essentially over Dover and a few minutes earlier than those made by *II/JG 51*, which were more to the north-east of the port.[137] This suggests that the two Me 109 formations, one *c.* 1,000 ft below and the other about the same height above 41 Squadron as it came in to intercept, belonged to *I/JG 51*. *II/JG 51* obviously attacked 41 Squadron later and further from Dover, so would logically have been the Me 109s seen flying higher up. *III/JG 26*, which, as already stated, was likely top cover to *JG 51* was probably too high for any interceptions. Claim times for the *III/JG 52* fighter sweep are later than most of those by *JG 51* and are mostly against Hurricanes rather than the exclusively Spitfire claims of *JG 51*;[138] so the *JG 52* sweep followed up at the end, to protect outgoing Stukas and escort Me 109s. They appear to have been involved mainly against 56 Squadron over Dover itself, this squadron thus being last to intercept of the four RAF units vectored against the Dover raid. 64 Squadron probably engaged elements of *I/JG 51* (possibly also from *II/JG 51*) in the Dover area just after 41 Squadron's interception, both these Spitfire squadrons also getting at some of the Ju 87s. 501 Squadron Hurricanes came in shortly after 64 Squadron, mostly attacking Ju 87s as they retreated back across the Channel and were largely spared Me 109 attentions[139] due to the actions of the two Spitfire squadrons, 41 and 64.

41 Squadron was flying with Blue Section in front, led by S/L Hood, followed by Red, then Yellow Sections, and Green was the rear-guard section, flying at *c.* 13,000 ft, above the rest at *c.* 12,000 ft.[140] Combat commenced at *c.* 07h35,[141] and available sources differ on exactly what happened at the start and what orders S/L Hood gave his men. Several sources claim that Hood ordered one flight, that he was leading, to go for the Ju 87s and the other, led by F/Lt Webster, to tackle the Me 109s of the second, higher formation, coming in from about 1,000 ft above.[142] However, as is clear from several other sources, all four sections went into line astern as S/L Hood had ordered, and then three of them, Blue, Red and Green, dove down to attack the lower Me 109 formation, flying about 1,000 m lower than them, with Yellow Section being led by P/O Bennions diving further down to attack three Ju 87s.[143]

As Hood led his men down into the attack on the lower Me 109s they saw the second Messerschmitt formation, coming out of the sun and turning in behind them from c. 1,000 ft above; he was faced with a dilemma. The Squadron Leader appears to have kept to his attack on the lower formation, and it was only F/Lt Webster who broke away from the squadron attack and turned to face the incoming Me 109s from above.[144] Webster opened fire on one of the Me 109s, closing from 200 to 50 yds, saw it catch fire and spin down, then observing it flatten out lower down and hit the sea near the South Goodwin lightship.[145] But the aircraft seen to hit the sea near the Goodwin Sands belonged to 41 Squadron itself, and was F/O Gamblen's Spitfire which was seen to fall flaming into the sea at that location by a searchlight post and some of the staff of a radar station at Leathercotes 1 km further up the coast, to the north-east of St Margaret's Bay.[146] Webster's 'victim' thus probably flattened out above the sea and made off for France at high speed just above the waves, with Webster melding the spin with the unfortunate F/O Gamblen's demise; thus does overclaiming of the perfectly innocent kind occur.

While the Squadron Commander's Report on Flying Battle Casualty for F/O Gamblen claims that no one saw what had happened to him, this is untrue. While Webster, Green 1, had broken away from the attack on the lower Me 109 formation to try and tackle the second higher German fighter formation coming in from behind, Green 2 P/O Wallens and Green 3 F/O Gamblen continued their dives and as the latter was within range and just about to open fire on a Me 109, Wallens saw two other Me 109s closing on Gamblen from above and behind; he screamed a warning to his friend to no avail.[147] Wallens observed the leading Messerschmitt hit Gamblen's Spitfire with a concentrated fire pattern that he thought must have killed the pilot immediately, and he could only break away himself rather violently and watch the stricken and smoking Spitfire dive down to hit the sea and break up before disappearing.[148] While Gamblen's Spitfire led to a false claim by Webster, Wallens' violent breakaway probably also misled the attacking German fighters to claim him in addition to Gamblen. Wally Wallens thus clearly saw what had happened to his friend F/O Gamblen and must have reported this on his return to base as well. However, the Casualty Report for Gamblen was written on 7 August 1940, some days after the events and this must have been forgotten by then by the squadron intelligence officer as the Battle continued unabated; Wallens was still an active squadron member then before being seriously wounded in early September 1940.

While Green Section at the rear of the 41 Squadron line astern formation was engaged as described above, S/L Hood, Blue 1, had an easier time of it at the front. Hood led his squadron down onto the lower Me 109 formation of *c.* twelve machines, and attacked the number two aircraft of the rear German section from a very close range he estimated at only twenty yards; giving off clouds of smoke this Me 109 evaded his further attentions to starboard and he did not see what happened to it.[149] P/O Morrogh-Ryan, Red 2 in the section immediately behind Hood's Blue Section, observed the Me 109 burst into flames and dive into the Channel.[150] However, no Messerschmitt lost that day fell into the sea, with losses confined to three machines which crashed with varying levels of damage in France.[151] Red 2 may thus also have seen Hood's Me 109 evade and dive down smoking from its engine under full throttle and then as it rapidly dived down he may, like F/Lt Webster, have seen the crash of Gamblen's Spitfire and misinterpreted this as being the Me 109.

S/L Hood meanwhile fastened onto another Messerschmitt, which dived vertically away in the Me 109's standard evasive manoeuvre, Hood following close behind at only 50 yards, but as he opened fire the enemy machine pulled out of its dive, forcing Hood to break violently away to avoid colliding with it.[152] By now S/L Hood was at low altitude and saw one of the retreating Ju 87s flying just above the sea, closed in again to 50 yards and expended his last 4 seconds of ammunition on it. He watched the dive bomber plunge into the sea about 7 miles off Dover.[153] Having no witness to his success, Hood was only able to claim an unconfirmed victory back at Hornchurch after landing.[154]

S/L Hood's leadership of his squadron can be examined here. It does not appear from the available records[155] that Hood had seen the second, higher Me 109 formation coming down from up-sun onto their tails as he ordered the attack on the lower Messerschmitts. Green and

Yellow Sections, the two rearmost sections of 41 Squadron, were clearly surprised by the second bunch of Me 109s from above and rear.[156] It was only F/Lt Webster leading the rear-guard Green Section who warned of this unexpected attack and broke away to face it.[157] Hood's leadership in attacking the lower Me 109 formation cannot be faulted, but multi-layer German fighter protection was often the norm in the July (and later) battles and up-sun was always the place to look for them; Hood might thus have taken more care before committing his men to the first attack on the lower formation. These first two German Me 109 formations, only 2,000 odd feet apart vertically, effectively constituted a decoy in the shape of the lower Me 109s, with ambush party above, as described by P/O 'Wally' Wallens, flying as Green 2.[158] This tactic worked for the Germans as they thoroughly disrupted the attack of the two rearmost sections, Green and Yellow of 41 Squadron and had all the hallmarks of the direct or indirect influence of *Jafü 2*, *Generalmajor* Theo Osterkamp. It was his firm policy as the effective fighter leader in *Luftflotte 2* during July 1940 to try and ensure that RAF casualties were to be five times those of their own, and all sorts of stratagems to improve successful ambush tactics were encouraged, discussed and implemented.[159]

Yellow Section of 41 Squadron led by P/O Bennions formed line astern and dived down on S/L Hood's orders, but went right past the lower Me 109 formation tackled by Hood and presumably most of Blue and Red Sections (though not all, P/O Shipman attacked a Ju 87, for example) and attacked six Ju 87s below.[160] As Bennions opened fire on a Ju 87 he was himself attacked by a Me 109 which he evaded after taking some hits and followed down to *c.* 8,000 ft where the Messerschmitt started to circle and climb slowly; unseen, Bennions closed in and opened fire at about 200 yards but due to the damage his Spitfire had suffered only his starboard guns were working.[161] After three bursts and closing to *c.* fifty yards range, he finally seemed to get some hits as the Me 109's engine gave off copious smoke; it then climbed almost vertically and its propeller ceased to turn, but as Bennions followed he was attacked again from behind and he half-rolled away, almost stalling.[162] Hit again, his oil pressure sank to zero, the engine temperature soared and he could smell burning metal, so he made for forward base at Manston where he had to land without flaps and with a punctured port tyre, making a set of fairly spectacular ground loops as a consequence.[163] Despite his best efforts, however, his Spitfire was a write-off.[164]

Like Yellow 1, number two in the section F/O Scott was also surprised by the Me 109s as he attacked the Stukas off Dover at *c.* 07h50 next to Bennions; the Me 109 got so close that Scott's Spitfire was hit in the wings by eight cannon shells, but the fuselage and pilot within were only slightly damaged.[165] The aircraft's undercarriage collapsed on landing at Manston and it was written off as a result.[166] The third member of

Yellow Section, Sgt Carr-Lewty, obviously managed to escape the attentions of the avenging Me 109s as he described seeing a Hurricane from 56 Squadron, coded US-K, in hot pursuit of a Me 109 in a shallow dive but with another unseen Messerschmitt to his own rear.[167] Getting himself directly behind this second Me 109, Yellow 3 gave it a five-second burst of fire, closing from 200 to 100 yds, and saw it spin violently down with black smoke issuing from both sides of the machine, as confirmed by a no doubt relieved Hurricane pilot.[168] Breaking away from this action at about 5,000 ft, Carr-Lewty ended with a brief and apparently ineffective attack on a Ju 87 flying alone away from Dover to the north-north-east,[169] a rather strange direction to take homewards. Carr-Lewty claimed the Me 109 destroyed, confirmed.

Apart from S/L Hood, the rest of Blue and Red Sections enjoyed little success in their attacks against, first, the lower Me 109 formation, and second against the lower-still Ju 87s. Together these two sections numbered only five Spitfires. One of them flown by P/O Shipman managed to get amongst some of the dive-bombers, but his intended target evaded him with a stall manoeuvre.[170] Another of these five Spitfires, that of P/O Mackenzie, tried to attack five Me 109s from below, but they turned on him damaging his machine badly and also jamming the hood; the pilot stayed calm, got rid of his attackers and located a field near Ringwould, south-west of Deal, which was free of anti-invasion obstacles, where he made a successful forced-landing and the Spitfire was salvaged.[171] F/Lt Webster after breaking away from Green Section to tackle the descending second formation of Me 109s saw some Ju 87s in line astern on their bombing run over Dover harbour; he closed fast on the slow Junkers and approaching to within 50 yards fired a long burst at the last one, which gave off smoke, but he was then driven off by several Me 109s, with whom he jousted having no ammunition left.[172] He managed to get rid of them, descended to sea level and made for home at full boost; but his aircraft had been damaged and crashed when he touched down at Manston, damaging it further.[173]

Although it is always a hazardous business assigning specific losses to individuals claiming victories, some educated guesses can be made in the case of 41 Squadron. As already suggested, *I/JG 51* with two formations of Me 109s, one *c.* 1,000 ft below, the other *c.* 1,000 ft above 41 Squadron initially, were likely the first opponents of this squadron, seeing action against them a bit earlier than *II/JG 51* and over Dover itself, approximately. This *Gruppe* claimed three Spitfires confirmed, two by *Oblt* Joppien of *1/JG 51* and the other by *Oblt* Terry of *Stab I/JG 51*, with two more being adjudged as probables only and one rejected by this unit applying the German claims system.[174] These could fit the losses of F/O Gamblen, killed, F/O Scott whose aircraft was written-off after crash-landing, and the first, earlier damaging of P/O Bennions' Spitfire.

II/JG 51 claimed three Spitfires a bit later (07h35, 07h40, 07h43) and a little way north-north-east of Dover: one confirmed Spitfire claimed each by *Hpt* Tietzen *5/JG 51*, *Oblt* Priller *6/JG 51* and *Uffz* Haase of the same *Staffel*.[175] These three confirmed claims could fit the losses of the Spitfires of P/O Bennions (second, later attack on him) which was written off after crash-landing at Manston, the damaged Spitfire of F/Lt Webster, also crash-landing at the same forward base, and P/O Mackenzie's machine which force-landed in a field south-west of Deal, damaged. *II/JG 51* is thus thought to have been the higher flying Me 109 formation seen by 41 Squadron, and logically attacked a bit later than the lower positioned *I/JG 51*. *II/JG 51* also claimed a confirmed Spitfire and another adjudged as a probable by the German system to the west of Cap Gris Nez, even later (08h55),[176] which will be discussed below.

In total, 41 Squadron claimed two Me 109s confirmed and two shot down unconfirmed, i.e. no witnesses.[177] These were all claimed over the sea near Dover, two being claimed to have been seen diving into the sea; however, *JG 51* had only three losses this day, all of which fell over France, two being written off and one damaged 50%.[178] Two of the Me 109s were from *II/JG 51*, one crash-landing at the coast near Calais, its pilot being killed (*Fw* Hemmerling, 6 *Staffel*), after claiming a confirmed victory west of Cap Gris Nez; the other Me 109 made it to Le Wast (inland from Boulogne), force-landing with a dead engine and was 50% damaged, the pilot unhurt.[179] Neither of these German losses logically fits any of 41 Squadron's claims, made over the Channel close to Dover, leaving only the third German loss as a possible victory for the squadron. This was the Me 109 flown by *Hptm* Erwin Aichele of *Stab I/JG 51*, who managed to get his badly damaged aircraft back to the French coast but crashed in flames and died when it turned over as he tried to do a wheels-down landing on the beach at Wissant.[180] Aichele was thirty-nine years old and a highly experienced pilot, having flown as a Messerschmitt works test pilot in 1932 already.[181]

As discussed previously, both S/L Hood's confirmed and F/Lt Webster's unconfirmed claims were seen smoking or on fire before plunging into the sea, and they very possibly saw the demise of the unfortunate F/O Gamblen of their own squadron, who did indeed hit the sea in flames. They likely saw their supposed Me 109 victims diving at full throttle, thereby giving off lots of smoke from their straining engines, and as they flattened out near the sea and were lost to view, they may have seen nearby the Spitfire crashing into the sea on fire.

Sgt Carr-Lewty saw the Me 109 he attacked spin violently down issuing smoke from both sides of the nose, again possibly not seriously damaged. P/O Bennions' unconfirmed claim against an Me 109 described following a diving Messerschmitt down which had previously attacked him and inflicted minor damage, whereupon it began to circle and climb slowly at about 8,000 ft, enabling him to close in unseen and obtain some hits which led to it giving off lots of smoke.[182] Its pilot then did a strange thing, climbing almost vertically upwards and then its propeller stopped turning, and Bennions saw no more as he was himself attacked for a second time and this time his Spitfire was seriously damaged.[183] Was this perhaps the highly experienced Aichele, former test pilot, doing a risky manoeuvre by climbing vertically at full throttle and then cutting his engine? It is possible; alternatively, he may have been wounded and his engine damaged by Bennions' attack. We will never know the truth. Someone, most likely from 41 Squadron, did mortally hit *Hptm* Aichele's Me 109, causing his fatal crash-landing at Wissant.

Overall, 41 Squadron had been thoroughly bested by *JG 51*'s tactics, no doubt inspired by *Jafü 2*, Theo Osterkamp's teachings and fighting philosophy: for an apparent maximum loss of only one Me 109 and its pilot to 41 Squadron, the German pilots had killed F/O Gamblen, and damaged four other Spitfires, two of which were written off in crash-landings at forward base, and another further damaged in a force-landing in a field.

Documentary information on 64 Squadron's experiences on this raid is thin, there being no IPR preserved in the available files; recourse must thus be had to second-hand published sources, printed and digital. S/L MacDonell, leading the eight Spitfires of 64 Squadron, recorded victories over a Stuka and an Me 109 in his logbook.[184] Three of the eight Spitfires appear only to have joined MacDonell once combat had begun, and the S/L apparently damaged a Me 109 as well.[185] One other pilot of this squadron is credited with victories, P/O O'Meara, who dispatched a Ju 87 into the sea off Dover, and followed this up by damaging two more, one of which was on fire.[186] F/Sgt Adrian Laws of 64 Squadron is described as having been part of an engagement against a flight of Me 109s near St Margaret's Bay, claiming a probable Me 109; one of his colleagues, F/Sgt E. M. Gilbert, recalled the squadron meeting twelve Me 109s and Laws setting his opponent on fire.[187] Apart from the squadron leader and O'Meara, at least one other pilot, Sgt Binham, got at the Stukas as well, but his Spitfire was damaged by return fire during combat over the Channel and he was escorted back to the coast by F/O Gibson of 501 Squadron, where Binham made a force-landing near St Margaret's Bay at 07h30, his aircraft being recoverable.[188] It is entirely possible that S/L MacDonell and F/Sgt Laws attacked the same Me 109, in succession, and this may well have been the one belonging to *4/JG 51* that force-landed in France with 50% damage.[189]

In the 501 Squadron IPR, their eleven Hurricanes are recorded as taking off from Hawkinge straight after 64 Squadron, who were to patrol *c.* 5,000 feet higher than the Hurricanes; the latter initially flew at 5,000 ft, which order was later changed to 8,000 ft.[190] Presumably then, 64 Squadron also increased their patrol altitude accordingly. 501 Squadron reported sighting the incoming Dover raid just as they turned south-westwards from their position above Sandwich,[191] which lies 18-20 km north-north-east of Dover. While 501 Squadron proceeded first south-west behind Dover, to avoid its effective anti-aircraft barrage as ordered by the controller, before turning north-east once more over the sea while flying south-west of and close to Dover,[192] it would appear that 64 Squadron flew directly towards Dover from the Sandwich area, getting at the Germans before 501 Squadron and from a more advantageous altitude of, presumably, *c.* 13,000 ft. This would imply that 64 Squadron's combat took place over St Margaret's Bay, as reported by Sgt Binham and F/Sgt Laws; their combat initially against a group of about twelve Me 109s and then against possibly still-diving and subsequently low-flying dive-bombers out over the sea would logically have expanded out over the Channel waters.

Using times in action[193] suggests that 64 Squadron attacked a few minutes after 41 Squadron, respectively, 07h25 and 07h22, followed by 501 Squadron very soon after that, at 07h26, and finally, 56 Squadron intercepted at *c.* 07h33, all in the greater Dover area and out to sea towards the French coast. With 41 Squadron reporting three Me 109 formations sighted and action with two of them,[194] it is logical that 64 Squadron benefitted from this, facing only the third formation, of *c.* twelve Messerschmitts, presumably from *II/JG 51*. With some of the 64 Squadron Spitfires tackling these Me 109s, others were able to get at some of the Stukas, as described above. 41 Squadron, a few minutes earlier dealing with two formations of German fighters, faced a more difficult task and were bounced by what appears to have been a deliberate German tactic, and paid the price in casualties. 501 Squadron following up on 64 Squadron, were fortunate, catching the retreating Stukas as they made off at low altitude over the Channel.[195] The final act of this raid was the arrival very soon after of 56 Squadron, to meet *III/JG 52*'s sweep out, designed to protect retreating Stukas and escort Me 109s from *JG 51*, now short of fuel and no longer able to protect their charges effectively. The times into action[196] suggest that all four RAF squadrons intercepted within about four minutes of each other; with the Spitfires, Hurricanes and their Me 109 opponents flying in excess of 300 mph and once fighting began, in highly divergent directions, the aircraft rapidly became dispersed all over the sky, leading to that well known and oft-reported phenomenon of violent action amongst many aircraft being quickly followed by pilots suddenly finding themselves completely alone.

The eleven Hurricanes of 501 Squadron were led on this occasion by P/O Lee flying as Blue 1, despite the presence of F/Lt Stoney flying in the Red 2 position in a section led by P/O Gibson, the senior officer on this mission. However, 501 Squadron had obtained a new squadron leader in Harry Hogan after leaving France late in June 1940, and he had introduced a new system, ignoring rank, whereby the most experienced and able pilot led a formation into action.[197] This showed leadership of a high order by the new commander, and was an innovation which would help to keep 501 Squadron flying throughout the Battle in the thick of things, maintaining high morale and effectiveness despite high casualties. When 501 Squadron first sighted the incoming Dover raid as the Hurricanes turned over Sandwich, north-north-east of Dover and some seven kilometres south-west of Margate, and headed south-west inland from Dover itself to avoid its anti-aircraft barrage, as advised by the controller, the wily P/O Lee did not head straight for the enemy as 64 Squadron, flying above them, apparently did.[198] 'Hawkeye' Lee led his men past Dover, turned south over the Channel and headed back up the coast in a north-easterly direction once more, making for a position offshore of Dover,[199] where he no doubt intended to meet the outgoing Stukas, heading out to sea at low level after bombing their target, and then vulnerable. All the while he also knew that 64 Squadron would have diverted at least some of the Me 109s; in the event, the combined activities of 41 and 64 Squadrons' Spitfires had diverted pretty much the entire escort from *I* and *II/JG 51*, leaving the field free to 501 Squadron to exact a price from the dive bombers.

P/O Lee led his Hurricanes down in a dive onto the Ju 87s and the squadron made a total claim of two Ju 87s confirmed, one destroyed unconfirmed, two probables and four damaged, plus one Me 109 confirmed; a massive haul for a single bullet through the wing of P/O Bland's Hurricane.[200] As would be the case with most Stuka parties in the Battle, the fighting was confusing, with whirling aircraft all over the place and attacking fighters often getting in each other's way; the Stukas being very slow were also manoeuvrable. P/O Lee hit one, saw it give off white smoke and then lost sight of it in the confusion.[201] F/Lt George Stoney, although a highly experienced pre-war airline pilot with over 5,000 flying hours, was new to air combat; in a later BBC radio broadcast, he described seeing one Ju 87 go down in flames under the attentions of six Hurricanes, and shared another with a colleague which blew up, and finally pursued several others out over the Channel for some 12 miles before being attacked himself and avoiding this, returned safely home.[202] P/O Lee reported the combat taking place as far as 10 miles south-east of Dover.[203]

Some Me 109s from *6/JG 51* from the Stuka escort managed to get away from the fight against the Spitfires just north-east of Dover and came to the aid of the hard-pressed dive bombers. Two of them reported victories over Spitfires west of Cap Gris Nez, placing them not far from the location reported by P/O Lee; only *Fw* Hemmerling's claim at 07h55 was confirmed.[204] Hemmerling's Me 109 was however hit, and he was killed in a subsequent crash-landing outside Calais,[205] probably the victim of F/Sgt Morfill of 501 Squadron, the only member of that unit to claim a Me 109. Who Hemmerling may have attacked from 501 Squadron for his victory claim is not clear, but F/Lt Stoney did report being shot at by a German aircraft far out, *c.* 12 miles over the Channel.[206]

At least one Spitfire of 64 Squadron was also mixed up in 501's combat during which P/O Gibson reporting shooting down a Ju 87 on the tail of a Spitfire – a very plucky Stuka pilot! – Gibson escorted Sgt Binham's damaged Spitfire back to the coast to a successful force-landing.[207]

Total claims noted above against the dive bombers amounted to two confirmed each to 64 and 501 Squadrons, one each unconfirmed to 41 and 501 Squadrons, two probably destroyed by 501 Squadron and one damaged by 41 Squadron, two more by 64 and four by 501 Squadron. These claims have to be balanced against actual casualties: two total losses of Ju 87s to *IV/LG 1*, both apparently shot down into the sea during fighter combat off Dover, both crews being lost; in addition, *II/StG 1* lost one shot down into the Channel by fighters from which the crew was rescued, another which was damaged by fighters and written off crash-landing at St Inglevert in France with one wounded aboard, and finally, one which made it back to its base, 30% damaged by fighters over the Channel, one crew member wounded.[208]

Despite all five Ju 87 casualties being ascribed to fighter combat, Dover's harbour master reported two shot down by the Dover defences; it was a significant anti-aircraft barrage and included some Z rocket batteries that fired a projectile which automatically opened a small parachute, beneath which dangled trailing wires with small explosive charges attached.[209] Curtains of such projectiles were observed to have entangled two Ju 87s, one of which suffered an explosion at low altitude; other ground observers noted a Stuka hit simultaneously by two ack-ack shells which blew it to pieces, with fragments seen raining down, and two more Stukas staggered and made out to sea trailing black smoke.[210]

F/Lt Stoney and P/O Duckenfield of 501 Squadron shared a confirmed Ju 87 which was observed to blow up;[211] possibly this was the Ju 87 seen to blow up from a double anti-aircraft strike. Then there were also the claims by 41 and 64 Squadrons close to Dover. Intense combat almost always led to over-claiming, and this was almost always unintentional; it would appear likely that two Stukas were shot down just off Dover (seen by ground observers) by some combination of fighters from the three squadrons and the ground defences; these may well have been the two lost by *IV/LG 1* where there were no survivors. The three casualties from *II/StG 1* – one shot down into the Channel with crew rescued by the *Luftwaffe*, one crashed and written off in France, one damaged – were likely the victims of 501 Squadron. One or more of them may also have been damaged by the Dover barrage prior to this, or by 64 Squadron or 41 Squadron closer to Dover before being finished off by 501 Squadron further out over the Channel as the Stukas made for France at low level.

Ten Hurricanes of 56 Squadron had been scrambled from Rochford at *c.* 07h10, twelve minutes before 41 Squadron's Spitfires were sent up from Manston.[212] The Hurricanes arrived over Dover probably not long after 41 and 64 Squadrons, the greater distance they had to fly to get there, at lower speed than Spitfires, being roughly balanced out by their earlier departure; the two fatal casualties, one to 41 and one to 56 Squadrons, were both observed crashing into the sea at *c.* 07h45, and at least one 41 Squadron pilot reported meeting a 56 Squadron aircraft in combat: Sgt Carr-Lewty was close enough to read the Hurricane's code letters US-K.[213] Two pilots of 56 Squadron also reported seeing Stukas bombing Dover harbour,[214] further supporting this squadron being engaged soon after 41 Squadron. It can be presumed that 41 Squadron's Spitfires were somewhat higher compared to the 56 Squadron Hurricanes as the 11 Group tactic encompassed sending in a Spitfire unit at greater altitude to take on the Me 109s, while the Hurricanes were vectored in at lower altitude and intended to go for the bombers. 56 Squadron records refer to Me 109s seen at 6,000-8,000 ft and at 11,000-12,000 ft but engagements with the Me 109s met appear to have been much less intense than those described by 41 Squadron.

It was only *III/JG 52*, flying a free chase over the Dover area, that reported combat with Hurricanes, bearing in mind the caveat of the Germans' very common confusion in action between the two principal RAF fighter types, plus what might be called 'Spitfire snobbery' on the part of *Luftwaffe* pilots.[215] The *III/JG 52* history, in contrast, reports confirmed and rejected claims against both Hurricanes and Spitfires.[216] *III/JG 52* was a rather unsuccessful unit against Fighter Command in late July, especially compared to *JG 51*, strongly influenced as the latter was by Theo Osterkamp's fighting philosophy, and this would fit much less intense combat for 56 Squadron than would likely have been the case if opposed by *I and II/JG 51*, which were probably kept busy enough by 41 Squadron to not have noticed 56 Squadron at lower altitudes.

The report on 56 Squadron's action is not over-informative. The formation of ten Hurricanes was led by F/Lt Coghlan who was instructed by the controller to orbit Dover; once there, they spotted various presumed enemy aircraft and the unit became separated in searching for and investigating them.[217] This can be judged as neither good tactics nor good leadership from F/Lt Coghlan. He reported seeing about six Me 109s between 6,000 and 8,000 ft, and a second much larger group of twenty-five to thirty at 12,000 ft, but all these enemy machines disappeared from his view when he went for the smaller formation lower down.[218] Coghlan also reported seeing a single Spitfire shoot down three Me 109s, one seen to be emitting flames, another glycol and the third giving off smoke and all three were observed to fall into the Channel.[219] No Me 109s were lost over the sea this day,[220] as already noted earlier, and what F/Lt Coghlan likely saw was some Me 109s from JG 51 dog-fighting with Spitfires from 41 Squadron, with several of the Messerschmitts performing their favourite escape from combat with a steep dive and flattening out above the sea, combined with the demise of the single Spitfire and single Hurricane lost by, respectively, 41 Squadron (F/O Gamblen) and 56 Squadron. The latter was F/Sgt C. J. Cooney, flying as Red 4 who went missing; F/Lt Weaver of his squadron saw a Hurricane going down giving off white smoke after an attack by a Me 109, and this machine was seen to hit the sea and explode by a searchlight post and the Leathercotes Signals Station, 10 miles off the coast at c. 07h45.[221] The signals station – Dover CH radar station Leathercotes – lies about 1 km up the coast to the north-east of St Margarets Bay, itself immediately north-east of Dover.

Percy Weaver claimed an Me 109 on fire about 10 miles east of Dover, witnessed by Sgts Smythe and Hillcoat and thus confirmed destroyed.[222] Once again, no Me 109s were lost over the Channel on this mission and a steeply diving, escaping Me 109 probably smoking heavily as its engine was over-boosted to escape is the likely explanation; once more, unintentional over-claiming. P/O Wicks and P/O Mounsdon observed Stukas dive-bombing Dover harbour, but inconclusive engagements with Me 109s up to twelve in number kept them away, Mounsdon's Hurricane being hit in the wing but he returned to base safely.[223] Bearing in mind limited effective radio ranges of the high frequency sets then in use by Fighter Command – 35 to 40 miles from sector controllers at sector stations, but extended by use of mobile radio relay stations, linked by landlines to sector control rooms[224] – once offshore of Dover, 56 Squadron would have been approaching average limits of contact with their controller at North Weald during this action.

Oberleutnant Günther Rall, acting Staffelkapitän 8/JG 52, recorded a combat with Hurricanes during which his Staffel claimed three shot down,[225] with the Gruppe history recording three Hurricanes and an equal number of Spitfires brought down in the Dover area at c. 07h40-07h45.[226] However, only two of them were confirmed including only one for *8/JG 52*, the balance being rejected.[227] *III/JG 52* would logically have been flying low enough to meet 56 Squadron, also at about the same altitude, bearing in mind their task to cover outgoing Stukas low over the water as they left Dover, and Me 109s of *JG 51*, now low on fuel and many having dived to sea level in the typical *Luftwaffe* escape tactic from a dogfight. The Stukas were effective, dispatching an armed yacht and two already damaged vessels in Dover harbour, the merchant ship *Gronland* (commodore's ship from Convoy CW 8 which had been damaged four days before in the Channel) and the *Sandhurst*, depot ship for the Dover destroyer flotilla, hit by high explosive and incendiary bombs at 07h25 with additional near misses by both bomb types causing further damage.[228]

29 July 1940: scattered small-scale shipping raids

Some hours after the Dover raid, an attack on ships off Dungeness was carried out by a few Ju 88s of *II/KG 76*, deliberately flying just above the sea to avoid British radar detection; despite sometimes being described as a convoy, neither the west-sailing CW nor the east-sailing CE convoys were running past Dungeness on 29 July 1940.[229] The raid took place at *c.* 13h00, apparently on some trawlers, and while causing no damage, lost a Junkers which hit a balloon cable, with another supposedly shot down by ship's anti-aircraft fire.[230] Only a single machine was lost, a Ju 88 of *4/KG 76* carrying a Staff *Major* as observer and three other crew members, who all disappeared into the sea.[231] Flying so low and hitting a balloon cable gave the crew no chance at all. The trawlers were probably minesweeping vessels, operating out of either Sheerness or Dover.

Having achieved surprise by flying so low, there was no RAF reaction until after the fact. Twelve Spitfires of 610 Squadron which were halfway between Biggin Hill and their forward base at Hawkinge at the time of the attack, upon their arrival over Hawkinge had the six aircraft of A Flight diverted to fly out over the Channel off Dungeness and investigate.[232] Having arrived off Dungeness they sighted a single Do 17 at *c.* 6,000 ft which hastily jettisoned its bombs, turned for France and dived to sea level.[233] Attacking from *c.* 7,000 ft, mainly from astern and in succession, the six Spitfires were only able to damage the Dornier despite four exhausting their ammunition, and the German kept up gentle evasive turns and a high speed necessitating the fighters to use full throttle to engage; the courageous dorsal rear gunner kept up fire and slightly damaged two Spitfires.[234] The damage state of the Dornier was not recorded in German records, but the observer *Oberstleutnant* Adolf Genth, *Gruppenkommandeur* of *III/KG 76*, was killed.[235] What exactly this single *III/KG 76* bomber was doing, heading at *c.* 6,000 ft for the site of the low level *II/KG 76* trawler attack about fifteen minutes thereafter, remains unknown. While the loss of a senior officer and commander was serious, 610 Squadron should have destroyed this lone bomber. This once again shows up the small-calibre 0.303 inch machine guns used by Fighter Command, and the relative difficulty in mortally wounding a Dornier with air-cooled radial engines.

An even more inconclusive encounter with the enemy was experienced by three Spitfires of 603 Squadron at about noon, flying at 18,000 ft, 12 miles south-east of Aberdeen, Scotland. Sgt Caister led the section to intercept, and while they spotted two He 111s dodging in and out of clouds, only Caister was able to open fire a couple of times but to no known effect.[236] About half an hour later and much further south, nine Hurricanes of 145 Squadron, led by S/L Peel had been sent aloft from Tangmere at 13h28 to patrol in the Selsey Bill area; in due course, some 5 miles south of the Bill they intercepted a lone Ju 88 which they pursued out to sea with Peel leading three other pilots to claim its destruction.[237] A likely candidate for this claim was a Ju 88 of *7/KG 51* which crashed and was written off along with the crew on an operational mission, at Nogent-le-Rotrou in France, which was approximately due south of Selsey Bill and *c.* 80 km west of its base at Etampes.[238]

The next set of actions would be aimed mainly against shipping off the East Coast, firstly with probing single Heinkels from *I/KG 53* at *c.* 14h45-15h15, and then a fast raid on a small convoy off Harwich by *EGr 210* at about 17h15, these units both being part of *Fliegerkorps II.* Blue Section of 66 Squadron, P/Os Oxspring, Studd and Pickering had taken off at 14h08 with orders to patrol Lowestoft at 15,000 ft; at *c.* 14h45 they caught sight of a single Heinkel 111 flying leisurely towards the north-north-west at the same height, 20 miles out from the coast at Lowestoft.[239] Surprisingly, it took no action for a couple of minutes before turning to the south as the three Spitfires closed in; each Spitfire made several attacks from rear, quarter and beam, silencing return fire after the first one, and observed their damaged opponent dive into cloud at *c.* 8,000 ft.[240] The Heinkel's undercarriage dropped and it descended to within about 600-1,200 ft above the North Sea; then three Hurricanes suddenly appeared, each making an astern attack before the Heinkel ditched, three crew members being seen to emerge and climb onto the fuselage before launching a dinghy.[241]

F/Lt Bayne, F/O Bird-Wilson and P/O Wissler of 17 Squadron had been on patrol at *c.* 4,000 ft further to the south-west, when at *c.* 15h10 they were vectored north-north-east, sighting a single Heinkel 111 flying south-east about 400 ft below cloud and being attacked by Spitfires, which did not seem to be firing at it.[242] Bayne led his section in line astern into a frontal attack out of the sun and followed this up with an astern attack, the one observed by 66 Squadron, who seem not to have witnessed the first, head-on attack; 17 Squadron also saw the undercarriage come down as the Heinkel's hydraulics were penetrated, bombs being jettisoned, pieces shed as both engines smoked heavily and oil covered Bayne's windscreen and wing leading edges.[243] The 17 Squadron trio managed to get in another frontal attack before the Heinkel hit the sea and were also witness to three of the crew taking to their dinghy,[244] but the five-man crew of *3/KG 53* all perished.[245] Under extended attack by 66 Squadron, the Heinkel had been flying south-south-east, basically heading towards their base at Vitry-en-Artois in France, and 17 Squadron's pilots had joined the fray by flying north-north-east from their patrol position further to the south-west. By this time the hapless Heinkel had progressed quite far to the south-south-east from its original position off Lowestoft, and its final demise was some 30 or 40 miles off Harwich.[246]

As the preceding action reached its finale and in the same general area about 40 or 50 miles off Felixstowe, at about 15h05 three Hurricanes of 85 Squadron were patrolling over the North Sea when one of their number, F/O Patrick Woods-Scawen, spotted a lone Do 17 at 8,000 ft, flying east.[247] He was unable to inform his two comrades due to R/T congestion, so broke away and made a quarter attack from out of the sun, giving an initial long burst as he closed in from 300 yds to 100 yds.[248] Several more attacks from astern and quarter saw the Dornier slow down, shed pieces from both engines and centre section and descend seawards with one wing low.[249] Return fire put a bullet through Woods-Scawen's airscrew, which penetrated through and into his port wing; he pursued his enemy until his ammunition ran out and he saw four German fighters approaching from the French coast, upon which he turned for home, having reported an inconclusive combat.[250] In fact, F/O Woods-Scawen had seriously damaged the Do 17, from *Stab/KG 2*, which managed to put down at St Inglevert in the Pas de Calais, one crew member wounded and the machine a write-off, 60% damaged.[251] The Dornier had been spotting for the planned convoy raid by *EGr 210*.[252]

While the above combat was still reaching its conclusion, Green Section of 66 Squadron led by F/Lt Burton with F/O Campbell-Colquoun and P/O Collingridge was on patrol over Hammonds Knoll, a six-mile sandbank 40 km off Cromer, Norfolk, when vectored onto a radar contact; they sighted a single He 111 of *I/KG 53* about 10 miles to the east at 9,000 ft.[253] Forming line astern they pursued an enemy who acted rather strangely: the He 111 turned slowly to port and suffered repeated stern and quarter attacks from the three Spitfires, losing height gradually as its port engine was put out of action. The

Heinkel then made for land, jettisoning its bomb load some 10 miles offshore of Yarmouth.[254] Weak and inaccurate return fire was opened whenever the 66 Squadron section came within *c.* 1,000 yds of it, and having almost reached the coast, the Heinkel turned to the east-south-east and made off, still losing height and then heading east.[255] The three Spitfires landed safely at base, but P/O Collingridge soon after giving in his combat report, took off on another interception, only to crash on the beach at Orfordness injuring himself and writing off his aircraft.[256] The Heinkel of *2/KG 53* and its crew were less fortunate, disappearing into the North Sea.[257]

29 July 1940: low-level shipping raid off Harwich by *EGr 210*

Convoy FN236 had left Southend, at the mouth of the Thames Estuary on its north shore, where northbound convoys assembled on 29 July 1940, bound for Methil where it arrived two days later; it was made up of six unescorted merchantmen.[258] The convoy was proceeding off Harwich when the 5,919 grt *Clan Monroe* struck a mine; she was eventually towed and beached.[259] The 12th Minesweeping Flotilla based in Harwich was active about 5 miles away, alas too late for *Clan Monroe*, and its three vessels were escorted by the sloop HMS *Guillemot* acting as anti-aircraft defence ship for the flotilla, and which vessel sailed to assist *Clan Monroe*.[260] On arrival it found another sloop, HMS *Hastings* there, which had been detached from another convoy to help; *Guillemot* sent a search party to what turned out to be the abandoned merchant ship as *Hastings* made to return to her convoy.[261] As the latter departed, the search party was rowing back towards *Guillemot* when events unfolded in very rapid succession at 17h14.[262]

A Dornier spotter plane, presumably the one from *Stab/KG 2* discussed above in action against a Hurricane from 85 Squadron, had reported a large convoy of sixty-odd ships making for the Thames Estuary, and lying somewhere off the Harwich area.[263] *EGr 210* was ordered to attack the convoy, dispatching eight bomb-carrying Me 110s of *2/EGr 210* covered by three fighter model Me 110 C-6s carrying a 30 mm cannon from *1 Staffel*; they left their forward base at St Omer at 16h35,[264] just as HMS *Guillemot* went to the aid of the mined *Clan Monroe*. Over Dunkirk *EGr 210* met thirty Me 110s from *III/ZG 26* who were to be their main escort and top cover.[265] *Lt* Erich Beudel and his gunner *Obergefreiter* Heinrich Diemer flew one of the fighter escorts from *1/EGr 210* and the former's eyewitness account of the subsequent action was found in his diary in the wreckage of his Me 110 when he was shot down and killed over England on 15 August 1940.[266]

Beudel records flying north at sea level to avoid detection after leaving Dunkirk, for thirty minutes followed by a climb to clouds at *c.* 4,500 ft, after which they attacked merchant shipping at 17h15 just to the north of Orfordness. The attack was actually made on the crippled *Clan Monroe* and the five warships near her: the two sloops, *Guillemot* and *Hastings*, plus three minesweepers.[267] One minute before the bombing attack, witnesses on board *Guillemot* saw nine RAF fighters approaching from the starboard side of the ship and almost immediately afterwards, an equal number of Me 110s coming in to port; the latter splitting into a group of five who dived onto the ships and a group of four who maintained their altitude higher up and were seen to be attacked by the friendly fighters.[268] The crew of the sloop then reported seeing four of the five diving bomb-carrying aircraft who flew across *Clan Monroe* and *Guillemot* from port to starboard, release two bombs each with the fifth aircraft being hit by oerlikon rounds from the sloop and immediately hitting the sea just twenty-five yards off the ship's starboard quarter and vanishing.[269] The crew of the *Guillemot* may have observed one of the Me 110s fly at very low level through the water geyser from one of the explosions, which might easily have been mistaken for it hitting the sea and vanishing as the spray subsided. None of the eight bombers was in fact lost or even hit seriously, while *Guillemot* was drenched in seawater; the crew also claimed hitting another Me 110, which was seen to make off at low level towards the horizon shovelling out black smoke.[270]

This, however, more likely relates to aerial combat described below. It is important to note that HMS *Guillemot* recorded a time lapse of a mere thirty seconds between first sighting the separation of the *EGr 210* formation, the subsequent dives of the incoming Me 110s and the explosion of the last bomb as they thundered away to the south.[271] This is an excellent example of the rapidity of aerial events, and how such fleeting scenes as observed by aerial and ground/seaborne witnesses could easily lead to mistaken impressions of damage and casualties to opposing aircraft.

While RAF controllers had scrambled a total of seventy-four fighters to oppose the *EGr 210* raid, only the nine Hurricanes of 151 Squadron intercepted.[272] They had taken off from North Weald at 16h44 with orders to patrol Felixstowe and were then vectored north to intercept the Me 110s; the Hurricane pilots, flying some distance offshore, saw the enemy on their port side and observed them dive-bombing a damaged ship being escorted by five naval vessels.[273] The nine Hurricanes split, three to take on the dive-bombing Me 110s while the other six made for the higher escorting Me 110s of *EGr 210*, which unit mistook them for two separate squadrons.[274] The six higher Hurricane pilots attacked the *EGr 210* escorts, claiming a probable by F/Lt Kenneth Blair, and two more damaged, with two of their own Hurricanes damaged: F/O Milne force-landed at Rochford, his machine slightly damaged and later flew back to North Weald, while F/O Whittingham force-landed at Martlesham Heath, his Hurricane with category 2 damage.[275] F/O Whittingham was seriously wounded by bullets, just making it to the nearby Martlesham Heath forward aerodrome some 11-12 km inland from where the action took place off Hollesley Bay; he only returned to 151 Squadron from hospital and then sick leave on 16 October 1940.[276]

Leutnant Beudel, *1/EGr 210*, recorded in his diary how he sighted the two groups of Hurricanes coming in to their left, upon which the three escort Me 110s climbed and turned hard for a height advantage, intending to hinder the lower three Hurricanes and thus protect the bombers.[277] This was not to be, as the higher six Hurricanes attacked these three Me 110s from their starboard side, one of them hitting Beudel's aircraft and seriously damaging it: with about thirty bullet strikes from above and to the right, and a wounded gunner, his starboard engine spurting oil after multiple hits, tyres shot through, trimming tabs shot off, flaps and wings hit multiple times. The cockpit was also hit several times, two rounds narrowly missing the heads of both crewmen, smashing the radio entirely and one round hitting a loaded magazine for the rear gun, exploding all the rounds.[278] Pulling up into the clouds, Beudel then emerged again, meeting up with his *Staffelkapitän* and two more Me 110s from *III/ZG 26*, but any thoughts of further combat were put off by his gunner's condition and he headed at low level for the Dutch coast, but later changed his mind and put down at their forward base of St Omer.[279] The damage state of his Me 110 was not recorded in the Quartermaster General's Loss Returns; this might be due to his having been picked up from St Omer next day by his *Staffelkapitän* and flown home to their base at Denain, his heavily damaged machine left behind and its damage state thus not recorded in the longer term by its parent unit.

While 151 Squadron's higher six Hurricanes successfully prevented the three escorting Me 110s from *EGr 210* getting at their three low level colleagues, they themselves were surprised by part of the higher Me 110 escort, *8/ZG 26*, only seeing them at the last minute; three claims were made by *Oblt* Mayer, *Staffelkapitän 8/ZG 26*, *Oblt* Baagoe and *Uffz* Scherer, between 17h24 and 17h25, all being confirmed.[280] Once more, the rapidity of aerial combat is underlined by the very narrow time span of these claims. With two 151 Squadron Hurricanes damaged and force-landed and three claims, possibly one machine was hit by two separate Me 110s; overclaiming is almost always a companion of the rapid and fleeting nature of high-speed aerial combat between fighters. The damaged Me 110 claimed by the machine gunners of HMS *Guillemot* and seen to fly off low over the horizon issuing black smoke (see above) most likely relates to a Me 110 damaged by 151 Squadron. Logically this was *Lt* Beudel's machine, the only *EGr 210* casualty. The 151 Squadron flight led by F/Lt Kenneth Blair had made an effective beam attack on some of the *EGr 210* Me 110s but were themselves then distracted by escorting Me 110s of *III/ZG 26* intervening.

A final victim of the Luftwaffe on 29 July 1940 was the destroyer HMS *Delight*, surprised after leaving Portland en route to Liverpool after a refit.[281] South-west of Portland, at 19h25, thirteen Ju 87s from *III/StG 2* pounced on her, leaving her shattered by direct hits and near misses and ravaged by fire; despite this and the loss of eighteen of her crew with another fifty-nine badly wounded, she managed to limp back to a position just outside Portland where she was abandoned, and subsequently exploded and sank during the night.[282] No RAF fighters had hindered the Stukas in their work.

9

30 July–7 August 1940: Single Aircraft Actions and Me 109 Incursions; Osterkamp's Tactics Succeed and Fail in Eastern Channel

30 July 1940: single aircraft actions

A day (Tuesday) not marked by any raids or major confrontations, but with armed reconnaissance missions being flown by the *Luftwaffe* along the east coast of England and Scotland. At fifteen minutes to noon, Green Section of 603 Squadron, F/Lt Rushmer leading P/O Berry, Green 2, and P/O Pease were scrambled from their forward base of Montrose and ordered to orbit over the North Sea 30 miles to the east at 12,000 ft.[1] They were vectored onto a single He 111 flying at 16,000 ft on a northerly heading; forming line astern they closed in, with the enemy turning to starboard and diving into thin cloud.[2] As the three Spitfires followed, F/Lt Rushmer came out of the cloud at about 10,000 ft and the Heinkel's dorsal rear gunner opened up at him from about 400 yds; Rushmer closed in from dead astern to about 250 yards before reciprocating and using all his ammunition in a single extended burst.[3] As he pulled away both engines of the bomber were seen to be smoking, as Green 2 came in next from astern, also firing off all his rounds, in three bursts, observing the undercarriage drop, indicating the Heinkel's hydraulic system had failed, as it dived down to *c.* 4,000 ft where it flattened out.[4] The third Spitfire now attacked, from rear and beam using deflection, and the He 111 from *8/KG 26* hit the sea and exploded into flames after jettisoning its bombs, killing the crew of four, about 40 miles south-east of Montrose; return fire hit two of the Spitfires with a few rounds but inflicted only slight damage.[5]

Another armed reconnaissance was carried out by two Me 110 C-6 aircraft from *1/EGr 210*, briefed to search the Thames Estuary and then proceed further north up the coast in search of shipping.[6] Finding convoy 'Pilot' 10 miles off Aldeburgh at *c.* 15h00, they attacked at very low level with their formidable 30 mm cannons, and as an escorting trawler replied with anti-aircraft fire, they were spotted by the convoy patrol of 85 Squadron, F/Lt Hamilton, F/Sgt Allard and Sgt Evans, who saw them speeding off to the east.[7] Hamilton took after the rapidly disappearing Me 110s who opened fire on him already at 1,500 yds, managed to close, and from a range of 250-200 yds fired two five second bursts from astern at the one enemy machine; as he broke off his attack he saw the Me 110 swerve left and drop its nose towards the sea just below before recovering slightly.[8]

As the enemy had turned eastwards at full speed with Hamilton in hot pursuit, the savvy and experienced F/Sgt Allard cut across the angle of the turn and attacked from quarter astern, opening fire from only 150 yards and closing to 25 yards with a single long burst; Allard saw the starboard engine break up and the rear gunner still firing, albeit unsuccessfully.[9] Flying an old model Hurricane, Sgt Evans was unable to catch up but along with Hamilton saw the Me 110 hit the sea, break into pieces and vanish, leaving a man visible in the water.[10] Thus perished *Lt* Herold and his plucky gunner *Ogefr* Lilienthal, who put about ten bullets into F/Lt Hamilton's Hurricane, damaging it slightly.[11] There is one further apparent combat casualty reported in German records from 30 July 1940, a Ju 88 of *6/KG 76* which belly-landed at Creil, France, 30% damaged, supposedly hit by British fighters, though no claims have been identified.[12]

31 July 1940: Dover balloon barrage attacked, single aircraft actions

A day of rather poor weather with cloudy conditions and often poor visibility giving rise to few clear-cut actions where results of combat could be observed; the one exception was in the afternoon when clear conditions over south-east Kent accommodated a perfect German bounce of some 74 Squadron Spitfires. As was usual, very early in the morning, various 11 Group sector stations dispatched squadrons to forward bases, among them 111 Squadron taking off from Croydon en route for Hawkinge at the unholy hour of 04h50.[13] From there section-strength patrols and scrambles were made, including the three Hurricanes flown by F/Lt Connors, P/O Copeman and Sgt Carnell sent up at 07h20 to intercept two raiders in mid-Channel to the south-east of Dungeness.[14] Arrived there they spotted a Ju 88 despite the generally poor visibility and after a flat-out chase managed to catch it and applying a series of rear and astern quarter attacks, used all their ammunition; the Ju 88 employed evasive turns and alternate short climbs and dives and Connors was subjected to intense return fire.[15] He observed dense smoke from both engines and after attacks by his two wingmen, who experienced no return fire, the

German machine vanished in a vertical dive into mist covering the sea.[16] While 111 squadron claimed a probable Ju 88, and probably doubted it had got home, *Luftwaffe* losses include 15% damage to a Ju 88 of *II/KG 76* on this date inflicted by fighter action over the Channel, one crewman perishing and two being wounded.[17] Little wonder that Copeman and Carnell experienced no return fire.

Very soon afterwards, further to the West, Red Section of 145 Squadron had been sent up to patrol Bembridge on the Isle of Wight at 7,000 ft and at *c.* 08h00 saw a single Do 215 about 5,000 ft beneath them; as their quarry vanished in the cloudy conditions, they dived down, coming out below the clouds to find their enemy circling four trawlers below, presumably intending to attack them.[18] Ostowicz was the only one to get in an attack, opening up from 400 yards, but then the bomber flew into cloud once more and despite two further short bursts, the German machine disappeared for good.[19] No such aircraft is mentioned in the *Luftwaffe* losses for this day. However, *I/KG 55* reported two of its Heinkel 111s as having been shot down in action with fighters on operational missions, with each crew safely bailing out over France.[20] It is possible one of these machines was damaged by F/O Ostowicz of 145 Squadron whose aim was rather better than his aircraft identification. The other was a likely victim of 1 Squadron some hours later, who may have suffered equally from recognition challenges.

F/O Matthews led the three Hurricanes of Red Section, 1 Squadron up from Tangmere at 10h17 to intercept a raid at 15,000 ft south of the Isle of Wight, but found nothing; after some more vectors they were guided onto a bogey several miles further south, at about 8,000 ft.[21] Identified as a Do 17, it dived to sea level and made off to the south, followed by the section in line astern, which made four astern attacks on the luckless bomber, Red 3 even getting in a fifth.[22] Despite the prodigious expenditure of 5,000 rounds, the three pilots left the bomber, its port engine now giving off lots of black smoke and running very slowly, some 70 miles south of the coast.[23] While no Dorniers appear in German losses for the day, two Heinkel 111s from *I/KG 55* do, as discussed above.

There was then a long break before further enemy activity occurred at about 15h45.[24] About fifty German aircraft were detected by radar building up over Cap Gris Nez at an estimated height of 30,000 ft.[25] About half of this Me 109 force went for the Dover balloon barrage,[26] leaving the other half to tackle any intercepting RAF fighters. The balloons generally hindered effective Ju 87 dive-bombing attacks on ships and ports at low level, hence their planned removal by the *Luftwaffe* fighters. No follow-up raid occurred but destruction of the balloons was for future operations. Eleven Group of Fighter Command responded by scrambling thirty Spitfires and twenty-four Hurricanes from six different squadrons and vectoring them to the Dover area, but only the twelve Spitfires of 74 Squadron, which were already airborne from their forward base at Manston, actually got close enough for aerial combat to occur.[27]

74 Squadron's A Flight was on patrol over Manston at 20,000 ft when the build-up over the Pas de Calais was first noted and as its size became evident, B Flight was sent up to help. Meanwhile A Flight was directed to Dover to engage the incoming enemy fighters ahead of what was thought to be a raid, but from their height they only saw some Me 109s far out to sea and did not make contact.[28] B Flight was led by its new flight commander, F/Lt Kelly, a Cranwell graduate but lacking fighter experience;[29] the dangerous skies above the Dover Straits were no place for a novice, even less so for one leading a flight. The hapless pilots of B Flight, still 2,000 ft below their colleagues, spotted Me 109s also at *c.* 20,000 ft on their port side; Kelly led them in a continued climb, in line astern, turning in towards the Me 109s on their sun side.[30] Going to the sunny side worked fine when *above* an enemy, masking one's presence due to the glare, but when *below* the enemy it helped not at all.

The experienced Germans from *II/JG 51* split into two groups of six and nine machines, and came in from the beam and soon after from astern; Green 1 leading the second section saw Blue 3, Sgt Eley, hit by the perfect beam attack, at almost full deflection and with long-range cannon fire, his Spitfire going down in flames.[31] There are two logical claimants for this impressive piece of shooting, *Hpt* Tietzen, *Staffelkapitän 5/JG 51* and *Oblt* Fözö, *Staffelkapitän 4/JG 51*, who made recognised claims over Dover and north-west of Dover, both at 16h55.[32] One of them shot down Sgt Eley and in view of the times of claims, the other presumably attacked F/Lt Kelly as described below. Fred Eley's burning Spitfire fell into the shallow water only *c.* 200 m from the shore just west of Folkestone harbour and once the major wreckage, twisted and burnt, was recovered, his body was found still firmly strapped to his seat in the shattered remains of the cockpit.[33]

The second German *Staffelkapitän* got on Kelly's tail as the latter turned trying to get on a Me 109's tail, and from close range hammered the Spitfire, leaving dents in the armour at the back of the seat, hitting the port wing, one cannon shell penetrated the port upper side of the petrol tank and another blew the armour plate above the tank clean off.[34] As petrol streamed into his cockpit, up to his ankles, F/Lt Kelly managed to pull his barely controllable aircraft out of a spin and gamely went for two Me 109s either side of him, but again spun down further, and then found himself with another pair of Me 109s, one tempting him below with a slow role and dive away, and another above waiting to pounce; however, when he climbed towards this one, he was forced by the damage to dive away westwards towards Hastings-Hawkinge, and managed to get his badly damaged machine back to Manston.[35] A very brave but unfortunately inexperienced man, F/Lt Kelly was lucky to escape Sgt Eley's fate. His other wingman would also not return.

P/O Gunn, an ex-Halton apprentice, was apparently shot down somewhat later in the dogfight and fell into the Channel further out than his colleague, Fred Eley; his body was later recovered by a German E-boat and he is buried in Ostende, Belgium.[36] Green Section of 74 Squadron observing the second group of nine Me 109s coming towards them from above, continued climbing to 23,000 ft and lost them, except for Green 3, Sgt Skinner, who became detached during the first climbing turn, and attacked one of a wide vic of three Me 109s he saw some 5,000 ft below, leaving it diving away giving off smoke and flames.[37] While he claimed a probable Me 109 and F/Lt Kelly another damaged, no relevant German machines appear in the Luftwaffe loss lists.[38] Apart from the first two claims mentioned above by the two *Staffelkapitäns*, two more by *4/JG 51* pilots were made, respectively one minute later and three minutes later, specifically north and west of Dover, both being confirmed by the *Luftwaffe* system; a fifth claim was not confirmed, being classified as a probable.[39] These four claims likely reflect the several attacks on F/Lt Kelly, and the two 74 Squadron Spitfires lost.

By c. 18h00-18h30 when the last action of the day began, the weather had greatly deteriorated with heavy cloud cover and poor radio contact between RAF fighters within a formation providing a backdrop to a confused and rather nebulous set of contacts.[40] Twelve Hurricanes of 501 Squadron up from their forward base at Hawkinge were detailed to fly a circuitous patrol line, Ashford–Lympne–Folkestone, which they repeated two or three times.[41] P/O Gibson during the course of two circuits of the patrol saw enemy aircraft in and out of the clouds three times; unable to contact his wingmen or the squadron leader due to poor radio conditions, on the last occasion he broke away, followed by another Hurricane; diving down on two presumed Do 17s Gibson made a brief astern attack on one and claimed it damaged, before it climbed and turned steeply into cloud,[42] a manoeuvrability suggesting a Me 110 rather than a Do 17. The other ten Hurricanes continued the patrol, but lost P/O Don's machine, the pilot bailing out and seriously injured.[43] No one had seen Don in any engagement, although another 501 Squadron pilot, reported being fired on inland of the Deal-Dover axis.[44]

1-7 August 1940: mostly single aircraft actions

The first seven days of August 1940 saw something of a lull in the air over the Channel and North Sea. Only on 5 August were there a couple of more intense actions, but for the rest of these seven days there were a limited number of individual battles between small formations, mostly sections of three RAF fighters and single German bombers.[45]

On 1 August, a convoy north-east off Hull was attacked by scattered German bombers in the half hour after 13h00, with sections each from 607 and 616 Squadrons intercepting but not achieving anything concrete; a Spitfire from 616 was slightly damaged by return fire from a Ju 88.[46] A Ju 88 of *1/KG 30* reported lost with its crew on a mission to Carlisle was probably the victim of anti-aircraft fire over Edinburgh.[47] Another two convoys off Norfolk were also vulnerable and distracted the Coltishall sector controller, W/Co Beisiegel, enough so that a lone bomber from *I/KG 4* penetrated inland in mid-afternoon hitting the Boulton Paul aircraft factory at Norwich; damage was slight but tragically casualties in the immediate area were high.[48] In the evening a section of Hurricanes from 242 Squadron intercepted a He 111 and a Ju 88 over a convoy off Lowestoft, claiming damage to the former and destruction of the latter; a *9/KG 4* Ju 88 reported lost with its crew off the English East coast in *Luftwaffe* loss records was most likely the victim of Sgt Richardson, but no damaged He 111 is identified in these records.[49]

At about 15h00 two sections of 145 Squadron had been vectored from Tangmere to a position south of Hastings, where the one section met a Ju 88 of Stab *II/KG 76*, which despite the attention of all three Hurricanes managed to get away with 15% damage. A crew member later succumbed to his wounds.[50] The other section was less fortunate, meeting a lone Hs 126 tactical reconnaissance aircraft and although this was shot down by the section leader with both crewmen killed, the brave and capable rear gunner shot down the second 145 Squadron Hurricane as it came in to attack, killing its pilot.[51] Just exactly what such a machine was doing snooping about the English southern coast is a moot question, although it is remotely possible it was engaged in reconnaissance activities related to the planned German invasion.

On 2 August 1940, there was little action, a section of 19 Squadron claiming damage to a He 111 over the Cromer Knoll Lightship off the north coast of Norfolk at c. 11h15; attacks by all three section members, using one eight machine gun and two cannon-armed Spitfires definitely appears to have damaged their opponent, as the starboard engine was hit and oil covered much of the windscreen of one attacker.[52] Despite some sources relating this to a damaged He 111 of *II/KG 55*, this unit from *Luftflotte 3* would be very unlikely to have operated far up the east coast. More logical candidates in the *Luftwaffe* loss lists would be two Dorniers of *8/KG 2* which crash-landed at Guines near the coast; one suffered 60% damage (a write-off), the other 20%, but no crew casualties were reported.[53] The less damaged one might have been hit in a rather fleeting attack by one member of Green Section, 66 Squadron, east of Lowestoft in the evening.[54] The possibly faulty aircraft recognition under cloudy conditions of rather fleeting sightings by 19 Squadron would be nothing very unusual.

There is no known evidence for any combat between Fighter Command single-engined fighters and the *Luftwaffe* on the succeeding two days,[55] but 5 August 1940 would see a number of combats between RAF fighters and Me 109s and will be explored below. On 6 August a section of Hurricanes of 85 Squadron dispatched a Do 17 of 7/KG 3 along with its crew, near a convoy off Lowestoft at *c.* 06h50 with a set of beam-quarter and astern attacks by all three fighters.[56] At about midday, two separate sections of 72 Squadron Spitfires had inconclusive actions against He 111s, which may well have been the same aircraft; return fire hit one Spitfire, severing the aileron cable and it crashed on landing, being written off and lightly injuring the pilot.[57] Some five hours later, a further inconclusive interception of a Ju 88 *c.* 20 miles north-east of Flamborough Head by three Spitfires of 616 Squadron occurred; two of the fighters were lightly dented by objects thrown out of the German bomber.[58] The IPR also notes the interception height as 29,500 ft and that the leading Spitfire reached a speed of about 520 mph in diving after the quarry; this was obviously a reconnaissance aircraft piloted by someone of some skill. Aerial combat on 7 August was limited to a single He 111 attacked by three Hurricanes of 87 Squadron and claimed destroyed by P/O Comely at about midnight; a Ju 88 of 9/LG 1 which crashed at Chateaudun airfield in France, killing the crew, may well have been the victim.[59]

5 August 1940: fighter duels, the Osterkamp tactics falter

Convoy CE 8 was approaching the Beachy Head-Dover segment fairly early that morning and would traverse the dangerous Straits of Dover in the early afternoon when a small *Luftwaffe* attack was attempted but not pushed home.[60] Any approaching German formations would be suspected by controllers of having designs on this convoy. The controller at Hornchurch put up twelve Spitfires from 65 Squadron at 08h50 with orders to land at their forward base at Manston, and his colleague at Kenley launched nine Spitfires of 64 Squadron bound for their forward base Hawkinge at exactly the same time.[61] En route both squadrons received orders to intercept incoming German formations, 65 to take on bombers approaching Dover, while 64 was vectored to intercept a raid behind Dover.[62] Both probably flew at normal cruising speed until the changed vectors were received when they would have speeded up. In fact,

64 Squadron, as they neared the coast, were ordered by S/L MacDonell to engage emergency boost as they went into a steep climb for altitude, having been ordered by their controller to fly a course of 130 degrees, get up to 20,000 ft and circle.[63]

Bearing in mind the greater distance from Kenley to Dover as compared to the Rochford–Dover route, 65 Squadron probably got to the coast about five minutes earlier, by about 08h40-45. 64 Squadron's C/O would not have been popular at higher headquarters if his order for an entire formation to engage emergency boost had become known; despite launching themselves steeply upwards at maximum possible climbing speed, this would almost certainly not have hastened their reaching the Dover area any quicker. As 65 Squadron's Spitfires crossed the Kent coast east of Dover, they met 74 Squadron and then spotted a small formation of bombers, but before they could get to them they espied the inevitable escort: twenty-five to thirty Me 109s, arranged in vics of five-seven machines, line astern, at a height of 18,000 ft.[64] Being some 3,000 ft lower as they were originally intended to intercept the bombers, 65 Squadron climbed to attack the escorts, broke into separate sections of three and a pursuit began; only three Spitfires actually got close enough to open fire.[65] What followed was typical of the tactics espoused by *Generalmajor* Theo Osterkamp, the *Luftflotte 2* fighter supremo: the enemy turned for France, scattering and then resuming their formations, while those few which 65 Squadron got close to carried out the classic Me 109 escape tactic, half roll and dive, as recorded in the squadron's IPR.

The bombers had by then vanished, clearly only decoys being empty of bombs and thus much faster than usual, but two of the 65 Squadron pilots managed to score against the retreating escorts: F/Sgt Franklin claimed a Me 109 confirmed and another damaged, while Sgt Kilner claimed a probable.[66] At the beginning of the engagement, one of the Messerschmitts hit the petrol tank in F/O Walker's machine, but he was able to evade further attentions and got his damaged aircraft down at Manston; a sprained shoulder attested to the violence of his avoiding action.[67] The latter probably encourage his assailant to claim the Spitfire as a victory. It would seem that *I/JG 54* were the 'raid' identified by the radar system north of Dover, and that they may have been responsible for attacking F/O Walker; this despite 64 Squadron having been vectored to intercept this particular raid.

Of the five *Luftwaffe* fighter claims made for this morning, four were between 08h55 and 08h59, with one much earlier, by *Oblt* Seiler, *Staffelkapitän* of 1/JG 54, given as over the Channel at '09h15'.[68] This must be an error of detail as at that time neither 65 nor 64 Squadron had yet taken off from their home bases.[69] It is perhaps more likely that

Seiler's claim was actually at *c.* 09h50 (a plausible error of transposing 0915 for 0950, equally easy to do in either English or German), but in any event was likely the first German claim that morning. Logically this would have been against 65 Squadron, not 64, the former having very likely reached the Dover area before the latter, as already discussed above. *I/JG 54* would thus have played the role of the ambushers against RAF fighters reacting to the well-escorted spoof raid made towards the east of Dover. Following their brief bounce of elements of 65 Squadron they would have made rapidly for the French coast, having already spent time and fuel just inland of Dover.

The claims of 65 Squadron pursuing the (intentionally) retreating escort of the fleeing German bombers would presumably have been against those Me 109s. 65 Squadron had reported them as twenty-five to thirty in number,[70] and thus a *Gruppe* in strength. There are two potential German fighter casualties to consider against the claims made by 65 Squadron: an Me 109 of *I/JG 51* lost over the Channel together with its pilot, *Ofw* Schmid, or an Me 109 of *8/JG 51* damaged 40% over the Channel which returned to base, its pilot safe.[71] A unit history of *JG 51*, however, ascribes the loss of Karl Schmid to a Beaufighter (sic) rear gunner, at approximately 14h25, British time.[72] Therefore, by a process of elimination, 65 Squadron was responsible for the damaged Me 109 of *8/JG 51*, presumably by F/Sgt Franklin. Inferring that 65 Squadron engaged with Me 109s of *III/JG 51* is also consistent with three claims 10 km south-west of Dover at 09h55-09h59, made by three pilots of *7/JG 51*.[73] Presumably, when *III/JG 51* escorted the decoy bombers across the Channel towards Dover they then turned round again once they had attracted the attention of 65 Squadron, thereby setting them up for attack from *I/JG 54* placed at altitude behind, i.e. north of Dover; *7 Staffel* likely carried on over the Dover area, most probably at higher altitude than the rest of *III/JG 51*. This set up another potential ambush situation for any further British fighter squadrons responding to the incoming decoy formation. And they were partly successful, as witnessed by 64 Squadron's experiences.

64 Squadron had been circling offshore of Dover as per controller's instructions, and while they were on a westerly course, supposedly at 09h10, at about 13,000 ft, S/L MacDonell, Red 1, as well as Yellow 1, F/O Woodward and Red 2, Sgt Binham, observed an aircraft about 4 miles behind them turn over and go down pouring out white smoke, which they thought afterwards might have been Sgt Isaacs who had been flying in the tail-end-Charlie position, as Blue 3 and was missing.[74] A distance of 4 miles astern equated to only about one minute's flying time for fast fighters like Me 109s or Spitfires. After landing back at base, the surviving members of 64 Squadron discussed what might have happened

to Sgt Isaacs, and decided that he must have seen some Me 109s coming in from above and behind to attack his squadron, and dutifully performed his tail-end function of turning into them and engaging them.[75] One of the 64 Squadron pilots claimed to have seen Isaacs being attacked by two Me 110s on his tail, but before this pilot could get there to help, they had shot him down with no chance of bailing out of his stricken machine.[76] There is no record of this in the 64 Squadron IRP, so this may have been the pilot of 64 Squadron who made an early return to Hawkinge, being recorded there as landing at 09h09, fifteen to twenty minutes before the rest.[77]

If the report of Isaacs being shot down as described in the IPR was accurate, then the time quoted in the IPR for the others having seen an aircraft go down astern of them pouring white smoke could not have been correct, and an earlier time would have applied; this would make it more like the 08h50 given for Sgt Isaac's demise by another source.[78] The fact that Sgt Isaacs was not shot down rapidly in a surprise attack and that the offending Me 109s (there were no known Me 110s involved in this entire raid) did not then pounce on the rest of 64 Squadron, flying only a minute ahead, suggests that Sgt Isaacs put up a fight and delayed them long enough to save his squadron mates from suffering a similar fate. This would negate accounts of Isaacs having merely been surprised and dispatched,[79] or that of his friend, Sgt Jackie Mann flying in Yellow 3 position (and who had briefly seen Isaac's paperwork on his commanding officer's desk, wherein stood the assessment of him as a pilot, as 'below average, but would improve with experience'), who expressed the opinion that poor Isaacs never got the chance to improve.[80] He was most probably in action with the Me 109s of *7/JG 51*, who made several claims in the area south-west of Dover.[81]

Sgt Reggie Isaacs seems to have done considerably better than expected and was not just a brave man but an effective fighting pilot also. It was a callous practice, but alas also a fairly widespread one amongst RAF fighter squadrons in the Battle of Britain, to put the newest, least experienced boys at the back of a formation in the tail-end-Charlie position as sacrificial lambs, serving the preservation of more experienced comrades deemed more valuable to the cause. It cannot be regarded as good squadron leadership.

With this event behind them, and enabled to do so by the sacrifice of Sgt Isaacs, the rest of 64 squadron kept on and soon spotted a few Me 109s making fast for France and 64, being most likely at a greater height, were able to catch up and attacked them some 8 miles north-east of Cap Gris Nez at 10,000-12,000 ft.[82] This can only have been retreating remnants of *I/JG 54*; most of *III/JG 51* had departed back across the Channel several minutes earlier and *7/JG 51* would soon enter the picture again, from behind 64 Squadron. S/L MacDonell fired a single burst from the rear quarter using some deflection into a Me 109, fired twice at another Messerschmitt he saw diving on a Spitfire, possibly that flown by Donahue, see below, which he left pouring black smoke, and briefly fired at a third fighter. By now he was much lower down as always happened in a dogfight, and at *c.* 5,000 ft over mid-Channel spotted a Hs 126 short-range reconnaissance machine, giving it a final burst to finish his ammunition.[83] Sgt Mann gave a Me 109 in the same formation a long burst when it was in a stall turn, and observed it hit the sea; he and MacDonell confirmed each other's victories.[84] F/O Woodward also attacked the same small Me 109 formation, which he saw turn towards their attackers, but he tackled one diving away using evasive action, firing on it several times and closing in to 150 yards, and saw its evasive manoeuvres cease, something break off from the rear of the port wing and smoke pouring from this spot as it plunged further down.[85] He also saw the Hs 126 attacked by another Spitfire (MacDonell), and then fired at it himself, silencing the rear gunner, but broke away as the French coast was now near and his ammunition almost spent.[86]

I/JG 54 suffered two casualties in combat over the Channel that morning: a 35% damaged Me 109 which crash-landed back in France, its pilot unhurt, and another which was shot down by fighters into the Channel, pilot *Oblt* Seiler seriously wounded and out of action for months to come.[87] While some sources list Seiler's Me 109 as merely damaged, the *Luftwaffe* loss lists clearly state its 100% loss, albeit on 4 August, out by a day; most casualties detailed in the loss returns were only submitted some days, even weeks after the event itself, a practice which led to errors. The distinct similarities in the accounts of S/L MacDonell and Sgt Mann suggests they shot down the same Me 109.[88] Assuming these two claims to relate to *Oblt* Seiler's parachute descent into the sea, the damaged Me 109 suffered by *I/JG 54* logically can be ascribed to F/O Woodward. While Mann and MacDonell had claimed confirmed victories, Woodward's was for a probable, as was MacDonell's second claim.[89]

There is one more piece to the 64 Squadron jigsaw of 5 August 1940. Red 3, P/O Donahue, an experienced barnstorming pilot from the USA but on his first combat mission, made the common mistake of haring off after a Me 109 on his own without much thought, and was closing in on it, about 400 yards away and about to open fire, when he himself was hit by cannon and machine gun fire.[90] The damage was severe: the starboard side of the Spitfire was torn open, control cables damaged, electrical leads to the gun sight damaged, and the sight failed, the adjacent wing was also damaged and his radio put out of action.[91] Following violent manoeuvres, feint attacks and firing several bursts to distract them, he was once more free of the attentions of two attacking Me 109s, and made for home across the Channel; however, he had barely started crossing back over the sea before more Me 109s were spotted following him again, this time making for England, like him.[92] Desperate and with a barely controllable machine, he turned into them, and they retreated back to France and he managed to fly his extensively damaged Spitfire back to Hawkinge.[93]

7/JG 51 made three claims for Spitfires shot down about 10 km south-west of Dover, at 09h55, 09h57 and 09h59, respectively by *Lt* Staiger, *Uffz* Limpert and the *Staffelkapitän Hpt* Oesau.[94] These most probably relate to the loss of Sgt Isaacs, perhaps the earliest-timed claim, and the damaged Spitfire brought back by P/O Donahue. Perhaps one of them was made against Donahue after the initial attack which badly damaged his machine, any *Luftwaffe* pilot firing at an enemy machine and observing the damage thereafter, inflicted by the earlier attack, and with it flying with poor control as a result, would be justified in thinking it was his achievement. A final German claim, by *Lt* Seegatz of *5/JG 51*[95] might well reflect the final Me 109s which chased Donahue back towards England, it being common *Jagdflieger* practice to have a fresh fighter unit (*II/JG 51*) meet returning ragged German formations over the French coast which were short of fuel, ammunition and sometimes damaged; once again, one of them firing at Donahue's poorly controllable and obviously damaged aircraft could be forgiven for thinking it was his effort, with a colleague likely confirming it could not get back to the UK in that state. This is how over-claiming occurs with no fault of the relevant 'victorious' pilots other than optimism and rapid observations made in the heat of combat.

While *Generalmajor* Theo Osterkamp had obviously had an influential hand in planning the morning series of *Luftwaffe* incursions, and they were his normal wily combination of a decoy to distract and attract RAF fighter attention, i.e. the small bomber formation and escort of *III/JG 51* excluding *7 Staffel*, which together turned tail and dived back for France, and an ambushing fighter formation in *I/JG 54*, even followed up by a second, *7/JG 51*, such complex combinations sometimes got their timing wrong. In this case, 65 Squadron was able to get at the bomber escort and was briefly attacked by *I/JG 54*; honours were even at a damaged fighter each side. However, it was never part of the plan that the ambushers, *I/ JG 54* should themselves be surprised, something 64 Squadron was able to achieve thanks to the bravery and dedication of tail-end-Charlie, Sgt Isaacs. The second ambushing party of *7/JG 51* was able to redress this unplanned-for event, shooting down poor Isaacs and severely damaging Art Donahue's Spitfire, but could not stop 64 Squadron getting Seiler and damaging the Messerschmitt of his colleague.

65 Squadron was ordered up from Manston at noon to patrol a Channel convoy, and once there at 15,000 ft, observed about thirty Me 109s in a tight formation of vics of three fighters coming their way at c. 13,000 ft.[96] F/Lt Olive, leading the squadron, climbed preparatory to attacking them, but they turned back for France in a shallow, long dive, and Olive, after firing unsuccessfully at the rear Me 109, ordered his men back to the convoy.[97] Sgt Orchard did not hear this instruction, and followed the enemy until almost the French coast where he fired at all three members of a lagging vic, claiming one of them as a probable as it descended streaming smoke from its fuselage.[98]

A final feint was made towards convoy 'Bosom' off Dover that afternoon; S/L Hood led six Spitfires of 41 Squadron up from their forward base at Manston at 13h50 to patrol over the ships. He wisely placed his small formation at 20,000 ft, below a cloud layer about 1,500 ft higher.[99] Radar must have picked up an assembly of enemy aircraft over the Pas de Calais and the controller ordered two more squadrons forward to intercept any approach to the convoy. At 14h30 nine Hurricanes of 151 Squadron were scrambled from Rochford, with instructions to intercept enemy aircraft off Dover, and 65 Squadron were also sent up and ordered to intercept there.[100] While at c. 19,000 ft off Dover, 151 Squadron met an estimated five Ju 88s and about thirty Me 109s, all flying south-west; leading section Red went for a Ju 88, while Yellow Section climbed and engaged the Me 109 escort at 20,000 ft and above.[101] Yellow leader F/O Blair gave a Messerschmitt a three-second burst and observed it fall into the sea, while Sub Lt Beggs, Red 2, pursued his prey across the Channel and opened up on the Ju 88 at about 500 yards, closing to 200-300 yards, and saw dense black smoke coming out of both engines as his quarry dived steeply over the French coast.[102] Blair claimed his Me 109 as confirmed, Beggs his bomber as a probable.

S/L Hood's six Spitfires meanwhile had been carrying out their convoy patrol when at 15h00 a dark camouflaged He 111 popped out of the cloud above them, saw them and hastily popped back up, making off fast to the east.[103] Hood wisely kept five of his patrol over the ships, as they had been warned by the controller of a fifteen-plus raid on the way in, letting F/Lt Webster, leader of his second section, go after the lone bomber.[104] Webster did so with alacrity and used all his ammunition in several quarter-astern attacks on the bomber as it flew rapidly eastwards, in and out of the cloud cover, and one engine appeared to have been put out of action; however, the He 111 maintained its course for France, slowly losing height.[105] Seeing Me 109s coming across the Channel towards him, Webster wisely beat a retreat back to his comrades; the Me 109s contented themselves with escorting the bomber back to France, Webster settling for a claim for a damaged quarry.[106]

151 Squadron also noted a reluctance of the Me 109s to engage in their action off Dover, seeing them dive away using evasive turns; they also noted their original formation as comprising vics of six, seven and five Messerschmitts, in stepped-up line astern arrangement, but observed them working in pairs once this broke up.[107] P/O Blomeley of 151 Squadron later recorded a Me 110 as hit but unsubstantiated in his logbook, but made no formal claim to the intelligence officer once he had landed.[108] He may have been nearer the truth as the only bomber casualty listed in German records was a 15%-damaged Do 17 of *3/KG 3* which landed safely without casualties.[109] Spitfires of 65 Squadron also got involved briefly with the retreating Me 109s, claiming one destroyed and another damaged by F/Sgt Franklin.[110] *I/JG 51* in fact lost the Me 109 flown by *Ofw* Karl Schmid over the Channel on this mission, top scorer at that time in the *Gruppe*, who was killed.[111] Whether he fell victim to 151 Squadron's F/O Blair or 65 Squadron's F/Sgt Franklin is unknown (bearing in mind the 'Beaufighter' given as his victor above). *Hpt* Brustellin, the *Gruppenkommandeur* of *I/JG 51* claimed a 'Curtiss' over the Channel,[112] though no RAF fighter is recorded as damaged or even as having been attacked.

10

Some Analysis of Fighter Command Squadron Tactics: 1 July–7 August 1940

The detailed examinations of the fighting presented in the preceding chapters, supported by the sources and references given in the chapter notes (and not given again here), are used as the basis for some analysis of tactics applied by RAF squadron leadership at the sharp end during the period 1 July-7 August 1940. This does entail a certain amount of repetition, for which I apologise. The aim is to remind the reader of the action previously described – chosen to illustrate a specific tactical aspect – and then explore that tactical feature.

While many of Fighter Command's pilots had gained very useful experience during the fighting over France, the Dunkirk beaches and a few even over Norway, there was no real time available to squadron leaders and their pilots for any meaningful tactical innovations during these campaigns, marked by much chaos and in the cases of France and Norway with mostly primitive frontline airfields lacking many if not most amenities. While all RAF fighter pilots experiencing combat realised very soon that they had to get in close, harmonise their guns at shorter distances, and rethink their fighting formations and attack methods, the continuous fighting soon led to exhaustion exacerbated by ongoing retreats, poor supply lines, a lack of radar guidance and inadequate ground support. There was just not time or opportunity to fix what many realised was not good enough.

It was only once back in the UK that squadrons were able to rebuild, replace losses, train the new pilots, in many cases welcome new commanding officers who had not necessarily partaken of the lessons over the Continent, replace and repair aircraft and equipment and generally reorganise themselves into efficient fighting units again. Only then could the pilots and squadron leadership get to work on correcting the tactical practices they had learned during the halcyon pre-war days of the 1930s. During July 1940 as the Battle of Britain began, with relatively limited *Luftwaffe* operations mainly involving convoy attacks and assaults on coastal naval targets, complex fighter missions as well as limited inland incursions, many of a reconnaissance nature, squadron leaders and their flight commanders as well as ordinary pilots began implementing the necessary changes and tactical innovations.

The so-called Fighter Area Attacks drummed into fighter pilots in the 1930s proved to be of very little use. Air Chief Marshal Dowding and his 11 Group commander, AV-M Keith Park both saw them as a mere framework that would rapidly change once faced by the realities of combat, and felt strongly that combat leaders should make their own decision as to tactics as best dictated by the action itself.[1] Dowding's basic framework of orders for conducting the Battle of Britain encompassed:[2] an overall battle of attrition over a long time; throughout, to preserve Fighter Command as a force in being; to intercept all raids and that before they bombed; the basic unit of interception/attack to be the squadron; and Group commanders to fight the actual tactical, daily battle. In other words, the independence of Group commanders was central to Dowding's conduct of the Battle; similarly, sector commanders were trusted to have their controllers vector their squadrons into suitable attacking positions, again independently. The inherent freedom of squadron leadership thus to formulate and adapt combat tactics was part of this widespread emphasis on independent command at all levels.[3] Park, a loyal and enthusiastic disciple of Dowding, felt particularly strongly about tactical flexibility.[4]

Fighter formations

Some squadrons did experiment with diverse combat formations with varying success, but others stuck to what they had been taught in peacetime. The Fighter Area Attacks and rigid, tight formations comprising four three-aircraft vics had been promulgated from the top in times when only bombers lacking any fighter escort were envisaged as threatening Britain from German bases. Once this comfortable scenario was shattered by the loss of France, with numerous German bases along the southern side of the Channel, high command should have recast their philosophy, preferably through stimulating consultation between station commanders and squadron leaders, after initial combat experience had shown how flawed these formations were. The onus to change really lay, in the first place, with the squadron leader. These men whose role in the Battle was to be so critical were predominantly long-serving regular officers, imbued with the strong discipline of the RAF. The Germans called the pervasive tight vic formations, '*Idiotenreihen*' a term that does not require translation. However, the German fighter pilot had a philosophy, also inculcated from their top command, which was to prove as damaging, not so much to the pilot casualty rates but to losing the Battle itself. They were obsessively focussed on scoring victories and in the end this habit cost them too many bomber casualties. And once the fighter pilots became operationally tired and were not relieved as were their RAF opponents, it cost them excessive Me 109 losses. The *Idioten* factor was at work on both sides of the Channel.

On 17 July a full-strength formation of 64 Squadron flying over Beachy Head in vics of three and with two weavers above and behind, in dangerous conditions of mixed cloudy and glaring sunny patches, was stalked and ambushed by two Me 109s from *3/JG 2* led by *Lt* Helmut Wick, a leading ace, losing the port weaver Spitfire whose pilot was seriously wounded. Upon taking command on 26 July, S/L MacDonell soon changed the tight vics used by 64 Squadron to much more open and loose groups of three Spitfires. Similarly, F/O Ritchie of 603 Squadron on 16 July led his section to attack a lone bomber in a wide, open vic formation. There were some distinct advantages in keeping the two sections traditionally making up a RAF fighter squadron flight; section leaders were typically experienced pilots who also acted as deputy flight commanders. A widely spaced section of three would have been similar to the famous 'finger-four' *Schwarm* formation used by the *Luftwaffe* in the Battle, in many ways being a *Schwarm* missing one machine, but enjoying many of its inherent advantages in observing danger approaching, mutual protection and easy break-up.

S/L Devitt of 152 Squadron was one of the early innovators who adopted pairs as the standard formation for his unit. This squadron had still been using standard three Spitfire sections in actions on 13, 18 and 20 July, and were bounced on the latter two occasions. On 18 July one of their sections, attacking a Do 17 in line astern, was bounced by *2/JG 2* but got away with only two damaged Spitfires – not all bouncing pilots were a Helmut Wick. In addition, the number three pilot had spotted the bounce in time to warn his comrades to take violent avoiding action.

On 20 July, however, B Flight of six machines, made up of Blue and Green Sections and with Green 3 flying as a lone weaver, performing sweeps back and forth above and behind the flight, was bounced by *3/ JG 27*, *Staffelkapitän Oblt* Homuth picking off the weaver who was killed. On 25 July 1940, S/L Devitt led his squadron of ten Spitfires in to attack a Stuka raid, A Flight ahead composed of three pairs, Red, Yellow and White sections, and B Flight of two pairs, Green and Black Sections. Sending B Flight up to distract a close escort of Me 109s, Devitt led the rest against the bombers, but they were attacked by Me 109s, possibly from a higher-flying unit of *III/JG 27* who could only damage Devitt's Spitfire. Though when flying towards an interception the squadron normally flew in two large, six-aircraft vics, one behind the other, thereby somewhat negating the advantage of the pairs.

They were not alone in changing to pairs. Twelve Hurricanes of 615 Squadron led by S/L Kayll flew in pairs on an operation on 27 July. On 28 July, S/L Hood led 41 Squadron into action over the Dover region, using four stepped-down sections each of three Spitfires, and with Green 2 from the rearmost section flying 1,000 ft below his section. An unusual formation but providing protection from any attack from below and also to a certain extent, from bouncing Me 109s from above who liked to pull up behind and below rearmost machines before opening fire. Despite having improved the fighting ability of 64 Squadron through loose vics of three machines, S/L MacDonell persisted in using weavers. As we have seen, on 5 August Sgt Reggie Isaacs, acting as the weaver for the squadron, put up a brave fight against descending Me 109s and saved his comrades from attack, but at the price of his own life. However, one cannot fault MacDonell as a leader; the Germans who invented the 'finger-four' formation still used a weaver section in fighting the 1941-1942 RAF sweeps over Northern France.

Fighter Command did not observe pervasive German use of the 'finger-four' in the Battle, and many Intelligence Patrol Reports in July contain references to Me 109s flying in vics. For example, 65 Squadron on 5 August saw an approaching Me 109 *Gruppe* comprised entirely of perfect vics of three fighters. 151 Squadron on the same day observed how the Me 109s they saw were arranged in vics of five, six and seven machines but noted further that they broke up into pairs for action. This is an important point to note: fighter units on both sides used more clumsy formations often when flying towards a target or interception, but before battle was joined, they reverted to a more efficient fighting formation. For the larger German standard unit, the *Gruppe* of about thirty machines, if they had flown at cruising speeds towards interceptions in spread-out 'finger-fours' the commander would not have been able to keep his *Staffeln* in sight within his overall spatial orientation when planning an attack on the enemy. Similarly, RAF fighter squadrons used tight vic formations to fly towards interceptions but on sighting the enemy and prior to the actual attack, most squadron leaders ordered their sections to separate and form line astern formations, and some even to break up into pairs just like the *Luftwaffe*. Of course, for both fighter forces, if surprised while flying their specific *'Idiotenreihen'* before transitioning to their fighting formations, the results were often grim.

Fighter Command ammunition

The ammunition loads carried by Fighter Command's Spitfires and Hurricanes were soon increased by the squadrons themselves, from the recommended standard of 2,400 rounds, or 300 per gun, early in July 1940: mostly up by *c.* 4-11%, and some up to 17% more rounds. Notably, 74 Squadron habitually carried 2,720 rounds and 603 Squadron, 2,800 rounds (Chart 2). While the former was mostly in action against Me 109s over the Straits of Dover, the latter fought mainly against lone German bombers off the Scottish coast; the perception of the need to increase ammunition load was thus likely a general feeling on fighter squadrons.

While RAF documents, especially IPRs, provide these interesting data for many squadrons, only one document gave details of the different ammunition types and their proportions: a 257 Squadron IPR for 19 July has percentage data, and knowing the RAF kept different ammunition types loaded in separate machine guns in the eight gun batteries of Hurricanes and Spitfires, it can be deduced easily that five guns were loaded exclusively with ball ammunition, two only with armour piercing rounds and the remaining machine gun carried a few tracer rounds and all the 'De Wilde' projectiles. The latter, also called Type VI ammunition, ignited only on impact and gave off a small ignition explosion in doing so, and were highly effective and very popular with pilots as they provided small flashes when they hit home; their limited proportion was due to production constraints.

The bomber problem: attacking the single aircraft in July 1940

Lone bombers seeking targets of opportunity or specific targets under favourable weather conditions, as well as armed reconnaissance and primary reconnaissance missions by bomber type machines, were common in July 1940. Interceptions from 1 July-7 August 1940 resulted in the destruction of seventy-one German aircraft, sixty-five bombers (and twenty-eight more damaged), two Me 110s, two He 59s and two Hs 126s. The number of attacking RAF fighters is known for sixty-two of these aircraft, averaging out at 2.95 British fighters, and a figure of 2.15 fighters for the twelve damaged machines where this is known. For twenty-four of the Luftwaffe losses, the ammunition expenditure of the RAF attackers is known: 4,949 rounds. While statistics must always be treated with some circumspection, especially for low data numbers, this essentially means that for each German lone bomber aircraft destroyed, attack by a full section of three RAF fighters was needed, firing an average of *c.* 5,000 rounds between them. However, bomber return fire also exacted high fighter casualties: eight Hurricanes lost and seventeen damaged, five Spitfires and another twelve damaged; four RAF pilots were killed and two wounded. A well fought bomber aircraft could wreak havoc on its attackers, sometimes: a Do 17 of *III/KG 76* attacked on 29 July managed to damage two of the four Spitfires attacking it, who in turn, despite firing off at least 9,600 rounds of ammunition largely from astern, only damaged it, killing one crew member.

The RAF attack method is known for twenty-four of the German losses: astern attacks 57%; quarter astern 16%; beam attacks 22%; head-on 5%. Once again, one should be wary of statistics, especially where data are limited. Innovation and adaptation of tactics applied against lone bombers began on the very first day of July 1940 and continued apace thereafter as new methods rapidly replaced the Fighter Area attacks. Three Spitfires of 602 Squadron carried out the first beam attack on a lone bomber on 1 July. The first simultaneous attacks, from astern and abeam on a lone bomber, were done by a section of 54 Squadron led by F/Lt 'Wonky' Way on 3 July. Thereafter, combinations of astern, quarter astern and beam attacks by sections of RAF fighters became relatively common, but were seldom performed simultaneously and rather carried out by one fighter after another in succession; for example, by 616 and 603 Squadrons on 3 July, or on 8 July by 602 and 74 Squadrons. 602 Squadron was a prolific initiator of new attack methods, demonstrated by their flying a combination of beam and head-on attacks by a section against a lone bomber on 7 July 1940. It is noticeable that most of this tactical innovation came either from 13 Group squadrons (602 and 603 Squadrons) or those from 11 Group's Hornchurch sector (54 and 74 Squadrons).

This experience during the 1 July-7 August 1940 period underlined for Fighter Command and for the squadrons involved what it would take to destroy German bombers: harmonise guns at shorter distances, get in close with all the attendant risks that brought and – possibly of greatest importance – that it would generally require multiple attacks by several fighters to destroy these larger machines. Gun harmonisation distance within Fighter Command was initially standardised at about 400 yards, concomitant with the lack of intensive gunnery training, and with Dowding's probably generally correct view that the average pilot could not shoot well. However, a wide spray of machine gun projectiles at such ranges would not lethally damage a bomber, and during July 1940 the realities of experienced combat soon brought change; P/O Colin Gray of 54 Squadron and F/Lt Sailor Malan of 74 Squadron were amongst those prominent in reducing the distance to about 250 yards. Interestingly, both flew out of Hornchurch Sector Station, and Malan was a leading innovator in Fighter Command in the Battle and afterwards.

A good example of realising the need to get in close, with its inherent risks to the attacking fighter, is given by F/Lt 'Pat' Hughes, leading luminary of 234 Squadron: on 27 July he led a section against a lone Ju 88 from *3(F)/121* south-west of Land's End, who fired off all their ammunition from 200-300 yards and while claiming an unconfirmed victory, their quarry successfully belly-landed at base, minus a gunner who tragically fell from the Junkers just above the sea. Early the very next day, Hughes again led a section of 234 Squadron Spitfires against another lone Ju 88, this time from *II/LG 1* near Plymouth, and led his colleagues in to fire from only 100-50 yards, seeing their victim crash into the sea on fire. Thus the realities and pressure of combat lead to very rapid changes in tactics. With the 0.303 calibre machine guns carried by the RAF's fighters, shorter harmonisation and closing in to short ranges were more or less essential to hit a bomber lethally, at the same time exposing the attacking pilot to much greater danger himself, and in time many an experienced and successful pilot paid for the successful tactic with his life, including Hughes, who was killed on 7 September 1940. Basically, whether assaulting a lone bomber or a formation of escorted bombers, risks to the attackers had to be accepted.

Attacking bomber formations

Many if not all involved in the aerial defence of the UK would have been mindful of what the future held, as mass raids by bombers in formation with large escorts were expected, and indeed became a reality from 11 August onwards. There was one distinct difference between attacking lone bombers and those in tight formations: manoeuvrability was basically the rule for lone aircraft who generally took effective evasive action, whereas those in formation had only limited possibilities for this. From 11 August onwards breaking up German bomber formations therefore became critical and attacks from astern and quarter astern, akin to the Fighter Area Attacks, would not be adequate.

During the first ten days of July 1940 there were seven *Luftwaffe* convoy attacks by small- to medium-sized Do 17 bomber formations over the Eastern Channel or off the Thames Estuary, mostly strongly escorted by one or two fighter *Gruppen*, either both Me 109s or one each of Me 109s and Me 110s. The Dorniers were exclusively from *KG 2*, the Me 110s from *ZG 26*, the Me 109s from *II and III/JG 51* and *I/LG 2*. These units fell under the *Kanalkampfführer, Oberst* Fink, simultaneously *Kommodore KG 2*, ably supported by *Oberst* Osterkamp, *Kommodore*

JG 51. At this stage of the Battle, in the Pas de Calais, the Germans only had *c.* 100-120 Me 109s available for operations (Chart 1), which latter soon brought those numbers down.

Fighter Command responses to these seven convoy raids varied between a section of three, a flight of six-eight machines, sixteen sent against the second raid, and a grand total of thirty-eight against the largest convoy raid on 10 July, Dowding's choice of the official opening day of the Battle of Britain, when the first major raid of the Battle was seriously countered by 11 Group. Of the seven Dornier convoy attacks, six were escorted; in four cases RAF fighters got at the bombers, despite the best efforts of the escorting Me 109s and Me 110s for three of them, the fourth being unescorted, and in a fifth case some fighters got at straggling retreating bombers. Total Dornier sorties on these seven raids totalled *c.* 186, with *c.* 270 escort sorties, of which about eighty were Me 110s, the rest Me 109s, and Fighter Command met them with eighty-four sorties of Spitfires and Hurricanes, of which about twenty-five to thirty actually got at the bombers. Casualties at this stage of the Battle were still low: four Dorniers lost and five damaged, four Me 110s destroyed and two damaged, one Me 109 lost and two damaged; Fighter Command lost five Hurricanes and three damaged, with four Spitfires lost, two damaged, and with six pilots dead, one wounded. Most losses were inflicted by the escorts, bombers apparently being responsible for destroying one Hurricane and damaging two, as well as one Spitfire, and killing its pilot; one Hurricane and pilot were lost to friendly fire from Spitfires.

The Fighter Command machines were outnumbered, overall, by about five and a half to one but as not all fighters sent up to tackle raids actually made contact, the odds effectively would have been higher. German escort fighters outnumbered their British opponents by about three to one. Overall, losses were quite different: almost 11% of aircraft for the RAF and six fighter pilots killed, and slightly less than 2% aircraft for the Germans, with ten fighter crewmen lost. These percentages are a direct reflection of the disparate aircraft numbers employed by each side. With much of the fighting over water and with the rather *ad hoc* British rescue system as opposed to an organised and capable German one, British fighter pilot losses in July, proportionately, were high.

Tactical innovation came not only from RAF unit leaders but also from the ranks of the ordinary line pilots. As an example, Sgt Cartwright DFM from 79 Squadron, on 4 July was part of the first RAF attack on an escorted raid in the Battle and was the first to carry out a beam attack, on two Dorniers, significantly damaging both and wounding two crew members in each before the German escorts intervened. German bombers had little to no armour to protect against beam fire. This was at the cost of Cartwright's own life taken by the rapidly descending Me 109 escorts involved. Four days later, two small Dornier convoy raids were each intercepted by small formations of 610 Squadron; they attacked the first from dead astern in the absence of escorts but lost a Spitfire to return fire while not causing any serious harm to any bombers, but did put the Dorniers off their aim, no ships being hit. The second, later raid was escorted, and P/O Norris led six Spitfires into an astern attack, but coming in for a second attack on the bombers they opened up their line astern formations of three aircraft into three machines flying abreast – basically a Fighter Area 'No. 3 attack' – thus splitting the return fire; a rapid innovation of tactics in the heat of battle.

In other raids, unit leadership played a critical role in ensuring a really aggressive assault against high odds. On 9 July 1940 F/Lt Hugh Ironside led six Hurricanes of 151 Squadron against *c.* 100 German aircraft, Dorniers, Me 110s and Me 109s, stepped successively up behind each other from 12,000 to 20,000 ft. Splitting his pitifully small force, Ironside ordered three to distract the escort (a tall order!) and the other three to go for the bombers, but the escort overwhelmed them all and battle was joined only between fighters. F/Lt Ironside received a hit on his cockpit canopy, sending splinters into one eye, but he managed to get out of the fight and get his aircraft home; another Hurricane was shot down into the sea but its pilot survived. North Weald's station commander, the ever-combative Wing Commander Victor Beamish, flying on Ironside's wing, knocked down an Me 110 with two other pilots and another Me 110 suffered severe damage with its gunner panicking and bailing out into the sea on the way home, being posted missing. The bombers also panicked, splitting up into six formations, only one of which found the convoy and scored no hits. It was the sheer determination of this attack carried out by a rather salty squadron that made the difference despite poor tactical conditions and high odds. 151 Squadron had lost a flight commander over Dunkirk who was shot down but made it on to a returning ship, only to have that sunk by an e-boat; its crew machine-gunned the survivors in the water. 151 Squadron was one of those units which attacked with intent to do harm.

65 Squadron, led by F/Lt Saunders, intercepted a second large raid on the same convoy later that day, meeting some seventy enemy machines, again bombers, Me 110s, Me 109s stepped up from 8,000 to 14,000 ft; Saunders had only seven Spitfires, flying in an innovative formation with a pair in front, then a section in vic and a pair at the back. Climbing up, they turned in and dived on some Me 109s below and dispatched one and its pilot for a Spitfire slightly damaged. This was typical of the tactics used by this squadron and reflects their belief in their role as tackling the escorts preferentially, while also lowering risk and losses. It was already

established 11 Group practice, when possible, to have Spitfires tackle top cover fighters and Hurricanes their lower altitude bomber charges. 65 Squadron had recently lost an entire section to the 109s in amongst cloud and their erstwhile C/O the next day under similar circumstances. The tactical approaches of 151 and 65 Squadrons were very different to each other, yet each, in its own way, worked.

For the last convoy raid in this 1-10 July period, on the last day, the Germans used a new method. With two bomber *Gruppen*, escorts of a Me 110 *Gruppe* and another of Me 109s, the escorts surged ahead of the bombers as they neared their convoy target, climbing and forming a massive rotating circle just past the target. The circle, a tactic that would be repeated, was meant to absorb the incoming British fighters, and did so. The RAF squadrons were very well controlled, 74 Squadron being sent up high, 56 Squadron at the level of the main part of the Me 110s and towards the end as the circle broke up and dived towards France, 64 Squadron was brought in at low level to chase these now fuel-challenged retreating enemies. F/Lt Measures led 74 Squadron above the topmost Me 109s and down into the middle of the German fighter circle in a rather spectacular spiral dive and latched onto various enemy machines. 56 Squadron preceded them by a few minutes and, approaching the still forming fighter circle, climbed and dived onto the Me 110s across the circle, with P/O Geoffrey Page climbing up the other side of the circle and then briefly flying in the opposite direction around the inside of it. Meanwhile, S/L John Thompson's nine Hurricanes of 111 Squadron were vectored on to the Dorniers from ahead and quite a bit higher, but there was no head-on attack as so pervasively reported in literature.

Thompson led his men past the bombers before turning in behind and performing a determined close-in 'No. 5 Fighter Area attack' – all sections, line astern, following each other in – as the bombing of the convoy began. Thompson's men made repeated and determined assaults on the Dorniers from astern, closing right in to 50-25 yards, one colliding with its victim and killing F/O Higgs, who may also have been hit by a Me 109 just before. They were able to dispatch two Do 17s into the Channel, another was written off in France and two more damaged; three Me 110s and crews were shot down and one Me 109 from the disintegrating fighter circles, for the loss of only two British Hurricanes and three more fighters damaged, Higgs being the only fatality. Just like 151 Squadron's attack on the previous day, Thompson led his men in with intent and determination and got in close; these were factors that made all the difference.

On 11 July, twelve He 111s of *I/KG 55* escorted by twelve Me 110s of *III/ZG 76* flew in from just west of the Isle of Wight, up the Solent to bomb Portsmouth dockyard, specifically the floating dock. 601 Squadron intercepted the raid halfway up the Solent, F/Lt Rhodes-Moorhouse leading his flight into an astern attack on the bombers after having ordered his other flight to climb and take on the escort. A combination of anti-aircraft fire and 601 Squadron's assault severely damaged two Heinkels, while the Me 110s shot down a Hurricane, whose wounded pilot was strafed on his parachute, fortunately without hitting him. 145 Squadron, scrambled once the raid was already in progress, intercepted an outgoing formation of 11 machines, one of which broke away as they did so; they finished this one off as well as the twelfth Heinkel. S/L Peel who had led them in an astern attack on the bombers was hit and his Hurricane badly damaged by return fire, nevertheless he chased a third Heinkel far out to sea, leaving it severely damaged and it crashed in France and was written off. Despite a failing engine, Peel got back almost to the coast before bailing out and being rescued just in time before he lost consciousness. He had set a fine example of sticking with the enemy for his squadron. 601 Squadron's attack as well as anti-aircraft fire saved the dockyard from any serious damage and the floating dock was not hit.

The next day, a convoy off Aldeburgh on the East Coast was attacked by three unescorted, small bomber formations within half an hour: twelve He 111s of *II/KG 53* flying in a single open vic formation; nine He 111s of 8/KG 53 in three vics, line astern; and a vic of three *II/KG 2* Do 17s. The controllers did excellent work as each German formation was intercepted; three pairs of 17 Squadron on convoy patrol to the north, the south and directly over the ships each intercepted one of the three successive German bomber formations. *II/KG 53* was met only by a pair of 17 Squadron Hurricanes, losing a Heinkel to astern attacks from below. 8/KG 53 was intercepted by the second 17 Squadron pair, which shot down the rearmost machine from the third vic through repeated quarter astern attacks. A beam attack by a reinforcement section of 85 Squadron, led by Sgt Jowitt who was hit by return fire and did not return, seriously damaged a second 8/KG 53 Heinkel, which was finished off by the first 17 Squadron pair, still in the vicinity of the convoy.

II/KG 2 was intercepted by ten Hurricanes of 151 Squadron led by S/L Donaldson who bored in fearlessly from astern, his men in line astern, each machine attacking singly in succession being exposed to the full and coordinated fire of all three bombers, who defended themselves peerlessly. Donaldson's machine was badly hit, as was the next one, flown by Wing Commander Beamish, North Weald station commander, but both got home unharmed after crippling one Dornier, which was finished off by four other Hurricanes. Three more Hurricanes hit a second Do 17 but at the cost of a Hurricane and pilot, and this bomber was shot down into the sea by the third 17 Squadron pair, with a number of quarter astern and head-on attacks.

The loss rates to the German bombers on 12 July 1940, 8% (*II/KG 53*), 22% (*8/KG 53*) and 67% (*II/KG 2*), were all unsustainable, but the five bombers lost in total cost two Hurricanes and pilots, two more damaged. These five bombers succumbed to attack by two Hurricanes each in two cases, four, five and six Hurricanes for the other three. Downing German bombers in formation using rifle calibre machine guns required multiple and dangerous close attacks. Use of *Luftwaffe* bombers in July tailed off thereafter, the last two attacks being on 24 July. Over the Western Channel, *Luftflotte 3* engaged in a number of limited raids by small Ju 88 formations on a wide variety of targets on 15, 16 and 18 July. On the latter day also, a flight of 609 Squadron patrolling a convoy off Swanage intercepted two Ju 88s and dispatched one and damaged the other with beam, quarter and astern attacks but had two Spitfires shot down by return fire, both pilots rescued uninjured.

Early on 24 July two formations of six Do 17s each from *II/KG 2* making for a convoy in the Dover Straits, were intercepted by a flight of Spitfires from 54 Squadron. The first wave bombed the ships but missed, but the second wave was attacked so intently from astern by Green Section led by P/O Gribble that they jettisoned their ordinance and fled before reaching the convoy. Return fire damaged two Spitfires, but the convoy suffered no losses. Simultaneously, Me 110s from *EGr 210* attacked naval trawlers and a Trinity House vessel standing by the convoy, sinking three trawlers and damaging the Trinity House ship; a flight from 64 Squadron intercepted, with inconclusive results. The controllers had done an excellent job getting fighters onto both of these coordinated formations in short order.

At midday the same day, a second two-part raid flew in over the sea off the Eastern Kent coast: eighteen Do 17s of *I/KG 2*, with close escort of *III/JG 52* and higher remote escort of *III/JG 26*, turned west off Margate en route to a convoy debouching into the Thames Estuary from the River Medway. The *EGr 210* Me 110s carried on north, aiming for another convoy off Harwich. F/Lt Deere led twelve 54 Squadron Spitfires from the beam into the six vics of three Do 17s each at *c.* 5,000 ft, stepped up with Me 109s above. However, the Messerschmitts kept them off the Dorniers, and splitting into sections line astern, 54 Squadron attacked individually, resulting in multiple small dogfights in which they had little trouble outmanoeuvring the Me 109s, and outpacing them by use of maximum engine boost. The Do 17s rapidly dropped one salvo of bombs and disappeared back to France. Six Spitfires of 65 Squadron half-heartedly attacked the bombers after 54 Squadron, from too far away, damaging one and then became involved with some of the escort.

A double menace: Stukas and Me 110 fighter bombers up until 23 July

The Me 110s made their first appearance on 9 July, both in the east over the Thames Estuary where they fought 151 Squadron as already related, and over the Western Channel where a sweep of six Me 110s was intercepted by a section of 43 Squadron led by S/L George Lott, south of the Isle of Wight. The Me 110s saw the Hurricanes approaching, turned back into them enabling a head-on confrontation where the heavy, centralised nose armament of the Me 110, additionally making aiming easy, proved formidable. Lott lost an eye due to splinters from a hit on his armoured windscreen, somehow flew back over the mainland and survived a parachute jump, but never flew in action again.

Later that day, *Luftflotte 3* launched the first Stuka attack of the Battle, *I/StG 77* attacking a convoy south-east of Portland, escorted by Me 110s of *13/LG 1* with top cover from some Me 109s of *I/JG 2*. Due to radar difficulties, only a single section from 609 Squadron intercepted, under cloudy conditions, but managed to kill the *Gruppenkommandeur* of the Stukas. However, their section leader fell victim to the Me 110s, who in turn lost one of their own aircraft. With minimal opposition, *I/StG 77* only damaged two steamers in the convoy despite fielding twenty-seven dive bombers, probably due to loss of their leader; in future the Stuka would prove a potent weapon against shipping and naval vessels. Stuka dive-bombers made eight more raids up till 23 July, one on Portland harbour, the other seven on convoys: four in the Dover Straits area and three in the Western Channel. Of these eight attacks, seven were intercepted by the RAF but in only four of them did the British fighters actually get at the Ju 87s (three were in the Dover area); in the other three cases the RAF fought the escort only. The controllers were thus much more successful in getting their fighters in amongst the Ju 87s in the Dover Straits, three times out of four, but their bases were much closer and they had radar observation over the Pas de Calais.

Over the Western Channel, controllers generally only spotted raids in about mid-Channel, which were already at height and coming in fast. Escorts in the Western Channel had much further to fly, thus they could only make a brief attack and then go home; consequently, they flew Me 109 sweeps just ahead of Stukas or tried to arrive over the target as the Ju 87s got there. Me 110s were used more as escorts in the Western Channel; they were not used in the Eastern Channel except for *EGr 210*, which often coordinated bombing with Ju 87s. Stukas flew in very slowly and so were very hard to escort directly. Over the narrow seas in the Dover Straits Me 109s were sent ahead, coincident with Ju 87 arrival over convoys or just behind, thus maintaining a Messerschmitt presence essentially in the Dover area to tackle any fighter attacks made on the Stukas.

There were two particularly advantageous times to attack a Stuka formation; one was when their speed was at a minimum as they pulled up from their dives. The second time was just before the Stukas dived onto their targets; they would then form a circle, normally each *Staffel* in turn, and then peel off individually from the circle, into a near-vertical dive with dive breaks on. If attacked while still in the circle, when their pilots' attention was focussed on their targets and an accurate dive, they were slow, possibly distracted and could be hit. Once their dives commenced, with dive breaks on, no modern fighter could stay with them as the fighters inevitably overtook their quarry. Stukas generally made difficult targets, their slow speed enabling quite clumsy and slow aerial manoeuvres, counter-intuitively making them hard to hit.

An action on 14 July involving 615 Squadron illustrates two different attacks on the Stukas. The convoy off Dover was protected by S/L Kayll's Red Section of 615 Squadron who saw the incoming Ju 87s at 12,000 ft with Me 109 escorts about 1,000 ft higher. Kayll led his small band into a climb and then descended onto the Stukas just as they were starting their dives; a confused combat followed between Hurricanes and Ju 87s briefly attacking each other, and with Me 109s mixing in also, and one Hurricane and pilot was lost. Meanwhile the other three sections of 615 Squadron had taken off from their forward base at Hawkinge and F/O Gayner led Yellow Section out towards the convoy, saw it being bombed, and they found themselves at only 3,000 ft with Stukas below them pulling out of their dives. They attacked immediately and downed two of them, killing the crews.

On 20 July Me 110s of *EGr 210* cooperated closely with the main Stuka raiding force, and both Me 110s and Ju 87s timed their attacks to converge on one of the convoy's escorting destroyers, leaving it sinking. This rather ominous step-up in raid coordination marked the onset of many more, multiple-unit, complex attacks, which became a common practice in *Luftflotte 2*. On this occasion, S/L John Worrall of 32 Squadron on 20 July led his men from 10,000 ft and out of the evening sun straight through lower escorting Me 109s, put his sections into line astern, throttled back to reduce speed in the dive and set about the Ju 87s as they began their dives. He took two of his three sections in with him, the third being detailed to take on and distract an upper Me 109 escort, which they did with the loss of one of their number. Meanwhile Worrall and his other two sections chased Stukas all over the sky, with escorting Me 109s doing the same to them, and a few Me 110s also mixing in. S/L Worrall's six Hurricanes hit and damaged four Stukas, and 32 Squadron dispatched a Me 109 and pilot; the cost was

Worrall himself crash-landing, slightly injuring him and destroying his aircraft, and another Hurricane damaged, its pilot slightly wounded.

Initiative was shown by the Germans on 11 July in a raid on Portland Harbour, when *III/StG 2* was escorted by *III/ZG 76*: one Me 110 *Staffel*, *9/ZG 76*, was placed *c.* 2,000-3,000 ft below the Stukas, to protect them when they slowed, put on dive breaks, circled and dove onto their targets – a vulnerable set of manoeuvres. By placing escorts a couple of thousand feet below, the Ju 87s could easily descend to and then through these escorts if need arose. A second *Staffel* was placed not far above the Stukas, intended to provide a close escort for when the Stukas pulled out of their bombing dives, another very vulnerable moment – these Me 110s would delay their descent until the right moment, to arrive where the Ju 87s pulled out of their dives at low level. The third Staffel of *III/ZG 76* was higher and behind the rest of the formation. RAF controllers assigned six separate RAF units to intercept, but only three made contact, two of their leaders demonstrating impressive tactical competency.

F/Lt Sir Archibald Hope had approached the incoming enemy formation from the east originally, but then led his flight towards the north-west as the Germans themselves turned east for Portland. Hope led his men in from the flank at the perfect moment, just as they turned over and dived, and though they claimed one Ju 87, plus five more probable and one damaged, only one was lost; however, their aim was greatly upset as only one ship was slightly damaged. Hope's six machines, as they dived after the Stukas, also became embroiled with the Me 110s of 9/ZG 76 who were trying to form a circle. As they did so, S/L Dewar skilfully placed his three Hurricanes of 87 Squadron between the sun and the enemy machines and attacking from the south, an unexpected direction, achieved surprise, and hit several of the Me 110s and negated formation of their protective circle. A 238 Squadron flight engaged various outgoing Me 110s; of the four Me 110s destroyed, two required five attackers, and one two attackers, while the fourth although only attacked by one Hurricane may also have been hit by anti-aircraft fire from Portland. Only one Hurricane was damaged. The potentially innovative Me 110 tactics might have saved the Ju 87s greater casualties, but at high cost to the escorts themselves, and the Stukas' bombing aim was put off. It was not repeated.

Fighter Command controllers also displayed tactical excellence. On 13 July, as a convoy escorted by a single old destroyer left Dover, six Stukas were launched from the Pas de Calais while their Me 109 escort took off from a base further south, intending to fly north a few miles inland and parallel to the French coast north of Boulogne, thus meeting up with the slow Stukas between Calais and Dover. The radar signals from these two formations of greatly differing speeds would have allowed the controller to distinguish them and decipher what the Germans intended. With conventional wisdom, the controller dispatched 56 Squadron from Rochford towards Calais, where they arrived before the Stukas, and then with commendable innovation he dispatched the 11 Hurricanes to the south from Calais, flying a few miles off the coast. After a quarter of an hour he had them reverse course and speed up; thus as the Me 109 escort proceeded north a few miles inland, they were being accompanied by the 56 Squadron Hurricanes flying a parallel course but a few miles out to sea. The British fighters were perfectly vectored behind and above the Stukas as they flew over the coast at Calais, and F/Lt John Coghlan promptly led them into a diving attack.

The controller's plan worked perfectly, the dive bombers seemingly paralysed for a few seconds at being attacked from the south over their own territory, then jettisoned their bombs, rolled over and dove for the sea, hotly pursued by the Hurricanes. The Hurricanes damaged two of the six Ju 87s, one crash-landing on the beach at Cap Gris Nez but paid the price for their temerity once the *II/JG 51* escort worked out what was happening and climbed in, killing two 56 Squadron pilots, with another Hurricane damaged and a fourth force-landing on the British coast (repairable). Most importantly, though, the raid was aborted before it even started.

While *EGr 210* was using Me 110 (and Me 109) fighter bombers to attack convoys and ports in the Eastern Channel and off the east coast, only a single attack by Me 110s was made over the Western Channel, and a Me 110 circle provided cover for a reconnaissance machine approaching Portland once, on 13 July. The latter action was the second RAF experience in the Battle against a circle, *V/LG 1* forming one at about 17,000 ft. They were intercepted by 238 Squadron led by F/Lt Walch, whose one section dispatched a Dornier, while Walch climbed the other three sections of Hurricanes to about 1,000 ft above the circle and up-sun of them but then waited rather aimlessly for the Me 110 circle to break up before attacking. Finally, two individual pilots took action, P/O Considine taking a risk and attacking from below, knocking one Me 110 out of the circle which then began to break up and a general engagement followed. Prior to this, Sgt Batt had climbed higher before diving headlong down into the circle, firing at a Me 110 and then pulling back up again to repeat the process. Two Spitfires from a section from 609 Squadron also attacked the outgoing Me 110s, and between them the two squadrons accounted for one Me 110 shot down into the Channel, another written off in France and two more damaged. Sgt Batt's method was similar to that employed by F/Lt Gracie of 56 Squadron in attacking the first circle encountered, on 10 July.

EGr 210 had flown their first operation of the Battle on 13 July, followed by six more attacks up to 23 July. Two of these seven attacks were not intercepted. Ten Me 110s of *EGr 210* attacked a convoy off Harwich on 15 July, being intercepted by a section of 56 Squadron on convoy patrol, led by F/Lt Gracie: despite claims, no Me 110s were lost. As was their typical method, the *EGr 210* machines came in fast and at only a few thousand feet, diving immediately on to the ships in vic formations; these were always difficult attacks to counter due to their speed – it took about fifteen minutes from their base to the convoy – and their straight-in-and-out attack method.

Three days later, a Me 110 *Staffel* of *EGr 210* flying an armed reconnaissance at sea level past the Thames Estuary and again off Harwich came across a group of naval trawlers, which, as was their wont, they attacked immediately. Two Blenheims accidently in the area tried to intercede but their poor performance led only to a loss of one to the Me 110s, which then carried out a second strafing attack with four of their machines armed with 30 mm cannon; these mostly jammed and the attack was unsuccessful. On 19 July, the *Gruppe* made two raids in the Dover Straits, one against destroyers off that port (not intercepted) and later, a second on Dover itself, by *EGr 210*'s Me 109 *Staffel*; despite their very rapid approach, the controllers did an excellent job, getting two of the three squadrons scrambled over Dover in time. The first, 32 Squadron led by S/L Worrall, engaged the 'dive-bombers' and were in turn engaged by the Me 109 escort, but did well despite being outnumbered and lower. One section of the second unit, 74 Squadron, also became involved in the dogfighting.

If *EGr 210*'s Me 110 raids were hard to counter, those by this unit's Me 109 *Staffel* were even more problematic due to their even greater speed. Next day, 32 Squadron again intercepted a fast *EGr 210* Me 110 raid on Dover; two of the Hurricanes pursued a couple of the Messerschmitts out across the Channel, resulting in one aircraft from each side being damaged. In an ominous development for Fighter Command, this raid on Dover appears to have been coordinated with a convoy attack off Swanage at the other end of the Channel, a fairly rare example of improved tactical coordination between *Luftflotten 2* and *3*.

The only similar attack over the Western Channel, carried out by a *Zerstörer Gruppe* escorted by another, plus a further *Gruppe* of Me 109s, targeted a convoy sailing west off the Isle of Wight. Controllers directed four different formations against the raiders but only a flight from 43 Squadron and subsequently a section from 238 Squadron made contact. S/L Badger split his six 43 Squadron Hurricanes, sending one section to distract the Me 109s while he attacked a large formation of what he interpreted as Do 17s, just as they were circling round prior to dive-bombing the ships. Badger turned into the half-circle and made a deflection attack, but both sections were basically overwhelmed by numbers. The 238 Squadron Hurricane section attacked the departing Me 110s from rear and above. While a collision between a Hurricane and an Me 109 cost each side a machine and pilot, the nine intercepting Hurricanes damaged one Me 110 severely, which was written off landing in France, killing its crew. Two Hurricanes were damaged but made it home, the pilots unhurt. The Me 110 bombers were effective, sinking one ship, seriously damaging another and hitting a third.

A continuous menace: Me 109 actions to 23 July

The influence of *Oberst* Osterkamp's emphasis on all possible dirty tricks to gain advantage and surprise and thus enhance enemy casualties shows in the three German bounce successes in the first ten days of July. In two actions they skilfully used clouds, in the other a decoy was used to distract the British pilots. But the RAF was learning and achieved two successful surprise attacks on Me 109s themselves on 8 July, which downed three Messerschmitts and pilots. Both were launched from below; leaders were Sgt Mould 74 Squadron, and F/Lt 'Wonky' Way 54 Squadron. The first ten days also saw eight dogfights between opposing fighters. In one, Sub Lt Frank Dawson-Paul, one of only three intercepting Spitfires of 64 Squadron, climbed up after an ascending *Gruppe*-strength Me 109 unit which formed a circle over the Channel at 32,000 ft, a height where the Spitfire struggled, and then flew round the circle in the opposite direction to their rotation and opened fire, but spun out due to the recoil. Subsequently, he aggressively chased a Me 109 right to Calais.

Increasing tactical innovation by RAF pilots was increasingly allied to aggression. On 9 July F/Lt Deere led a flight of 54 Squadron to attack an escorted He 59 rescue seaplane, sending one section down against the seaplane, while his section remained as top cover. When twelve more Messerschmitts joined the lower battle, Deere came down with his one wingman, but left his remaining wingman as a final top cover. The latter was able to perform two disrupting dive and zoom-climb attacks on the Me 109s, but, the 54 Squadron flight was badly outnumbered and suffered the loss of three machines and two pilots. Deere himself carried out a head-on attack on a Me 109 and neither pilot gave way; in the resulting collision the Me 109 suffered minor damage but Deere's Spitfire had two propeller blades forced back against the fuselage and his canopy pushed down. The incredible New Zealander was trapped in a burning machine but managed a crash-landing and used his bare hands to escape the ruined cockpit. The same day, Hurricanes of 79 Squadron dived on a

Staffel of Me 109s over the Channel and two of the Hurricanes pursued their opponents right to the French coast; panicky over-boosting of strained Daimler-Benz engines led to much black smoke being given off, but despite 79 Squadron's claims, no Me 109 was hit; pilot morale was probably another matter.

On 19 July, over the Dover Straits, 141 Squadron's nine Defiants were attacked by about twenty Me 109s of *III/JG 51* from high up-sun; however, S/L Richardson and his men were not surprised, and Richardson led them into a steep left turn, trying to form a circle, but they were hit before it could be completed. This then broke up before Richardson led the survivors to perform steep left and right turns into the attackers, which worked. The unequal combat led to four Defiants shot down into the sea, two more crashed on land and one was damaged, four pilots and six gunners lost; however, in reply one Me 109 crashed in France, its pilot mortally wounded and two more were damaged. The same day off Selsey Bill 43 Squadron was on patrol, A Flight being above B Flight, as ten to fifteen Me 109s from *III/JG 27* emerged from clouds, obviously intending to bounce the lower group of Hurricanes. F/Lt Simpson led A Flight up into the sun on seeing them and then ordered his men to break up and attack the Me 109s below. Despite an advantageous tactical situation, they only managed to damage one Messerschmitt and wound its pilot, while losing two Hurricanes shot down, one pilot killed, one wounded and a third damaged. 141 Squadron had done better under much more challenging conditions.

24-29 July 1940: heavier and more complex, multi-unit attacks

The 24 July ushered in a new phase in the Battle, marked by the operational debut of the first German radar station on the Channel coast, at Cap Blanc Nez, and also marked by significant reinforcements to the Me 109 resources in the Pas de Calais. Two days earlier, the fresh *III/ JG 52* had replaced *III/JG 3*, and the whole of JG 26 which had been stationed at its new Channel bases since 15 July became fully operational for the first time (Chart 1). Consequently, Kesselring commanding *Luftflotte* 2 and his fighter boss, *Generalmajor* Theo Osterkamp, could stage more complex and larger forays over south-eastern Kent, focussed on British naval assets on five out of six days. Combinations of the various *Luftwaffe* components became the norm in this intense period of fighting: bombers, Stukas, fighter bombers and escorts interacted in complex multi-element operations, which tried the talents of RAF controllers and fighter leaders alike. In the west, *Luftflotte 3* on four out of the six days, staged only a daily Stuka attack and some small fighter actions in an essentially unimaginative set of predictable missions. Granted in the Western Channel, Me 109 assets were limited for July 1940 to an effective four *Gruppen* with a fifth only becoming available from 28 July (Chart 1), and the wide Channel and slow speeds of the Ju 87s meant that continuous close escort was not possible, being replaced instead by fighter sweeps timed to precede closely or coincide with the arrival of raids over their shipping or port targets. The Me 109 menace so prevalent over the narrow Straits of Dover could not be replicated over the Western Channel waters. Of the four western Stuka raids, two were not intercepted by the RAF, and the other two resulted mainly in rather desultory fighter activity by both sides.

As already discussed earlier under bomber operations, 24 July saw an early small Do 17 convoy raid in concert with Me 110s from *EGr 210* attacking naval support vessels. Midday saw a larger two-part raid by Dorniers on a convoy in the Thames Estuary and by *EGr 210* Me 110s on shipping off Harwich. Complex Me 109 sorties accompanied the Estuary raid; a sweep ahead by ten Me 109s of *II/JG 26* was met by nine Spitfires of 610 Squadron over the Dover area, who killed their *Gruppenkommandeur*. The Do 17s had a direct escort of *III/JG 52* and higher remote escort of *III/JG 26*. 54 Squadron and a flight from 65 Squadron attacked the Dorniers, but they were prevented by *III/JG 52* from making effective assaults on them, and elements of *III/JG 26* appear to have attacked 54 Squadron's rear section. After landing and a rapid turnaround, nine 610 Squadron Spitfires led again by F/Lt Ellis also became involved in this intense dogfight. 54 Squadron lost one pilot, had another wounded in a damaged aircraft, and a third was written off in a crash-landing (possibly related to the *EGr 210* raid). III/JG 52 suffered four machines and pilots dispatched into the Channel, including their *Gruppenkommandeur* and two *Staffelkapitäns*, with *III/JG 26* losing two aircraft and pilots. Both German units were on their first missions in the Battle; *III/JG 52* had suffered a shattering experience and left the Channel for good a few days later. The Spitfire squadrons had done excellent work; the Me 109 menace could be tamed. While the massive dogfight raged off North Foreland, *EGr 210* sneaked off at low level to Harwich where they attacked a group of naval trawlers, sinking one but losing a Me 110 to anti-aircraft fire.

Next day, 25 July, shortly before noon, *EGr 210* Me 109 fighter-bombers made a rapid low-level light raid on Dover harbour, and were not intercepted, but their top cover, probably from *III/JG 52* and *II/JG 51*, became involved in a number of small dogfights with thirty-two intercepting RAF fighters from 32, 65 and 615 Squadrons. For the loss of a Hurricane, pilot wounded, two Me 109s were dispatched, one pilot PoW, the other wounded. The low level Me 109 bombing was an unexpected surprise, and the top cover achieved the desired German objective of luring Fighter Command into battle, but then lost two Me 109s to one Hurricane force-landed, not the sort of result favoured by *Generalmajor* Osterkamp at all.

Another, this time very large raid followed a couple of hours later, on convoy CW 8 offshore between Dover and Folkestone, apparently by three *Gruppen* of Stukas in three waves, with six Me 109 *Gruppen* escorting them. The attack was made purposely where the navigable waters were narrow, between the shore and the treacherous Goodwin Sands. Five Spitfires of 54 Squadron were on convoy patrol and F/Lt Way led them fearlessly into a mass of escorting Me 109s, probably in total comprising all three *Gruppen* of *JG 51*; Way himself was soon shot down and killed, and another Spitfire was also lost. Two more sections of 54 Squadron arrived to help, one being kept at altitude by the controller and the other skirmishing with some Me 109s. Clearly, 54 Squadron was simply overwhelmed and the raid hit the ships successfully.

While the first wave was still bombing, eleven Spitfires of 64 Squadron were vectored onto the approaching second wave, S/L MacDonell cleverly attacking the Stukas from above and out of the sun as they rolled over and dove, also avoiding the escort – very effective leadership. He led his section onto the diving Ju 87s, rolling over, cutting power and having a brief squirt as they dove past the dive-bombers; unbeknownst to him his other eight Spitfires climbed and fought against the escort of *III/JG 26*, while *7/JG 26* also dove after and then past the Stukas to try and protect them. MacDonell shot down one retreating Stuka and one of his section went missing; when the squadron leader got back to the convoy he was attacked by the escort, his machine seriously damaged but he managed to put it down at Hawkinge as the engine cut, his cockpit full of fumes and his canopy jammed. In that state he witnessed S/L Smith's machine (610 Squadron) crash as it came in, killing him. F/Lt Ellis had led nine Spitfires of 610 Squadron head-on into the escort of the third wave of Stukas, *III/JG 52* and while he dispatched the *Staffelkapitän 7/ JG 52*, S/L Smith's machine was mortally hit and another damaged. Two further squadrons were sent in as reinforcements, a full dozen Hurricanes from 111 Squadron skirmishing with *III/JG 26* and six Spitfires of 74 Squadron fighting a few Me 109s.

The convoy was hit hard: one ship sunk, two damaged and towed in to Dover and a fourth damaged and beached (later salvaged); they could not manoeuvre well in the restricted waters between shore and Goodwin Sands, but shot down one Stuka. A further dive-bomber was damaged in the general action. What was really remarkable about this large and complex action was that the controllers, from three sector stations,

Hornchurch, Biggin Hill and Kenley, managed to get fresh fighters vectored in to each of the three waves; great credit was also due to the 11 Group Controller coordinating this response and getting his timing of ordering the various sector responses at just the right times. Despite overwhelming escorts, the RAF fighters managed to contain their losses to two and a pilot from 54 Squadron, one aircraft and pilot plus another damaged for each of 64 and 610 Squadrons. The battle of attrition planned by Dowding and executed by Park and his sector controllers was working. Two Stukas were lost, another probably damaged in this action, and a Me 109 possibly shot down in this set of combats, or perhaps later.

Convoy CW 8 had progressed westwards to a position off Folkestone when attacked again by Stukas diving out of the afternoon sun, which sank four ships and damaged two more. This time the controllers did not get a perfect result: only eight Spitfires of 64 Squadron (led by F/Lt Henstock) out of three squadrons scrambled, made contact, and in dogfights against escorting Me 109s including elements from both *JG 26* and *JG 51*, lost one Spitfire and pilot and two more damaged for one Me 109 and pilot dispatched. The dive-bombers were not intercepted. Yet another raid on this unfortunate convoy was made at about 18h00, and the Stukas bombed without RAF interference, soon followed up by German E-boats, which were driven off in their turn by two destroyers and some MTBs that sortied from Dover. The two destroyers rashly got too close to the enemy coast and were caught while racing back to safety by a Me 110 *Staffel* from *EGr 210* and then a *Gruppe* of Ju 87s who both attacked again out of the afternoon sun, seriously damaging both vessels, which had to be towed back to Dover. Ten Spitfires of 54 Squadron lost an aircraft and pilot to *JG 51* which escorted the Me 110s.

Soon after, S/L Manton leading nine Hurricanes of 56 Squadron onto the scene, sent six of his machines down to catch the Stukas at their most vulnerable moment as they pulled out of their dives, shooting down one, while he himself led the remaining section into the escorting Me 109s of *III/JG 52* to protect the other six, his Hurricane being damaged and he slightly wounded. With their attention on 56 Squadron, elements of *III/JG 52* were surprised by seven Spitfires of 610 Squadron who downed two Me 109s and killed their pilots. The Fighter Command squadrons had done well – against approximately two *Gruppen* of Me 109s and one of Stukas, they had accounted for two Messerschmitts and their pilots and one Stuka, for the loss of one Spitfire and pilot and a lightly damaged Hurricane. The RAF squadrons were fast gaining experience and were doing increasingly well in the battle of attrition. With 11 Group and sector controllers now well versed in the intricacies of their job, they were ensuring that the British squadrons intercepted most raids and were placed in tactical situations where they could more than hold their own.

The Dowding system was working, with Park's very capable hands on the daily clashes.

After a relatively quiet day on the 26th, 27 July was marked by fast attacks, all by *EGr 210*, against naval assets in Dover harbour and off Harwich. Six fast Me 109 fighter-bombers sneaked in at low level after lunch, cleverly coming in from the landward side and damaging a destroyer and hitting barracks; there was no interception – understandably. A second attack on Dover harbour in the early evening, again by Me 109s, this time coming in at 7,000 ft from Folkestone, dive-bombed ships in the harbour, sinking an already damaged destroyer, damaging a depot vessel, and then after releasing roared back towards France just above the sea. A dozen Hurricanes of 501 Squadron vectored in from the opposite direction, saw the bombing but only a few got close to the fast-retreating Me 109s; F/Lt Cox, leading the squadron appears to have been shot down by *3/EGr 210* members who turned back to help their rearmost machine, under attack by Cox. One pilot from a flight of 41 Squadron also vectored in to this raid as it came in, broke away from his formation and skirmished with a few of the retreating Messerschmitts, to no avail. About an hour earlier, the two Me 110-equipped *Staffeln* of *EGr 210* hit a naval group off Aldeburgh on the East coast, two destroyers protecting six minesweeper trawlers. One destroyer was sunk, the other damaged with one Me 110 and crew obliterated by a direct anti-aircraft hit. Due to these further naval losses on this day, and signs of the Germans erecting long range guns near Calais, Dover was abandoned by the Royal Navy as an anti-invasion base on 27 July, the vulnerable and valuable destroyers being relocated to Harwich and Sheerness.[5]

On 28 July there was one major and complex set of engagements between mainly Spitfires and Me 109s around Dover. Following an initial feint attack at about noon, some ninety minutes later over sixty decoy He 111s came in, turning back when near the coast, having lured four RAF squadrons into the air. The escort of four *Staffeln* of *JG 51* and top cover from *III/JG 26*, however, carried on inland over the Dover area. F/Lt 'Sailor' Malan, seeing a *Staffel* of Me 109s from *JG 51* diving down towards unsuspecting Hurricanes from 111 Squadron, skilfully led his first two sections in a surprise attack on their rear, while aware of more Me 109s coming in behind. He accepted this unfavourable tactical situation to save the Hurricanes from a bad bounce. There was also definite determination on Malan's part to get at the Me 109s, which is what the RAF fighters really had to do, accepting at the same time the likelihood of being outnumbered and attacked by more German fighters when they did go in. The British fighters could never have won the Battle if they, like the Germans often did, attacked only when favourable conditions pertained. To attack bombers or Me 109s, RAF unit leaders had to accept tactical risks.

Malan's 74 Squadron became embroiled with three *Staffeln* of JG 51, losing two Spitfires, one pilot dead and the other wounded, with two more aircraft damaged; they shot down one Messerschmitt, pilot killed, with another damaged. The Germans had claimed two confirmed victories and another unconfirmed, with minor elements likely of all four *Staffeln* becoming involved with a few of 74 Squadron's Spitfires pursuing them back across the Channel to France. Outnumbered approximately 2:1, 74 Squadron had done well, and their leader had performed in an exemplary fashion.

In a somewhat strange action, the *Kommodore* of *JG 51*, the famous Werner Mölders and his wingman, lingered over the Dover area after the above combats, and bounced the lead section of 41 Squadron, climbing in a spiral near Dover and using a stepped down, from front to back, formation of successive vics of three Spitfires, one machine being placed beneath to protect from below. At least this was an attempt at something new on behalf of the squadron leader, 'Robin' Hood, who had already earned himself a DFC for leadership over Dunkirk. By late July 1940, also, 41 Squadron had begun to harmonise their guns at 150 yards, and to apply a wider line-abreast vic formation when action appeared imminent.[6] While the two lone German pilots succeeded in hitting one Spitfire from the lead section of 41 Squadron, pilot wounded, they were very rapidly set upon by much of the following sections, attacking aggressively, and Mölders was wounded and very lucky to make it back to the French coast in a failing aircraft, which was a write-off.

While the normal German method involved a unit leader attacking vulnerable RAF fighters under an umbrella of followers, Mölders on his first operation of the Battle was behaving in an arrogant and dangerous manner, and despite having been warned by his wingman of other Spitfires behind, had persisted with his attack; he paid the price for this and was lucky to have survived. The RAF fighters were becoming more innovative, more skilled at finely timed and executed attacks, and much more aggressive, all boding well, and in fact essential for what was to come when the large raids began in August 1940. 111 Squadron, who had been saved by Malan's action, destroyed two rescue He 59 floatplanes over the Channel.

The *III/JG 26* top cover appear to have followed the norm when *Gruppenkommandeur* Galland and his wingman *Oblt* Müncheberg made a two-man bounce of the rear Hurricane in a 257 Squadron formation as it changed formation while turning, the machine crashing and being written off, the pilot only suffering minor injury. While such relatively safe bounce tactics beneath protective cover were common and in fact much admired on the German side, it always raises the question why a larger attack from the inherently favourable tactical position was not carried out to inflict greater casualties and disperse the RAF formations attacked.

29 July was marked by a fast-paced German raid on Dover, *c.* eighty Me 109s and forty-eight Ju 87s were opposed by thirty-eight British fighters, resulting in four Stukas being lost and two Me 109s, one more of each being damaged. The loss rate of the Stukas at 8.3% was significantly above generally accepted sustainable losses, about 5%; Fighter Command losses were one Hurricane and one Spitfire destroyed, two damaged Spitfires written off in crash landings, two more force-landed in fields, damaged, and another two Hurricanes at least back at base in a damaged state. Each side lost two fighter pilots killed, and the Stukas two complete crews plus two men wounded.

Interestingly, the raid had a lower escort, another one *c.* 1,000 ft higher, then an upper escort and finally a top cover (which didn't engage as they were too high), and in a new development, there was a low-level sweep-out to protect retreating Ju 87s and escorts. The controllers did an excellent job, getting all four RAF squadrons into contact with enemy aircraft within about four minutes. While the Stukas and escort swept in out of the sun from north-east of Dover, 41 and 64 Spitfire squadrons were placed well above the bombers and close to the level of the first escort by the controllers; S/L Hood attacked the lower escort, which was close below his level but 41 Squadron was hard hit by the second escort layer about 1,000 ft higher. However, this enabled some pilots of 64 Squadron to get at the dive-bombers. 501 Squadron, very cleverly led by P/O Lee, circled over Dover and pounced on the Stukas as they pulled up out of their dives and headed home. 56 Squadron was vectored straight onto the sweep-out.

German escorts were becoming more complex and dangerous, but 11 Group controllers were by now well versed in their craft, and many unit leaders by now were also fully capable of taking advantage of their placement vis-à-vis the incoming enemy formations by the controllers, and even successfully dealing with less favourable tactical situations that pertained. Vectoring Spitfires onto escorts and Hurricanes onto bombers, as seen here to an extent, was already a well-established RAF norm. In such raids as 29 July, the escorting Me 109s also had the advantage of being at the correct chosen heights, top cover at high altitude, lower cover(s) closer to their charges. RAF controllers in contrast had much less time to get their fighters to high altitude to provide protection from the bounce and ensure advantage in fighter versus fighter combats; however, they generally aimed at placing their fighters at the same altitude or somewhat above incoming bomb-carrying *Luftwaffe* formations and their direct escorts.

Time and distances involved in operations over south-east Kent meant they would never be able to place their fighter squadrons above all of the enemy formations, a point often misconstrued by 'big wing' protagonists. Some RAF unit leaders when scrambled from a forward base flew an essentially reciprocal course inland when vectored towards enemy raids approaching the coast, before turning back towards the enemy but now at a more favourable altitude; the first such example in the records was led by F/Lt Brian Smith of 610 Squadron on 18 July. It was, however a potentially dangerous tactic, as if they significantly exceeded the controller's designated height they could miss getting at the raid by being too high, and also possibly place themselves closer to a second, higher-flying direct escort, such as that experienced by 41 Squadron above.

30 July-7 August 1940: a lull before the storm

Following the intense action that characterised the 24-29 July period, the subsequent nine days witnessed a relative lull in the air over the Channel and North Sea, apart from 5 August when fighter combats heated up. The complex operations set up by *Generalmajor* Theo Osterkamp necessitating perfect timing and the smooth working of all parts of the plan, as in any military situation, always had the potential to go awry, as indeed happened on 5 August.

German bombers were also encumbered with extra weight from July 1940 onwards, thereby reducing bomb loads in time, as escalating casualties necessitated some changes. An increase in bomber defensive armament began as combat experience was gained over the British Isles during July. The limited amount of documented data available on the number of MG 15 machine guns carried by bombers necessitates examining a longer period, 1 July-15 September 1940, to provide enough cumulative data to give an estimation of increases (Chart 3).[7] Overall, at least for He 111s and Do 17s, there appears to be an increase in extra guns mounted, with fewer data points for the Ju 88s, insufficient for a meaningful conclusion. Among the first extra weapons installed in Do 17s and He 111s were side-mounted MG 15s (Illustration 39), to counter RAF beam attacks, which showed an increase in frequency even in July 1940.[8] Other extra guns were mounted in some aircraft in the glass nose in front of the pilot, firing obliquely upwards (Illustration 30);[9] how he was supposed to handle this in addition to his other tasks has to be considered. Also, in the confined personnel spaces of the German bombers the noise levels from extra guns must have been very high, never mind cordite gasses and discarded cartridge cases.

Armour carried by the German machines also increased,[10] in parallel with enhanced fire power. Initially in the Battle, most German bombers had armour protection for the pilot; this was later expanded to the dorsal rear gunner, rather than the ventral position, and then also for the observer's position adjacent to the pilot. A final step was to provide armoured bulkheads across the section of the aircraft. In the He 111s this generally was placed with one side gunner behind its protection while the other, less fortunate one, had the bulkhead, uselessly, at his back.[11] Such are the fortunes of war. A caveat is that data on both guns and armour carried is derived from bomber crash sites in the United Kingdom; with high impact crashes, heavy components like engines, oleo legs, armour and guns tend to get deeply buried and reliable counting then becomes impossible for RAF intelligence investigators examining *Luftwaffe* crashes.

A final word

Fighter Command was learning and adapting, and under Dowding's and Park's wise, sure and patient leadership, and the influence of increasingly expert controllers, had started out on the long path to winning the battle of attrition during July 1940. Station commanders and squadron leaders were each saddled with much responsibility in the face of daily danger. The hard-learned tactical expertise of the squadron leader in getting at enemy bomber formations encompassed balancing risk against aggressive success for the squadron, enduring painful casualties yet maintaining squadron morale. He had his own personal battle for survival and was also the person writing the letters to next of kin, a hard psychological burden to be borne, in addition to a high administrative load.

To the author's mind, these were the absolutely critical heroes of the victory that Fighter Command achieved against long odds. These enormous responsibilities left little time for some details on occasion, and these must have included things like combat formations and other elements of their hectic lives at the time. For any misplaced criticism levelled here, *mea culpa*.

Notes

Dedication

1. *Hometown Battlefield* is a concept based on a song of that title by noted Canadian musician and singer, J.P. Cormier; www.jp-cormier.com

Preface

1. Lucas, Laddie, *Out of the Blue* (London: Hutchinson, 1985), see p. 31.
2. Dowding, Air Chief Marshal Sir Hugh C. T., *The Battle of Britain*, despatch submitted to the Secretary of State for Air 20 August 1941 and published in 1946 (London: His Majesty's Stationary Office, Supplement to The London Gazette, 10 September 1946), pp. 4543-4571.
3. Park, Air Vice-Marshal K. R., *German Air Attacks on England – 8th Aug.–10th Sept.*, RAF Report from Headquarters No. 11 Group to Headquarters, Fighter Command, 12 September 1940. National Archives Air 16/635-4A, or Air 2/7355.
4. Unknown author, *German plans for the Invasion of England, 1940; Operation "Sealion"*.

   Declassified CIA document, Declassified Documents RG 263, Entry ZZ17, RC Box # 3, RC location 230/902/64/1; downloaded from www.cia.gov. The entire document is based on the German Naval Staff record mainly, plus also some material from OKW records.
5. *ibid.*
6. Eriksson, Patrick G., *Alarmstart* (Stroud: Amberley, 2017). *Major Trübenbach's descriptions of September 1940 raids and the role of his JG 52 escorts in this volume bear this out*; pp. 114-15 and 117-19.
7. Unknown author, *German Bombing Formations 1939/40*, RAF Tactical Committee (General) Paper No. 10 (T.C. 10), Air Ministry, 16 December 1940, National Archives Air 16/300, 5 pages and 11 figures; compare

with Dierich, Wolfgang, *Kampfgeschwader 51 "Edelweiss"* (Stuttgart: Motorbuch Verlag, 1974), see p. 36.

8. Books providing a foundation for this volume: Osterkamp, Theo, *Durch Höhen und Tiefen jagt ein Herz* (Heidelberg: Kurt Vowinckel Verlag, 1952); Wood, Derek and Dempster, Derek, *The Narrow Margin* (London: Arrow Books, 1967); Mason, Francis K., *Battle over Britain* (London: McWhirter Twins, 1969); Ramsey, Winston. G. (ed.), *The Battle of Britain: Then and Now* (London: Battle of Britain Prints International Ltd., 1982); James, T. Cecil G., *The Battle of Britain* (Abingdon: Routledge, 2012); Parker, Nigel, *Luftwaffe Crash Archive*, Vol. 1 (Walton on Thames: Red Kite Books, Air Research Publications, 2013); Cull, Brian, *First of the Few* (Stroud: Fonthill, 2013); Wynn, Kenneth G., *Men of the Battle of Britain: a Biographical Directory of the Few* (Barnsley: Frontline, 2015; West Malling: The Battle of Britain Memorial Trust, 2015); Cull, Brian, *Battle for the Channel* (Stroud: Fonthill, 2017). In addition the website: 'Tony Wood's Combat Claims and Casualties Lists'; accessed via Don Caldwell's website: don-caldwell.we.bs/claims/tonywood.htm (with many succeeding repeats and relatively minor edits by fellow historians). These claims lists are not complete and contain gaps, some large, especially for certain Me 110 units in 1940; however, they do reflect accredited *Luftwaffe* victory claims and not just submitted and unverified claims.

1. *The learning curve of July 1940: the first nine days*

1. Dowding, Air Chief Marshal Sir Hugh C. T., *The Battle of Britain*, despatch submitted to the Secretary of State for Air, 20 August 1941 and published in 1946 (London: His Majesty's Stationary Office, Supplement to *The London Gazette*, 10 September 1946), pp. 4543-4571; Mason, Francis K., *Battle over Britain* (London: McWhirter Twins, 1969).

2. Mason, Francis, *op. cit.* (pp. 131-155); Cull, Brian, *First of the Few* (Stroud: Fonthill, 2013) (pp. 133-193).

3. Data from relevant squadron Fighter Command Combat Reports (also called Form 'F', often sub-headed as Intelligence Patrol Report; Air 16/955 files of the National Archives; reference will generally be made to the 'F' Forms as Intelligence Patrol Reports, abbreviated to IPRs in this volume; these were written by the Squadron Intelligence Officer and sometimes by the Sector Intelligence Officer); Mason, Francis, *op. cit.* (pp. 131-155); Cull, Brian, *op. cit.* (pp. 133-193).

4. Standard ammunition loads per either Spitfire or Hurricane Mark 1 aircraft were 300 rounds per gun, thus 2,400 rounds in total for the eight machine guns each machine carried: Price, Alfred, *The Hardest Day; The Battle of Britain 18 August 1940* (London: Arrow Books, 1990),

see p. 23. Higher ammunition loads per gun noted from respective IPRs from the eight individual squadrons, Air 16/955 files.

5. Data for attacks on lone German bombers during 1–9 July period derived from squadron IPRs (Air 16/955 records, National Archives).

6. IPRs for 602 Squadron on 1 July 1940, and for 54 Squadron on 3 July 1940 (Air 16/955 records, National Archives).

7. IPRs for 616 and 603 Squadrons on 3 July 1940, and for 74 and 602 Squadrons on 8 July 1940 (Air 16/955 records, National Archives).

8. IPR, 602 Squadron, 7 July 1940 (Air 16/955 records, National Archives).

9. Mason, Francis, *op. cit.* (pp. 139-140).

10. Cull, Brian, *op. cit.* (pp. 157-158); Prien, Jochen, *Geschichte des Jagdgeschwaders 77, Teil 1, 1934-1941* (Eutin: Struve-Druck, 1992) (p. 331).

11. Note 9, *op. cit.*

12. Cull, Brian, *op. cit.* (pp. 157-158).

13. *ibid.*

14. Cull, Brian, *op. cit.* (p. 161); Prien, Jochen, *op. cit.* (p. 331).

15. Website, Wood, Tony, *Tony Wood's Combat Claims and Casualties Lists*: accessed via Don Caldwell's website: don-caldwell.we.bs/claims/tonywood.htm.

16. Stones, Donald, *A Pilot's Passion* (Rennes: Adrian Burt, 2014) (p. 49); Mason, Francis, *op. cit.* (p. 141).

17. Stones, Donald, *op. cit.* (p. 49). RDF, Radio Direction Finding, early name for radar.

18. Note 12, *op. cit.*

19. IPR, 54 Squadron, 4 July 1940 (Air 16/955 records, National Archives).

20. *ibid.*

21. IPR, 32 Squadron, 4 July 1940 (Air 16/955 records, National Archives).

22. IPR, 32 Squadron, 4 July 1940 (Air 16/955 records, National Archives); Cull, Brian, *op. cit.* (pp. 159-160); Mason, Francis, *op. cit.* (pp. 140-141).

23. Mason, Francis, *op. cit.* (p. 141).

24. Cull, Brian, *op. cit.* (pp. 159-161).

25. Prien, Jochen, *op. cit.* (p. 331).

26. Mason, Francis, *op. cit.* (p. 142); Cull, Brian, *op. cit.* (pp. 162-164).

27. Squadron Commander's Report on Flying Battle Casualty, P/O D. K. Milne, 64 Squadron, 5 July 1940 (Air 81 records, National Archives).

28. Cull, Brian, *op. cit.* (p. 162).

29. *ibid.*

30. *ibid.*

31. *ibid.*

32. Note 15, *op. cit.*

33. Cull, Brian, *op. cit.* (pp. 162-163); Mason, Francis, *op. cit.* (p. 142).

34. Mason, Francis, *op. cit.* (p. 142); Website, Holm, Michael, *The Luftwaffe, 1933-1945*; www.ww2.dk.

35. Mason, Francis, *op. cit.* (pp. 144-145).

36. Mason, Francis, *op. cit.* (p. 145).

37. Cull, Brian, *op. cit.* (p. 168, p. 173); Mason, Francis, *op. cit.* (p. 145).

38. Cull, Brian, *op. cit.* (p. 168, p. 171); Mason, Francis, *op. cit.* (pp. 145-146).

39. Note 15, *op. cit.*

40. Deere, Alan C., *Nine Lives* (London: Coronet, 1974) (pp. 86-88).

41. Osterkamp, Theo, *Durch Höhen und Tiefen jagt ein Herz* (Heidelberg: Kurt Vowinckel Verlag, 1952) (pp. 318-323).

42. *ibid.*

43. Mason, Francis, *op. cit.* (p. 146).

44. Mason, Francis, *op. cit.* (pp. 145-146); Cull, Brian, *op. cit.* (pp. 168-172).

45. IPR, 65 Squadron, 7 July 1940 (Air 16/955 records, National Archives).

46. IPR, 65 Squadron, 7 July 1940 (Air 16/955 records, National Archives); Combat Report (abbreviated to CR in this volume), F/Lt Gerald Saunders, 65 Squadron, 7 July 1940 (Air 50 records, National Archives). CRs are generally headed Form 'F', just as for IPRs but they are distinct documents.

47. CRs, F/Lt Gerald Saunders and F/Sgt William Franklin, 65 Squadron, 7 July 1940 (Air 50 records, National Archives).

48. Note 15, *op. cit.*

49. Stones, Donald, *op. cit.* (p. 49); Cull, Brian, *op. cit.* (p. 169).

50. Report by F/O R. B. Knowles, Hawkinge Duty Pilot, 7 July 1940 in S/L Joslin's casualty file (Air 81 records, National Archives); Mason, Francis, *op. cit.* (p. 146).

51. IPR, 65 Squadron, 7 July 1940 (Air 16/955 records, National Archives); Mason, Francis, *op. cit.* (p. 146).

52. IPR, 54 Squadron, 7 July 1940 (Air 16/955 records, National Archives).

53. Note 15, *op. cit.*

54. Cull, Brian, *op. cit.* (pp. 168-172).

55. Cull, Brian, *op. cit.* (pp. 168-172); IPR, 65 Squadron, 7 July 1940 (Air 16/955 records, National Archives).

56. Mason, Francis, *op. cit.* (p. 146); Cull, Brian, *op. cit.* (pp. 168-172).

57. Cull, Brian, *op. cit.* (p. 175); Mason, Francis, *op. cit.* (pp. 147-150).

58. Bailey, David J., *610 (County of Chester) Auxiliary Air Force Squadron, 1936-1940* (Stroud: Fonthill, 2018) (pp. 209-212); Mason, Francis, *op. cit.* (p. 147).

59. Mason, Francis, *op. cit.*; Wood, Derek and Dempster, Derek, *The Narrow Margin* (London: Arrow Books, 1967); and many other classic Battle of Britain texts.

60. IPR, 610 Squadron, 8 July 1940 (Air 16/955 records, National Archives) (take off time *c.* 15h00; was another, earlier IPR this day, take off time c. 14h00).

61. IPR, 610 Squadron, 8 July 1940 (Air 16/955 records, National Archives) (take off time *c.* 15h00); Prien, Jochen, *op. cit.* (p. 333).

62. IPR, 610 Squadron, 8 July 1940 (Air 16/955 records, National Archives) (take off time *c.* 15h00).

63. *ibid.*

64. *ibid.*

65. Cull, Brian, *op. cit.* (p. 180).

66. Prien, Jochen, *op. cit.* (p. 333).

67. IPR, 610 Squadron, 8 July 1940 (Air 16/955 records, National Archives) (take off time *c.* 15h00).

68. Cumming, Anthony, *The Royal Navy and the Battle of Britain* (Annapolis, Maryland: Naval Institute Press, 2013) (pp. 60-62, p. 69); Gustin, Emmanuel and Williams, Anthony G., *Flying Guns: The Development of Aircraft Guns, Ammunition and Installations, 1933-45* (Shrewsbury: Airlife, 2003) (p. 23); Williams, Anthony, G., *The Battle of Britain: Armament of the competing fighters* (article on his website: Quarryhs. co.uk/BoB.htm, 2004, revised 2005); Kaplan, Philip, *Fighter Aces of the RAF in the Battle of Britain* (Philadelphia, Pennsylvania: Casemate, 2008) (pp. 20-21).

69. Mason, Francis, *op. cit.* (pp. 147-148).

70. Multiple examples of these tactics are given in many sources, for example: Cull, Brian, *op. cit.*; Wood, Derek and Dempster, Derek, *op. cit.*; Mason, Francis, *op. cit.*; Jullian, Marcel, *The Battle of Britain* (London: Jonathan Cape, 1967); McKee, Alexander, *Strike from the Sky* (London: New English Library, 1969).

71. Stones, Donald, *op. cit.* (pp. 49-51).

72. Note 15, *op. cit.*; Stones, Donald, *op. cit.* (pp. 49-51).

73. Stones, Donald, *op. cit.* (pp. 49-51); Mason, Francis, *op. cit.* (p. 147).

74. Tidy, Douglas, *I fear no Man; the Story of No 74 (Fighter) Squadron Royal Flying Corps and Royal Air Force* (Cape Town: Purnell, 1972) (p. 76); IPR, 74 Squadron, 8 July 1940 (Air 16/955 records, National Archives).

75. Knight, Dennis, *Harvest of Messerschmitts: The Chronicle of a Village at War, 1940* (London: Frederick Warne, 1981) (pp. 64-66); IPRs, 74 and 32 Squadrons, 8 July 1940 (Air 16/955 records, National Archives).

76. Mason, Francis, *op. cit.* (p. 150); Cull, Brian, *op. cit.* (p. 180).

77. IPR, 32 Squadron, 8 July 1940 (Air 16/955 records, National Archives).

78. IPR, 32 Squadron, 8 July 1940 (Air 16/955 records, National Archives); Note 15, *op. cit.*

79. Cull, Brian, *op. cit.* (p. 180); Note 15, *op. cit.*

80. IPR, 32 Squadron, 8 July 1940 (Air 16/955 records, National Archives).

81. IPR, 65 Squadron, 8 July 1940 (Air 16/955 records, National Archives).

82. *ibid.*

83. Parker, Nigel, *Luftwaffe Crash Archive,* Vol. 1 (Walton on Thames: Red Kite Books, Air Research Publications, 2013); Cull, Brian, *op. cit.* (p. 180); IPR, 65 Squadron, 8 July 1940 (Air 16/955 records, National Archives); Knight, Dennis, *op. cit.* (p. 66).

84. Note 15, *op. cit.*

85. Mason, Francis, *op. cit.* (p. 150); Cull, Brian, *op. cit.* (p. 180).

86. Prien, Jochen, *op. cit.* (p. 333); IPR, 54 Squadron, 8 July 1940 (Air 16/955 records, National Archives); Cull, Brian, *op. cit.* (p. 177).

87. Prien, Jochen, *op. cit.* (p. 333).

88. IPR, 54 Squadron, 8 July 1940 (Air 16/955 records, National Archives); Cull, Brian, *op. cit.* (p. 180).

89. IPR, 43 Squadron, 9 July 1940 (Air 16/955 records, National Archives).

90. *ibid.*

91. *ibid.*

92. Mason, Francis, *op. cit.* (pp. 152-155); Cull, Brian, *op. cit.* (p. 182).

93. IPR, 43 Squadron, 9 July 1940 (Air 16/955 records, National Archives).

94. For example: Mason, Francis, *op. cit.* (p. 155); Cull, Brian, *op. cit.* (p. 182, p. 189).

95. Von Eimannsberger, Ludwig, *Zerstörer Gruppe: A History of V./(Z) LG 1 – I./NJG 3 1939-1941* (Atglen, Pennsylvania: Schiffer, 1998).

96. Cull, Brian, *op. cit.* (p. 187).

97. Website, *aufhimmelzuhause.com/id99.htm*; Von Eimannsberger, Ludwig, *op. cit.* (p. 92).

98. Archives, Imperial War Museum, London: *Luftwaffe Quartermaster General Loss Returns* (a very large document). Electronic copy kindly provided by Nigel Parker, from original at the Museum.

99. Ramsey, Winston. G. (ed.), *The Battle of Britain: Then and Now* (London: Battle of Britain Prints International Ltd., 1982; this source largely has things corrected for 10 July, see RAF entry for that day. Cull's two excellent and detailed studies of the July 1940 fighting also have this largely corrected for both 9 and 10 July: Cull, Brian, 2013, *op. cit.* (pp. 191-192); Cull, Brian, *Battle for the Channel* (Stroud: Fonthill, 2017), (p. 49).

100. Von Eimannsberger, Ludwig, *op. cit.* (p. 92).

101. Mason, Francis, *op. cit.* (p. 151).

102. Mason, Francis, *op. cit.* (pp. 151-152).

103. Mason, Francis, *op. cit.* (p. 152).

104. Prien, Jochen, *op. cit.* (p. 334).

105. Mason, Francis, *op. cit.* (pp. 152-155); Wynn, Kenneth G., *Men of the Battle of Britain: A Biographical Directory of the Few* (Barnsley:

Frontline, 2015; West Malling: The Battle of Britain Memorial Trust, 2015) (p. 34, p. 173, p. 216, p. 367).

106. Illustrations of F/Lt Ironside's pilot's logbook pages for 9 July 1940 can be found on the web: https://pinterest.com/pin/532409987179110049/

107. *ibid.*

108. Note 98, *op. cit.*; Mason, Francis, *op. cit.* (pp. 152-155).

109. Cull, Brian, 2013, *op. cit.* (p. 192).

110. Cull, Brian, 2013, *op. cit.* (pp. 189-190).

111. Mason, Francis, *op. cit.* (p. 152); https://pinterest.com/pin/532409987179110049/; Darlow, Steve, *Five of the Few* (London: Grub Street, 2010) (p. 62).

112. Mason, Francis, *op. cit.* (p. 152); Cull, Brian, 2013, *op. cit.* (p. 182).

113. Prien, Jochen, *op. cit.* (p. 334).

114. Darlow, Steve, *op. cit.* (p. 67).

115. For example, multiple entries in: James, T. Cecil G., *The Battle of Britain* (Abingdon: Routledge, 2012).

116. IPR, 65 Squadron, 9 July 1940 (Air 16/955 records, National Archives).

117. IPRs, 65 and 79 Squadrons, 9 July 1940 (Air 16/955 records, National Archives).

118. IPR, 79 Squadron, 9 July 1940 (Air 16/955 records, National Archives); note 98, *op. cit.*; Mason, Francis, *op. cit.* (p. 153).

119. IPR, 79 Squadron, 9 July 1940 (Air 16/955 records, National Archives).

120. *ibid.*

121. *ibid.*

122. CRs, F/Lt Gerald Saunders and F/O W. H. Maitland-Walker, 65 Squadron, 9 July 1940 (Air 50 records, National Archives); IPR, 65 Squadron, 9 July 1940 (Air 16/955 records, National Archives).

123. IPR, 65 Squadron, 9 July 1940 (Air 16/955 records, National Archives).

124. IPR, 65 Squadron, 9 July 1940 (Air 16/955 records, National Archives); Prien, Jochen, *op. cit.* (p. 334).

125. CRs, F/Lt Gerald Saunders, F/Sgt N. T. Phillips and F/O W. H. Maitland-Walker, 65 Squadron, 9 July 1940 (Air 50 records, National Archives); IPR, 65 Squadron, 9 July 1940 (Air 16/955 records, National Archives).

126. Note 15, *op. cit.*

127. Prien, Jochen, *op. cit.* (p. 334); Note 15, *op. cit.*

128. CR, F/Sgt Robert MacPherson, 65 Squadron, 9 July 1940 (Air 50 records, National Archives).

129. Cull, Brian, 2013, *op. cit.* (p. 191); Parker, Nigel, *op. cit.* (entry for 9 July 1940).

130. IPR, 65 Squadron, 9 July 1940 (Air 16/955 records, National Archives).

131. *ibid.*

132. Website, de Zeng, Henry L. IV and Stankey, Douglas G., *Luftwaffe Officer Career Summaries* (2014 updated version), accessed via Michael

Holm's website, *The Luftwaffe 1933-1945*: www.ww2.dk; this source at www.ww2.dk/lwoffz.html; Mason, Francis, *op. cit.* (p. 154-155).

133. IPR, 609 Squadron, 9 July 1940 (Air 16/955 records, National Archives).
134. Mason, Francis, *op. cit.* (p. 154); IPR, 609 Squadron, 9 July 1940 (Air 16/955 records, National Archives).
135. IPR, 609 Squadron, 9 July 1940 (Air 16/955 records, National Archives).
136. *ibid.*
137. *ibid.*
138. *ibid.*
139. *ibid.*
140. *ibid.*
141. *ibid.*
142. Website, de Zeng, Henry L. IV and Stankey, Douglas G., *op. cit.*
143. *Seenotdienst* is the German air-sea rescue service; webpage, *aufhimmelzuhause.com, op. cit.*
144. Note 15, *op. cit.*
145. *ibid.*
146. Cull, Brian, 2013, *op. cit.* (p. 187).
147. Mason, Francis, *op. cit.* (p. 153); IPR, 54 Squadron, 9 July 1940 (Air 16/955 records, National Archives).
148. IPR, 54 Squadron, 9 July 1940 (Air 16/955 records, National Archives).
149. *ibid.*
150. Parker, Nigel, *op. cit.* (entry for 9 July 1940).
151. IPR, 54 Squadron, 9 July 1940 (Air 16/955 records, National Archives).
152. *ibid.*
153. IPR, 54 Squadron, 9 July 1940 (Air 16/955 records, National Archives); CR, F/Lt Alan Deere, 54 Squadron, 9 July 1940 (Air 50 records, National Archives).
154. Cull, Brian, 2013, *op. cit.* (p. 184, p. 191).
155. IPR, 54 Squadron, 9 July 1940 (Air 16/955 records, National Archives); Operations Record Book (abbreviated to ORB in this volume; also known as Form 540), 54 Squadron, 9 July 1940 (Air 27 records, National Archives); CR, F/Lt Alan Deere, 54 Squadron, 9 July 1940 (Air 50 records, National Archives).
156. IPR, 54 Squadron, 9 July 1940 (Air 16/955 records, National Archives).
157. *ibid.*
158. Deere, Alan C., *op. cit.* (p. 93).
159. Squadron Commander's Report on Flying Battle Casualty, P/O J. W. Garton, 54 Squadron, 9 July 1940 (Air 81 records, National Archives).
160. Note 15, *op. cit.*
161. Bergström, Christer, *The Battle of Britain: an epic conflict revisited* (Oxford: Casemate, 2015; Eskilstuna: Vaktel, 2015) (p. 70); Cull, Brian, 2013, *op. cit.* (p. 184).
162. Mason, Francis, *op. cit.* (p. 155).

2. 10 July 1940: the official start of the Battle of Britain

1. Dowding, Air Chief Marshal Sir Hugh C. T., *The Battle of Britain*, despatch submitted to the Secretary of State for Air 20 August 1941 and published in 1946 (London: His Majesty's Stationary Office, Supplement to *The London Gazette*, 10 September 1946), pages 4543-4571.

2. Mason, Francis K., *Battle over Britain* (London: McWhirter Twins, 1969) (p. 156); Ramsey, Winston. G. (ed.), *The Battle of Britain: then and now* (London: Battle of Britain Prints International Ltd., 1982) (entries for 10 July 1940); Website, Wood, Tony, 'Tony Wood's Combat Claims and Casualties Lists'; accessed via Don Caldwell's website: don-caldwell. we.bs/claims/tonywood.htm.

3. Mason, Francis, *op. cit.* (pp. 156-157); Archives, Imperial War Museum, London: *Luftwaffe Quartermaster General Loss Returns*; Website, Holm, Michael, *The Luftwaffe, 1933-1945*; www.ww2.dk.

4. Cull, Brian, *Battle for the Channel* (Stroud: Fonthill, 2017) (p. 50).

5. IPR, 74 Squadron, 10 July 1940 (Air 16/955 records, National Archives) (take off time *c.* 10h30, was also a later IPR).

6. *ibid.*

7. Website, Wood, Tony, *op. cit.*; Mason, Francis, *op. cit.* (p. 157); Ramsey, Winston (ed.), *op. cit.* (*Luftwaffe* entry for 10 July 1940).

8. Mason, Francis, *op. cit.* (p. 157); Ramsey, Winston (ed.), *op. cit.* (RAF entry for 10 July 1940).

9. Website, Wood, Tony, *op. cit.*

10. Cull Brian, *op. cit.* (p. 45 and pp. 48-49).

11. Obermaier, Ernst, *Die Ritterkreuzträger der Luftwaffe* (Mainz: Verlag Dieter Hoffmann, 1966) (p. 182).

12. *Luftwaffe Quartermaster General Loss Returns, op. cit.*; Goss, Chris, *Dornier Do 17 Units of World War 2* (Oxford: Osprey, 2019) (pp. 35-36); Cull Brian, *op. cit.* (p. 42).

13. Website, de Zeng, Henry L. IV and Stankey, Douglas G., *Luftwaffe Officer Career Summaries* (2014 updated version), accessed via Michael Holm's website, *The Luftwaffe 1933-1945*: www.ww2.dk; this source at www.ww2.dk/lwoffz.html.

14. Goss, Chris, *op. cit.* (p. 35).

15. *Luftwaffe Quartermaster General Loss Returns, op. cit.*; Goss, Chris, *op. cit.* (p. 36).

16. Website, de Zeng, Henry L. IV and Stankey, Douglas G., *op. cit.*

17. Website, de Zeng, Henry L. IV, *Luftwaffe Airfields 1935-1945*, accessed via Michael Holm's website, *The Luftwaffe 1933-1945*: www.ww2.dk; this source at www.ww2.dk/lwairfields.html.

18. *ibid.*

19. Cull Brian, *op. cit.* (p. 42, p. 47).

20. Bungay, Stephen, *The Most Dangerous Enemy* (London: Aurum Press, 2009) (p. 252).
21. Wynn, Kenneth G., *Men of the Battle of Britain: A Biographical Directory of the Few* (Barnsley: Frontline, 2015; West Malling: The Battle of Britain Memorial Trust, 2015) (pp. 348-349).
22. IPR, 66 Squadron, 10 July 1940 (Air 16/955 records, National Archives); Cull Brian, *op. cit.* (p. 35).
23. IPR, 66 Squadron, 10 July 1940 (Air 16/955 records, National Archives).
24. *ibid.*
25. *ibid.*
26. IPR, 242 Squadron, 10 July 1940 (Air 16/955 records, National Archives).
27. *ibid.*
28. *ibid.*
29. *ibid.*
30. Cull Brian, *op. cit.* (p. 36).
31. IPR, 92 Squadron, 10 July 1940 (Air 16/955 records, National Archives).
32. *ibid.*
33. *ibid.*
34. *Luftwaffe Quartermaster General Loss Returns, op. cit.*
35. Ramsey, Winston (ed.), *op. cit.* (*Luftwaffe* entry for 10 July 1940); Cull Brian, *op. cit.* (p. 50); *Luftwaffe Quartermaster General Loss Returns, op. cit.*
36. Prien, Jochen, *Geschichte des Jagdgeschwaders 77, Teil 1, 1934-1941* (Eutin: Struve-Druck, 1992) (p. 335); Aders, Gebhard and Held, Werner, *Jagdgeschwader 51 'Mölders'* (Stuttgart: Motorbuch, 1985) (p. 57).
37. IPR, 74 Squadron, 10 July 1940 (Air 16/955 records, National Archives) (take off time *c.* 13h40, was an earlier IPR).
38. Reeve, Jonathan, *Battle of Britain Voices* (Stroud: Amberley, 2015) (pp. 121-122).
39. Page, Geoffrey, *Tale of a Guinea Pig* (London: Corgi, 1983) (pp. 54-59).
40. Mason, Francis, *op. cit.*; Jullian, Marcel, *The Battle of Britain* (London: Jonathan Cape, 1967); Osterkamp, Theo, *Durch Höhen und Tiefen jagt ein Herz* (Heidelberg: Kurt Vowinckel Verlag, 1952); Knight, Dennis, *Harvest of Messerschmitts: The Chronicle of a Village at War, 1940* (London: Frederick Warne, 1981) (pp. 67-68).
41. Prien, Jochen, *op. cit.* (pp. 335-336); Website, de Zeng, Henry L. IV and Stankey, Douglas G., *op. cit.*; Parker, Nigel, *Luftwaffe Crash Archive,* Vol. 1 (Walton on Thames: Red Kite Books, Air Research Publications, 2013) (entry for 10 July 1940); Knight, Dennis, *op. cit.* (pp. 67-68); Cull, Brian, *op. cit.* (p. 49). III/ZG 26 numbers reported variously as eighteen or thirty Me 110s: Bergström, Christer, *The Battle of Britain: An Epic Conflict Revisited* (Oxford: Casemate, 2015;

Eskilstuna: Vaktel, 2015) (p. 73); Aders, Gebhard and Held, Werner, *op. cit.* (p. 57).

42. Bergström, Christer, *op. cit.* (p. 73).

43. Prien, Jochen, *op. cit.* (pp. 335-336); Knight, Dennis, *op. cit.* (pp. 67-68).

44. Orange, Vincent, *Park; the Biography of Air Chief Marshal Sir Keith Park* (London: Grub Street, 2013); Wood, Derek and Dempster, Derek, *The Narrow Margin* (London: Arrow Books, 1967); Mason, Francis, *op. cit.*

45. James, T. Cecil G., *The Battle of Britain* (Abingdon: Routledge, 2012) (p. 27).

46. Mason, Francis, *op. cit.* (p. 157); Thomas, Nick, *Hurricane Squadron Ace* (Barnsley: Pen and Sword, 2014) (pp. 67-68); Bungay, Stephen, *op. cit.* (p. 150); James, T. Cecil G., *op. cit.* (p. 27).

47. IPR, 32 Squadron, 10 July 1940 (Air 16/955 records, National Archives).

48. *ibid.*

49. IPR, 32 Squadron, 10 July 1940 (Air 16/955 records, National Archives); James, T. Cecil G., *op. cit.* (p. 27); CR, F/O J. B. W. Humpherson, 32 Squadron, 10 July 1940 (Air 50 records, National Archives), quoted partially in Thomas, Nick, *op. cit.* (p. 68).

50. IPR, 32 Squadron, 10 July 1940 (Air 16/955 records, National Archives); CRs, F/O J. B. W. Humpherson and Sgt L. H. B. Pearce, 32 Squadron, 10 July 1940 (Air 50 records, National Archives), both quoted partially in Thomas, Nick, *op. cit.* (p. 68).

51. James, T. Cecil G., *op. cit.* (p. 27).

52. Wood, Derek and Dempster, Derek, *op. cit.* (pp. 431-465).

53. IPR, 74 Squadron, 10 July 1940 (Air 16/955 records, National Archives) (take off time *c.* 13h40); CR, F/Lt E. J. Gracie, 56 Squadron, 10 July 1940 (Air 50 records, National Archives); Page, Geoffrey, *op. cit.* (pp. 55-57); CR, Sub Lt F. Dawson-Paul, 64 Squadron, 10 July 1940 (Air 50 records, National Archives), quoted partially in Cull, Brian, *op. cit.* (p. 39).

54. IPR, 111 Squadron, 10 July 1940 (Air 16/955 records, National Archives); CR, S/L J. M. Thompson, 111 Squadron, 10 July 1940 (Air 50 records, National Archives); IPR, 74 Squadron, 10 July 1940 (Air 16/955 records, National Archives) (take off time *c.* 13h40).

55. Parker, Nigel, *op. cit.* (entry for 10 July 1940).

56. Mason, Francis, *op. cit.* (p. 157).

57. CR, F/Lt E. J. Gracie, 56 Squadron, 10 July 1940 (Air 50 records, National Archives).

58. *ibid.*

59. *ibid.*

60. *ibid.*

61. *ibid.*

62. *ibid.*

63. Page, Geoffrey, *op. cit.* (pp. 54-59).
64. *ibid.*
65. *ibid.*
66. Cull, Brian, *op. cit.* (p. 46).
67. Eriksson, Patrick G., *Alarmstart* (Stroud: Amberley, 2017) (p. 91).
68. Thomas, Nick, *op. cit.* (p. 68).
69. Mason, Francis, *op. cit.* (p. 157).
70. Cull, Brian, *op. cit.* (p. 46).
71. IPR, 74 Squadron, 10 July 1940 (Air 16/955 records, National Archives) (take off time *c.* 13h40).
72. *ibid.*
73. *ibid.*
74. *ibid.*
75. Knight, Dennis, *op. cit.* (pp. 67-68).
76. Cull, Brian, *op. cit.* (p. 45).
77. Mason, Francis, *op. cit.* (p. 158).
78. Cull, Brian, *op. cit.* (p. 46); CR, Sub Lt F. Dawson-Paul, 64 Squadron, 10 July 1940 (Air 50 records, National Archives), quoted partially in Cull, Brian, *op. cit.* (p. 39).
79. Mason, Francis, *op. cit.* (p. 158); Bungay, Stephen, *op. cit.* (p. 150).
80. Mason, Francis, *op. cit.* (p. 157); IPR, 111 Squadron, 10 July 1940 (Air 16/955 records, National Archives).
81. For example: Bungay, Stephen, *op. cit.* (p. 150); Cull, Brian, *op. cit.* (p. 38); Hough, Richard and Richards, Denis, *The Battle of Britain* (Sevenoaks: Coronet, 1990) (pp. 125-126).
82. A copy of the Operational Record Book entry for 10 July 1940 is given in: Mason, Francis, *op. cit.* (p. 157).
83. IPR, 111 Squadron, 10 July 1940 (Air 16/955 records, National Archives).
84. Reeve, Jonathan, *op. cit.* (pp. 121-122); IPR, 111 Squadron, 10 July 1940 (Air 16/955 records, National Archives); CR, S/L J. M. Thompson, 111 Squadron, 10 July 1940 (Air 50 records, National Archives).
85. *ibid.*
86. CR, S/L J. M. Thompson, 111 Squadron, 10 July 1940 (Air 50 records, National Archives).
87. IPR, 111 Squadron, 10 July 1940 (Air 16/955 records, National Archives); CR, S/L J. M. Thompson, 111 Squadron, 10 July 1940 (Air 50 records, National Archives).
88. CR, S/L J. M. Thompson, 111 Squadron, 10 July 1940 (Air 50 records, National Archives).
89. Reeve, Jonathan, *op. cit.* (pp. 121-122).
90. *ibid.*

91. CR, S/L J. M. Thompson, 111 Squadron, 10 July 1940 (Air 50 records, National Archives).

92. IPR, 111 Squadron, 10 July 1940 (Air 16/955 records, National Archives).

93. CR, S/L J. M. Thompson, 111 Squadron, 10 July 1940 (Air 50 records, National Archives).

94. IPR, 111 Squadron, 10 July 1940 (Air 16/955 records, National Archives).

95. Cull, Brian, *op. cit.* (p. 46).

96. IPR, 111 Squadron, 10 July 1940 (Air 16/955 records, National Archives); Knight, Dennis, *op. cit.* (pp. 67-68); Reeve, Jonathan, *op. cit.* (pp. 121-122).

97. Bergström, Christer, *op. cit.* (pp. 74-75).

98. Website, Wood, Tony, *op. cit.*

99. Ramsey, Winston (ed.), *op. cit.* (RAF and *Luftwaffe* entries for 10 July 1940).

100. Prien, Jochen, *op. cit.* (pp. 335-336).

101. IPR, 74 Squadron, 10 July 1940 (Air 16/955 records, National Archives) (take off time *c.* 13h40).

102. Bergström, Christer, *op. cit.* (pp. 73-74).

103. IPRs, 32, 56, 64, 74 and 111 Squadrons, 10 July 1940 (Air 16/955 records, National Archives); Cull, Brian, *op. cit.* (pp. 45-46).

104. Ramsey, Winston (ed.), *op. cit.* (*Luftwaffe* entry for 10 July 1940); Parker, Nigel, *op. cit.* (entry for 10 July 1940).

105. Parker, Nigel, *op. cit.* (entry for 10 July 1940).

106. Ramsey, Winston (ed.), *op. cit.* (*Luftwaffe* entry for 10 July 1940); Bergström, Christer, *op. cit.* (pp. 74-75).

107. Ramsey, Winston (ed.), *op. cit.* (*Luftwaffe* entry for 10 July 1940).

108. Ramsey, Winston (ed.), *op. cit.* (*Luftwaffe* entry for 10 July 1940); Parker, Nigel, *op. cit.* (entry for 10 July 1940).

109. *ibid.*

110. Parker, Nigel, *op. cit.* (entry for 10 July 1940).

3. 11 July 1940: shipping raids in the Western Channel

1. James, T. Cecil G., *The Battle of Britain* (Abingdon: Routledge, 2012) (p. 28).

2. IPR, 66 Squadron, 11 July 1940 (Air 16/955 records, National Archives); Cull, Brian, *Battle for the Channel* (Stroud: Fonthill, 2017) (p. 59).

3. IPR, 66 Squadron, 11 July 1940 (Air 16/955 records, National Archives).

4. IPR, 242 Squadron, 11 July 1940 (Air 16/955 records, National Archives).

5. *ibid.*

6. Cull, Brian, *op. cit.* (pp. 52-53 and p. 62).

7. IPRs, 66 and 242 Squadrons, 11 July 1940 (Air 16/955 records, National Archives).

8. IPR, 85 Squadron, 11 July 1940 (Air 16/955 records, National Archives); Townsend, Peter, *Duel of Eagles* (London: Weidenfeld and Nicolson, 1970) (pp. 263-268).

9. *ibid.*

10. *ibid.*

11. *ibid.*

12. Townsend, Peter, *op. cit.* (pp. 263-268).

13. Townsend, Peter, *op. cit.* (pp. 263-268); Ramsey, Winston. G. (ed.), *The Battle of Britain: Then and Now* (London: Battle of Britain Prints International Ltd., 1982) (entries for 11 July 1940).

14. James, T. Cecil G., *op. cit.* (p. 28).

15. James, T. Cecil G., *op. cit.* (p. 28); Squadron Commander's Report on Flying Battle Casualty, Sgt F. J. P. Dixon, 501 Squadron, 11 July 1940 (Air 81 records, National Archives).

16. James, T. Cecil G., *op. cit.* (p. 28); IPR, 609 Squadron, 11 July 1940 (Air 16/955 records, National Archives).

17. Squadron Commander's Report on Flying Battle Casualty, Sgt F. J. P. Dixon, *op. cit.*

18. Squadron Commander's Report on Flying Battle Casualty, Sgt F. J. P. Dixon, *op. cit.*; Ramsey, Winston. G. (ed.), *op. cit.* (RAF entry for 11 July 1940).

19. James, T. Cecil G., *op. cit.* (p. 28).

20. Bergström, Christer, *The Battle of Britain: An Epic Conflict Revisited* (Oxford: Casemate, 2015; Eskilstuna: Vaktel, 2015) (p. 75).

21. Website, Wood, Tony, 'Tony Wood's Combat Claims and Casualties Lists': accessed via Don Caldwell's website: don-caldwell.we.bs/claims/tonywood.htm.

22. Ramsey, Winston. G. (ed.), *op. cit.* (RAF entry for 11 July 1940).

23. James, T. Cecil G., *op. cit.* (p. 28).

24. IPR, 609 Squadron, 11 July 1940 (Air 16/955 records, National Archives).

25. *ibid.*

26. *ibid.*

27. *ibid.*

28. Squadron Commander's Report on Flying Battle Casualty, P/O G. T. M. Mitchell, 609 Squadron, 11 July 1940 (Air 81 records, National Archives); Crook, David M., *Spitfire Pilot* (London: Grub Street, 2010) (p. 76).

29. Website, Wood, Tony, *op. cit.*; Ramsey, Winston. G. (ed.), *op. cit.* (RAF entry for 11 July 1940).

30. IPR, 609 Squadron, 11 July 1940 (Air 16/955 records, National Archives); James, T. Cecil G., *op. cit.* (p. 28).

31. IPR, 609 Squadron, 11 July 1940 (Air 16/955 records, National Archives).

32. *ibid.*

33. Crook, David M., *op. cit.* (pp. 70-72); IPR, 609 Squadron, 11 July 1940 (Air 16/955 records, National Archives).

34. *ibid.*

35. Crook, David M., *op. cit.* (pp. 70-72).

36. Crook, David M., *op. cit.* (pp. 70-72); Ramsey, Winston. G. (ed.), *op. cit.* (RAF entry for 11 July 1940).

37. IPR, 609 Squadron, 11 July 1940 (Air 16/955 records, National Archives); Cull, Brian, *op. cit.* (p. 59).

38. Ramsey, Winston. G. (ed.), *op. cit.* (Luftwaffe entry for 11 July 1940).

39. Bergström, Christer, *op. cit.* (p. 75); however, no source for this interpretation is given.

40. Website, Holm, Michael, *The Luftwaffe, 1933-1945*, www.ww2.dk; see also most general Battle of Britain histories, e.g. Ramsey, Winston. G. (ed.), *The Battle of Britain: Then and Now* (London: Battle of Britain Prints International Ltd., 1982), or Mason, Francis K., *Battle over Britain* (London: McWhirter Twins, 1969).

41. Archives, Imperial War Museum, London: *Luftwaffe Quartermaster General Loss Returns*.

42. IPR, 609 Squadron, 11 July 1940 (Air 16/955 records, National Archives).

43. Website, Wood, Tony, *op. cit.*; Ramsey, Winston (ed.), *op. cit.* (*Luftwaffe* entry for 11 July 1940).

44. Website, Wood, Tony, *op. cit.*; as a caveat, however, this list is not complete, at least for certain units.

45. James, T. Cecil G., *op. cit.* (p. 28); Mason, Francis K., *op. cit.* (pp. 161-162); Cull, Brian, *op. cit.* (p. 59).

46. Wynn, Kenneth G., *Men of the Battle of Britain: A Biographical Directory of the Few* (Barnsley: Frontline, 2015; West Malling: The Battle of Britain Memorial Trust, 2015) (p. 49, p. 139); James, T. Cecil G., *op. cit.* (p. 28); Mason, Francis K., *op. cit.* (pp. 161-162); Cull, Brian, *op. cit.* (p. 59).

47. James, T. Cecil G., *op. cit.* (pp. 28-29).

48. James, T. Cecil G., *op. cit.* (p. 30).

49. *ibid.*

50. See map section at beginning of this book.

51. James, T. Cecil G., *op. cit.* (pp. 28-29).

52. Lanchbery, Edward, *Against the Sun* (London: Pan, 1957) (pp. 44-45); Gleed, Ian, *Arise to Conquer* (London: Severn House, 1975) (p. 53); CR, P/O D. T. Jay, 87 Squadron, 11 July 1940 (Air 50 records, National Archives); James, T. Cecil G., *op. cit.* (pp. 28-29).

53. James, T. Cecil G., *op. cit.* (pp. 28-29).

54. Saunders, Andy, *Stuka Attack!* (London: Grub Street, 2013) (pp. 26-31).

55. *ibid.*

56. CR, F/Lt Sir Archibald Hope, 601 Squadron, 11 July 1940 (Air 50 records, National Archives); James, T. Cecil G., *op. cit.* (pp. 28-29).

57. Saunders, Andy, *op. cit.* (pp. 26-31); Goss, Chris, *Luftwaffe Fighters' Battle of Britain* (Manchester: Crécy, 2010) (pp. 23-26).

58. CR, F/Lt Sir Archibald Hope, 601 Squadron, 11 July 1940 (Air 50 records, National Archives); James, T. Cecil G., *op. cit.* (pp. 28-29); CR, P/O P. Chaloner-Lindsey, 601 Squadron, 11 July 1940 (Air 50 records, National Archives); CR, S/L J. S. Dewar, 87 Squadron, 11 July 1940 (Air 50 records, National Archives), quoted partially on website of The King's School, Canterbury Alumni Association, www.oks.org.uk; Eriksson, Patrick G., *Alarmstart* (Stroud: Amberley, 2017) (p. 94).

59. Ramsey, Winston (ed.), op. *cit.* (*Luftwaffe* entry for 11 July 1940).

60. CRs, F/Lt Sir Archibald Hope, P/O P. Chaloner-Lindsey, F/O C. J. H. Riddle and F/Sgt A. H. D. Pond, 601 Squadron, 11 July 1940 (Air 50 records, National Archives) (take off time *c.* 11h12, was a later CR for Pond).

61. CR, S/L J. S. Dewar, 87 Squadron, 11 July 1940 (Air 50 records, National Archives).

62. Wynn, Kenneth G., *op. cit.* (pp. 248-249).

63. CR, F/Lt Sir Archibald Hope, 601 Squadron, 11 July 1940 (Air 50 records, National Archives).

64. CR, F/Sgt A. H. D. Pond, 601 Squadron, 11 July 1940 (Air 50 records, National Archives) (take off time *c.* 11h12).

65. CR, F/O C. J. H. Riddle, 601 Squadron, 11 July 1940 (Air 50 records, National Archives).

66. *ibid.*

67. Wynn, Kenneth G., *op. cit.* (p. 321).

68. CR, P/O P. Chaloner-Lindsey, 601 Squadron, 11 July 1940 (Air 50 records, National Archives). His handwritten report is difficult in places to unravel, and the author has inserted a full stop followed by a capital letter just before '50' therein, as it appears to be the start of a new sentence; several others in the original report also begin with a small letter and are again corrected here, to enable better comprehension of what he is saying. No doubt excitement and combat nerves could easily affect someone's handwriting straight after a mission.

69. CR, F/Sgt A. H. D. Pond, 601 Squadron, 11 July 1940 (Air 50 records, National Archives) (take off time *c.* 11h12).

70. Saunders, Andy, *op. cit.* (pp. 26-31); James, T. Cecil G., *op. cit.* (pp. 28-29).

71. James, T. Cecil G., *op. cit.* (pp. 28-29); Parry, Simon W., *Battle of Britain Combat Archive,* Vol. 1, 10 July–22 July 1940 (Walton on Thames: Red Kite Books, 2015) (pp. 32-33).

72. Saunders, Andy, *op. cit.* (pp. 26-31); Ramsey, Winston (ed.), *op. cit.* (*Luftwaffe* entry for 11 July 1940); Parker, Nigel, *Luftwaffe Crash*

Archive, Vol. 1 (Walton on Thames: Red Kite Books, Air Research Publications, 2013) (entry for 11 July 1940).

73. CR, S/L J. S. Dewar, 87 Squadron, 11 July 1940 (Air 50 records, National Archives). Corrections not made to CR for linguistic errors.

74. Wynn, Kenneth G., *op. cit.* (pp. 133-134).

75. CRs, F/Lt Sir Archibald Hope and F/O C. J. H. Riddle, 601 Squadron, 11 July 1940 (Air 50 records, National Archives).

76. Website, *The Encyclopaedia of Portland History,* www.portlandhistory. co.uk.

77. CR, P/O D. T. Jay, 87 Squadron, 11 July 1940 (Air 50 records, National Archives).

78. Wynn, Kenneth G., *op. cit.* (p. 271).

79. Alexander, Kristen, *Australia's Few and the Battle of Britain* (Barnsley: Pen and Sword, 2015) (pp. 169-172).

80. CR, F/O R. L. Glyde, 87 Squadron, 11 July 1940 (Air 50 records, National Archives).

81. *ibid.*

82. CR, F/Lt S. C. Walch, 238 Squadron, 11 July 1940 (Air 50 records, National Archives).

83. *ibid.*

84. *ibid.*

85. *ibid.*

86. Alexander, Kristen, *op. cit.* (pp. 169-172); CR, F/Lt S. C. Walch, 238 Squadron, 11 July 1940 (Air 50 records, National Archives).

87. Alexander, Kristen, *op. cit.* (pp. 169-172).

88. *ibid.*

89. *ibid.*

90. *ibid.*

91. CR, P/O P. Chaloner-Lindsey, 601 Squadron, 11 July 1940 (Air 50 records, National Archives).

92. Parry, Simon W., *op. cit.* (pp. 32-33); Ramsey, Winston (ed.), *op. cit.* (*Luftwaffe* entry for 11 July 1940).

93. Eriksson, Patrick G., *op. cit.* (p. 94).

94. Eriksson, Patrick G., *op. cit.* (p. 94); Saunders, Andy, *op. cit.* (pp. 26-31); Ramsey, Winston (ed.), *op. cit.* (*Luftwaffe* entry for 11 July 1940).

95. Eriksson, Patrick G., *op. cit.* (p. 94); Saunders, Andy, *op. cit.* (p. 31).

96. Eriksson, Patrick G., *op. cit.* (p. 94).

97. Saunders, Andy, *op. cit.* (pp. 26-31); Goss, Chris, *op. cit.* (pp. 23-26).

98. *ibid.*

99. Ramsey, Winston (ed.), *op. cit.* (*Luftwaffe* entry for 11 July 1940).

100. Parry, Simon W., *op. cit.* (pp. 32-33).

101. Goss, Chris, *op. cit.* (pp. 23-26).

102. Second part of report, CR, S/L J. S. Dewar, 87 Squadron, 11 July 1940 (Air 50 records, National Archives).
103. Cull, Brian, *op. cit.* (p. 61); Ramsey, Winston (ed.), *op. cit.* (*Luftwaffe* entry for 11 July 1940).
104. Saunders, Andy, *op. cit.* (pp. 26-31).
105. CR, P/O D. T. Jay, 87 Squadron, 11 July 1940 (Air 50 records, National Archives).
106. *ibid.*
107. *ibid.*
108. *ibid.*
109. CR, F/O R. L. Glyde, 87 Squadron, 11 July 1940 (Air 50 records, National Archives).
110. Ramsey, Winston (ed.), *op. cit.* (*Luftwaffe* entry for 11 July 1940).
111. *ibid.*
112. CR, S/L J. S. Dewar, 87 Squadron, 11 July 1940 (Air 50 records, National Archives); see first part of combat report, quoted in the text above.
113. CR, S/L J. S. Dewar, 87 Squadron, 11 July 1940 (Air 50 records, National Archives).
114. Ramsey, Winston (ed.), *op. cit.* (*Luftwaffe* entry for 11 July 1940).
115. James, T. Cecil G., *op. cit.* (pp. 28-29).
116. Ramsey, Winston (ed.), *op. cit.* (*Luftwaffe* entry for 11 July 1940).
117. Cull, Brian, *op. cit.* (p. 54).
118. Ramsey, Winston (ed.), *op. cit.* (RAF entry for 11 July 1940).
119. Website, Wood, Tony, *op. cit.*
120. Mahlke, Helmut, *Memoirs of a Stuka Pilot* (London: Frontline, 2013) (p. 117).
121. Von Eimannsberger, Ludwig, *Zerstörer Gruppe: A history of V./(Z)LG 1 – I./NJG 3 1939-1941* (Atglen: Schiffer, 1998) (p. 92).
122. Website, *Wrecksite*, www.wrecksite.eu/wreck.aspx?4678.
123. Mahlke, Helmut, *op. cit.* (p. 117).
124. Note 122, *op. cit.*
125. *ibid.*
126. CR, F/Sgt A. H. D. Pond, 601 Squadron, 11 July 1940 (Air 50 records, National Archives) (take off time *c.* 11h12).
127. *ibid.*
128. Parry, Simon W., *op. cit.* (pp. 32-33); Cull, Brian, *op. cit.* (p. 54).
129. James, T. Cecil G., *op. cit.* (pp. 29-31); Mason, Francis K., *op. cit.* (pp. 161-162); Bergström, Christer, *op. cit.* (p. 76).
130. James, T. Cecil G., *op. cit.* (pp. 29-31); Mason, Francis K., *op. cit.* (pp. 161-162).
131. Parker, Nigel, *op. cit.* (entry for 11 July 1940).
132. Parker, Nigel, *op. cit.* (entry for 11 July 1940); James, T. Cecil G., *op. cit.* (pp. 29-31).

133. Mason, Francis K., *op. cit.* (pp. 161-162); James, T. Cecil G., *op. cit.* (pp. 29-31).

134. *ibid.*

135. Parker, Nigel, *op. cit.* (entry for 11 July 1940).

136. *ibid.*

137. Mason, Francis K., *op. cit.* (p. 162, footnote thereon).

138. James, T. Cecil G., *op. cit.* (pp. 29-31); Parker, Nigel, *op. cit.* (entry for 11 July 1940).

139. Mason, Francis K., *op. cit.* (pp. 161-162).

140. *ibid.*

141. Parker, Nigel, *op. cit.* (entry for 11 July 1940).

142. Parker, Nigel, *op. cit.* (entry for 11 July 1940); Ramsey, Winston (ed.), *op. cit.* (*Luftwaffe* entry for 11 July 1940).

143. Ramsey, Winston (ed.), *op. cit.* (*Luftwaffe* entry for 11 July 1940).

144. Parker, Nigel, *op. cit.* (entry for 11 July 1940).

145. James, T. Cecil G., *op. cit.* (pp. 29-31).

146. Mason, Francis K., *op. cit.* (pp. 161-162); Cull, Brian, *op. cit.* (p. 60).

147. Bergström, Christer, *op. cit.* (p. 76).

148. For example: Mason, Francis K., *op. cit.* (pp. 161-162); James, T. Cecil G., *op. cit.* (pp. 29-31).

149. Ramsey, Winston (ed.), *op. cit.* (RAF entry for 11 July 1940).

150. A copy of Sgt Arthur Woolley's formal report on being shot down on 11 July 1940, was posted on Facebook on 11 July 2017 by the Kent Battle of Britain Museum; Squadron Commander's Report on Flying Battle Casualty, Sgt A. W. Woolley, 601 Squadron, 11 July 1940 (Air 81 records, National Archives) (copy of pilot's report and that of Commanding Officer).

151. *ibid.*

152. *ibid.*

153. *ibid.*

154. *ibid.*

155. *ibid.*

156. Mason, Francis K., *op. cit.* (pp. 161-162); Cull, Brian, *op. cit.* (p. 61).

157. Parker, Nigel, *op. cit.* (entry for 11 July 1940).

158. Cull, Brian, *op. cit.* (p. 56); James, T. Cecil G., *op. cit.* (pp. 29-31).

159. *ibid.*

160. James, T. Cecil G., *op. cit.* (pp. 29-31).

161. Parker, Nigel, *op. cit.* (entry for 11 July 1940).

162. *ibid.*

163. *ibid.*

164. *ibid.*

165. Ramsey, Winston (ed.), *op. cit.* (*Luftwaffe* entry for 11 July 1940).

166. Cull, Brian, *op. cit.* (p. 56).

167. *ibid.*
168. Parker, Nigel, *op. cit.* (entry for 11 July 1940).
169. Cull, Brian, *op. cit.* (p. 56).
170. Mason, Francis K., *op. cit.* (pp. 161-162).
171. Pitchfork, Graham, *Shot down in the drink: true stories of RAF and Commonwealth aircrews saved from the sea in WWII* (Oxford: Osprey, 2017).
172. Ramsey, Winston (ed.), op. *cit.* (RAF entry for 11 July 1940).
173. *ibid.*
174. James, T. Cecil G., *op. cit.* (pp. 29-31); Cull, Brian, *op. cit.* (p. 60).
175. Ramsey, Winston (ed.), op. *cit.* (*Luftwaffe* entry for 11 July 1940).
176. James, T. Cecil G., *op. cit.* (p. 32).
177. *ibid.*
178. *ibid.*
179. *ibid.*

4. 12-15 July 1940: activity shifts to Dover Straits and East Coast convoys; EGr 210 enters the fray

1. Mason, Francis K., *Battle over Britain* (London: McWhirter Twins, 1969) (pp. 163-164); Website, Holdoway, Mike, *Convoy Web*; www.convoyweb.org.uk.
2. Relevant RAF records detailed below; James, T. Cecil G., *The Battle of Britain* (Abingdon: Routledge, 2012) (p. 33).
3. IPRs, 17 Squadron (two in number, one for P/O Manger/Sgt Griffiths and one for P/O Pittman/Sgt Fopp), 85 and 151 Squadrons, 12 July 1940 (Air 16/955 records, National Archives).
4. Ramsey, Winston. G. (ed.), *The Battle of Britain: Then and Now* (London: Battle of Britain Prints International Ltd., 1982) (entries for 12 July 1940); Parker, Nigel, *Luftwaffe Crash Archive*, Vol. 1 (Walton on Thames: Red Kite Books, Air Research Publications, 2013) (entry for 12 July 1940).
5. Wood, Derek and Dempster, Derek, *The Narrow Margin* (London: Arrow Books, 1967) (pp. 105-121).
6. IPR, 151 Squadron, 12 July 1940 (Air 16/955 records, National Archives).
7. Cull, Brian, *Battle for the Channel* (Stroud: Fonthill, 2017) (p. 300).
8. Mason, Francis K., *op. cit.* (pp. 163-164); IPR, 17 Squadron, 12 July 1940, for P/O Pittman/Sgt Fopp (Air 16/955 records, National Archives).
9. IPRs, 17 Squadron (two in number, one for P/O Manger/Sgt Griffiths and one for P/O Pittman/Sgt Fopp), 151 Squadron, 12 July 1940 (Air 16/955 records, National Archives); Franks, Norman L., *Double Mission: RAF Fighter Ace and SOE Agent* (London: William Kimber, 1976) (pp. 57-58).

10. Mason, Francis K., *op. cit.* (pp. 163-164); James, T. Cecil G., *op. cit.* (p. 33); IPR, 17 Squadron, 12 July 1940, for P/O Manger/Sgt Griffiths (Air 16/955 records, National Archives); Website, Holdoway, Mike, *op. cit.*

11. IPR, 17 Squadron, 12 July 1940, for P/O Manger/Sgt Griffiths (Air 16/955 records, National Archives).

12. *ibid.*

13. Parker, Nigel, *op. cit.* (entry for 12 July 1940).

14. IPR, 85 Squadron, 12 July 1940 (Air 16/955 records, National Archives).

15. IPR, 17 Squadron, 12 July 1940, for P/O Pittman/Sgt Fopp (Air 16/955 records, National Archives).

16. Mason, Francis K., *op. cit.* (pp. 163-164).

17. Parker, Nigel, *op. cit.* (entry for 12 July 1940); this author made extensive use of the so-called 'K reports', Air Intelligence reports resulting from interrogation of captured *Luftwaffe* aircrew. The specific report here comes from Air Ministry (A.I.(K)) Prisoner of War Reports, Volume 4, AIR 40/2397, No's. 101 – 200, 21 May–24 July 1940. Here they will be referred to as 'K reports'.

18. Parker, Nigel, *op. cit.* (entry for 12 July 1940); Website, de Zeng, Henry L. IV and Stankey, Douglas G., *Luftwaffe Officer Career Summaries* (2014 updated version), accessed via Michael Holm's website, *The Luftwaffe 1933-1945*: www.ww2.dk; this source at www.ww2.dk/lwoffz.html.

19. IPR, 17 Squadron, 12 July 1940, for P/O Pittman/Sgt Fopp (Air 16/955 records, National Archives).

20. IPR, 17 Squadron, 12 July 1940, for P/O Pittman/Sgt Fopp (Air 16/955 records, National Archives); Parker, Nigel, *op. cit.* (entry for 12 July 1940).

21. Parker, Nigel, *op. cit.* (entry for 12 July 1940).

22. Cull, Brian, *op. cit.* (pp. 63-64).

23. *ibid.*

24. *ibid.*

25. Hunt, Leslie, *Twenty-One Squadrons: the History of the Royal Auxiliary Air Force: 1925-1957* (London: Garnstone Press, 1972) (p. 317); Cull, Brian, *op. cit.* (pp. 63-64).

26. Website, *wo2vpr*, https://sites.google.com/site/wo2vpr1/home/11-07-1940-avro-anson-oostvoorne.

27. *ibid.*

28. IPR, 85 Squadron, 12 July 1940 (Air 16/955 records, National Archives); Wynn, Kenneth G., *Men of the Battle of Britain: a biographical directory of the Few* (Barnsley: Frontline, 2015; West Malling: The Battle of Britain Memorial Trust, 2015) (p. 44, p. 280, p. 456).

29. Ramsey, Winston (ed.), op. cit. (RAF entry for 12 July 1940).

30. Wynn, Kenneth G., *op. cit.* (p. 44); IPR, 85 Squadron, 12 July 1940 (Air 16/955 records, National Archives); Cull, Brian, *op. cit.* (pp. 67-68).

31. IPR, 85 Squadron, 12 July 1940 (Air 16/955 records, National Archives).

32. IPR, 17 Squadron, 12 July 1940, for P/O Manger/Sgt Griffiths (Air 16/955 records, National Archives).

33. *ibid.*

34. Parker, Nigel, *op. cit.* (entry for 12 July 1940); Ramsey, Winston (ed.), op. *cit.* (*Luftwaffe* entry for 12 July 1940).

35. Parker, Nigel, *op. cit.* (entry for 12 July 1940).

36. Parker, Nigel, *op. cit.* (entry for 12 July 1940); IPR, 85 Squadron, 12 July 1940 (Air 16/955 records, National Archives).

37. For example: Mason, Francis K., *op. cit.* (pp. 163-164); Bergström, Christer, *The Battle of Britain: an Epic Conflict Revisited* (Oxford: Casemate, 2015; Eskilstuna: Vaktel, 2015) (pp. 76-77).

38. IPR, 151 Squadron, 12 July 1940 (Air 16/955 records, National Archives); Franks, Norman L., *op. cit.* (pp. 57-58).

39. Website, de Zeng, Henry L. IV and Stankey, Douglas G., *op. cit.*

40. IPR, 151 Squadron, 12 July 1940 (Air 16/955 records, National Archives); Ramsey, Winston (ed.), *op. cit.* (entries for 12 July 1940).

41. Mason, Francis K., *op. cit.* (pp. 163-164); IPR, 151 Squadron, 12 July 1940 (Air 16/955 records, National Archives).

42. Stokes, Doug, *Wings Aflame: The Biography of Group Captain Victor Beamish DSO and Bar, DFC, AFC* (Manchester: Goodall/Crécy, 1998).

43. IPR, 151 Squadron, 12 July 1940 (Air 16/955 records, National Archives).

44. *ibid.*

45. *ibid.*

46. Website, *The Battle of Britain London Monument*, The Airmen's Stories – F/Lt R L Smith (p. 8), www.bbm.org.uk/airmen/SmithRL.htm.

47. IPR, 151 Squadron, 12 July 1940 (Air 16/955 records, National Archives); Ramsey, Winston (ed.), op. *cit.* (RAF entry for 12 July 1940).

48. IPR, 151 Squadron, 12 July 1940 (Air 16/955 records, National Archives).

49. Franks, Norman L., *op. cit.* (pp. 57-58); Mason, Francis K., *op. cit.* (pp. 163-164).

50. *ibid.*

51. Mason, Francis K., *op. cit.* (pp. 163-164).

52. Parker, Nigel, *op. cit.* (entry for 12 July 1940); Ramsey, Winston (ed.), *op. cit.* (*Luftwaffe* entry for 12 July 1940).

53. IPR, 151 Squadron, 12 July 1940 (Air 16/955 records, National Archives); Ramsey, Winston (ed.), *op. cit.* (*Luftwaffe* entry for 12 July 1940); Parker, Nigel, *op. cit.* (entry for 12 July 1940).

54. Ramsey, Winston (ed.), *op. cit.* (*Luftwaffe* entry for 12 July 1940); Parker, Nigel, *op. cit.* (entry for 12 July 1940). The former source names one 5/ *KG 2* survivor and the latter source, two 5/*KG 2* survivors who perfectly match the names of two survivors from the 8/*KG 53* He 111 shot down by P/O Pittman and Sgt Fopp of 17 Squadron earlier; obviously an error in the primary records on survivors rescued from the sea.

55. Mason, Francis K., *op. cit.* (pp. 163-164).
56. Cull, Brian, *op. cit.* (p. 65, p. 69).
57. Ramsey, Winston (ed.), op. *cit.* (*Luftwaffe* entry for 12 July 1940); Cull, Brian, *op. cit.* (p. 71).
58. IPR, 603 Squadron, 12 July 1940 (Air 16/955 records, National Archives).
59. *ibid*
60. *ibid.*
61. IPR, 603 Squadron, 12 July 1940 (Air 16/955 records, National Archives); Ramsey, Winston (ed.), op. *cit.* (*Luftwaffe* entry for 12 July 1940).
62. Note 58, *op. cit.*
63. *ibid.*
64. IPR, 603 Squadron, 12 July 1940 (Air 16/955 records, National Archives); Ramsey, Winston (ed.), op. *cit.* (*Luftwaffe* entry for 12 July 1940).
65. Archives, Imperial War Museum, London: *Luftwaffe Quartermaster General Loss Returns.*
66. Squadron Commander's Report on Flying Battle Casualty, P/O D. A. Hewitt, 501 Squadron, 12 July 1940 (Air 81 records, National Archives).
67. Letter to the father of P/O Hewitt, Dr S. R. D. Hewitt at the Saint John General Hospital, New Brunswick, from the Director of Personal Services of the RAF. From the Casualty File of P/O D. A. Hewitt (Air 81 records, National Archives).
68. Cull, Brian, *op. cit.* (p. 69).
69. Ramsey, Winston (ed.), *op. cit.* (*Luftwaffe* entry for 12 July 1940); Cull, Brian, *op. cit.* (p. 69).
70. Dalton-Morgan, Tom, *Tommy Leader* (Wendover: Griffon International, 2007) (p. 38); Ramsey, Winston (ed.), *op. cit.* (*Luftwaffe* entry for 12 July 1940).
71. Dalton-Morgan, Tom, *op. cit.* (p. 38).
72. Note 70, *op. cit.*
73. Cull, Brian, *op. cit.* (p. 65-66).
74. Parker, Nigel, *op. cit.* (entry for 12 July 1940).
75. *ibid.*
76. Website, *Battle of Britain London Monument,* bbm.org.uk/airmen/Dalton-Morgan.htm.
77. IPR, 74 Squadron, 12 July 1940 (Air 16/955 records, National Archives).
78. *ibid.*
79. *ibid.*
80. *ibid.*
81. *ibid.*
82. *Luftwaffe Quartermaster General Loss Returns, op. cit.* This damaged machine is not included amongst the day's losses given by several sources, e.g. Cull, Brian, *op. cit.*, Ramsey, Winston (ed.), *op. cit.* (*Luftwaffe* entry for 12 July 1940); however, it is listed in Mason, Francis K., *op. cit.*

83. IPR, 74 Squadron, 12 July 1940 (Air 16/955 records, National Archives).
84. IPR, 234 Squadron, 12 July 1940 (Air 16/955 records, National Archives).
85. *ibid*.
86. *ibid*.
87. *Luftwaffe Quartermaster General Loss Returns, op. cit.*
88. Cull, Brian, *op. cit.* (p. 69).
89. Mason, Francis K., *op. cit.* (pp. 164-165).
90. Mason, Francis K., *op. cit.* (pp. 164-165); Cull, Brian, *op. cit.* (p. 66); Ramsey, Winston (ed.), op. *cit.* (*Luftwaffe* entry for 12 July 1940).
91. Cull, Brian, *op. cit.* (p. 69).
92. Von Eimannsberger, Ludwig, *Zerstörer Gruppe: A history of V./(Z)LG 1 – I./NJG 3 1939-1941* (Atglen: Schiffer, 1998) (p. 92, p. 208).
93. Vasco, John, *Messerschmitt Bf 110 Bombsights over England: Erprobungsgruppe 210 in the Battle of Britain* (Atglen: Schiffer, 2002) (p. 16).
94. Cull, Brian, *op. cit.* (p. 300).
95. Vasco, John, *op.cit.* (p. 16); Barbas, Bernd, *Die Geschichte der I. Gruppe des Jagdgeschwaders 52* (Überlingen: self-published, undated) (p. 93).
96. Vasco, John, *op. cit.* (p. 16).
97. Cull, Brian, *op. cit.* (p. 79).
98. *Luftwaffe Quartermaster General Loss Returns, op. cit.*
99. Cull, Brian, *op. cit.* (p. 72, p. 78); Mason, Francis K., *op. cit.* (p. 167).
100. Cull, Brian, *op. cit.* (p. 76); Dalton-Morgan, Tom, *op. cit.* (p. 40).
101. Dalton-Morgan, Tom, *op. cit.* (p. 40).
102. *ibid*.
103. Ramsey, Winston (ed.), *op. cit.* (*Luftwaffe* entry for 13 July 1940).
104. Dalton-Morgan, Tom, *op. cit.* (p. 40).
105. Ramsey, Winston (ed.), *op. cit.* (RAF entry for 13 July 1940).
106. Burt, Danny, *A Battle of Britain Spitfire Squadron: the Men and Machines of 152 Squadron in the Summer of 1940* (Barnsley: Pen and Sword, 2018) (p. 243).
107. IPR, 152 Squadron, 13 July 1940 (Air 16/955 records, National Archives).
108. Ramsey, Winston (ed.), *op. cit.* (*Luftwaffe* entry for 13 July 1940).
109. Website, Holm, Michael, *The Luftwaffe, 1933-1945*; www.ww2.dk.
110. Mason, Francis K., *op. cit.* (p. 166).
111. IPR, combined, 238 and 609 Squadrons, 13 July 1940 (Air 16/955 records, National Archives).
112. Alexander, Kristen, *Australia's Few and the Battle of Britain* (Barnsley: Pen and Sword, 2015) (pp. 173-175); Mason, Francis K., *op. cit.* (p. 166); IPR, combined, 238 and 609 Squadrons, 13 July 1940 (Air 16/955 records, National Archives).
113. Von Eimannsberger, Ludwig, *op. cit.* (p. 93).

114. For example, Mason, Francis K., *op. cit.* (p. 166); Bergström, Christer, *op. cit.* (pp. 77-78).
115. Von Eimannsberger, Ludwig, *op. cit.* (p. 93).
116. IPR, combined, 238 and 609 Squadrons, 13 July 1940 (Air 16/955 records, National Archives).
117. *ibid.*
118. Von Eimannsberger, Ludwig, *op. cit.* (pp. 207-208).
119. Mason, Francis K., *op. cit.* (pp. 131-166).
120. Mason, Francis K., *op. cit.* (p. 166).
121. IPR, combined, 238 and 609 Squadrons, 13 July 1940 (Air 16/955 records, National Archives).
122. *ibid.*
123. IPR, combined, 238 and 609 Squadrons, 13 July 1940 (Air 16/955 records, National Archives); Alexander, Kristen, *op. cit.* (pp. 173-175).
124. Wynn, Kenneth G., *op. cit.* (pp. 287-288 and p. 541).
125. Note 121, *op. cit.*
126. Alexander, Kristen, *op. cit.* (pp. 173-175).
127. Alexander, Kristen, *op. cit.* (pp. 173-175); IPR, combined, 238 and 609 Squadrons, 13 July 1940 (Air 16/955 records, National Archives).
128. *ibid.*
129. Alexander, Kristen, *op. cit.* (pp. 173-175); Ramsey, Winston (ed.), *op. cit.* (RAF entry for 13 July 1940).
130. Website, Dorset Crashes, dorset.hampshireairfields.co.uk.
131. Note 121, *op. cit.*
132. *ibid.*
133. *ibid.*
134. *ibid.*
135. Batt, L. Gordon, *Scramble! A Flying Memoir of one of the Few* (Gunthorpe: The Battle of Britain Historical Society, 2001) (pp. 43-44).
136. *ibid.*
137. Wynn, Kenneth G., *op. cit.* (pp. 107-108).
138. Von Eimannsberger, Ludwig, *op. cit.* (p. 93).
139. *ibid.*
140. Von Eimannsberger, Ludwig, *op. cit.* (p. 93); Ramsey, Winston (ed.), *op. cit.* (*Luftwaffe* entry for 13 July 1940).
141. Ramsey, Winston (ed.), op. *cit.* (*Luftwaffe* entry for 13 July 1940).
142. IPR, combined, 238 and 609 Squadrons, 13 July 1940 (Air 16/955 records, National Archives); Cull, Brian, *op. cit.* (pp. 72-73).
143. IPR, combined, 238 and 609 Squadrons, 13 July 1940 (Air 16/955 records, National Archives); Von Eimannsberger, Ludwig, *op. cit.* (p. 93).
144. IPR, combined, 238 and 609 Squadrons, 13 July 1940 (Air 16/955 records, National Archives); Batt, L. Gordon, *op. cit.* (pp. 43-44).

145. IPR, combined, 238 and 609 Squadrons, 13 July 1940 (Air 16/955 records, National Archives); Batt, L. Gordon, *op. cit.* (pp. 43-44); Von Eimannsberger, Ludwig, *op. cit.* (p. 93).

146. IPR, combined, 238 and 609 Squadrons, 13 July 1940 (Air 16/955 records, National Archives); Cull, Brian, *op. cit.* (pp. 72-73).

147. Ramsey, Winston (ed.), *op. cit.* (*Luftwaffe* entry for 13 July 1940).

148. IPR, combined, 238 and 609 Squadrons, 13 July 1940 (Air 16/955 records, National Archives).

149. *ibid.*

150. Cull, Brian, *op. cit.* (pp. 72-73); Foreman, John, *RAF Fighter Command Air Victory Claims of World War Two, Part One 1939-1940* (Walton-on-Thames: Red Kite, 2003) (p. 102).

151. Mason, Francis K., *op. cit.* (pp. 166-167); Knight, Dennis, *Harvest of Messerschmitts: The Chronicle of a Village at War, 1940* (London: Frederick Warne, 1981) (p. 69); Saunders, Andy, *Stuka Attack!* (London: Grub Street, 2013) (pp. 34-35); Cull, Brian, *op. cit.* (pp. 72-74); Bergström, Christer, *op. cit.* (pp. 78-79); Ramsey, Winston (ed.), op. *cit.* (entries for 13 July 1940).

152. Website, Smith, Gordon and co-workers, naval-history.net; www.naval-history.net/xDKWW2-4007-20JUL01.htm.

153. Mason, Francis K., *op. cit.* (pp. 166-167); Page, Geoffrey, *Tale of a Guinea Pig* (London: Corgi, 1983) (pp. 67-70); Saunders, Andy, *op. cit.* (pp. 34-35).

154. Saunders, Andy, *op. cit.* (pp. 34-35); Bergström, Christer, *op. cit.* (pp. 78-79); Cull, Brian, *op. cit.* (pp. 72-74); Aders, Gebhard and Held, Werner, *Jagdgeschwader 51 'Mölders'* (Stuttgart: Motorbuch, 1985) (p. 249).

155. Website, Holm, Michael, *op. cit.*

156. Squadron Commander's Report on Flying Battle Casualty, Sgt J. R. Cowsill, 56 Squadron, 13 July 1940 (Air 81 records, National Archives); Squadron Commander's Report on Flying Battle Casualty, Sgt J. J. Whitfield, 56 Squadron, 13 July 1940 (Air 81 records, National Archives); Mason, Francis K., *op. cit.* (pp. 166-167); Page, Geoffrey, *op. cit.* (pp. 67-70); Cull, Brian, *op. cit.* (pp. 72-74).

157. Page, Geoffrey, *op. cit.* (pp. 67-70).

158. Page, Geoffrey, *op. cit.* (p. 67, p. 74).

159. Page, Geoffrey, *op. cit.* (pp. 67-70).

160. *ibid.*

161. Mason, Francis K., *op. cit.* (pp. 166-167).

162. Page, Geoffrey, *op. cit.* (pp. 67-70).

163. Saunders, Andy, *op. cit.* (pp. 34-35).

164. CR, F/Lt Coghlan, 56 Squadron, 13 July 1940 (Air 50 records, National Archives); Bergström, Christer, *op. cit.* (pp. 78-79).

165. Bergström, Christer, *op. cit.* (pp. 78-79).

166. Saunders, Andy, *op. cit.* (pp. 34-35).
167. Bergström, Christer, *op. cit.* (pp. 78-79); Website, Wood, Tony, 'Tony Wood's Combat Claims and Casualties Lists': accessed via Don Caldwell's website: don-caldwell.we.bs/claims/tonywood.htm; Ramsey, Winston (ed.), *op. cit.* (RAF entry for 13 July 1940).
168. Saunders, Andy, *op. cit.* (pp. 34-35).
169. *ibid.*
170. Website, Wood, Tony, *op. cit.*
171. Cull, Brian, *op. cit.* (pp. 75-77).
172. Saunders, Andy, *op. cit.* (p. 183); Ramsey, Winston (ed.), *op. cit.* (*Luftwaffe* entry for 13 July 1940).
173. Cull, Brian, *op. cit.* (pp. 72-74).
174. Ramsey, Winston (ed.), *op. cit.* (RAF entry for 13 July 1940).
175. *ibid.*
176. Squadron Commander's Report on Flying Battle Casualty, Sgt J. R. Cowsill, 56 Squadron, 13 July 1940 (Air 81 records, National Archives).
177. Saunders, Andy, *op. cit.* (pp. 34-35).
178. Website, Wood, Tony, *op. cit.*
179. Ramsey, Winston (ed.), *op. cit.* (RAF entry for 13 July 1940).
180. *ibid.*
181. Squadron Commander's Report on Flying Battle Casualty, Sgt J. J. Whitfield, 56 Squadron, 13 July 1940 (Air 81 records, National Archives).
182. Page, Geoffrey, *op. cit.* (pp. 67-70).
183. *ibid.*
184. *ibid.*
185. Saunders, Andy, *op. cit.* (pp. 34-35).
186. *Kanalkampfführer* = Channel Battle Leader.
187. Saunders, Andy, *op. cit.* (p. 183).
188. Osterkamp, Theo, *Durch Höhen und Tiefen jagt ein Herz* (Heidelberg: Kurt Vowinckel Verlag, 1952) (pp. 343-348); Bergström, Christer, *op. cit.* (pp. 78-79).
189. Osterkamp, Theo, *op. cit.* (pp. 343-348).
190. IPR, 54 Squadron, 13 July 1940 (Air 16/955 records, National Archives); Cull, Brian, *op. cit.* (pp. 71-72 and p. 75).
191. IPR, 54 Squadron, 13 July 1940 (Air 16/955 records, National Archives); Cull, Brian, *op. cit.* (p. 71).
192. Website, Helgason, Gudmundur, *uboat.net*, uboat.net/allies/warships/ship/5455.html. HMS *Vanessa* was repaired at Sheerness and returned to duty only on 4 November 1940.
193. Saunders, Andy, *op. cit.* (p. 183).
194. IPR, 54 Squadron, 13 July 1940 (Air 16/955 records, National Archives); signed by the Intelligence Officer at Rochford.
195. Cull, Brian, *op. cit.* (p. 71).

196. IPR, 54 Squadron, 13 July 1940 (Air 16/955 records, National Archives).
197. *ibid.*
198. Using times from Ramsey, Winston (ed.), *op. cit.* (*Luftwaffe* entry for 13 July 1940).
199. Ramsey, Winston (ed.), *op. cit.* (*Luftwaffe* entry for 13 July 1940).
200. Cull, Brian, *op. cit.* (p. 72).
201. *ibid.*
202. *ibid.*
203. Cull, Brian, *op. cit.* (p. 78).
204. Ramsey, Winston (ed.), *op. cit.* (RAF entry for 13 July 1940); Cull, Brian, *op. cit.* (p. 71).
205. Cull, Brian, *op. cit.* (pp. 71-72 and p. 75).
206. Cull, Brian, *op. cit.* (p. 75).
207. Morgan, Eric B. and Shacklady, Edward, *Spitfire: The History* (Stamford: Key Publishing, 1987) (p. 121).
208. Morgan, Eric B. and Shacklady, Edward, *op. cit.* (p. 80).
209. Cull, Brian, *op. cit.* (pp. 71-72).
210. Osterkamp, Theo, *op. cit.* (pp. 343-348). This autobiographical book in German is long out of print and difficult to locate; the present author is highly indebted to the late *Oberst a. D.* Hanns Trübenbach, who led first *I/LG 2* and then *JG 52* in the Battle of Britain, who very kindly donated his personal copy to him.
211. *ibid.*
212. *ibid.*
213. *ibid.*
214. *ibid.*
215. *ibid.*
216. Churchill, Winston, S., *The Second World War, vol. II, Their Finest Hour* (London: Cassell, 1949) (p. 241).
217. IPRs, 151, 610 and 615 Squadrons, 14 July 1940 (Air 16/955 records, National Archives); Bergström, Christer, *op. cit.* (p. 79); Mason, Francis K., *op. cit.* (pp. 169-170); Website, Wood, Tony, *op. cit.*; Cull, Brian, *op. cit.* (p. 83-84); Prien, Jochen and Stemmer, Gerhard, *Messerschmitt Bf 109 im Einsatz bei der III./Jagdgeschwader 3* (Eutin: Struve-Druck, 1995) (p. 38); Ramsey, Winston (ed.), *op. cit.* (entries for 14 July 1940).
218. *ibid.*
219. *ibid.*
220. One Ju 87 loss given in: Ramsey, Winston (ed.), *op. cit.* (*Luftwaffe* entry for 14 July 1940); good evidence for a second Ju 87 loss in Cull, Brian, *op. cit.* (p. 84).
221. Website, Wood, Tony, *op. cit.*: lists Stange as claimant of a probable Hurricane; Prien, Jochen and Stemmer, Gerhard, *op. cit.* (p. 38) gives Trebing a victory over a Hurricane.

222. IPR, 615 Squadron, 14 July 1940 (Air 16/955 records, National Archives).
223. *ibid.*
224. *ibid.*
225. *ibid.*
226. Squadron Commander's Report on Flying Battle Casualty, P/O M. R. Mudie, 615 Squadron, 14 July 1940 (Air 81 records, National Archives); also further details elsewhere in his Air 81 Casualty File; IPR, 615 Squadron, 14 July 1940 (Air 16/955 records, National Archives).
227. Ramsey, Winston (ed.), *op. cit.* (RAF entry for 14 July 1940).
228. Prien, Jochen and Stemmer, Gerhard, *op. cit.* (p. 38).
229. *ibid.*
230. Website, Wood, Tony, *op. cit.*; Cull, Brian, *op. cit.* (pp. 83-84).
231. *ibid.*
232. IPR, 615 Squadron, 14 July 1940 (Air 16/955 records, National Archives).
233. *ibid.* No linguistic corrections made to wording of report.
234. Ramsey, Winston (ed.), *op. cit.* (*Luftwaffe* entry for 14 July 1940).
235. IPR, 615 Squadron, 14 July 1940 (Air 16/955 records, National Archives).
236. Website, Wood, Tony, *op. cit.*
237. IPR, 615 Squadron, 14 July 1940 (Air 16/955 records, National Archives).
238. *ibid.*
239. IPRs, 151 and 610 Squadrons, 14 July 1940 (Air 16/955 records, National Archives).
240. IPR, 151 Squadron, 14 July 1940 (Air 16/955 records, National Archives).
241. *ibid.* No linguistic corrections made to wording of report.
242. *ibid.*
243. *ibid.*
244. *ibid.*
245. Website, Wood, Tony, *op. cit.*; Prien, Jochen and Stemmer, Gerhard, *op. cit.* (p. 38, p. 475).
246. Prien, Jochen and Stemmer, Gerhard, *op. cit.* (p. 38, p. 445).
247. IPR, 151 Squadron, 14 July 1940 (Air 16/955 records, National Archives).
248. Website, Wood, Tony, *op. cit.*
249. Website, en.wikipedia.org/wiki/Dover_Strait_coastal_guns.
250. IPR, 610 Squadron, 14 July 1940 (Air 16/955 records, National Archives).
251. *ibid.*
252. As described in: IPRs, 151 and 610 Squadrons, 14 July 1940 (Air 16/955 records, National Archives).
253. IPR, 610 Squadron, 14 July 1940 (Air 16/955 records, National Archives).
254. *ibid.*
255. Prien, Jochen and Stemmer, Gerhard, *op. cit.* (p. 38, p. 445).
256. Cull, Brian, *op. cit.* (p. 80); Website, *Wrecksite,* www.wrecksite.eu/wreck.aspx?283080; Website, military.wikia.org/wiki/List_of_shipwrecks_in_July_1940.

257. Cull, Brian, *op. cit.* (p. 80).

258. *ibid.*

259. Wood, Derek and Dempster, Derek, *op. cit.* (p. 252); Mason, Francis K., *op. cit.* (pp. 170-171); Cull, Brian, *op. cit.* (p. 85).

260. IPR, 56 Squadron, 15 July 1940 (Air 16/955 records, National Archives).

261. James, T. Cecil G., *op. cit.* (p. 33, p. 41).

262. Cull, Brian, *op. cit.* (p. 85); Vasco, John, *op. cit.* (p. 16).

263. Website, Smith, Gordon and co-workers, *op. cit.*

264. IPR, 56 Squadron, 15 July 1940 (Air 16/955 records, National Archives).

265. IPR, 56 Squadron, 15 July 1940 (Air 16/955 records, National Archives); Revell, Alex, *Fighter Aces! The Constable Maxwell Brothers: Fighter Pilots in Two World Wars* (Barnsley: Pen and Sword, 2010) (p. 121).

266. Vasco, John, *op.cit.* (p. 16); IPR, 56 Squadron, 15 July 1940 (Air 16/955 records, National Archives).

267. Revell, Alex, *op. cit.* (p. 121).

268. Vasco, John, *op. cit.* (p. 16).

269. IPR, 56 Squadron, 15 July 1940 (Air 16/955 records, National Archives).

270. Cull, Brian, *op. cit.* (p. 89); Note 46, *op. cit.*

271. Note 46, *op. cit.*

272. Cull, Brian, *op. cit.* (p. 89).

273. IPR, 603 Squadron, 15 July 1940 (Air 16/955 records, National Archives).

274. *ibid.*

275. Cull, Brian, *op. cit.* (p. 86).

276. Cull, Brian, *op. cit.* (pp. 86-89).

277. Ramsey, Winston (ed.), *op. cit.* (RAF entry for 15 July 1940).

278. Wood, Derek and Dempster, Derek, *op. cit.* (p. 252).

279. Cull, Brian, *op. cit.* (p. 88); Mason, Francis K., *op. cit.* (pp. 170-171).

280. Mason, Francis K., *op. cit.* (pp. 170-171).

281. IPR, 92 Squadron, 15 July 1940 (Air 16/955 records, National Archives).

282. IPR, 92 Squadron, 15 July 1940 (Air 16/955 records, National Archives); Cull, Brian, *op. cit.* (p. 89).

283. Cull, Brian, *op. cit.* (p. 89).

284. Website, Holm, Michael, *op. cit.*

285. For example: Ramsey, Winston (ed.), *op. cit.* (*Luftwaffe* entry for 15 July 1940).

286. IPR, 145 Squadron, 15 July 1940 (Air 16/955 records, National Archives).

287. Website, Wood, Tony, *op. cit.*

288. IPR, 56 Squadron, 15 July 1940 (Air 16/955 records, National Archives).

5. 16-19 July 1940: small raids in Western Channel; Dover and shipping attacked by EGr 210 in East

1. IPR, 603 Squadron, 16 July 1940 (Air 16/955 records, National Archives); Cull, Brian, *Battle for the Channel* (Stroud: Fonthill, 2017) (p. 91, p. 93).

2. IPR, 603 Squadron, 16 July 1940 (Air 16/955 records, National Archives).

3. IPR, 603 Squadron, 16 July 1940 (Air 16/955 records, National Archives); Cull, Brian, *op. cit.* (p. 93).

4. Note 2, *op. cit.*

5. Cull, Brian, *op. cit.* (pp. 91-93); Parker, Nigel, *Luftwaffe Crash Archive,* Vol. 1 (Walton on Thames: Red Kite Books, Air Research Publications, 2013) (entry for 16 July 1940); Mason, Francis K., *Battle over Britain* (London: McWhirter Twins, 1969) (p. 173).

6. Hunt, Leslie, *Twenty-One Squadrons: the History of the Royal Auxiliary Air Force: 1925-1957* (London: Garnstone Press, 1972) (p. 76).

7. Cull, Brian, *op. cit.* (p. 91); Parker, Nigel, *op. cit.* (entry for 16 July 1940).

8. Cull, Brian, *op. cit.* (p. 91).

9. Cull, Brian, *op. cit.* (p. 93).

10. Cull, Brian, *op. cit.* (pp. 94-96).

11. See: Mason, Francis K., *op. cit.* (p. 174).

12. Cull, Brian, *op. cit.* (p. 96); Mason, Francis K., *op. cit.* (p. 174).

13. Cull, Brian, *op. cit.* (pp. 95-96).

14. Mombeek, Eric and Roba, Jean-Louis, with Goss, Chris, *Am Himmel Frankreichs; die Geschichte des JG 2 "Richthofen", Band 2: 1940-1941* (Linkebeek: ASBL La Porte d'Hoves, 2013) (pp. 18-19).

15. Website, Holm, Michael, *The Luftwaffe, 1933-1945*, www.ww2.dk; Mombeek, Eric and Roba, Jean-Louis, with Goss, Chris, *op. cit.* (pp. 18-19).

16. Mombeek, Eric and Roba, Jean-Louis, with Goss, Chris, *op. cit.* (pp. 18-19).

17. Webpage, Ranter, Harro and Lujan, Fabian, *Aviation Safety Network*, aviation-safety.net/wikibase/229943.

18. Mombeek, Eric and Roba, Jean-Louis, with Goss, Chris, *op. cit.* (pp. 18-19).

19. Ramsey, Winston. G. (ed.), *The Battle of Britain: Then and Now* (London: Battle of Britain Prints International Ltd., 1982) (RAF entry for 17 July 1940).

20. Details in F/O D. M. Taylor's casualty file (Air 81/1131, Air 81 Records, National Archives).

21. Imperial War Museum Sound Archive, World War 1939-1945, London; iwm.org.uk/collections/sound; P/O R. L. Jones, IWM Sound Archive item #20497; MacDonell, Donald, *From Dogfight to Diplomacy: A Spitfire Pilot's Log 1932-1958* (Barnsley: Pen and Sword, 2009) (p. 44).

22. Imperial War Museum Sound Archive, World War 1939-1945, IWM Sound Archive item #20497, *op. cit.*

23. For example: Eriksson, Patrick G., *Alarmstart* (Stroud: Amberley, 2017) (p. 13, p. 33).

24. For example: Eriksson, Patrick G., *op. cit.* (pp. 149-150 and p. 166).

25. Cull, Brian, *op. cit.* (p. 95, p. 97).

26. Website, de Zeng, Henry L. IV and Stankey, Douglas G., *Luftwaffe Officer Career Summaries* (2014 updated version), accessed via Michael Holm's website, *The Luftwaffe 1933-1945*: www.ww2.dk; this source at www.ww2.dk/lwoffz.html.

27. Cull, Brian, *op. cit.* (p. 95, p. 97); Ramsey, Winston. G. (ed.), *op. cit.* (*Luftwaffe* entry for 17 July 1940).

28. Ramsey, Winston. G. (ed.), *op. cit.* (RAF entry for 17 July 1940); Cull, Brian, *op. cit.* (p. 97).

29. Cull, Brian, *op. cit.* (p. 96).

30. At *c.* 14h10: Cull, Brian, *op. cit.* (p. 95).

31. Cull, Brian, *op. cit.* (p. 98).

32. Osterkamp, Theo, *Durch Höhen und Tiefen jagt ein Herz* (Heidelberg: Kurt Vowinckel Verlag, 1952) (pp. 318-323); see also discussions of this topic under 4 and 7 July 1940.

33. Mason, Francis K., *op. cit.* (pp. 175-177).

34. *ibid.*

35. *ibid.*

36. Bailey, David J., *610 (County of Chester) Auxiliary Air Force Squadron, 1936-1940* (Stroud: Fonthill, 2018) (pp. 228-229).

37. Bailey, David J., *op. cit.* (pp. 228-231).

38. *ibid.*

39. Mason, Francis K., *op. cit.* (pp. 175-177).

40. Bailey, David J., *op. cit.* (pp. 228-231).

41. Mason, Francis K., *op. cit.* (pp. 175-177).

42. Squadron Commander's Report on Flying Battle Casualty, P/O P. Litchfield, 610 Squadron, 18 July 1940 (Air 81 records, National Archives).

43. Website, Wood, Tony, *Tony Wood's Combat Claims and Casualties Lists*: accessed via Don Caldwell's website: don-caldwell.we.bs/claims/tonywood.htm; Bailey, David J., *op. cit.* (pp. 228-231).

44. Wood, Derek and Dempster, Derek, *The Narrow Margin* (London: Arrow Books, 1967) (pp. 253-254).

45. Obermaier, Ernst, *Die Ritterkreuzträger der Luftwaffe* (Mainz: Verlag Dieter Hoffmann, 1966) (p. 220).

46. Vasco, John, *Messerschmitt Bf 110 Bombsights over England: Erprobungsgruppe 210 in the Battle of Britain* (Atglen: Schiffer, 2002) (pp. 16-17).

47. *ibid.*

48. National Archives: War Cabinet, Weekly Resumé (No. 46) of the Naval, Military, and Air Situation from 12 noon July 11th to 12 noon July 18th, 1940; Website, Smith, Gordon and co-workers, naval-history.net, www.naval-history.net/xDKWW2-4007-20JUL01.htm; Website, Harwich & Dovercourt - A time gone by; harwich_and_dovercourt.co.uk/warships/trawlers/.

49. Vasco, John, *op. cit.* (pp. 16-17).

50. Vasco, John, *op. cit.* (pp. 16-17 and p. 168).

51. Cull, Brian, *op. cit.* (pp. 99-100).

52. Wood, Derek and Dempster, Derek, *op. cit.* (pp. 253-254); Website, Chen, Peter C., *World War II Database*, ww2db.com/event/today/7/18/1940.

53. Cull, Brian, *op. cit.* (pp. 100-101 and p. 104); Burt, Danny, *A Battle of Britain Spitfire Squadron: The Men and Machines of 152 Squadron in the Summer of 1940* (Barnsley: Pen and Sword, 2018) (p. 221); Operations Record Book (ORB), 152 Squadron, 18 July 1940 (Air 27 records, National Archives).

54. Cull, Brian, *op. cit.* (pp. 100-101 and p. 104); Burt, Danny, *op. cit.* (p. 221).

55. Mombeek, Eric and Roba, Jean-Louis, with Goss, Chris, *op. cit.* (pp. 19-20); Ramsey, Winston. G. (ed.), *op. cit.* (RAF entry for 18 July 1940).

56. Cull, Brian, *op. cit.* (pp. 100-101); Burt, Danny, *op. cit.* (p. 221).

57. Cull, Brian, *op. cit.* (pp. 100-101 and p. 104); Burt, Danny, *op. cit.* (p. 221).

58. Cull, Brian, *op. cit.* (p. 104); Ramsey, Winston. G. (ed.), *op. cit.* (*Luftwaffe* entry for 18 July 1940).

59. Mombeek, Eric and Roba, Jean-Louis, with Goss, Chris, *op. cit.* (pp. 19-20); Website, Wood, Tony, *op. cit.*; Cull, Brian, *op. cit.* (p. 106).

60. IPR, 603 Squadron, 18 July 1940 (Air 16/955 records, National Archives) (take off time *c.* 10h21; were two other, later 603 Squadron IPRs this day).

61. *ibid.*

62. Mason, Francis K., *op. cit.* (pp. 175-177).

63. Details in RAF Montrose's casualty file for 18 July 1940 (Air 81 Records, National Archives).

64. *Supplement to the London Gazette*, 4 October 1940, p. 5879; Dix Noonan Webb Auctioneers, dnw.co.uk/auction-archive/past-catalogues/lot.php?auction_id=5338lot_uid=373763; *Stornoway Gazette* of 26 July 1940 and 2 August 1940.

65. Website: lewistributes-3945.blogspot.com/2011/08/alexander-maciver-41b-north-tolsta.html.

66. Ramsey, Winston. G. (ed.), *op. cit.* (*Luftwaffe* entry for 18 July 1940).

67. Combat Report (CR), F/Lt Boyd, 145 Squadron, 18 July 1940 (Air 50 records, National Archives).

68. *ibid.*

69. Ramsey, Winston. G. (ed.), *op. cit.* (RAF entry for 18 July 1940).

70. IPR, 609 Squadron, 18 July 1940 (Air 16/955 records, National Archives).

71. *ibid.*

72. *ibid.*

73. *ibid.*

74. *ibid.*

75. *ibid.*

76. *ibid.*

77. Cull, Brian, *op. cit.* (p. 101); Ramsey, Winston. G. (ed.), *op. cit.* (RAF entry for 18 July 1940).

78. Website, Royal Air Force Museum: Battle of Britain blog, 2015, by Elliott, Peter on diary entries of P/O John Bisdee, 609 Squadron, https://www. rafmuseum.org.uk/blog/category/john_bisdees_battle_of_britain/.

79. *ibid.*

80. Cull, Brian, *op. cit.* (pp. 101-102).

81. IPR, 609 Squadron, 18 July 1940 (Air 16/955 records, National Archives).

82. Cull, Brian, *op. cit.* (p. 102, p. 104, p. 107).

83. Mason, Francis K., *op. cit.* (p. 177); Cull, Brian, *op. cit.* (p. 102, p. 107).

84. IPR, 603 Squadron, 18 July 1940 (Air 16/955 records, National Archives) (take off time *c.* 14h17; were two other 603 Squadron IPRs this day, one earlier, another later).

85. *ibid.*

86. *ibid.*

87. *ibid.*

88. *ibid.*

89. MacDonell, Donald, *op. cit.* (p. 44); see also discussion thereof under 17 July 1940.

90. IPR, 603 Squadron, 18 July 1940 (Air 16/955 records, National Archives) (take off time *c.* 18h55; were two other, earlier 603 Squadron IPRs this day).

91. *ibid.*

92. *ibid.*

93. IPR, 603 Squadron, 18 July 1940 (Air 16/955 records, National Archives) (take off time *c.* 18h55); Ramsey, Winston. G. (ed.), *op. cit.* (RAF entry for 18 July 1940).

94. Ramsey, Winston. G. (ed.), *op. cit.* (*Luftwaffe* entry for 18 July 1940).

95. Cull, Brian, *op. cit.* (p. 102, p. 106); Ramsey, Winston. G. (ed.), *op. cit.* (*Luftwaffe* entry for 18 July 1940).

96. IPR, 92 Squadron, 18 July 1940 (Air 16/955 records, National Archives); Cull, Brian, *op. cit.* (p. 104).

97. IPR, 92 Squadron, 18 July 1940 (Air 16/955 records, National Archives).

98. *ibid.*

99. Mason, Francis K., *op. cit.* (p. 174); Ramsey, Winston. G. (ed.), *op. cit.* (RAF entry for 18 July 1940).

100. Cull, Brian, *op. cit.* (p. 100).

101. Mason, Francis K., *op. cit.* (pp. 175-177).

102. Morgan, M. S., *The Southern Gate: RAF Kenley during the Battle of Britain* (Independently published, 2021) (p. 15).

103. Website, Holm, Michael, *op. cit.*

104. Mason, Francis K., *op. cit.* (pp. 177-181).

105. Cull, Brian, *op. cit.* (p. 113, p. 117, p. 119).

106. For example: Mason, Francis K., *op. cit.* (pp. 177-181); Ramsey, Winston. G. (ed.), *op. cit.* (*Luftwaffe* entry for 19 July 1940).

107. IPR, 257 Squadron, 19 July 1940 (Air 16/955 records, National Archives).

108. *ibid.*

109. *ibid.*

110. *ibid.*

111. McKinstry, Leo, *Hurricane: Victor of the Battle of Britain* (London: John Murray, 2011) (p. 133); Williams, Anthony, G., The development of RAF guns and ammunition from World War 1 to the present day (*RAF Historical Society Journal*, volume 45, 2009, pp. 37-58); Website, article by Williams, Anthony G., 2004 (revised 2005): The Battle of Britain: Armament of the competing fighters, Quarryhs.co.uk/BoB.htm.

112. *ibid.*

113. Williams, Anthony, G., 2009, *op. cit.*; Website, Williams, Anthony G., article, 2004 (revised 2005), *op. cit.*

114. IPR, 257 Squadron, 19 July 1940 (Air 16/955 records, National Archives).

115. Mason, Francis K., *op. cit.* (p. 177).

116. Mason, Francis K., *op. cit.* (p. 551).

117. James, T. Cecil G., *The Battle of Britain* (Abingdon: Routledge, 2012) (pp. 35-36).

118. James, T. Cecil G., *op. cit.* (pp. 35-36); Bergström, Christer, *The Battle of Britain: An Epic Conflict Revisited* (Oxford: Casemate, 2015; Eskilstuna: Vaktel, 2015) (pp. 79-81).

119. James, T. Cecil G., *op. cit.* (pp. 35-36); Harkins, Hugh, *Defiant Mk. I Combat Log: Fighter Command May–September 1940* (Glasgow: Centurion Publishing, 2014) (p. 54).

120. IPR, 111 Squadron, 19 July 1940 (Air 16/955 records, National Archives).

121. *ibid.*

122. Vasco, John, *op. cit.* (p. 17); Website, Smith, Gordon and co-workers, *op. cit.*

123. Website, Smith, Gordon and co-workers, *op. cit.*

124. Vasco, John, *op. cit.* (p. 17).

125. Knight, Dennis, *Harvest of Messerschmitts: The Chronicle of a Village at War, 1940* (London: Frederick Warne, 1981) (pp. 32-34).

126. Cull, Brian, *op. cit.* (pp. 109-110).

127. IPR, 141 Squadron, 19 July 1940 (Air 16/955 records, National Archives); not corrected in any way.

128. *ibid*; details before body of report which was cited.

129. Ramsey, Winston. G. (ed.), *op. cit.* (RAF entry for 19 July 1940).

130. IPR, 141 Squadron, 19 July 1940 (Air 16/955 records, National Archives).

131. *ibid.*
132. Knight, Dennis, *op. cit.* (pp. 72-74).
133. Bishop, Patrick, *Battle of Britain* (London: Quercus, 2010) (pp. 111-112).
134. Cull, Brian, *op. cit.* (p. 107).
135. Cull, Brian, *op. cit.* (pp. 107-109).
136. Cull, Brian, *op. cit.* (pp. 108-109).
137. For example: Eriksson, Patrick G., *op. cit.* (p. 93).
138. Website, Wood, Tony, *op. cit.*
139. Ramsey, Winston. G. (ed.), *op. cit.* (*Luftwaffe* entry for 19 July 1940), only records the loss of Heilmann; Cull, Brian, *op. cit.* (p. 119).
140. IPR, 111 Squadron, 19 July 1940 (Air 16/955 records, National Archives).
141. James, T. Cecil G., *op. cit.* (pp. 35-36).
142. IPR, 111 Squadron, 19 July 1940 (Air 16/955 records, National Archives).
143. *ibid.*
144. *ibid.*
145. Archives, Imperial War Museum, London: *Luftwaffe Quartermaster General Loss Returns.*
146. Website, Wood, Tony, *op. cit.*
147. IPR, 111 Squadron, 19 July 1940 (Air 16/955 records, National Archives).
148. For example, Mason, Francis K., *op. cit.* (p. 179); Cull, Brian, *op. cit.* (p. 107).
149. Wood, Derek and Dempster, Derek, *op. cit.* (p. 254).
150. Vasco, John, *op. cit.* (p. 17, p. 172).
151. Cull, Brian, *op. cit.* (p. 300).
152. Vasco, John, *op. cit.* (p. 172).
153. Morgan, M. S., *op. cit.* (pp. 16-17).
154. IPRs, 32 and 74 Squadrons, 19 July 1940 (Air 16/955 records, National Archives).
155. IPR, 32 Squadron, 19 July 1940 (Air 16/955 records, National Archives).
156. *ibid.*
157. Ramsey, Winston. G. (ed.), *op. cit.* (RAF entry for 19 July 1940).
158. IPR, 32 Squadron, 19 July 1940 (Air 16/955 records, National Archives).
159. Combat Report (CR), P/O Smythe, 32 Squadron, 19 July 1940 (Air 50 records, National Archives).
160. CR, P/O Gillman, 32 Squadron, 19 July 1940 (Air 50 records, National Archives).
161. CR, Sgt Henson, 32 Squadron, 19 July 1940 (Air 50 records, National Archives).
162. *ibid.*
163. IPR, 32 Squadron, 19 July 1940 (Air 16/955 records, National Archives).
164. IPRs, 32 and 74 Squadrons, 19 July 1940 (Air 16/955 records, National Archives); no corrections made.
165. IPR, 74 Squadron, 19 July 1940 (Air 16/955 records, National Archives).

166. For example: Bickers, Richard Townshend, and co-authors, *The Battle of Britain: The Greatest Battle in the History of Air Warfare* (London: Salamander, 1990) (pp. 68-69).

167. Tidy, Douglas, *I Fear No Man: The History of No. 74 (Fighter) Squadron Royal Flying Corps and Royal Air Force (The Tigers)* (Cape Town: Purnell, 1972) (pp. 46-47).

168. IPR, 32 Squadron, 19 July 1940 (Air 16/955 records, National Archives).

169. Morgan, M. S., *op. cit.* (pp. 16-17).

170. Cull, Brian, *op. cit.* (p. 113, p. 120).

171. Mason, Francis K., *op. cit.* (p. 181); Parker, Nigel, *op. cit.* (entry for 19 July 1940).

172. Morgan, M. S., *op. cit.* (pp. 16-17).

173. *ibid.*

174. *ibid.*

175. *ibid.*

176. Cull, Brian, *op. cit.* (p. 116).

177. Ramsey, Winston. G. (ed.), *op. cit.* (*Luftwaffe* entry for 19 July 1940).

178. *ibid.*

179. Website, Wood, Tony, *op. cit.*

180. IPR, 32 Squadron, 19 July 1940 (Air 16/955 records, National Archives).

181. IPR, 43 Squadron, 19 July 1940 (Air 16/955 records, National Archives).

182. *ibid.*

183. *ibid.*

184. *ibid.*

185. *ibid.*

186. *ibid.*

187. *ibid.*

188. *ibid.*

189. *ibid.*

190. Townsend, Peter, *Duel of Eagles* (London: Weidenfeld and Nicolson, 1970) (p. 297, p. 377).

191. Bolitho, Hector, *Combat Report: The Story of a Fighter Pilot* (London: B. T. Batsford, 1943) (pp. 80-84).

192. *ibid.*

193. *ibid.*

194. IPR, 43 Squadron, 19 July 1940 (Air 16/955 records, National Archives).

195. Cull, Brian, *op. cit.* (p. 111).

196. *ibid.*

197. Cull, Brian, *op. cit.* (p. 111); Saunders, Andy, *Stuka Attack!* (London: Grub Street, 2013) (p. 38).

198. Ring, Hans and Girbig, Werner, *Jagdgeschwader 27: Die Dokumentation über den Einsatz an allen Fronten 1939-1945* (Stuttgart: Motorbuch, 1975) (p. 50).

199. Ramsey, Winston. G. (ed.), *op. cit.* (RAF entry for 19 July 1940).

200. Website, Wood, Tony, *op. cit.*; Ramsey, Winston. G. (ed.), *op. cit.* (RAF entry for 19 July 1940).

201. Ramsey, Winston. G. (ed.), *op. cit.* (*Luftwaffe* entry for 19 July 1940).

202. Kimbell, Andrew, *The One History Forgot: David Alwyne Pemberton – A Life Story* (Independently published, 2018) (pp. 39-40).

203. *ibid.*

204. Gretzyngier, Robert, *Poles in Defence of Britain: A Day-by-Day Chronology of Polish Day and Night Fighter Pilot Operations: July 1940–June 1941* (London: Grub Street, 2016) (p. 8).

205. *ibid.*

206. *ibid.*

207. Ramsey, Winston. G. (ed.), *op. cit.* (entries for 19 July 1940); Mason, Francis K., *op. cit.* (p. 179).

208. Cull, Brian, *op. cit.* (pp. 118-119); Ramsey, Winston. G. (ed.), *op. cit.* (entries for 19 July 1940); Vasco, John, *op. cit.* (p. 17); Website, Helgason, Gudmundur, *uboat.net*, uboat.net/allies/warships/ship/6866. html; Website, *Wrecksite*, wrecksite.eu/wreck.aspx?1257; islandeye. co.uk/history/shipwrecks/Crestflower_hmt.html.

6. 20-23 July 1940: convoy attacks in Western Channel and Dover Straits; the RAF fighter rear-guard problem

1. IPR, 56 Squadron, 20 July 1940 (Air 16/955 records, National Archives).

2. *ibid.*

3. *ibid.*

4. Cull, Brian, *Battle for the Channel* (Stroud: Fonthill, 2017) (p. 121).

5. IPR, 54 Squadron, 20 July 1940 (Air 16/955 records, National Archives); Cull, Brian, *op. cit.* (p. 128).

6. IPR, 54 Squadron, 20 July 1940 (Air 16/955 records, National Archives).

7. *ibid.*

8. Ramsey, Winston. G. (ed.), *The Battle of Britain: Then and Now* (London: Battle of Britain Prints International Ltd., 1982) (*Luftwaffe* entry for 20 July 1940).

9. Cull, Brian, *op. cit.* (pp. 121-122).

10. IPR, 85 Squadron, 20 July 1940 (Air 16/955 records, National Archives).

11. Cull, Brian, *op. cit.* (p. 129).

12. Ramsey, Winston. G. (ed.), *op. cit.* (*Luftwaffe* entry for 20 July 1940).

13. IPR, 603 Squadron, 20 July 1940 (Air 16/955 records, National Archives).

14. IPR, 603 Squadron, 20 July 1940 (Air 16/955 records, National Archives); Cull, Brian, *op. cit.* (pp. 120-121).

15. Cull, Brian, *op. cit.* (p. 120).

16. IPR, 66 Squadron, 20 July 1940 (Air 16/955 records, National Archives).

17. Alexander, Kristen, *Australia's Few and the Battle of Britain* (Barnsley: Pen and Sword, 2015) (pp. 184-185).

18. *ibid.*

19. Burt, Danny, *A Battle of Britain Spitfire Squadron: the Men and Machines of 152 Squadron in the Summer of 1940* (Barnsley: Pen and Sword, 2018) (pp. 185-189); Website, de Zeng, Henry L. IV, *Luftwaffe Airfields 1935-1945*, accessed via Michael Holm's website, *The Luftwaffe 1933-1945*: www.ww2.dk; this source at www.ww2.dk/lwairfields.html.

20. IPR, Red Section of 238 Squadron, 20 July 1940 (Air 16/955 records, National Archives).

21. Burt, Danny, *op. cit.* (pp. 185-189); www.deeperdorset.co.uk, a website with copies of several reports from P/O Posener's casualty file (152 Squadron), or Air 81 file, kept in the National Archives – Air 81/1163: detailed reports by P/Os Beaumont and Williams, 152 Squadron, on what happened on this flight, a summary report by S/L Devitt, commander of 152 Squadron, as well as an action report by F/Lt Turner of 238 Squadron. This is an unusually detailed file, such files normally containing only the often brief summarising Squadron Commander's Report on Flying Battle Casualties.

22. Wynn, Kenneth G., *Men of the Battle of Britain: a Biographical Directory of the Few* (Barnsley: Frontline, 2015; West Malling: The Battle of Britain Memorial Trust, 2015) (p. 36, p. 423, p. 566).

23. Reports by P/Os Beaumont and Williams, 152 Squadron in P/O Posener's Air 81/1163 casualty file, via www.deeperdorset.co.uk.

24. Report by F/Lt Turner, 238 Squadron in P/O Posener's Air 81/1163 casualty file, via www.deeperdorset.co.uk.

25. IPR, Red Section of 238 Squadron, 20 July 1940 (Air 16/955 records, National Archives).

26. *ibid.*

27. Cull, Brian, *op. cit.* (p. 123).

28. Note 25, *op. cit.*

29. Alexander, Kristen, *op. cit.* (pp. 184-185).

30. *ibid.*

31. Reports by P/O's Beaumont and Williams, 152 Squadron in P/O Posener's Air 81/1163 casualty file, via www.deeperdorset.co.uk.

32. *ibid.*

33. Report by F/Lt Turner, 238 Squadron in P/O Posener's Air 81/1163 casualty file, via www.deeperdorset.co.uk.

34. Website, Smith, Gordon and co-workers, naval-history.net, www.naval-history.net/xDKWW2-4007-20JUL02.htm.

35. Website, Wood, Tony, 'Tony Wood's Combat Claims and Casualties Lists': accessed via Don Caldwell's website: don-caldwell.we.bs/claims/tonywood.htm; Cull, Brian, *op. cit.* (p. 123, p. 131).

36. Ramsey, Winston. G. (ed.), *op. cit.* (*Luftwaffe* entry for 20 July 1940); Ring, Hans and Girbig, Werner, *Jagdgeschwader 27: Die Dokumentation über den Einsatz an allen Fronten 1939-1945* (Stuttgart: Motorbuch, 1975) (pp. 50-51).

37. Cull, Brian, *op. cit.* (p. 123).

38. Report by P/O Williams, 152 Squadron in P/O Posener's Air 81/1163 casualty file, via www.deeperdorset.co.uk.

39. Thomas, Nick, *Hurricane Squadron Ace* (Barnsley: Pen and Sword, 2014) (pp. 75-79); IPR, 32 Squadron, 20 July 1940 (Air 16/955 records, National Archives) (take off time *c.* 13h00; there was a later 32 Squadron IPR this day).

40. James, T. Cecil G., *The Battle of Britain* (Abingdon: Routledge, 2012) (p. 37).

41. IPR, 32 Squadron, 20 July 1940 (Air 16/955 records, National Archives) (take off time *c.* 13h00).

42. *ibid.*

43. *ibid.*

44. *ibid.*

45. For example: Mason, Francis K., *Battle over Britain* (London: McWhirter Twins, 1969) (p. 183); Ramsey, Winston. G. (ed.), *op. cit.* (*Luftwaffe* entry for 20 July 1940) (p. 542).

46. Cull, Brian, *op. cit.* (pp. 122-123). Note that on p. 79 of this source, under 13 July 1940, this damaged Me 110 is listed as well; this is likely an error reflecting the nature of the German loss records.

47. IPR, 32 Squadron, 20 July 1940 (Air 16/955 records, National Archives) (take off time *c.* 13h00); Cull, Brian, *op. cit.* (pp. 122-123).

48. Cull, Brian, *op. cit.* (pp. 122-123).

49. Vasco, John, *Messerschmitt Bf 110 Bombsights over England: Erprobungsgruppe 210 in the Battle of Britain* (Atglen: Schiffer, 2002) (p. 159).

50. Vasco, John, *op. cit.* (p. 17).

51. Cull, Brian, *op. cit.* (p. 122).

52. Archives, Imperial War Museum, London: *Luftwaffe Quartermaster General Loss Returns.*

53. Vasco, John, *op. cit.* (p. 17 and pp. 172-173).

54. Saunders, Andy, *Stuka Attack!* (London: Grub Street, 2013) (p. 38); Cull, Brian, *op. cit.* (pp. 122-123); Hewitt, Nick, *Coastal Convoys 1939-1945: the Indestructible Highway* (Barnsley: Pen and Sword Maritime, 2019) (pp. 91-92).

55. Website, Smith, Gordon and co-workers, *op. cit.*

56. Ramsey, Winston. G. (ed.), *op. cit.* (entries for 20 July 1940); Cull, Brian, *op. cit.* (pp. 122-123); Mason, Francis K., *op. cit.* (p. 182); Thomas, Nick, *op. cit.* (pp. 75-79); IPR, 32 Squadron, 20 July 1940 (Air 16/955 records,

National Archives) (take off time *c.* 17h00; was an earlier 32 Squadron IPR this day).

57. Thomas, Nick, *op. cit.* (pp. 75-79); IPR, 32 Squadron, 20 July 1940 (Air 16/955 records, National Archives) (take off time *c.* 17h00).

58. *ibid.*

59. Knight, Dennis, *Harvest of Messerschmitts: The Chronicle of a Village at War, 1940* (London: Frederick Warne, 1981) (pp. 74-75); Thomas, Nick, *op. cit.* (pp. 75-79); IPR, 32 Squadron, 20 July 1940 (Air 16/955 records, National Archives) (take off time *c.* 17h00).

60. IPR, 32 Squadron, 20 July 1940 (Air 16/955 records, National Archives) (take off time *c.* 17h00).

61. Bailey, David J., *610 (County of Chester) Auxiliary Air Force Squadron, 1936-1940* (Stroud: Fonthill, 2018) (pp. 232-235); IPR, 32 Squadron, 20 July 1940 (Air 16/955 records, National Archives) (take off time *c.* 17h00).

62. Bailey, David J., *op. cit.* (pp. 232-235).

63. *ibid.*

64. IPR, 65 Squadron, 20 July 1940 (Air 16/955 records, National Archives).

65. *ibid.*

66. *ibid.*

67. *ibid.*

68. Website, Wood, Tony, *op. cit.*

69. Saunders, Andy, *op. cit.* (p. 38); Ramsey, Winston. G. (ed.), *op. cit.* (*Luftwaffe* entry for 20 July 1940); IPR, 32 Squadron, 20 July 1940 (Air 16/955 records, National Archives) (take off time *c.* 17h00).

70. Website, Smith, Gordon and co-workers, naval-history.net, www.naval-history.net/xGM-Chrono-10DD-15B-HMS_Brazen.htm.

71. Ramsey, Winston. G. (ed.), *op. cit.* (*Luftwaffe* entry for 20 July 1940); Cull, Brian, *op. cit.* (p. 131).

72. IPR, 65 Squadron, 20 July 1940 (Air 16/955 records, National Archives).

73. IPR, 32 Squadron, 20 July 1940 (Air 16/955 records, National Archives) (take off time *c.* 17h00).

74. Cull, Brian, *op. cit.* (pp. 123-124).

75. IPR, 238 Squadron, Green Section, 20 July 1940 (Air 16/955 records, National Archives).

76. *ibid.*

77. Ramsey, Winston. G. (ed.), *op. cit.* (*Luftwaffe* entry for 20 July 1940).

78. IPR, 501 Squadron, 20 July 1940 (Air 16/955 records, National Archives); Cull, Brian, *op. cit.* (p. 123); Squadron Commander's Report on Flying Battle Casualty, P/O E. J. H. Sylvester, 501 Squadron, 20 July 1940 (Air 81 records, National Archives), copy of this report from P/O Sylvester's Air 81/1173 casualty file on website: www.deeperdorset.co.uk.

79. Squadron Commander's Report on Flying Battle Casualty, P/O E. J. H. Sylvester, 501 Squadron, 20 July 1940, *op. cit.*

80. IPR, 501 Squadron, 20 July 1940 (Air 16/955 records, National Archives).

81. *ibid.*

82. Ramsey, Winston. G. (ed.), *op. cit.* (*Luftwaffe* entry for 20 July 1940).

83. Website, Wood, Tony, *op. cit.*

84. Squadron Commander's Report on Flying Battle Casualty, P/O E. J. H. Sylvester, 501 Squadron, 20 July 1940, *op. cit.*; Ramsey, Winston. G. (ed.), *op. cit.* (RAF entry for 20 July 1940); IPR, 501 Squadron, 20 July 1940 (Air 16/955 records, National Archives).

85. Cull, Brian, *op. cit.* (p. 124); Website, Battle of Britain London Monument, bbm.org.uk/airmen/Haworth.htm; Ramsey, Winston. G. (ed.), *op. cit.* (RAF entry for 20 July 1940).

86. Cull, Brian, *op. cit.* (p. 124, p. 129).

87. Cull, Brian, *op. cit.* (p. 124); Ramsey, Winston. G. (ed.), *op. cit.* (*Luftwaffe* entry for 20 July 1940).

88. Mason, Francis K., *op. cit.* (p. 185); Cull, Brian, *op. cit.* (p. 133).

89. Cull, Brian, *op. cit.* (pp. 134-135).

90. IPR, 238 Squadron, 21 July 1940 (Air 16/955 records, National Archives) (take off time *c.* 10h05; there were two later 238 Squadron IPRs this day); Cull, Brian, *op. cit.* (p. 135); Ramsey, Winston. G. (ed.), *op. cit.* (*Luftwaffe* entry for 21 July 1940).

91. IPR, 238 Squadron, 21 July 1940 (Air 16/955 records, National Archives) (take off time *c.* 10h05).

92. As an example among several sources: Cull, Brian, *op. cit.* (pp. 133-134 and p. 140).

93. For example: Franks, Norman L. R., *Royal Air Force Fighter Command Losses of the Second World War, Volume 1, Operational Losses: Aircraft and Crews 1939-1941* (Leicester: Midland, 1997) (p. 46); Morgan, M. S., *The Southern Gate: RAF Kenley During the Battle of Britain* (Independently published, 2021) (p. 18).

94. Website, *Historical RFA*, Royal Fleet Auxiliary Historical Society, www.historicalrfa.org.

95. Website, Holdoway, Mike, Convoy Web, www.convoyweb.org.uk/cw/index.html?cw.php?convoy=7!~cwmain.

96. Combat Report (CR), S/L J. V. C. Badger, 43 Squadron, 21 July 1940 (Air 50 records, National Archives); Dalton-Morgan, Tom, *Tommy Leader* (Wendover: Griffon International, 2007) (p. 41).

97. *ibid.*

98. CR, S/L J. V. C. Badger, 43 Squadron, 21 July 1940 (Air 50 records, National Archives); Cull, Brian, *op. cit.* (pp. 136-137); Dalton-Morgan, Tom, *op. cit.* (p. 41).

99. Dalton-Morgan, Tom, *op. cit.* (p. 41).

100. Cull, Brian, *op. cit.* (pp. 136-137).

101. Nowarra, Heinz J., *Luftschlacht um England: Verlorener Sieg* (Friedberg: Podzun-Pallas-Verlag, 1978) (p. 21); Ramsey, Winston. G. (ed.), *op. cit.* (entries for 21 July 1940).

102. Website, Wood, Tony, *op. cit.*

103. Cull, Brian, *op. cit.* (pp. 136-137).

104. Website, *Wrecksite*, www.wrecksite.eu/wreck.aspx?1279; Website, Smith, Gordon and co-workers, naval-history.net, www.naval-history.net/xDKWW2-4007-20JKL02.htm.

105. IPR, 238 Squadron, 21 July 1940 (Air 16/955 records, National Archives) (take off time *c.* 15h15; were two earlier 238 Squadron IPRs this day).

106. *ibid.*

107. *ibid.*

108. *ibid.*

109. *ibid.*

110. Alexander, Kristen, *op. cit.* (pp. 185-186).

111. Mason, Francis K., *op. cit.* (p. 551).

112. Ramsey, Winston. G. (ed.), *op. cit.* (*Luftwaffe* entry for 21 July 1940); Website, Wood, Tony, *op. cit.*; Cull, Brian, *op. cit.* (pp. 136-137).

113. For example: Mason, Francis K., *op. cit.* (p. 184).

114. Von Eimannsberger, Ludwig, *Zerstörer Gruppe: A history of V./(Z)LG 1 – I./NJG 3 1939-1941* (Atglen: Schiffer, 1998) (pp. 93-94).

115. Mason, Francis K., *op. cit.* (p. 184).

116. Von Eimannsberger, Ludwig, *op. cit.* (pp. 93-94); Ramsey, Winston. G. (ed.), *op. cit.* (*Luftwaffe* entry for 21 July 1940).

117. Cull, Brian, *op. cit.* (pp. 136-137 and p. 140).

118. Cull, Brian, *op. cit.* (p. 140); IPR, 238 Squadron, 21 July 1940 (Air 16/955 records, National Archives) (take off time *c.* 15h15).

119. Von Eimannsberger, Ludwig, *op.cit.* (pp. 93-94 and p. 208).

120. Vasco, John, *op. cit.* (p. 17).

121. IPR, 238 Squadron, 21 July 1940 (Air 16/955 records, National Archives) (take off time *c.* 15h15).

122. Vasco, John, *op. cit.* (p. 11).

123. Website, Lawson, Siri, warsailors.com, https://www.warsailors.com/singleships/Kollskegg.html; Cull, Brian, *op. cit.* (pp. 136-137 and p. 300).

124. James, T. Cecil G., *op. cit.* (p. 36).

125. Ramsey, Winston. G. (ed.), *op. cit.* (*Luftwaffe* entry for 21 July 1940); IPR, 238 Squadron, 21 July 1940 (Air 16/955 records, National Archives) (take off time *c.* 14h20; there were two other 238 Squadron IPRs this day, one earlier, one later); Parker, Nigel, *Luftwaffe Crash Archive*, Vol. 1 (Walton on Thames: Red Kite Books, Air Research Publications, 2013) (entry for 21 July 1940).

126. IPR, 238 Squadron, 21 July 1940 (Air 16/955 records, National Archives) (take off time *c.* 14h20).

127. IPR, 46 Squadron, 22 July 1940 (Air 16/955 records, National Archives).

128. *ibid.*

129. *ibid.*

130. Goss, Chris, *Dornier Do 17 Units of World War 2* (Oxford: Osprey, 2019) (p. 50).

131. IPR, 46 Squadron, 22 July 1940 (Air 16/955 records, National Archives).

132. IPR, 66 Squadron, 22 July 1940 (Air 16/955 records, National Archives).

133. *ibid.*

134. Cull, Brian, *op. cit.* (p. 144, p. 147).

135. Mason, Francis K., *op. cit.* (pp. 185-186).

136. *ibid.*

137. Bergström, Christer, *The Battle of Britain: an Epic Conflict Revisited* (Oxford: Casemate, 2015; Eskilstuna: Vaktel, 2015) (p. 83).

138. Mason, Francis K., *op. cit.* (pp. 187-188).

139. Website of de Zeng, Henry L. IV and Stankey, Douglas G., *Luftwaffe Officer Career Summaries* (2014 updated version), accessed via Michael Holm's website, *The Luftwaffe 1933-1945*: www.ww2.dk; this source at www.ww2.dk/lwoffz.html.

140. Cull, Brian, *op. cit.* (pp. 145-146); Mason, Francis K., *op. cit.* (pp. 187-188); *Luftwaffe Quartermaster General Loss Returns, op. cit.*

141. IPR, 603 Squadron, 23 July 1940 (Air 16/955 records, National Archives).

142. *ibid.*

143. Goss, Chris, *op. cit.* (pp. 50-51).

144. IPR, 603 Squadron, 23 July 1940 (Air 16/955 records, National Archives).

145. *Luftwaffe Quartermaster General Loss Returns, op. cit.*; Cull, Brian, *op. cit.* (p. 152).

146. Website, de Zeng, Henry L. IV and Stankey, Douglas G., *op. cit.*; Mason, Francis K., *op. cit.* (p. 188).

147. Mason, Francis K., *op. cit.* (p. 188); Cull, Brian, *op. cit.* (p. 148, p. 152).

148. Website, Holm, Michael, *The Luftwaffe, 1933-1945,* www.ww2.dk.

149. IPR, 242 Squadron, 23 July 1940 (Air 16/955 records, National Archives).

150. *ibid.*

7. *24-26 July 1940: multiple convoy attacks in Eastern Channel and East Coast; limited action in Western Channel*

1. IPR, 92 Squadron, 24 July 1940 (Air 16/955 records, National Archives).

2. Ramsey, Winston. G. (ed.), *The Battle of Britain: Then and Now* (London: Battle of Britain Prints International Ltd., 1982) (*Luftwaffe* entry for 24 July 1940).

3. IPR, 92 Squadron, 24 July 1940 (Air 16/955 records, National Archives).

4. *ibid.*

5. Ramsey, Winston. G. (ed.), *op. cit.* (*Luftwaffe* entry for 24 July 1940).

6. Bergström, Christer, *The Battle of Britain: an epic conflict revisited* (Oxford: Casemate, 2015; Eskilstuna: Vaktel, 2015) (pp. 83-85).

7. *ibid.*

8. Website, Holdoway, Mike, Convoy Web, www.convoyweb.org.uk.

9. *ibid.*

10. Mason, Francis K., *Battle over Britain* (London: McWhirter Twins, 1969) (pp. 190-191).

11. For example: Wood, Derek and Dempster, Derek, *The Narrow Margin* (London: Arrow Books, 1967) (p. 258); Deighton, Len, *Fighter: The True Story of the Battle of Britain* (St Albans: Triad/Panther, 1979) (pp. 171-173).

12. Vasco, John, *Messerschmitt Bf 110 Bombsights over England: Erprobungsgruppe 210 in the Battle of Britain* (Atglen: Schiffer, 2002) (p. 18).

13. Cull, Brian, *Battle for the Channel* (Stroud: Fonthill, 2017) (p. 159).

14. Mason, Francis K., *op. cit.* (pp. 190-191); Wood, Derek and Dempster, Derek, *op. cit.* (p. 258); Bergström, Christer, *op. cit.* (pp. 83-85); Ramsey, Winston. G. (ed.), *op. cit.* (RAF entry for 24 July 1940).

15. Mason, Francis K., *op. cit.* (pp. 190-191); Bergström, Christer, *op. cit.* (pp. 83-85); Bishop, Patrick, *Battle of Britain* (London: Quercus, 2010) (pp. 123-124); Operations Record Book (ORB), 54 Squadron, 24 July 1940 (Air 27 records, National Archives).

16. ORB, 54 Squadron, 24 July 1940, *op. cit.*

17. *ibid.*

18. *ibid.*

19. Barbas, Bernd, *Die Geschichte der III. Gruppe des Jagdgeschwaders 52* (Überlingen: self-published, undated) (p. 19).

20. Ramsey, Winston. G. (ed.), *op. cit.* (RAF entry for 24 July 1940).

21. Barbas, Bernd, *op. cit.* (p. 19).

22. Website, Smith, Gordon, and co-workers, naval-history.net, www.naval-history.net; Wikipedia, List of shipwrecks, July 1940, https://en.wikipedia.org/wiki/List_of_shipwrecks_in_July_1940.

23. Website, Pocock, Michael W., *Maritime Quest*, www.maritimequest.com/daily_event_archive/2012/07_july/24_hm_trawler_fleming.htm; Cull, Brian, *op. cit.* (pp. 154-163 and p. 301).

24. Cull, Brian, *op. cit.* (pp. 154-163).

25. Morgan, M. S., *The Southern Gate: RAF Kenley during the Battle of Britain* (Independently published, 2021) (p. 18).

26. *ibid.*

27. IPR, 504 Squadron, 24 July 1940 (Air 16/955 records, National Archives).

28. *ibid.*

29. Caldwell, Donald L., *JG 26 Luftwaffe Fighter Wing Diary, 1939-1942*, Vol. 1 (Mechanicsburg: Stackpole Books, 2012) (pp. 47-49).

30. For example: Bergström, Christer, *op. cit.* (pp. 83-85); Caldwell, Donald L., *op. cit.* (pp. 47-49).

31. Website, de Zeng, Henry L. IV and Stankey, Douglas G., *Luftwaffe Officer Career Summaries* (2014 updated version), accessed via Michael Holm's website, *The Luftwaffe 1933-1945*: www.ww2.dk; this source at www.ww2.dk/lwoffz.html.

32. Caldwell, Donald L., *op. cit.* (pp. 47-49); Priller, Josef, *J.G. 26: Geschichte eines Jagdgeschwaders* (Stuttgart: Motorbuch, 1980) (pp. 330-345).

33. Caldwell, Donald L., *op. cit.* (p. 47).

34. Priller, Josef, *op. cit.* (p. 88, p. 221).

35. Ramsey, Winston G. (ed.), *op. cit.* (*Luftwaffe* entry for 24 July 1940).

36. Website, de Zeng, Henry L. IV and Stankey, Douglas G., *op. cit.*

37. IPR, 610 Squadron, 24 July 1940 (Air 16/955 records, National Archives) (take off time *c.* 11h12; was one later 610 Squadron IPR this day).

38. *ibid.*

39. See also: Cull, Brian, *op. cit.* (pp. 154-163).

40. Note 37, *op. cit.*

41. Caldwell, Donald L., *op. cit.* (pp. 47-49).

42. Note 37, *op. cit.*; Cull, Brian, *op. cit.* (pp. 154-163).

43. See detailed discussion of this point: Bailey, David J., *610 (County of Chester) Auxiliary Air Force Squadron, 1936-1940* (Stroud: Fonthill, 2018) (pp. 236-238 and p. 242).

44. Cull, Brian, *op. cit.* (pp. 154-163); Bailey, David J., *op. cit.* (p. 238).

45. Mason, Francis K., *op. cit.* (pp. 190-191); Deighton, Len, *op. cit.* (pp. 171-173).

46. Cull, Brian, *op. cit.* (pp. 154-163).

47. Bergström, Christer, *op. cit.* (pp. 83-85); Barbas, Bernd, *op. cit.* (p. 19).

48. IPRs, 54 and 65 Squadrons, 24 July 1940 (Air 16/955 records, National Archives); ORB, 54 Squadron, 24 July 1940, *op. cit.*

49. Vasco, John, *op. cit.* (p. 18).

50. Bergström, Christer, *op. cit.* (pp. 83-85); Caldwell, Donald L., *JG 26: Top Guns of the Luftwaffe* (New York: Orion Books, 1991) (pp. 32-33).

51. IPR, 54 Squadron, 24 July 1940 (Air 16/955 records, National Archives); Cull, Brian, *op. cit.* (pp. 154-163).

52. Rall, Günther, *Mein Flugbuch* (Moosburg, Germany: NeunundzwanzigSechs Verlag, 2004) (pp. 52-54).

53. Barbas, Bernd, *op. cit.* (p. 19); Caldwell, Donald L., 2012, *op. cit.* (pp. 47-49).

54. IPRs, 54 and 65 Squadrons, 24 July 1940 (Air 16/955 records, National Archives); Cull, Brian, *op. cit.* (pp. 154-163).

55. IPR, 54 Squadron, 24 July 1940 (Air 16/955 records, National Archives).

56. *ibid.*

57. *ibid.*

58. *ibid.*

59. *ibid.*

60. Numerous photographs appear in unit history: e.g., Barbas, Bernd, *op. cit.* (pp. 36-37 and pp. 40-41).

61. IPR, 54 Squadron, 24 July 1940 (Air 16/955 records, National Archives).

62. IPR, 54 Squadron, 24 July 1940 (Air 16/955 records, National Archives); ORB, 54 Squadron, 24 July 1940, *op. cit.*

63. Vasco, John, *op. cit.* (p. 18).

64. IPR, 54 Squadron, 24 July 1940 (Air 16/955 records, National Archives).

65. Bergström, Christer, *op. cit.* (pp. 83-85).

66. Galland, Adolf, *The First and the Last* (London: Fontana/Collins, 1970) (pp. 26-27).

67. Goss, Chris, *Luftwaffe Fighters' Battle of Britain* (Manchester: Crécy, 2010) (pp. 28-29).

68. Cull, Brian, *op. cit.* (pp. 154-163); Website, Wood, Tony, 'Tony Wood's Combat Claims and Casualties Lists': accessed via Don Caldwell's website: don-caldwell.we.bs/claims/tonywood.htm.

69. Caldwell, Donald L., 2012, *op. cit.* (pp. 47-49).

70. Ramsey, Winston G. (ed.), *op. cit.* (*Luftwaffe* entry for 24 July 1940); Parker, Nigel, *Luftwaffe Crash Archive,* Vol. 1 (Walton on Thames: Red Kite Books, Air Research Publications, 2013) (entry for 24 July 1940).

71. Parker, Nigel, *op. cit.* (entry for 24 July 1940).

72. IPR, 54 Squadron, 24 July 1940 (Air 16/955 records, National Archives); ORB, 54 Squadron, 24 July 1940, *op. cit.*

73. Barbas, Bernd, *op. cit.* (p. 19); Rall, Günther, *op. cit.* (pp. 52-54); Cull, Brian, *op. cit.* (pp. 154-163); Ramsey, Winston G. (ed.), *op. cit.* (*Luftwaffe* entry for 24 July 1940); Parker, Nigel, *op. cit.* (entry for 24 July 1940).

74. Barbas, Bernd, *op. cit.* (p. 19); Website, Wood, Tony, *op. cit.*; Cull, Brian, *op. cit.* (pp. 154-163).

75. IPR, 65 Squadron, 24 July 1940 (Air 16/955 records, National Archives).

76. Bailey, David J., *op. cit.* (p. 241).

77. Cull, Brian, *op. cit.* (pp. 154-163).

78. Combat Report, F/Lt John Ellis, 610 Squadron, 24 July 1940 (Air 50 records, National Archives), via Bailey, David J., *op. cit.* (p. 240).

79. *ibid.*

80. IPR, 610 Squadron, 24 July 1940 (Air 16/955 records, National Archives) (take off time *c.* 12h34; was one earlier 610 Squadron IPR this day), document mistakenly dated 25 July 1940 and headed 615 Squadron; Bailey, David J., *op. cit.* (pp. 238-244).

81. *ibid.*

82. IPR, 65 Squadron, 24 July 1940 (Air 16/955 records, National Archives).

83. *ibid.*

84. IPR, 65 Squadron, 24 July 1940 (Air 16/955 records, National Archives); Cull, Brian, *op. cit.* (pp. 154-163).

85. Cull, Brian, *op. cit.* (pp. 154-163); Ramsey, Winston G. (ed.), *op. cit.* (*Luftwaffe* entry for 24 July 1940); Parker, Nigel, *op. cit.* (entry for 24 July 1940).

86. IPR, 65 Squadron, 24 July 1940 (Air 16/955 records, National Archives).

87. Vasco, John, *op. cit.* (p. 18); Cull, Brian, *op. cit.* (pp. 154-163).

88. Website, Smith, Gordon and co-workers, *op. cit.*; Website, Holdoway, Mike, *op. cit.*; Website, Pocock, Michael W., *Maritime Quest, op. cit.*

89. Website, Pocock, Michael W., *Maritime Quest, op. cit.*

90. Vasco, John, *op. cit.* (p. 18).

91. Wikipedia, List of shipwrecks, July 1940, *op. cit.*

92. Diary quoted in: Cull, Brian, *op. cit.* (p. 159).

93. IPR, 74 Squadron, 24 July 1940 (Air 16/955 records, National Archives).

94. This is evident from 54 Squadron documents, such as IPRs, CRs etc.

95. Hewitt, Nick, *Coastal Convoys 1939-1945: the Indestructible Highway* (Barnsley: Pen and Sword Maritime, 2019) (p. 93); Bergström, Christer, *op. cit.* (pp. 85-87).

96. James, T. Cecil G., *The Battle of Britain* (Abingdon: Routledge, 2012) (pp. 37-39).

97. *ibid.*

98. IPR, 222 Squadron, 25 July 1940 (Air 16/955 records, National Archives).

99. *ibid.*

100. *ibid.*

101. Ramsey, Winston G. (ed.), *op. cit.* (*Luftwaffe* entry for 25 July 1940).

102. Website, Holm, Michael, *The Luftwaffe, 1933-1945*; www.ww2.dk.

103. IPR, 3 Squadron, 25 July 1940 (Air 16/955 records, National Archives).

104. Ramsey, Winston G. (ed.), *op. cit.* (*Luftwaffe* entry for 25 July 1940).

105. Cull, Brian, *op. cit.* (pp. 166-172).

106. *ibid.*

107. Barbas, Bernd, *op. cit.* (pp. 20-21); Rall, Günther, *op. cit.* (p. 54).

108. Bergström, Christer, *op. cit.* (pp. 85-87).

109. Cull, Brian, *op. cit.* (pp. 166-172).

110. Deighton, Len, *op. cit.* (pp. 175-177); Cull, Brian, *op. cit.* (pp. 166-172).

111. Knight, Dennis, *Harvest of Messerschmitts: The Chronicle of a Village at War, 1940* (London: Frederick Warne, 1981) (pp. 77-79).

112. Vasco, John, *op. cit.* (p. 18).

113. Mason, Francis K., *op. cit.* (pp. 191-193); IPR, 65 Squadron, 25 July 1940 (Air 16/955 records, National Archives).

114. IPR, 65 Squadron, 25 July 1940 (Air 16/955 records, National Archives). No corrections made to IPR excerpt.

115. *ibid.*

116. IPRs, 32 and 615 Squadrons, 25 July 1940 (Air 16/955 records, National Archives).

117. Thomas, Nick, *Hurricane Squadron Ace* (Barnsley: Pen and Sword, 2014) (pp. 79-81); IPR, 32 Squadron, 25 July 1940 (Air 16/955 records, National Archives).

118. Ramsey, Winston G. (ed.), *op. cit.* (entries for 25 July 1940); Website, Holm, Michael, *op. cit.*

119. IPR, 32 Squadron, 25 July 1940 (Air 16/955 records, National Archives). No corrections made to IPR excerpt.

120. Note 117, *op. cit.*

121. IPR, 32 Squadron, 25 July 1940 (Air 16/955 records, National Archives).

122. IPR, 615 Squadron, 25 July 1940 (Air 16/955 records, National Archives).

123. Ramsey, Winston G. (ed.), *op. cit.* (*Luftwaffe* entry for 25 July 1940); Parker, Nigel, *op. cit.* (entry for 25 July 1940).

124. IPR, 32 Squadron, 25 July 1940 (Air 16/955 records, National Archives); CR, F/Lt M. N. Crossley, 32 Squadron, 25 July 1940 (Air 50 records, National Archives).

125. Barbas, Bernd, *op. cit.* (pp. 20-21 and p. 298); Parker, Nigel, *op. cit.* (entry for 25 July 1940); latter source gives much later time of loss – *c.* 18h40 – than the former.

126. Parker, Nigel, *op. cit.* (entry for 25 July 1940).

127. For example: Ramsey, Winston G. (ed.), *op. cit.* (*Luftwaffe* entry for 25 July 1940); Parker, Nigel, *op. cit.* (entry for 25 July 1940).

128. Barbas, Bernd, *op. cit.* (pp. 20-21).

129. Archives, Imperial War Museum, London: *Luftwaffe Quartermaster General Loss Returns*; Barbas, Bernd, *op. cit.* (pp. 20-21).

130. IPR, 32 Squadron, 25 July 1940 (Air 16/955 records, National Archives); Ramsey, Winston G. (ed.), *op. cit.* (RAF entry for 25 July 1940).

131. Website, Wood, Tony, *op. cit.*

132. *ibid.*

133. Ramsey, Winston G. (ed.), *op. cit.* (*Luftwaffe* entry for 25 July 1940).

134. Cull, Brian, *op. cit.* (p. 174).

135. Website, en.wikipedia.org/wiki/ Gloster_Aircraft_Company.

136. Cull, Brian, *op. cit.* (p. 174).

137. *ibid.*

138. CR, F/Lt P. P. Hanks, 5 OTU, 25 July 1940 (Air 50 records, National Archives), excerpt therefrom given in: IPR, 5 OTU, 25 July 1940 (Air 16/955 records, National Archives). OTU = Operational Training Unit.

139. Cull, Brian, *op. cit.* (p. 174); Ramsey, Winston G. (ed.), *op. cit.* (*Luftwaffe* entry for 25 July 1940).

140. Saunders, Andy, *Stuka Attack!* (London: Grub Street, 2013) (p. 38); Hewitt, Nick, *op. cit.* (pp. 93-96); Knight, Dennis, *op. cit.* (pp. 77-79).

141. McKee, Alexander, *Strike from the Sky* (London: New English Library, 1969) (pp. 42-48).

142. *ibid.*

143. Mason, Francis K., *op. cit.* (pp. 191-193); Caldwell, Donald L., 2012, *op. cit.* (pp. 48-49); Saunders, Andy, *op. cit.* (p. 38); Jullian, Marcel, *The Battle of Britain* (London: Jonathan Cape, 1967) (pp. 78-81).

144. Hewitt, Nick, *op. cit.* (pp. 93-96).

145. Saunders, Andy, *op. cit.* (p. 38).

146. Operations Record Book (ORB), 54 Squadron, 25 July 1940 (Air 27 records, National Archives).

147. Saunders, Andy, *op. cit.* (p. 38).

148. Hewitt, Nick, *op. cit.* (pp. 93-96); Holland, James, *The Battle of Britain; Five months that Changed History May-October 1940* (London: Corgi, 2011) (pp. 564-566).

149. Website, Holm, Michael, *op. cit.*

150. Saunders, Andy, *op. cit.* (p. 33).

151. Website, Holm, Michael, *op. cit.*

152. Bergström, Christer, *op. cit.* (pp. 85-87).

153. Website, Wood, Tony, *op. cit.*

154. Knight, Dennis, *op. cit.* (pp. 77-79); Mason, Francis K., *op. cit.* (pp. 191-193); Deighton, Len, *op. cit.* (pp. 175-177).

155. IPR, 64 Squadron, 25 July 1940 (Air 16/955 records, National Archives) (take off time *c.* 14h50; there was one later 64 Squadron IPR this day); MacDonell, Donald, *From Dogfight to Diplomacy: a Spitfire Pilot's Log 1932-1958* (Barnsley: Pen and Sword, 2009) (pp. 48-50).

156. Deighton, Len, *op. cit.* (pp. 175-177); IPR, 111 Squadron, 25 July 1940 (Air 16/955 records, National Archives).

157. Caldwell, Donald L., 2012, *op. cit.* (pp. 48-49).

158. *ibid.*

159. Mason, Francis K., *op. cit.* (pp. 191-193).

160. McKee, Alexander, *op. cit.* (pp. 42-48).

161. Website, Wood, Tony, *op. cit.*

162. Jullian, Marcel, *op. cit.* (pp. 78-81).

163. ORB, 54 Squadron, 25 July 1940 (Air 27 records, National Archives); Wynn, Kenneth G., *Men of the Battle of Britain: a Biographical Directory of the Few* (Barnsley: Frontline, 2015; West Malling: The Battle of Britain Memorial Trust, 2015) (p. 550); Ramsey, Winston G. (ed.), *op. cit.* (RAF entry for 25 July 1940).

164. Bergström, Christer, *op. cit.* (pp. 85-87); ORB, 54 Squadron, 25 July 1940 (Air 27 records, National Archives); Hough, Richard and Richards, Denis, *The Battle of Britain* (Sevenoaks: Coronet, 1990) (p. 132).

165. Hough, Richard and Richards, Denis, *op. cit.* (p. 132).

166. ORB, 54 Squadron, 25 July 1940 (Air 27 records, National Archives).

167. Jullian, Marcel, *op. cit.* (pp. 78-81).

168. IPR, 64 Squadron, 25 July 1940 (Air 16/955 records, National Archives) (take off time *c.* 14h50).

169. MacDonell, Donald, *op. cit.* (pp. 48-50); IPR, 64 Squadron, 25 July 1940 (Air 16/955 records, National Archives) (take off time *c.* 14h50).

170. *ibid.*

171. *ibid.*

172. *ibid.*

173. *ibid.*

174. *ibid.*

175. *ibid.*

176. MacDonell, Donald, *op. cit.* (pp. 48-50).

177. Caldwell, Donald L., 2012, *op. cit.* (pp. 48-49).

178. Caldwell, Donald L., 2012, *op. cit.* (pp. 48-49); MacDonell, Donald, *op. cit.* (pp. 48-50).

179. IPR, 610 Squadron, 25 July 1940 (Air 16/955 records, National Archives) (take off time *c.* 14h58; was one later 610 Squadron IPR this day).

180. *ibid.*

181. CR, F/Lt J. Ellis, 610 Squadron, 25 July 1940 (Air 50 records, National Archives), excerpt therefrom given in: Bailey, David J., *op. cit.* (p. 245); IPR, 610 Squadron, 25 July 1940 (Air 16/955 records, National Archives) (take off time *c.* 14h58).

182. Cull, Brian, *op. cit.* (pp. 166-172).

183. Bailey, David J., *op. cit.* (p. 248-251).

184. Bailey, David J., *op. cit.* (p. 20-21).

185. IPR, 610 Squadron, 25 July 1940 (Air 16/955 records, National Archives) (take off time *c.* 14h58).

186. Barbas, Bernd, *op. cit.* (pp. 20-21).

187. James, T. Cecil G., *op. cit.* (pp. 37-39); IPR, 111 Squadron, 25 July 1940 (Air 16/955 records, National Archives).

188. Jullian, Marcel, *op. cit.* (pp. 78-81); McKee, Alexander, *op. cit.* (pp. 42-48).

189. *ibid.*

190. Cull, Brian, *op. cit.* (pp. 166-172).

191. Hewitt, Nick, *op. cit.* (pp. 93-96); Saunders, Andy, *op. cit.* (p. 38).

192. Jullian, Marcel, *op. cit.* (pp. 78-81).

193. Ramsey, Winston G. (ed.), *op. cit.* (*Luftwaffe* entry for 25 July 1940).

194. *ibid.*

195. Mason, Francis K., *op. cit.* (pp. 191-193).

196. Knight, Dennis, *op. cit.* (pp. 77-79).

197. Hewitt, Nick, *op. cit.* (pp. 93-96); Mason, Francis K., *op. cit.* (pp. 191-193); Saunders, Andy, *op. cit.* (p. 38).

198. James, T. Cecil G., *op. cit.* (p. 39).

199. Knight, Dennis, *op. cit.* (pp. 77-79).
200. Website, Holm, Michael, *op. cit.*
201. Bergström, Christer, *op. cit.* (pp. 85-87).
202. Caldwell, Donald L., 2012, *op. cit.* (pp. 48-49); Ramsey, Winston G. (ed.), *op. cit.* (*Luftwaffe* entry for 25 July 1940).
203. Website, Wood, Tony, *op. cit.*
204. Thomas, Nick, *op. cit.* (pp. 79-81).
205. ORB, 54 Squadron, 25 July 1940 (Air 27 records, National Archives).
206. IPR, 64 Squadron, 25 July 1940 (Air 16/955 records, National Archives) (take off time *c.* 16h30; there was one earlier 64 Squadron IPR this day).
207. *ibid.*
208. IPR, 64 Squadron, 25 July 1940 (Air 16/955 records, National Archives) (take off time *c.* 16h30); Ramsey, Winston G. (ed.), *op. cit.* (RAF entry for 25 July 1940).
209. IPR, 64 Squadron, 25 July 1940 (Air 16/955 records, National Archives) (take off time *c.* 16h30).
210. Note 208, *op. cit.*
211. Website, Wood, Tony, *op. cit.*
212. Hewitt, Nick, *op. cit.* (pp. 93-96).
213. James, T. Cecil G., *op. cit.* (pp. 37-39); Hewitt, Nick, *op. cit.* (pp. 93-96).
214. McKee, Alexander, *op. cit.* (pp. 42-48).
215. Mason, Francis K., *op. cit.* (pp. 191-193).
216. McKee, Alexander, *op. cit.* (pp. 42-48).
217. *ibid.*
218. Hewitt, Nick, *op. cit.* (pp. 93-96); McKee, Alexander, *op. cit.* (pp. 42-48).
219. Vasco, John, *op. cit.* (p. 18); Saunders, Andy, *op. cit.* (p. 38).
220. Vasco, John, *op. cit.* (p. 18).
221. Bergström, Christer, *op. cit.* (pp. 85-87); Vasco, John, *op. cit.* (p. 18).
222. Hewitt, Nick, *op. cit.* (pp. 93-96).
223. Saunders, Andy, *op. cit.* (p. 38).
224. Cull, Brian, *op. cit.* (pp. 166-172).
225. Bergström, Christer, *op. cit.* (pp. 85-87); Barbas, Bernd, *op. cit.* (pp. 20-21).
226. Website, de Zeng, Henry L. IV, *Luftwaffe Airfields 1935-1945*, accessed via Michael Holm's website, *The Luftwaffe 1933-1945*: www.ww2.dk; this source at www.ww2.dk/lwairfields.html.
227. Bergström, Christer, *op. cit.* (pp. 85-87).
228. Website, Holm, Michael, *op. cit.*
229. Ramsey, Winston G. (ed.), *op. cit.* (*Luftwaffe* entry for 25 July 1940).
230. Saunders, Andy, *op. cit.* (p. 184).
231. Mahlke, Helmut, *Memoirs of a Stuka Pilot* (London: Frontline, 2013) (pp. 119-120 and p. 280).
232. Barbas, Bernd, *op. cit.* (pp. 20-21); Rall, Günther, *op. cit.* (p. 54).

233. Barbas, Bernd, *op. cit.* (pp. 20-21).

234. Website, Wood, Tony, *op. cit.*

235. IPRs, 54 and 56 Squadrons, 25 July 1940 (Air 16/955 records, National Archives); James, T. Cecil G., *op. cit.* (pp. 37-39).

236. ORB, 54 Squadron, 25 July 1940 (Air 27 records, National Archives).

237. IPR, 54 Squadron, 25 July 1940 (Air 16/955 records, National Archives).

238. *ibid.*

239. Ramsey, Winston G. (ed.), *op. cit.* (RAF entry for 25 July 1940); IPR, 54 Squadron, 25 July 1940 (Air 16/955 records, National Archives).

240. Wynn, Kenneth G., *op. cit.* (p. 167).

241. IPR, 54 Squadron, 25 July 1940 (Air 16/955 records, National Archives).

242. IPR, 56 Squadron, 25 July 1940 (Air 16/955 records, National Archives); Page, Geoffrey, *Tale of a Guinea Pig* (London: Corgi, 1983) (pp. 74-77).

243. IPR, 56 Squadron, 25 July 1940 (Air 16/955 records, National Archives); Mason, Francis K., *op. cit.* (pp. 191-193); CR, F/Lt E. J. Gracie, 56 Squadron, 25 July 1940 (Air 50 records, National Archives); Sutton, Barry, *Fighter Boy: Life as a Battle of Britain Pilot* (Stroud: Amberley, 2010) (pp. 145-148).

244. James, T. Cecil G., *op. cit.* (pp. 37-39).

245. CR, F/Lt E. J. Gracie, 56 Squadron, 25 July 1940 (Air 50 records, National Archives); Sutton, Barry, *op. cit.* (pp. 145-148); Page, Geoffrey, *op. cit.* (pp. 74-77).

246. IPR, 56 Squadron, 25 July 1940 (Air 16/955 records, National Archives); CR, F/Lt E. J. Gracie, 56 Squadron, 25 July 1940 (Air 50 records, National Archives); Sutton, Barry, *op. cit.* (pp. 145-148); Page, Geoffrey, *op. cit.* (pp. 74-77).

247. *ibid.*

248. Ramsey, Winston G. (ed.), *op. cit.* (*Luftwaffe* entry for 25 July 1940).

249. *ibid.*

250. IPR, 56 Squadron, 25 July 1940 (Air 16/955 records, National Archives); Ramsey, Winston G. (ed.), *op. cit.* (RAF entry for 25 July 1940).

251. Website, Wood, Tony, *op. cit.*; Barbas, Bernd, *op. cit.* (pp. 20-21).

252. Barbas, Bernd, *op. cit.* (pp. 20-21); Rall, Günther, *op. cit.* (p. 54).

253. Barbas, Bernd, *op. cit.* (pp. 20-21).

254. IPR, 610 Squadron, 25 July 1940 (Air 16/955 records, National Archives) (take off time *c.* 18h27; was one earlier 610 Squadron IPR this day).

255. James, T. Cecil G., *op. cit.* (p. 39).

256. Mahlke, Helmut, *op. cit.* (pp. 119-120).

257. Ramsey, Winston G. (ed.), *op. cit.* (*Luftwaffe* entry for 25 July 1940).

258. Cull, Brian, *op. cit.* (pp. 172-173).

259. *ibid.*

260. Mahlke, Helmut, *op. cit.* (pp. 119-120).

261. *ibid.*

262. ORB, 152 Squadron, 25 July 1940 (Air 27 records, National Archives); IPR, 152 Squadron, 25 July 1940 (Air 16/955 records, National Archives).

263. Burt, Danny, *A Battle of Britain Spitfire Squadron: the Men and Machines of 152 Squadron in the Summer of 1940* (Barnsley: Pen and Sword, 2018) (pp. 15-17).

264. *ibid.*

265. IPR, 152 Squadron, 25 July 1940 (Air 16/955 records, National Archives).

266. ORB, 152 Squadron, 25 July 1940 (Air 27 records, National Archives); Burt, Danny, *op. cit.* (p. 94, p. 138).

267. Burt, Danny, *op. cit.* (p. 138).

268. Website, Wood, Tony, *op. cit.*

269. Ramsey, Winston G. (ed.), *op. cit.* (RAF entry for 25 July 1940).

270. ORB, 152 Squadron, 25 July 1940 (Air 27 records, National Archives); IPR, 152 Squadron, 25 July 1940 (Air 16/955 records, National Archives).

271. *ibid.*

272. ORB, 152 Squadron, 25 July 1940 (Air 27 records, National Archives).

273. Ramsey, Winston G. (ed.), *op. cit.* (*Luftwaffe* entry for 25 July 1940).

274. ORB, 152 Squadron, 25 July 1940 (Air 27 records, National Archives).

275. ORB, 152 Squadron, 25 July 1940 (Air 27 records, National Archives); IPR, 152 Squadron, 25 July 1940 (Air 16/955 records, National Archives); Burt, Danny, *op. cit.* (pp. 84-85).

276. *ibid.*

277. ORB, 152 Squadron, 25 July 1940 (Air 27 records, National Archives); Burt, Danny, *op. cit.* (pp. 84-85); Ramsey, Winston G. (ed.), *op. cit.* (RAF entry for 25 July 1940).

278. Burt, Danny, *op. cit.* (pp. 112-114); IPR, 152 Squadron, 25 July 1940 (Air 16/955 records, National Archives).

279. Burt, Danny, *op. cit.* (p. 247); IPR, 152 Squadron, 25 July 1940 (Air 16/955 records, National Archives).

280. Burt, Danny, *op. cit.* (p. 247); ORB, 152 Squadron, 25 July 1940 (Air 27 records, National Archives).

281. IPR, 152 Squadron, 25 July 1940 (Air 16/955 records, National Archives); Ramsey, Winston G. (ed.), *op. cit.* (*Luftwaffe* entry for 25 July 1940).

282. *ibid.*

283. IPR, 87 Squadron, 25 July 1940 (Air 16/955 records, National Archives).

284. *ibid.*

285. *ibid.*

286. IPRs, 87 and 152 Squadrons, 25 July 1940 (Air 16/955 records, National Archives).

287. Shaw, Michael, *Twice Vertical: the History of No. 1 (Fighter) Squadron RAF* (London: Macdonald, 1971) (p. 153); Cull, Brian, *op. cit.* (pp. 166-172).

288. Ramsey, Winston G. (ed.), *op. cit.* (*Luftwaffe* entry for 25 July 1940).

289. IPR, 92 Squadron, 25 July 1940 (Air 16/955 records, National Archives).

290. *ibid.*

291. Wood, Derek and Dempster, Derek, *op. cit.* (pp. 259-260).

292. Website, Bond, Bill and others, Battle of Britain Historical Society: Battle of Britain 1940, Chronology (p. 22), battleofbritain1940.net/0022.html.

293. Mason, Francis K., *op. cit.* (p. 194); Ramsey, Winston G. (ed.), *op. cit.* (RAF entry for 26 July 1940).

294. Wynn, Kenneth G., *op. cit.* (p. 321).

295. Website, Wood, Tony, *op. cit.*

296. Ramsey, Winston G. (ed.), *op. cit.* (RAF entry for 26 July 1940).

297. Von Eimannsberger, Ludwig, *Zerstörer Gruppe: A history of V./(Z)LG 1 – I./NJG 3 1939-1941* (Atglen: Schiffer, 1998) (p. 94, p. 204, p. 208).

298. Cull, Brian, *op. cit.* (pp. 184-188); Alexander, Kristen, *Australia's Few and the Battle of Britain* (Barnsley: Pen and Sword, 2015) (p. 187).

299. Alexander, Kristen, *op. cit.* (p. 187).

300. *ibid.*

301. Ramsey, Winston G. (ed.), *op. cit.* (*Luftwaffe* entry for 26 July 1940).

302. Ramsey, Winston G. (ed.), *op. cit.* (RAF entry for 26 July 1940); Cull, Brian, *op. cit.* (pp. 184-188).

303. Von Eimannsberger, Ludwig, *op. cit.* (p. 94, p. 204, p. 208).

304. IPR, 65 Squadron, 26 July 1940 (Air 16/955 records, National Archives); Cull, Brian, *op. cit.* (pp. 184-188).

305. IPR, 65 Squadron, 26 July 1940 (Air 16/955 records, National Archives).

306. Cull, Brian, *op. cit.* (pp. 184-188).

307. Ramsey, Winston G. (ed.), *op. cit.* (*Luftwaffe* entry for 26 July 1940); *Luftwaffe Quartermaster General Loss Returns*, *op. cit.*; IPR, 92 Squadron, 26 July 1940 (Air 16/955 records, National Archives).

308. Parker, Nigel, *op. cit.* (entry for 26 July 1940).

309. James, T. Cecil G., *op. cit.* (p. 36).

8. *27-29 July 1940: repeated attacks on harbour and naval vessels at Dover; limited attacks on convoys and naval vessels off Harwich and in Western Channel*

1. Mason, Francis K., *Battle over Britain* (London: McWhirter Twins, 1969) (pp. 195-196); Saunders, Andy, *Stuka Attack!* (London: Grub Street, 2013) (pp. 38-39).

2. *ibid.*

3. Cull, Brian, *Battle for the Channel* (Stroud: Fonthill, 2017) (pp. 188-194); IPR, 609, 145 and 238 Squadrons combined, 27 July 1940 (Air 16/955 records, National Archives).

4. Mason, Francis K., *op. cit.* (pp. 195-196).

5. IPR, 609, 145 and 238 Squadrons combined, 27 July 1940 (Air 16/955 records, National Archives).

6. *ibid.*

7. *ibid.*
8. *ibid.*
9. *ibid.*
10. *ibid.*
11. *ibid.*
12. Crook, David M., *Spitfire Pilot* (London: Grub Street, 2010) (pp. 78-79).
13. Note 5, *op. cit.*
14. *ibid.*
15. IPR, 609, 145 and 238 Squadrons combined, 27 July 1940 (Air 16/955 records, National Archives); Ramsey, Winston G. (ed.), *The Battle of Britain: Then and Now* (London: Battle of Britain Prints International Ltd., 1982) (entries for 27 July 1940); Saunders, Andy, *op. cit.* (pp. 38-39).
16. Ramsey, Winston G. (ed.), *op. cit.* (RAF entry for 27 July 1940).
17. Note 5, *op. cit.*
18. Mason, Francis K., *op. cit.* (pp. 195-196).
19. Mason, Francis K., *op. cit.* (pp. 195-196); IPRs, 41, 501 and 615 Squadrons, 27 July 1940 (Air 16/955 records, National Archives).
20. James, T. Cecil G., *The Battle of Britain* (Abingdon: Routledge, 2012) (p. 41); Wood, Derek and Dempster, Derek, *The Narrow Margin* (London: Arrow Books, 1967) (p. 260); Cull, Brian, *op. cit.* (pp. 188-194); Vasco, John, *Messerschmitt Bf 110 Bombsights over England: Erprobungsgruppe 210 in the Battle of Britain* (Atglen: Schiffer, 2002) (pp. 18-19).
21. Saunders, Andy, *op. cit.* (pp. 38-39).
22. IPRs, 41 and 501 Squadrons, 27 July 1940 (Air 16/955 records, National Archives); Brew, Steve, *Blood, Sweat and Courage: 41 Squadron RAF 1939-1942* (Stroud: Fonthill, 2014) (pp. 122-123).
23. Vasco, John, *op. cit.* (pp. 18-19).
24. IPR, 501 Squadron, 27 July 1940 (Air 16/955 records, National Archives).
25. *ibid.*
26. IPR, 41 Squadron, 27 July 1940 (Air 16/955 records, National Archives); Brew, Steve, *op. cit.* (pp. 122-123).
27. Vasco, John, *op. cit.* (pp. 18-19 and pp. 176-177); Website, Wood, Tony, *Tony Wood's Combat Claims and Casualties Lists*: accessed via Don Caldwell's website: don-caldwell.we.bs/claims/tonywood. htm.
28. Ramsey, Winston G. (ed.), *op. cit.* (RAF entry for 27 July 1940); Barbas, Bernd, *Die Geschichte der III. Gruppe des Jagdgeschwaders 52* (Überlingen: self-published, undated) (p. 21).
29. IPR, 615 Squadron, 27 July 1940 (Air 16/955 records, National Archives).
30. Mason, Francis K., *op. cit.* (pp. 195-196).
31. *ibid.*

32. Website, en.wikipedia.org/wiki/HMS_Wren_(1919); Website, *The Battle of Britain Historical Timeline*, battleofbritain1940.com/entry/Saturday-27-july-1940.

33. Website, en.wikipedia.org/wiki/HMS_Wren_(1919).

34. Bergström, Christer, *The Battle of Britain: An Epic Conflict Revisited* (Oxford: Casemate, 2015; Eskilstuna: Vaktel, 2015) (pp. 87-88); Kiehl, Heinz, *Kampfgeschwader 53 "Legion Condor": The Complete History of KG 53 in World War II* (Atglen: Schiffer, 2013) (pp. 265-266).

35. Vasco, John, *op. cit.* (pp. 18-19 and pp. 176-177); Cull, Brian, *op. cit.* (pp. 188-194).

36. Website, *Wrecksite*, www.wrecksite.eu/wreck.aspx?469.

37. IPR, 234 Squadron, 27 July 1940 (Air 16/955 records, National Archives); Cull, Brian, *op. cit.* (pp. 188-194).

38. *ibid.*

39. Newton, Dennis, *A Spitfire Pilot's Story: Pat Hughes Battle of Britain Top Gun* (Stroud: Amberley, 2016) (pp. 182-194).

40. IPR, 234 Squadron, 28 July 1940 (Air 16/955 records, National Archives); Mason, Francis K., *op. cit.* (pp. 196-197).

41. IPR, 234 Squadron, 28 July 1940 (Air 16/955 records, National Archives).

42. *ibid.*

43. Ramsey, Winston G. (ed.), *op. cit.* (*Luftwaffe* entry for 28 July 1940).

44. Bishop, Patrick, *Battle of Britain* (London: Quercus, 2010) (pp. 133-134); Wood, Derek and Dempster, Derek, *op. cit.* (p. 261).

45. *ibid.*

46. IPR, 74 Squadron, 28 July 1940 (Air 16/955 records, National Archives); CR, F/Lt D. P. D. G. Kelly, 74 Squadron, 28 July 1940 (Air 50 records, National Archives); CR, F/Lt A. G. Malan, 74 Squadron, 28 July 1940 (Air 50 records, National Archives), copy in Bergström, Christer, *op. cit.* (pp. 88-89).

47. CR, F/Lt A. G. Malan, 74 Squadron, 28 July 1940, *op. cit.*

48. IPR, 74 Squadron, 28 July 1940 (Air 16/955 records, National Archives).

49. *ibid.*

50. *ibid.*

51. CR, F/Lt D. P. D. G. Kelly, 74 Squadron, 28 July 1940 (Air 50 records, National Archives).

52. *ibid.*

53. IPR, 74 Squadron, 28 July 1940 (Air 16/955 records, National Archives).

54. Ramsey, Winston G. (ed.), *op. cit.* (RAF entry for 28 July 1940); IPR, 74 Squadron, 28 July 1940 (Air 16/955 records, National Archives).

55. IPR, 74 Squadron, 28 July 1940 (Air 16/955 records, National Archives).

56. Cull, Brian, *op. cit.* (pp. 200-201); Website, Wood, Tony, *op. cit.*; Website, *Jagdgeschwader 51 "Mölders" Victory Claims 1939-1945*, Luftwaffe.cz/jg51_victories.html (last update 19.11.2001).

57. Squadron Commander's Report on Flying Battle Casualty, Sgt E. A. Mould, 74 Squadron, 28 July 1940 (Air 81 records, National Archives); Ramsey, Winston G. (ed.), *op. cit.* (RAF entry for 28 July 1940); Knight, Dennis, *Harvest of Messerschmitts: The Chronicle of a village at War, 1940* (London: Frederick Warne, 1981) (pp. 79-81).

58. Website, *Jagdgeschwader 51 "Mölders" Victory Claims 1939-1945*, *op. cit.* Website, Wood, Tony, *op. cit.*

59. Aders, Gebhard and Held, Werner, *Jagdgeschwader 51 'Mölders'* (Stuttgart: Motorbuch, 1985) (p. 248); Website, *Jagdgeschwader 51 "Mölders" Victory Claims 1939-1945, op. cit.*

60. Kershaw, Alex, *The Few* (London: Penguin, 2008) (p. 71-74).

61. Squadron Commander's Report on Flying Battle Casualty, P/O H. R. Young, 74 Squadron, 28 July 1940 (Air 81 records, National Archives).

62. Ramsey, Winston G. (ed.), *op. cit.* (RAF entry for 28 July 1940).

63. Squadron Commander's Report on Flying Battle Casualty, P/O H. R. Young, 74 Squadron, 28 July 1940 (Air 81 records, National Archives).

64. For example, Ramsey, Winston G. (ed.), *op. cit.* (RAF entry for 28 July 1940).

65. Mason, Francis K., *op. cit.* (pp. 196-197); Bungay, Stephen, *The Most Dangerous Enemy* (London: Aurum Press, 2009) (p. 159); claims listed by *JG 51* for 28 July 1940 identify the four *Staffeln* of *JG 51* as 1, 2, 3 and 6/*JG 51*: Website, *Jagdgeschwader 51 "Mölders" Victory Claims 1939-1945, op. cit.*

66. Osterkamp, Theo, *Durch Höhen und Tiefen jagt ein Herz* (Heidelberg: Kurt Vowinckel Verlag, 1952) (pp. 318-323).

67. Website, Holm, Michael, *The Luftwaffe, 1933-1945,* www.ww2.dk.

68. Kiehl, Heinz, *op. cit.* (pp. 253-289).

69. *Tiger News* No 40, on *No 74 (F) Tiger Squadron Association* website, www.74squadron.org.uk (news section itself probably an excerpt from Paul Trickett's article on P/O Freeborn in *World War II Magazine*.)

70. IPR, 74 Squadron, 28 July 1940 (Air 16/955 records, National Archives); Cull, Brian, *op. cit.* (pp. 199).

71. IPR, 74 Squadron, 28 July 1940 (Air 16/955 records, National Archives).

72. Note 58, *op. cit.*

73. Mason, Francis K., *op. cit.* (pp. 196-197); IPRs, 257 and 74 Squadrons, 28 July 1940 (Air 16/955 records, National Archives).

74. IPR, 74 Squadron, 28 July 1940 (Air 16/955 records, National Archives).

75. IPR, 111 Squadron, 28 July 1940 (Air 16/955 records, National Archives).

76. IPR, 257 Squadron, 28 July 1940 (Air 16/955 records, National Archives).

77. *ibid.*

78. *ibid.*

79. *ibid.*

80. *ibid.*

81. Ramsey, Winston G. (ed.), *op. cit.* (RAF entry for 28 July 1940).

82. IPR, 257 Squadron, 28 July 1940 (Air 16/955 records, National Archives).

83. Mason, Francis K., *op. cit.* (pp. 196-197); Bungay, Stephen, *op. cit.* (p. 159).

84. Caldwell, Donald L., *JG 26 Luftwaffe Fighter Wing Diary, 1939-1942*, Vol. 1 (Mechanicsburg: Stackpole Books, 2012) (pp. 49-50); Website, Wood, Tony, *op. cit.*

85. *ibid.*

86. *ibid.*

87. Von Forell, Fritz, *Werner Mölders: Flug zur Sonne; Die Geschichte des grossen Jagdfliegers* (Leoni Am Starnberger See: Druffel Verlag, 1976) (pp. 135-136); Kershaw, Alex, *op. cit.* (pp. 71-74).

88. For example: IPR, 41 Squadron, 28 July 1940 (Air 16/955 records, National Archives); CR, P/O G. H. Bennions, 41 Squadron, 28 July 1940 (Air 50 records, National Archives), copy in: Thomas, Nick, *Ben Bennions DFC: Battle of Britain Fighter Ace* (Barnsley: Pen & Sword, 2011) (p. 102).

89. Von Forell, Fritz, *op. cit.* (pp. 135-136).

90. *ibid.*

91. Von Forell, Fritz, *op. cit.* (pp. 135-136); Kershaw, Alex, *op. cit.* (pp. 71-74).

92. Ramsey, Winston G. (ed.), *op. cit.* (*Luftwaffe* entry for 28 July 1940).

93. Kershaw, Alex, *op. cit.* (pp. 71-74), Kirchner's story therein is sourced from another book: Mombeek, Eric, Wadman, David and Creek, Eddie J., *Jagdwaffe: Battle of Britain: Phase One: July–August 1940 (Luftwaffe Colours: Volume Two, Section 1)* (Crowborough: Classic Publications, 2001) (p. 40).

94. *ibid.*

95. *ibid.*

96. IPR, 41 Squadron, 28 July 1940 (Air 16/955 records, National Archives).

97. Brew, Steve, *op. cit.* (pp. 124-125); Shipman, John, *One of 'The Few': The Memoirs of Wing Commander Ted 'Shippy' Shipman AFC* (Barnsley: Pen & Sword, 2008) (pp. 83-85).

98. Brew, Steve, *op. cit.* (pp. 124-125).

99. Thomas, Nick, *op. cit.* (p. 102); Shipman, John, *op. cit.* (pp. 83-85).

100. Brew, Steve, *op. cit.* (pp. 124-125).

101. IPR, 41 Squadron, 28 July 1940 (Air 16/955 records, National Archives); Brew, Steve, *op. cit.* (pp. 124-125); Thomas, Nick, *op. cit.* (pp. 100-104); Shipman, John, *op. cit.* (pp. 83-85); Ramsey, Winston G. (ed.), *op. cit.* (RAF entry for 28 July 1940).

102. IPR, 41 Squadron, 28 July 1940 (Air 16/955 records, National Archives).

103. *ibid.*

104. *ibid.*

105. Confirmation report of P/O Wallens, annotated directly on Bennions' Combat Report: CR, P/O G. H. Bennions, 41 Squadron, 28 July 1940 (Air 50 records, National Archives), copy in Thomas, Nick, *op. cit.* (pp. 102). The confirmation report is an unusual feature in such records.

106. Note 88, *op. cit.*

107. IPR, 41 Squadron, 28 July 1940 (Air 16/955 records, National Archives); Brew, Steve, *op. cit.* (pp. 124-125).

108. Website, Wood, Tony, *op. cit.*

109. Note 58, *op. cit.*

110. Mason, Francis K., *op. cit.* (pp. 196-197).

111. IPR, 111 Squadron, 28 July 1940 (Air 16/955 records, National Archives).

112. IPR, 111 Squadron, 28 July 1940 (Air 16/955 records, National Archives); Cull, Brian, *op. cit.* (p. 197, p. 202); Ramsey, Winston G. (ed.), *op. cit.* (*Luftwaffe* entry for 28 July 1940); Parker, Nigel, *Luftwaffe Crash Archive*, Vol. 1 (Walton on Thames: Red Kite Books, Air Research Publications, 2013) (entry for 28 July 1940).

113. Cull, Brian, *op. cit.* (p. 197, p. 202).

114. Cull, Brian, *op. cit.* (p. 197); Ramsey, Winston G. (ed.), *op. cit.* (*Luftwaffe* entry for 28 July 1940).

115. Website, *Wrecksite*, www.wrecksite.eu/wreck.aspx?15051; Website, Edgar, Scott, *Northern Ireland during the Second World War*, Wartimeni. com/person/john-mcneill; Web forum, *Ships Nostalgia*, shipsnostalgia. com/archive/index.php/t-3152.html.

116. National Archives, discovery.nationalarchives.gov.uk/details/r/ C10818948.

117. Cull, Brian, *op. cit.* (p. 202).

118. Website, Holm, Michael, *op. cit.*

119. Ramsey, Winston G. (ed.), *op. cit.* (RAF entry for 28 July 1940).

120. Mason, Francis K., *op. cit.* (pp. 198-199); Cull, Brian, *op. cit.* (pp. 203-206).

121. Mason, Francis K., *op. cit.* (pp. 198-199); Thomas, Nick, *op. cit.* (pp. 104-108); Knight, Dennis, *op. cit.* (p. 81).

122. Cull, Brian, *op. cit.* (pp. 203-206).

123. Saunders, Andy, *op. cit.* (pp. 39-43).

124. Note 120, *op. cit.*; Caldwell, Donald L., *op. cit.* (pp. 49-50).

125. Rall, Günther, *Mein Flugbuch* (Moosburg, Germany: NeunundzwanzigSechs Verlag, 2004) (p. 54).

126. Caldwell, Donald L., *op. cit.* (pp. 49-50).

127. IPRs, 56 and 41 Squadrons, 29 July 1940 (Air 16/955 records, National Archives); Cull, Brian, *op. cit.* (pp. 203-206); Brew, Steve, *op. cit.* (pp. 125-128); Foreman, John, *RAF Fighter Command Air Victory Claims of World War Two, Part One 1939-1940* (Walton-on-Thames: Red Kite, 2003) (entry for 29 July 1940); Thomas, Nick, *Their Finest Hour: Stories*

of the Men who Won the Battle of Britain (Barnsley: Pen & Sword, 2016) (Kindle version: chapter on P/O E. G. Gilbert, 64 Squadron).

128. IPR, 501 Squadron, 29 July 1940 (Air 16/955 records, National Archives).
129. Ramsey, Winston G. (ed.), *op. cit.* (RAF entry for 29 July 1940).
130. Cull, Brian, *op. cit.* (pp. 203-206).
131. Mason, Francis K., *op. cit.* (pp. 198-199).
132. *ibid.*
133. Squadron Commander's Report on Flying Battle Casualty, F/O D. H. Gamblen, 41 Squadron, 29 July 1940 (Air 81 records, National Archives); Brew, Steve, *op. cit.* (pp. 125-128).
134. Thomas, Nick, 2011, *op. cit.* (pp. 104-108); IPR, 41 Squadron, 29 July 1940 (Air 16/955 records, National Archives); Brew, Steve, *op. cit.* (pp. 125-128).
135. IPR, 41 Squadron, 29 July 1940 (Air 16/955 records, National Archives).
136. Note 134, *op. cit.*
137. Website, Wood, Tony, *op. cit.*
138. *ibid.*
139. IPR, 501 Squadron, 29 July 1940 (Air 16/955 records, National Archives).
140. Notes 133 and 134, *op. cit.*
141. Note 133, *op. cit.*
142. Mason, Francis K., *op. cit.* (pp. 198-199); Shipman, John, *op. cit.* (p. 85).
143. Notes 133 and 134, *op. cit.*
144. Note 134, *op. cit.*
145. Brew, Steve, *op. cit.* (pp. 125-128).
146. Squadron Commander's Report on Flying Battle Casualty, F/Sgt C. J. Cooney, 56 Squadron, 29 July 1940 (Air 81 records, National Archives).
147. Wallens, R. W. 'Wally', *Flying Made My Arms Ache* (Upton-upon-Severn: The Self-Publishing Association Ltd., 1990) (pp. 119-120).
148. *ibid.*
149. Brew, Steve, *op. cit.* (pp. 125-128).
150. *ibid.*
151. Ramsey, Winston G. (ed.), *op. cit.* (*Luftwaffe* entry for 29 July 1940).
152. Brew, Steve, *op. cit.* (pp. 125-128).
153. *ibid.*
154. IPR, 41 Squadron, 29 July 1940 (Air 16/955 records, National Archives).
155. Squadron Commander's Report on Flying Battle Casualty, F/O D. H. Gamblen, 41 Squadron, 29 July 1940 (Air 81 records, National Archives); IPR, 41 Squadron, 29 July 1940 (Air 16/955 records, National Archives).
156. Wallens, R. W. 'Wally', *op. cit.* (pp. 119-120); Thomas, Nick, 2011, *op. cit.* (pp. 104-108).
157. Thomas, Nick, 2011, *op. cit.* (pp. 104-108).
158. Wallens, R. W. 'Wally', *op. cit.* (pp. 119-120).
159. Osterkamp, Theo, *op. cit.* (pp. 318-323).

160. IPR, 41 Squadron, 29 July 1940 (Air 16/955 records, National Archives); CR, P/O G. H. Bennions, 41 Squadron, 29 July 1940 (Air 50 records, National Archives), copy in Thomas, Nick, 2011, *op. cit.* (pp. 104-108).

161. *ibid.*

162. *ibid.*

163. *ibid.*

164. Ramsey, Winston G. (ed.), *op. cit.* (RAF entry for 29 July 1940).

165. Thomas, Nick, 2011, *op. cit.* (pp. 104-108); IPR, 41 Squadron, 29 July 1940 (Air 16/955 records, National Archives).

166. Note 164, *op. cit.*

167. Thomas, Nick, 2011, *op. cit.* (pp. 104-108); Brew, Steve, *op. cit.* (pp. 125-128).

168. Brew, Steve, *op. cit.* (pp. 125-128).

169. *ibid.*

170. IPR, 41 Squadron, 29 July 1940 (Air 16/955 records, National Archives).

171. Note 167, *op. cit.*

172. Brew, Steve, *op. cit.* (pp. 125-128).

173. Ramsey, Winston G. (ed.), *op. cit.* (RAF entry for 29 July 1940); Brew, Steve, *op. cit.* (pp. 125-128).

174. Website, Wood, Tony, *op. cit.*

175. *ibid.*

176. *ibid.*

177. IPR, 41 Squadron, 29 July 1940 (Air 16/955 records, National Archives).

178. Brew, Steve, *op. cit.* (pp. 125-128); Ramsey, Winston G. (ed.), *op. cit.* (*Luftwaffe* entry for 29 July 1940).

179. Ramsey, Winston G. (ed.), *op. cit.* (*Luftwaffe* entry for 29 July 1940).

180. Aders, Gebhard and Held, Werner, *op. cit.* (p. 58).

181. Marek J. Murawski, *Messerschmitt Bf 109 A-D*, article on Kagero Publishing website, www.kagero.pl.

182. Note 160, *op. cit.*

183. *ibid.*

184. MacDonell, Donald, *From Dogfight to Diplomacy: A Spitfire Pilot's Log 1932-1958* (Barnsley: Pen and Sword, 2009) (p. 52).

185. Morgan, M. S., *The Southern Gate: RAF Kenley during the Battle of Britain* (Independently published, 2021) (pp. 22-23); Wynn, Kenneth G., *Men of the Battle of Britain: a Biographical Directory of the Few* (Barnsley: Frontline, 2015; West Malling: The Battle of Britain Memorial Trust, 2015) (p. 335).

186. Website dedicated to the memory of Squadron Leader James Joseph "Orange" O'Meara D.S.O., D.F.C., jjomeara.com. Website no longer accessible.

187. Wikipedia, Adrian Francis Laws, en.wikipedia.org/wiki/Adrian_Francis_Laws; Thomas, Nick, 2016, *op. cit.*

188. Ramsey, Winston G. (ed.), *op. cit.* (RAF entry for 29 July 1940).
189. *ibid.*
190. IPR, 501 Squadron, 29 July 1940 (Air 16/955 records, National Archives).
191. *ibid.*
192. *ibid.*
193. Cull, Brian, *op. cit.* (pp. 203-206).
194. IPR, 41 Squadron, 29 July 1940 (Air 16/955 records, National Archives).
195. IPR, 501 Squadron, 29 July 1940 (Air 16/955 records, National Archives).
196. Cull, Brian, *op. cit.* (pp. 203-206).
197. Darlow, Steve, *Five of the Few* (London: Grub Street, 2010) (p. 27).
198. CR, P/O K. N. T. Lee, 501 Squadron, 29 July 1940 (Air 50 records, National Archives), copy in: Darlow, Steve, *op. cit.* (p. 34); IPR, 501 Squadron, 29 July 1940 (Air 16/955 records, National Archives).
199. *ibid.*
200. IPR, 501 Squadron, 29 July 1940 (Air 16/955 records, National Archives); Saunders, Andy, *op. cit.* (pp. 39-43); Ramsey, Winston G. (ed.), *op. cit.* (RAF entry for 29 July 1940).
201. Note 198, *op. cit.*
202. Saunders, Andy, *op. cit.* (pp. 39-43).
203. Note 198, *op. cit.*
204. Website, Wood, Tony, *op. cit.*
205. Ramsey, Winston G. (ed.), *op. cit.* (*Luftwaffe* entry for 29 July 1940).
206. Saunders, Andy, *op. cit.* (pp. 39-43).
207. IPR, 501 Squadron, 29 July 1940 (Air 16/955 records, National Archives); Ramsey, Winston G. (ed.), *op. cit.* (RAF entry for 29 July 1940).
208. Ramsey, Winston G. (ed.), *op. cit.* (*Luftwaffe* entry for 29 July 1940).
209. Cull, Brian, *op. cit.* (pp. 203-206).
210. *ibid.*
211. Saunders, Andy, *op. cit.* (pp. 39-43); Cull, Brian, *op. cit.* (pp. 203-206).
212. IPR, 56 Squadron, 29 July 1940 (Air 16/955 records, National Archives); Cull, Brian, *op. cit.* (pp. 203-206).
213. Squadron Commander's Report on Flying Battle Casualty, F/Sgt C. J. Cooney, 56 Squadron, 29 July 1940 (Air 81 records, National Archives); Brew, Steve, *op. cit.* (pp. 125-128); IPR, 56 Squadron, 29 July 1940 (Air 16/955 records, National Archives).
214. IPR, 56 Squadron, 29 July 1940 (Air 16/955 records, National Archives).
215. Rall, Günther, *op. cit.* (p. 54).
216. Barbas, Bernd, *op. cit.* (p. 22, p. 326).
217. IPR, 56 Squadron, 29 July 1940 (Air 16/955 records, National Archives).
218. *ibid.*
219. *ibid.*
220. Ramsey, Winston G. (ed.), *op. cit.* (*Luftwaffe* entry for 29 July 1940).
221. Note 213, *op. cit.*

222. IPR, 56 Squadron, 29 July 1940 (Air 16/955 records, National Archives).

223. IPR, 56 Squadron, 29 July 1940 (Air 16/955 records, National Archives); Ramsey, Winston G. (ed.), *op. cit.* (RAF entry for 29 July 1940).

224. See detailed discussions by Brimmicombe-Wood, Lee on his game website, *The Burning Blue*, airbattle.co.uk, particularly his research notes, p. 3.

225. Rall, Günther, *op. cit.* (p. 54).

226. Barbas, Bernd, *op. cit.* (p. 22).

227. Rejected at unit level: Barbas, Bernd, *op. cit.* (p. 326); Website, Wood, Tony, *op. cit.*, comprises essentially confirmed successes while also listing rejections (and probables), shows the two confirmed victories but only two of the four rejected claims.

228. Bergström, Christer, *op. cit.* (p. 89); Saunders, Andy, *op. cit.* (pp. 39-43).

229. Mason, Francis K., *op. cit.* (pp. 199-200); Saunders, Andy, *Convoy Peewit; August 8, 1940: The first day of the Battle of Britain?* (London: Grub Street, 2010) (pp. 204-205).

230. Website, *The Battle of Britain Historical Timeline*, battleofbritain1940. com/entry/Monday-29-july-1940.

231. Ramsey, Winston G. (ed.), *op. cit.* (*Luftwaffe* entry for 29 July 1940).

232. IPR, 610 Squadron, 29 July 1940 (Air 16/955 records, National Archives).

233. IPR, 610 Squadron, 29 July 1940 (Air 16/955 records, National Archives); CRs, F/Lt E. B. B. Smith, F/O S. C. Norris, Sgt R. F. Hamlyn, 610 Squadron, 29 July 1940 (Air 50 records, National Archives), copies in: Bailey, David J., *610 (County of Chester) Auxiliary Air Force Squadron, 1936-1940* (Stroud: Fonthill, 2018) (pp. 274-279).

234. Bailey, David J., *op. cit.* (pp. 274-279).

235. Ramsey, Winston G. (ed.), *op. cit.* (*Luftwaffe* entry for 29 July 1940).

236. IPR, 603 Squadron, 29 July 1940 (Air 16/955 records, National Archives).

237. Cull, Brian, *op. cit.* (p. 212).

238. Cull, Brian, *op. cit.* (p. 215); Website, Holm, Michael, *op. cit.*; Ramsey, Winston G. (ed.), *op. cit.* (*Luftwaffe* entry for 29 July 1940).

239. IPR, 66 Squadron, Blue Section, 29 July 1940 (Air 16/955 records, National Archives).

240. *ibid.*

241. *ibid.*

242. IPR, 17 Squadron, 29 July 1940 (Air 16/955 records, National Archives).

243. *ibid.*

244. *ibid.*

245. Cull, Brian, *op. cit.* (p. 215).

246. IPR, 17 Squadron, 29 July 1940 (Air 16/955 records, National Archives).

247. IPR, 85 Squadron, 29 July 1940 (Air 16/955 records, National Archives).

248. *ibid.*

249. *ibid.*

250. *ibid.*

251. Ramsey, Winston G. (ed.), *op. cit.* (*Luftwaffe* entry for 29 July 1940).
252. Vasco, John, *op. cit.* (pp. 19-20).
253. IPR, 66 Squadron, Green Section, 29 July 1940 (Air 16/955 records, National Archives).
254. *ibid.*
255. *ibid.*
256. Ramsey, Winston G. (ed.), *op. cit.* (RAF entry for 29 July 1940).
257. Cull, Brian, *op. cit.* (p. 215).
258. Website, Holdoway, Mike, *Convoy Web*; www.convoyweb.org.uk.
259. Website, *Wrecksite*: www.wrecksite.eu/wreck.aspx?31585.
260. Vasco, John, *op. cit.* (pp. 19-20).
261. *ibid.*
262. *ibid.*
263. Cull, Brian, *op. cit.* (p. 208).
264. Vasco, John, *op. cit.* (pp. 19-20 and pp. 163-164).
265. Vasco, John, *op. cit.* (pp. 19-20).
266. Erich Beudel's account in: ORB, 151 Squadron, 14 September 1940 (Air 27 records, National Archives); Vasco, John, *op. cit.* (pp. 19-20); see also, Cull, Brian, *op. cit.* (pp. 208-9).
267. Vasco, John, *op. cit.* (pp. 19-20).
268. *ibid.*
269. *ibid.*
270. *ibid.*
271. *ibid.*
272. Wood, Derek and Dempster, Derek, *op. cit.* (p. 262).
273. Website, *Battle of Britain London Monument*, bbm.org.uk/airmen/Whittingham.htm; IPR, 151 Squadron, 29 July 1940 (Air 16/955 records, National Archives); Vasco, John, *op. cit.* (pp. 19-20).
274. IPR, 151 Squadron, 29 July 1940 (Air 16/955 records, National Archives); Vasco, John, *op. cit.* (pp. 19-20); Cull, Brian, *op. cit.* (pp. 208-209).
275. Cull, Brian, *op. cit.* (pp. 212-213); IPR, 151 Squadron, 29 July 1940 (Air 16/955 records, National Archives); Website, *Battle of Britain London Monument*, bbm.org.uk/airmen/Whittingham.htm; Ramsey, Winston G. (ed.), *op. cit.* (RAF entry for 29 July 1940); Wynn, Kenneth G., *op. cit.* (p. 48).
276. Wynn, Kenneth G., *op. cit.* (p. 561).
277. Note 266, *op. cit.*
278. ORB, 151 Squadron, 14 September 1940 (Air 27 records, National Archives).
279. ORB, 151 Squadron, 14 September 1940 (Air 27 records, National Archives); Ramsey, Winston G. (ed.), *op. cit.* (*Luftwaffe* entry for 29 July 1940).
280. Cull, Brian, *op. cit.* (pp. 208-209); Vasco, John, *op. cit.* (pp. 19-20); Bergström, Christer, *op. cit.* (p. 89); Website, Wood, Tony, *op. cit.*
281. Hewitt, Nick, *Coastal Convoys 1939-1945: the Indestructible Highway* (Barnsley: Pen and Sword Maritime, 2019) (p. 97).

282. Saunders, Andy, 2013, *op. cit.* (p. 43); Hewitt, Nick, *op. cit.* (p. 97).

9. 30 July-7 August 1940: single aircraft actions and Me 109 incursions; Osterkamp's tactics succeed and fail in Eastern Channel

1. IPR, 603 Squadron, 30 July 1940 (Air 16/955 records, National Archives).
2. *ibid.*
3. *ibid.*
4. *ibid.*
5. IPR, 603 Squadron, 30 July 1940 (Air 16/955 records, National Archives); Cull, Brian, *Battle for the Channel* (Stroud: Fonthill, 2017) (pp. 215-219).
6. Vasco, John, *Messerschmitt Bf 110 Bombsights over England: Erprobungsgruppe 210 in the Battle of Britain* (Atglen: Schiffer, 2002) (p. 20).
7. Vasco, John, *op. cit.* (p. 20); IPR, 85 Squadron, 30 July 1940 (Air 16/955 records, National Archives).
8. IPR, 85 Squadron, 30 July 1940 (Air 16/955 records, National Archives).
9. *ibid.*
10. *ibid.*
11. Note 7, *op. cit.*
12. Cull, Brian, *op. cit.* (p. 219); Ramsey, Winston G. (ed.), *The Battle of Britain: Then and Now* (London: Battle of Britain Prints International Ltd., 1982) (*Luftwaffe* entry for 30 July 1940).
13. IPR, 111 Squadron, 31 July 1940 (Air 16/955 records, National Archives).
14. *ibid.*
15. *ibid.*
16. *ibid.*
17. Archives, Imperial War Museum, London: *Luftwaffe Quartermaster General Loss Returns*; Cull, Brian, *op. cit.* (p. 223); Mason, Francis K., *Battle over Britain* (London: McWhirter Twins, 1969) (p. 202).
18. CR, F/O A. Ostowicz , 145 Squadron, 31 July 1940 (Air 50 records, National Archives), copy in: Gretzyngier, Robert, *Poles in Defence of Britain: A Day-by-Day Chronology of Polish Day and Night Fighter Pilot Operations: July 1940–June 1941* (London: Grub Street, 2016) (p. 9); IPR, 145 Squadron, 31 July 1940 (Air 16/955 records, National Archives).
19. *ibid.*
20. *Luftwaffe Quartermaster General Loss Returns, op. cit.*
21. IPR, 1 Squadron, 31 July 1940 (Air 16/955 records, National Archives); Shaw, Michael, *Twice Vertical: The History of No. 1 (Fighter) Squadron RAF* (London: Macdonald, 1971) (p. 153).
22. *ibid.*
23. *ibid.*
24. Knight, Dennis, *Harvest of Messerschmitts: The Chronicle of a Village at War, 1940* (London: Frederick Warne, 1981) (p. 82).

25. James, T. Cecil G., *The Battle of Britain* (Abingdon: Routledge, 2012) (p. 37); Mason, Francis K., *op. cit.* (pp. 201-202).

26. *ibid.*

27. Mason, Francis K., *op. cit.* (pp. 201-202).

28. IPR, 74 Squadron, 31 July 1940 (Air 16/955 records, National Archives).

29. Wynn, Kenneth G., *Men of the Battle of Britain: A Biographical Directory of the Few* (Barnsley: Frontline, 2015; West Malling: The Battle of Britain Memorial Trust, 2015) (p. 286).

30. IPR, 74 Squadron, 31 July 1940 (Air 16/955 records, National Archives).

31. IPR, 74 Squadron, 31 July 1940 (Air 16/955 records, National Archives); Knight, Dennis, *op. cit.* (p. 82); Cull, Brian, *op. cit.* (pp. 223-225).

32. Aders, Gebhard and Held, Werner, *Jagdgeschwader 51 'Mölders'* (Stuttgart: Motorbuch, 1985) (p. 249); Website, Wood, Tony, *Tony Wood's Combat Claims and Casualties Lists*: accessed via Don Caldwell's website: don-caldwell.we.bs/claims/tonywood.htm; Cull, Brian, *op. cit.* (pp. 223-225).

33. Knight, Dennis, *op. cit.* (p. 82 and pp. 85-86).

34. IPR, 74 Squadron, 31 July 1940 (Air 16/955 records, National Archives); Knight, Dennis, *op. cit.* (p. 82); Tidy, Douglas, *I Fear No Man: The History of No. 74 (Fighter) Squadron Royal Flying Corps and Royal Air Force (The Tigers)* (Cape Town: Purnell, 1972) (pp. 80-82).

35. Note 34, *op. cit.*; Ramsey, Winston G. (ed.), *op. cit.* (RAF entry for 31 July 1940).

36. Rideout, Brian, article on P/O Gunn in the Remembrance Edition of The Haltonian, news magazine of The RAF Halton Apprentices Association, oldhaltonians.co.uk; copy accessed via Tiger News No. 62, May 2013, of the No. 74 (F) Tiger Squadron Association, www.74squadron.org.uk; Wynn, Kenneth G., *op. cit.* (p. 211).

37. IPR, 74 Squadron, 31 July 1940 (Air 16/955 records, National Archives).

38. *Luftwaffe Quartermaster General Loss Returns, op. cit.*

39. Website, Wood, Tony, *op. cit.*

40. IPR, 501 Squadron, 31 July 1940 (Air 16/955 records, National Archives).

41. *ibid.*

42. *ibid.*

43. Note 40, *op. cit.*; Ramsey, Winston G. (ed.), *op. cit.* (RAF entry for 31 July 1940).

44. Note 40, *op. cit.*

45. Cull, Brian, *op. cit.* (pp. 230-250); Mason, Francis K., *op. cit.* (pp. 206-213); Ramsey, Winston G. (ed.), *op. cit.* (entries for 1–7 August 1940).

46. IPRs, 607 and 616 Squadrons, 1 August 1940 (Air 16/955 records, National Archives).

47. Mason, Francis K., *op. cit.* (p. 207).

48. Mason, Francis K., *op. cit.* (p. 206); Cull, Brian, *op. cit.* (pp. 226).

49. Mason, Francis K., *op. cit.* (p. 207); IPR, 242 Squadron, 1 August 1940 (Air 16/955 records, National Archives); *Luftwaffe Quartermaster General Loss Returns, op. cit.*

50. IPR, 145 Squadron, 1 August 1940 (Air 16/955 records, National Archives); Cull, Brian, *op. cit.* (p. 227, p. 232).

51. IPR, 145 Squadron, 1 August 1940 (Air 16/955 records, National Archives); Cull, Brian, *op. cit.* (pp. 227-228); Mason, Francis K., *op. cit.* (p. 206).

52. IPR, 19 Squadron, 2 August 1940 (Air 16/955 records, National Archives).

53. *Luftwaffe Quartermaster General Loss Returns, op. cit.*

54. IPR, 66 Squadron, 2 August 1940 (Air 16/955 records, National Archives); Cull, Brian, *op. cit.* (p. 233).

55. Mason, Francis K., *op. cit.* (pp. 209-210); Cull, Brian, *op. cit.* (pp. 236-241).

56. IPR, 85 Squadron, 6 August 1940 (Air 16/955 records, National Archives); Mason, Francis K., *op. cit.* (p. 212); Cull, Brian, *op. cit.* (pp. 246-247).

57. IPR, 72 Squadron, 6 August 1940 (Air 16/955 records, National Archives).

58. IPR, 616 Squadron, 6 August 1940 (Air 16/955 records, National Archives).

59. Cull, Brian, *op. cit.* (pp. 248-250).

60. Hewitt, Nick, *Coastal Convoys 1939-1945: the Indestructible Highway* (Barnsley: Pen and Sword Maritime, 2019) (pp. 102-103); Mason, Francis K., *op. cit.* (pp. 210-211).

61. IPRs, 64 and 65 Squadrons, 5 August 1940 (Air 16/955 records, National Archives) (take off time for 65 Squadron *c.* 08h50; was one later 65 Squadron IPR this day).

62. *ibid.*

63. Donahue, Arthur G., *Tally-Ho! Yankee in a Spitfire* (New York: McMillan, 1941) (p. 35); Kershaw, Alex, *The Few* (London: Penguin, 2008) (pp. 82-86).

64. IPR, 65 Squadron, 5 August 1940 (Air 16/955 records, National Archives) (take off time *c.* 08h50).

65. *ibid.*

66. *ibid.*

67. *ibid.*

68. Website, Wood, Tony, *op. cit.*

69. Note 61, *op cit.*

70. Note 64, *op cit.*

71. *Luftwaffe Quartermaster General Loss Returns, op. cit.*; Ramsey, Winston G. (ed.), *op. cit.* (*Luftwaffe* entry for 5 August 1940).

72. Aders, Gebhard and Held, Werner, *op. cit.* (pp. 63-64).

73. Website, Wood, Tony, *op. cit.*

74. IPR, 64 Squadron, 5 August 1940 (Air 16/955 records, National Archives).

75. Kershaw, Alex, *op. cit.* (pp. 82-86).

76. *ibid.*

77. IPR, 64 Squadron, 5 August 1940 (Air 16/955 records, National Archives).

78. Ramsey, Winston G. (ed.), *op. cit.* (RAF entry for 5 August 1940).

79. For example: Wynn, Kenneth G., *op. cit.* (pp. 265-266).

80. Mann, Jackie and Mann, Sunnie with Stimson, Tess, *Yours till the End* (London: Mandarin, 1992) (p. 134).

81. Website, Wood, Tony, *op. cit.*

82. IPR, 64 Squadron, 5 August 1940 (Air 16/955 records, National Archives).

83. *ibid.*

84. *ibid.*

85. *ibid.*

86. *ibid.*

87. Ramsey, Winston G. (ed.), *op. cit.* (*Luftwaffe* entry for 5 August 1940); *Luftwaffe Quartermaster General Loss Returns, op. cit.*; Goss, Chris, *Luftwaffe Fighters' Battle of Britain* (Manchester: Crécy, 2010) (p. 32); Held, Werner, Trautloft, Hannes and Bob, Ekkehard, *Die Grünherzjäger: Bildchronik des Jagdgeschwaders 54* (Friedberg: Podzun-Pallas-Verlag, 1985) (p. 68).

88. MacDonell, Donald, *From Dogfight to Diplomacy: A Spitfire Pilot's Log 1932-1958* (Barnsley: Pen and Sword, 2009) (p. 52); Note 80, *op. cit.*

89. Note 82, *op. cit.*

90. Kershaw, Alex, *op. cit.* (pp. 82-86); IPR, 64 Squadron, 5 August 1940 (Air 16/955 records, National Archives); Cull, Brian, *op. cit.* (p. 242).

91. IPR, 64 Squadron, 5 August 1940 (Air 16/955 records, National Archives); Kershaw, Alex, *op. cit.* (pp. 82-86).

92. *ibid.*

93. *ibid.*

94. Website, Wood, Tony, *op. cit.*

95. *ibid.*

96. IPR, 65 Squadron, 5 August 1940 (Air 16/955 records, National Archives) (take off time *c.* 12h00; was one earlier 65 Squadron IPR this day).

97. *ibid.*

98. *ibid.*

99. Brew, Steve, *Blood, Sweat and Courage: 41 Squadron RAF 1939-1942* (Stroud: Fonthill, 2014) (pp. 131-132).

100. IPR, 151 Squadron, 5 August 1940 (Air 16/955 records, National Archives); Cull, Brian, *op. cit.* (p. 244).

101. IPR, 151 Squadron, 5 August 1940 (Air *16/955* records, National Archives).

102. IPR, 151 Squadron, 5 August 1940 (Air *16/955* records, National Archives); CR, Sub Lt H. W. Beggs, 151 Squadron, 5 August 1940 (Air 50 records, National Archives), copy in: Cull, Brian, *op. cit.* (p. 243).

103. Brew, Steve, *op. cit.* (pp. 131-132).

104. *ibid.*

105. *ibid.*

106. *ibid.*

107. IPR, 151 Squadron, 5 August 1940 (Air *16/955* records, National Archives).

108. Cull, Brian, *op. cit.* (pp. 243-244).

109. Ramsey, Winston G. (ed.), *op. cit.* (*Luftwaffe* entry for 5 August 1940); *Luftwaffe Quartermaster General Loss Returns, op. cit.*

110. Cull, Brian, *op. cit.* (p. 244).

111. Note 109, *op. cit.*; Aders, Gebhard and Held, Werner, *op. cit.* (pp. 63-64).

112. Website, Wood, Tony, *op. cit.*; Aders, Gebhard and Held, Werner, *op. cit.* (pp. 63-64).

10. Some analysis of Fighter Command squadron tactics: 1 July-7 August 1940

1. Orange, Vincent, *Dowding of Fighter Command: Victor of the Battle of Britain* (London: Grub Street, 2011) (p. 121).

2. Orange, Vincent, *op. cit.*; Ray, John, *The Battle of Britain: Dowding and the First Victory, 1940* (London: Cassell, 2002).

3. Ray, John, *op. cit.* (pp. 109-110).

4. Orange, Vincent, *op. cit.* (p. 189).

5. Mason, Francis K., *Battle over Britain* (London: McWhirter Twins, 1969) (pp. 195-196).

6. Wallens, R. W. 'Wally', *Flying Made My Arms Ache* (Upton-upon-Severn: The Self-Publishing Association Ltd., 1990) (p. 118).

7. Parker, Nigel, *Luftwaffe Crash Archive, Vol. 1, 1st September 1939 to 14th August 1940* (Walton on Thames: Red Kite Books, Air Research Publications, 2013); and successive volumes: *Vol. 2, 15th August 1940 to 29th August 1940*, 2013; *Vol. 3, 30th August 1940 to 9th September 1940*, 2013; *Vol. 4, 10th September 1940 to 27th September 1940*, 2014.

8. *ibid.*

9. *ibid.*

10. *ibid.*

11. *ibid.*

Bibliography

Aders, Gebhard and Held, Werner, *Jagdgeschwader 51 'Mölders'* (Stuttgart: Motorbuch, 1985)

Alexander, Kristen, *Australia's Few and the Battle of Britain* (Barnsley: Pen and Sword, 2015)

Bailey, David J., *610 (County of Chester) Auxiliary Air Force Squadron, 1936-1940* (Stroud: Fonthill, 2018)

Barbas, Bernd, *Die Geschichte der I. Gruppe des Jagdgeschwaders 52* (Überlingen: self-published, undated)

Barbas, Bernd, *Die Geschichte der III. Gruppe des Jagdgeschwaders 52* (Überlingen: self-published, undated)

Batt, L. Gordon, *Scramble! A Flying Memoir of one of the Few* (Gunthorpe: The Battle of Britain Historical Society, 2001)

Bergström, Christer, *The Battle of Britain: An Epic Conflict Revisited* (Oxford: Casemate, 2015 and Eskilstuna: Vaktel, 2015)

Bickers, Richard Townshend, and co-authors, *The Battle of Britain: The Greatest Battle in the History of Air Warfare* (London: Salamander, 1990)

Bishop, Patrick, *Battle of Britain* (London: Quercus, 2010)

Bolitho, Hector, *Combat Report: The Story of a Fighter Pilot* (London: B. T. Batsford, 1943)

Brew, Steve, *Blood, Sweat and Courage: 41 Squadron RAF 1939-1942* (Stroud: Fonthill, 2014)

Bungay, Stephen, *The Most Dangerous Enemy* (London: Aurum Press, 2009)

Burt, Danny, *A Battle of Britain Spitfire Squadron: The Men and Machines of 152 Squadron in the Summer of 1940* (Barnsley: Pen and Sword, 2018)

Caldwell, Donald L., *JG 26: Top Guns of the Luftwaffe* (New York: Orion Books, 1991)

Caldwell, Donald L., *JG 26 Luftwaffe Fighter Wing Diary, 1939-1942*, Vol. 1 (Mechanicsburg: Stackpole Books, 2012)

Churchill, Winston, S., *The Second World War, vol. II, Their Finest Hour* (London: Cassell, 1949)

Crook, David M., *Spitfire Pilot* (London: Grub Street, 2010)

Cull, Brian, *First of the Few* (Stroud: Fonthill, 2013)

Cull, Brian, *Battle for the Channel* (Stroud: Fonthill, 2017)

Cumming, Anthony, *The Royal Navy and the Battle of Britain* (Annapolis, Maryland: Naval Institute Press, 2013)

Dalton-Morgan, Tom, *Tommy Leader* (Wendover: Griffon International, 2007)

Darlow, Steve, *Five of the Few* (London: Grub Street, 2010)

Deere, Alan C., *Nine Lives* (London: Coronet, 1974)

Deighton, Len, *Fighter: The True Story of the Battle of Britain* (St Albans: Triad/Panther, 1979)

Dierich, Wolfgang, *Kampfgeschwader 51 "Edelweiss"* (Stuttgart: Motorbuch Verlag, 1974)

Donahue, Arthur G., *Tally-Ho! Yankee in a Spitfire* (New York: McMillan, 1941)

Dowding, Air Chief Marshal Sir Hugh C. T., *The Battle of Britain* (London: HMSO, 1946)

Eriksson, Patrick G., *Alarmstart* (Stroud: Amberley, 2017)

Foreman, John, *RAF Fighter Command Air Victory Claims of World War Two, Part One 1939-1940* (Walton-on-Thames: Red Kite, 2003)

Franks, Norman L., *Double Mission: RAF fighter Ace and SOE Agent: Manfred Czernin, DSO, MC, DFC* (London: William Kimber, 1976)

Franks, Norman L. R., *Royal Air Force Fighter Command Losses of the Second World War, Volume 1, Operational Losses: Aircraft and Crews 1939-1941* (Leicester: Midland, 1997)

Galland, Adolf, *The First and the Last* (London: Fontana/Collins, 1970)

Gleed, Ian, *Arise to Conquer* (London: Severn House, 1975)

Goss, Chris, *Luftwaffe Fighters' Battle of Britain* (Manchester: Crécy, 2010)

Goss, Chris, *Dornier Do 17 Units of World War 2* (Oxford: Osprey, 2019)

Gretzyngier, Robert, *Poles in Defence of Britain: A Day-by-Day Chronology of Polish Day and Night Fighter Pilot Operations: July 1940–June 1941* (London: Grub Street, 2016)

Gustin, Emmanuel and Williams, Anthony G., *Flying Guns: The Development of Aircraft Guns, Ammunition and Installations, 1933-45* (Shrewsbury: Airlife, 2003)

Harkins, Hugh, *Defiant Mk. I Combat Log: Fighter Command May–September 1940* (Glasgow: Centurion Publishing, 2014)

Held, Werner, Trautloft, Hannes and Bob, Ekkehard, *Die Grünherzjäger: Bildchronik des Jagdgeschwaders 54* (Friedberg: Podzun-Pallas-Verlag, 1985)

Hewitt, Nick, *Coastal Convoys 1939-1945: the Indestructible Highway* (Barnsley: Pen and Sword Maritime, 2019)

Holland, James, *The Battle of Britain; Five Months that Changed History May-October 1940* (London: Corgi, 2011)

Hough, Richard and Richards, Denis, *The Battle of Britain* (Sevenoaks: Coronet, 1990)

Hunt, Leslie, *Twenty-One Squadrons: The History of the Royal Auxiliary Air Force: 1925-1957* (London: Garnstone Press, 1972)

James, T. Cecil G., *The Battle of Britain* (Abingdon: Routledge, 2012)

Jullian, Marcel, *The Battle of Britain* (London: Jonathan Cape, 1967)

Kaplan, Philip, *Fighter Aces of the RAF in the Battle of Britain* (Philadelphia, Pennsylvania: Casemate, 2008)

Kershaw, Alex, *The Few* (London: Penguin, 2008)

Kiehl, Heinz, *Kampfgeschwader 53 "Legion Condor": The Complete History of KG 53 in World War II* (Atglen: Schiffer, 2013)

Kimbell, Andrew, *The One History Forgot: David Alwyne Pemberton – A Life Story* (Independently published, 2018)

Knight, Dennis, *Harvest of Messerschmitts: The Chronicle of a Village at War, 1940* (London: Frederick Warne, 1981)

Lanchbery, Edward, *Against the Sun* (London: Pan, 1957)

Lucas, Laddie, *Out of the Blue* (London: Hutchinson, 1985)

MacDonell, Donald, *From Dogfight to Diplomacy: A Spitfire Pilot's Log 1932-1958* (Barnsley: Pen and Sword, 2009)

Mahlke, Helmut, *Memoirs of a Stuka Pilot* (London: Frontline, 2013)

Mann, Jackie, Mann, Sunnie with Stimson, Tess, *Yours till the End* (London: Mandarin, 1992)

Mason, Francis K., *Battle over Britain* (London: McWhirter Twins, 1969)

McKee, Alexander, *Strike from the Sky* (London: New English Library, 1969)

McKinstry, Leo, *Hurricane: Victor of the Battle of Britain* (London: John Murray, 2011)

Mombeek, Eric, Wadman, David and Creek, Eddie J., *Jagdwaffe: Battle of Britain: Phase One: July–August 1940 (Luftwaffe Colours: Volume Two, Section 1)* (Crowborough: Classic Publications, 2001)

Mombeek, Eric and Roba, Jean-Louis, with Goss, Chris, *Am Himmel Frankreichs; die Geschichte des JG 2 "Richthofen", Band 2: 1940-1941* (Linkebeek: ASBL La Porte d'Hoves, 2013)

Morgan, Eric B. and Shacklady, Edward, *Spitfire: The History* (Stamford: Key Publishing, 1987)

Morgan, M. S., *The Southern Gate: RAF Kenley during the Battle of Britain* (Independently published, 2021)

Newton, Dennis, *A Spitfire Pilot's Story: Pat Hughes Battle of Britain Top Gun* (Stroud: Amberley, 2016)

Nowarra, Heinz J., *Luftschlacht um England: Verlorener Sieg* (Friedberg: Podzun-Pallas-Verlag, 1978)

Obermaier, Ernst, *Die Ritterkreuzträger der Luftwaffe* (Mainz: Verlag Dieter Hoffmann, 1966)

Orange, Vincent, *Dowding of Fighter Command: Victor of the Battle of Britain* (London: Grub Street, 2011)

Orange, Vincent, *Park; the Biography of Air Chief Marshal Sir Keith Park* (London: Grub Street, 2013)

Osterkamp, Theo, *Durch Höhen und Tiefen jagt ein Herz* (Heidelberg: Kurt Vowinckel Verlag, 1952)

Page, Geoffrey, *Tale of a Guinea Pig* (London: Corgi, 1983)

Parker, Nigel, *Luftwaffe Crash Archive, Vol. 1, 1st September 1939 to 14th August 1940* (Walton on Thames: Red Kite Books, Air Research Publications, 2013)

Parker, Nigel, *Luftwaffe Crash Archive, Vol. 2, 15th August 1940 to 29th August 1940* (Walton on Thames: Red Kite Books, Air Research Publications, 2013)

Parker, Nigel, *Luftwaffe Crash Archive, Vol. 3, 30th August 1940 to 9th September 1940* (Walton on Thames: Red Kite Books, Air Research Publications, 2013)

Parker, Nigel, *Luftwaffe Crash Archive, Vol. 4, 10th September 1940 to 27th September 1940* (Walton on Thames: Red Kite Books, Air Research Publications, 2014)

Parry, Simon W., *Battle of Britain Combat Archive, Vol. 1, 10 July–22 July 1940* (Walton on Thames: Red Kite Books, 2015)

Pitchfork, Graham, *Shot Down in the Drink: True Stories of RAF and Commonwealth Aircrews Saved from the Sea in WWII* (Oxford: Osprey, 2017)

Price, Alfred, *The Hardest Day; the Battle of Britain 18 August 1940* (London: Arrow Books, 1990)

Prien, Jochen, *Geschichte des Jagdgeschwaders 77, Teil 1, 1934-1941* (Eutin: Struve-Druck, 1992)

Prien, Jochen and Stemmer, Gerhard, *Messerschmitt Bf 109 im Einsatz bei der III./Jagdgeschwader 3* (Eutin: Struve-Druck, 1995)

Priller, Josef, *J.G. 26: Geschichte eines Jagdgeschwaders* (Stuttgart: Motorbuch Verlag, 1980)

Rall, Günther, *Mein Flugbuch* (Moosburg, Germany: NeunundzwanzigSechs Verlag, 2004)

Ramsey, Winston. G. (ed.), *The Battle of Britain: Then and Now* (London: Battle of Britain Prints International Ltd., 1982)

Ray, John, *The Battle of Britain: Dowding and the First Victory, 1940* (London: Cassell, 2002)

Reeve, Jonathan, *Battle of Britain Voices* (Stroud: Amberley, 2015)

Revell, Alex, *Fighter Aces! The Constable Maxwell Brothers: Fighter Pilots in Two World Wars* (Barnsley: Pen and Sword, 2010)

Ring, Hans and Girbig, Werner, *Jagdgeschwader 27: Die Dokumentation über den Einsatz an allen Fronten 1939-1945* (Stuttgart: Motorbuch Verlag, 1975)

Saunders, Andy, *Convoy Peewit; August 8, 1940: The First Day of the Battle of Britain?* (London: Grub Street, 2010)

Saunders, Andy, *Stuka Attack!* (London: Grub Street, 2013)

Shaw, Michael, *Twice Vertical: The History of No. 1 (Fighter) Squadron RAF* (London: Macdonald, 1971)

Shipman, John, *One of 'The Few': The Memoirs of Wing Commander Ted 'Shippy' Shipman AFC* (Barnsley: Pen & Sword, 2008)

Stokes, Doug, *Wings Aflame: The Biography of Group Captain Victor Beamish DSO and Bar, DFC, AFC* (Manchester: Goodall/Crécy, 1998)

Stones, Donald, *A Pilot's Passion* (Rennes: Adrian Burt, 2014)

Sutton, Barry, *Fighter Boy: Life as a Battle of Britain Pilot* (Stroud: Amberley, 2010)

Thomas, Nick, *Ben Bennions DFC: Battle of Britain Fighter Ace* (Barnsley: Pen & Sword, 2011)

Thomas, Nick, *Hurricane Squadron Ace* (Barnsley: Pen and Sword, 2014)

Thomas, Nick, *Their Finest Hour: Stories of the Men who Won the Battle of Britain* (Barnsley: Pen & Sword, 2016)

Tidy, Douglas, *I fear no Man; the story of No 74 (Fighter) Squadron Royal Flying Corps and Royal Air Force* (Cape Town: Purnell, 1972)

Townsend, Peter, *Duel of Eagles* (London: Weidenfeld and Nicolson, 1970)

Vasco, John, *Messerschmitt Bf 110 Bombsights over England: Erprobungsgruppe 210 in the Battle of Britain* (Atglen: Schiffer, 2002)

Von Eimannsberger, Ludwig, *Zerstörer Gruppe: A History of V./(Z) LG 1 – I./ NJG 3 1939-1941* (Atglen: Schiffer, 1998)

Von Forell, Fritz, *Werner Mölders: Flug zur Sonne; Die Geschichte des grossen Jagdfliegers* (Leoni Am Starnberger See: Druffel Verlag, 1976)

Wallens, R. W. 'Wally', *Flying Made My Arms Ache* (Upton-upon-Severn: The Self-Publishing Association Ltd, 1990)

Wood, Derek and Dempster, Derek, *The Narrow Margin* (London: Arrow Books, 1967)

Wynn, Kenneth G., *Men of the Battle of Britain: A Biographical Directory of the Few* (Barnsley: Frontline, 2015; West Malling: The Battle of Britain Memorial Trust, 2015)

Websites

aufhimmelzuhause.com/id99.htm

Battle of Britain Historical Timeline, battleofbritain1940.com/entry/Saturday-27-july-1940; entry/Monday-29-july-1940

Bond, Bill and others, Battle of Britain Historical Society, *Battle of Britain 1940, Chronology,* battleofbritain1940.net/0022.html, page 22

Brimmicombe-Wood, Lee, *The Burning Blue,* airbattle.co.uk, particularly research notes, p. 3

Chen, Peter C., *World War II Database,* ww2db.com/event/today/7/18/1940

deZeng, Henry L. IV, *Luftwaffe Airfields 1935-1945,* www.ww2.dk/lwairfields.html

deZeng, Henry L. IV and Stankey, Douglas G., *Luftwaffe Officer Career Summaries* (2014 updated version), www.ww2.dk/lwoffz.html

Dix Noonan Webb Auctioneers, archive of past catalogues, dnw.co.uk/auction-archive/past-catalogues/lot.php?auction_id=5338lot_uid=373763

Dorset Crashes dorset.hampshireairfields.co.uk

Edgar, Scott, *Northern Ireland during the Second World War* wartimeni.com/person/john-mcneill

Gloster_Aircraft_Company, en.wikipedia.org/wiki/

Harwich & Dovercourt – A time gone by, harwich_and_dovercourt.co.uk/warships/trawlers/

Helgason, Gudmundur, *uboat.net*, uboat.net/allies/warships/ship/5455.html

Holdoway, Mike, *Convoy Web*, www.convoyweb.org.uk.

Holm, Michael, *The Luftwaffe, 1933-1945*, www.ww2.dk

islandeye.co.uk/history/shipwrecks/Crestflower_hmt.html

Jagdgeschwader 51 "Mölders" Victory Claims 1939-1945, Luftwaffe.cz/jg51_victories.html (last update 19.11.2001)

Kagero Publishing, article by Murawski, Marek J., *Messerschmitt Bf 109 A-D*, www.kagero.pl

Knott, Grahame, *Deeper Dorset*, www.deeperdorset.co.uk, reports by P/Os Beaumont and Williams, and S/L Devitt all of 152 Squadron, and F/Lt Turner of 238 Squadron on the loss of P/O F H Posener, 152 Squadron, on 20 July 1940, all from his RAF Casualty File, Air 81/1163, National Archives; Squadron Commander's Report on Flying Battle Casualty, P/O E J H Sylvester, 501 Squadron, killed 20 July 1940, from his RAF Casualty File, Air 81/1173, National Archives

Lawson, Siri, *warsailors.com*, https://www.warsailors.com/singleships/Kollskegg.html

lewistributes-3945.blogspot.com/2011/08/alexander-maciver-41b-north-tolsta.html

No 74 (F) Tiger Squadron Association, *Tiger News* No 40, www.74squadron.org.uk, news section, which appears to be an excerpt from an article on P/O Freeborn in *World War II Magazine* by Paul Trickett; *Tiger News* No 62, www.74squadron.org.uk, *Remembrance Edition of The Haltonian*, news magazine of The RAF Halton Apprentices Association (oldhaltonians.co.uk), Rideout, Brian, article on P/O Gunn

pinterest.com/pin/532409987179110049/, pilot's logbook, F/Lt Hugh Ironside, 151 Squadron, pages for 9 July 1940

Pocock, Michael W., *Maritime Quest*, www.maritimequest.com/daily_event_archive/2012/07_july/24_hm_trawler_fleming.htm

Ranter, Harro and Lujan, Fabian, *Aviation Safety Network*, aviation-safety.net/wikibase/229943

Royal Air Force Museum, Elliot, Peter, *Battle of Britain blog, 2015*, on diary entries of P/O John Bisdee, 609 Squadron, https://www.rafmuseum.org.uk/blog/category/john_bisdees_battle_of_britain/

Royal Fleet Auxiliary Historical Society, *Historical RFA*, www.historicalrfa.org

Ships Nostalgia, shipsnostalgia.com/archive/index.php/t-3152.html (web forum)

Smith, Gordon and co-workers, *naval-history.net*, www.naval-history.net/xDKWW2-4007- 20JUL01.htm; www.4007-20JUL02.htm; www.naval-history.net/xGM-Chrono-10DD-15B-HMS_Brazen.htm

The Battle of Britain London Monument, *The Airmen's Stories* – F/Lt R L Smith, www.bbm.org.uk/airmen/SmithRL.htm; – F/Lt T Dalton-Morgan, bbm.org. uk/airmen/Dalton-Morgan.htm; – F/O J F J Haworth, bbm.org.uk/airmen/ Haworth.htm; – P/O C D Whittingham, bbm.org.uk/airmen/Whittingham.htm

The Encyclopaedia of Portland History, www.portlandhistory.co.uk

The King's School, Canterbury Alumni Association, www.oks.org.uk

The memory of Squadron Leader James Joseph "Orange" O'Meara D.S.O., D.F.C., jjomeara.com, no longer accessible

Wikipedia; list of shipwrecks, July 1940, https://en.wikipedia.org/wiki/List_of_ shipwrecks_in_July_1940; coastal guns, Dover Strait, en.wikipedia.org/wiki/ Dover_Strait_coastal_guns; HMS *Wren*, en.wikipedia.org/wiki/HMS_Wren_ (1919); Adrian Francis Laws, en.wikipedia.org/wiki/Adrian_Francis_Laws

Williams, Anthony, G., *The Battle of Britain: Armament of the competing fighters* (2004, revised 2005), Quarryhs.co.uk/BoB.htm

wo2vpr, https://sites.google.com/site/wo2vpr1/home/11-07-1940-avro-anson-oostvoorne

Wood, Tony, *Tony Wood's Combat Claims and Casualties Lists,* don-caldwell. we.bs/claims/tonywood.htm

Wrecksite; www.wrecksite.eu/wreck.aspx?4678; aspx?1257; aspx?1279; aspx?469; aspx?15051; aspx?31585; aspx?283080

Facebook post: Kent Battle of Britain Museum, 11 July 2017; copy of Sgt Arthur Woolley's report on being shot down, 11 July 1940

Archives

UK National Archives, AIR set of records

Air 16/300: RAF Tactical Committee (General) Paper No. 10 (T.C. 10), Air Ministry, 16 December 1940, Unknown author, *German Bombing Formations 1939/40.*

Air 16/635-4A (also in Air 2/7355): RAF Report from Headquarters No. 11 Group to Headquarters Fighter Command, 12 September 1940, Park, Air Vice-Marshal K. R., *German Air Attacks on England – 8th Aug–10th Sept.*

Air 16/955: Fighter Command Combat Reports (also called Form 'F', often sub-headed as Intelligence Patrol Report; one for each action by each squadron, per day). Termed Intelligence Patrol Reports, abbreviated to IPRs, in this volume. Authored mainly by the Squadron Intelligence Officer, and sometimes by the Sector Intelligence Officer.

Air 27: Operations Record Book (also known as Form 540 and Form 541); abbreviated to ORB in this volume. One for each squadron, comprises daily record of aircraft and pilots in action; authored mainly by Squadron Adjutant with input from Intelligence Officer.

Air 40/2397: Air Ministry (A.I.(K)) Prisoner of War Reports; Volume 4, Nos. 101–200, 21 May–24 July 1940.

Air 50: Combat Report (abbreviated to CR in this volume; CRs are generally headed Form 'F', as are IPRs but they are distinct documents). One for each pilot making a claim in each squadron action. Collected by Squadron Intelligence Officer.

Air 81: RAF Casualty Files; include Squadron Commander's Reports on Flying Battle Casualties. One for each personnel or aircraft casualty.

Imperial War Museum

Archives, Imperial War Museum, London: *Luftwaffe Quartermaster General Loss Returns*

Imperial War Museum Sound Archive, World War 1939-1945, London iwm.org.uk/collections/sound; P/O R. L. Jones, IWM Sound Archive item #20497

UK National Archives

National Archives, discovery.nationalarchives.gov.uk/details/r/C10818948

War Cabinet, Weekly Resumé (No. 46) of the Naval, Military, and Air Situation from 12 noon July 11th to 12 noon July 18th, 1940

USA Archives

Declassified CIA document, *German plans for the Invasion of England, 1940; Operation "Sealion".* Declassified Documents RG 263, Entry ZZ17, RC Box #3, RC location 230/902/64/1; downloaded from www.cia.gov; unknown author

Newspapers

Stornoway Gazette, 26 July 1940 and 2 August 1940
Supplement to *The London Gazette,* 4 October 1940, p. 5879

Citations from documents held by national archives

A number of short citations from documents held in the National Archives appear in this book. They are drawn mainly from the following RAF document sets held in the National Archives:

Intelligence Patrol Reports/Fighter Command Combat Reports; Air 16/955;

Operational Record Books; Air 27;

Combat Reports; Air 50;

RAF Casualty Files; Air 81.

The book thus contains public sector information licensed under the Open Government License v.3.0 (http://www.nationalarchives.gov.uk/ information-management/re-using-public-sector-information/uk-government-licensing-framework/).

Acknowledgements

RAF veterans of the Battle of Britain with whom I corresponded provided critical insights into the fighting of the late summer and autumn of 1940. I was greatly privileged to have talked to or corresponded with the following: Sir Douglas Bader, squadron leader of 242 Squadron; Air Commodore Alan Deere, Flight Lieutenant in 54 Squadron, who also sent me a signed copy of his autobiography *Nine Lives*; Air Commodore James Coward, Flying Officer in 19 Squadron; Wing Commander Michael Crossley, who led a flight in and then took command of 32 Squadron; Group Captain David Haysom who led a flight in 79 Squadron; and his compatriot, Air Commodore Edward 'Teddy' Morris, Flying Officer in 79 Squadron. From the *Luftwaffe*, *Oberst* Hanns Trübenbach, erstwhile *Kommandeur* of I/LG 2, and subsequently *Kommodore* of JG 52, a true gentleman and wise warrior, who was totally honest in discussing fighter leadership on the German side, and who gave me his personal copy of Theo Osterkamp's autobiography, *Durch Hohen und Tiefen jagd ein Herz*, amongst other unobtainable volumes.

I received enormous support and very generous help, especially in the form of documents relating to the Battle, from several excellent historians and authors: Nigel Parker and Robert Forsyth (UK), Juha Vaittinen (Finland), and Lothair Vanoverbeke (Belgium). I owe them all a significant debt of gratitude, for friendship, advice and copious quantities of original material. Shaun Barrington of Amberley Publishing is thanked most sincerely for his encouragement, support and ongoing enthusiasm. Kerry Pentz of Penzil Advertising is acknowledged for her drafting skills.

My heartfelt gratitude goes to my wife, Mariánne, a well-published, talented writer and illustrator of her own series of children's books, for her love and support, and for allowing me long absences buried in my study. My brother, Dr Andrew Eriksson, was a great help in many ways: storing back-ups, reading several chapters, and addressing my ignorance of computers. A final thanks to my parents who gave me flying lessons as a youth and provided a critical and growing Second World War library from an early age.

Credits

Illustration 1, first published in Joubert de la Ferté, Philip, *The Third Service* (London: Thames and Hudson, 1955) as Plate 27; original source therein given as the Admiralty; the photograph is thus Crown Copyright, now in the public domain as it is pre-1.6.1957. All photographs from the Imperial War Museum (IWM) are Crown Copyright. Photos from the German Federal Archives (Bundesarchiv) are also in the public domain, under licence CC-BY-SA 3.0. Illustration 21 has few details as to primary source, but the original is held by the Air Historical Branch of the RAF, and is thus Crown Copyright. Illustration 31 has the indicated source: Royal Air Force Battle of Britain campaign diaries, on Wikimedia Commons; it is also Crown Copyright. Illustration 32, source given as Battle of Britain London Monument (https://www.bbm.org.uk/airmen/PageAG.htm) on Wikimedia Commons; photo originally taken by RAF official photographer and is Crown Copyright.

July 1940

		1	2	3	4	5	6	7	8	9	10	11	12	13	14	15	16	17	18
JG 2	I	■	■	■	■	■	■	■	■	■	■	■	■	■	■	■	■	■	■
	II	■	■	■	■	■	■	■	■	■	■	■	■	■	■	■	■	■	■
	III																		
JG 3	I																		
	II																		
	III	▨	▨	▨	▨								■	■	■	■	■	■	
JG 26	I														▨	▨	▨	▨	▨
	II																		
	III																		
JG 27	I		■	■	■	■	■	■	■	■	■	■	■	■	■	■	■	■	■
	II																		
	III	■	■	■	■	■	■	■	■	■	■	■	■	■	■	■	■	■	■
JG 51	I												■	■	■	■	■	■	■
	II	■	■	■	■	■	■	■	■	■	■	■	■	■	■	■	■	■	■
	III	■	■	■	■	■	■	■	■	■	■	■	■	■	■	■	■	■	■
JG 52	I																		
	II																		
	III																		
JG 53	I	■	■	■	■	■	■	■	■	■	■	■	■	■	■	■	■	■	■
	II																		
	III																		
JG 54	I																		
	II																		
	III																		
LG 2	I	■	■	■	■	■	■	■	■	■	■	■							

Dark grey = in place and active operationally; light grey = in place but not active operationally; white = unit absent from Channel region. *Geschwader* and subordinate *Gruppen* designations at left.

Chart 1. Chart summarising German fighter *Gruppen* stationed at French operational bases along the Channel during the Battle of Britain, from 1 July – 7 August 1940. Sources of data on chart in Bibliography: Website, Holm, Michael; fighter Geschwader histories: Mombeek, Eric and co-authors, JG 2, volume 2 (2013); Prien, Jochen and Stemmer, Gerhard, III/JG 3 (1995); Caldwell, Donald, JG 26, volume 1 (2012); Ring, Hans and Girbig, Werner, JG 27 (1975); Aders, Gebhard and Held, Werner, JG 51 (1985); Barbas, Bernd, I/JG 52 (undated); Barbas, Bernd, III/JG 52 (undated); Held, Werner and co-authors, JG 54 (1985); Prien, Jochen, JG 77, volume 1 (1992). Additional sources, not in Bibliography: Barbas, Bernd, *Die Geschichte*

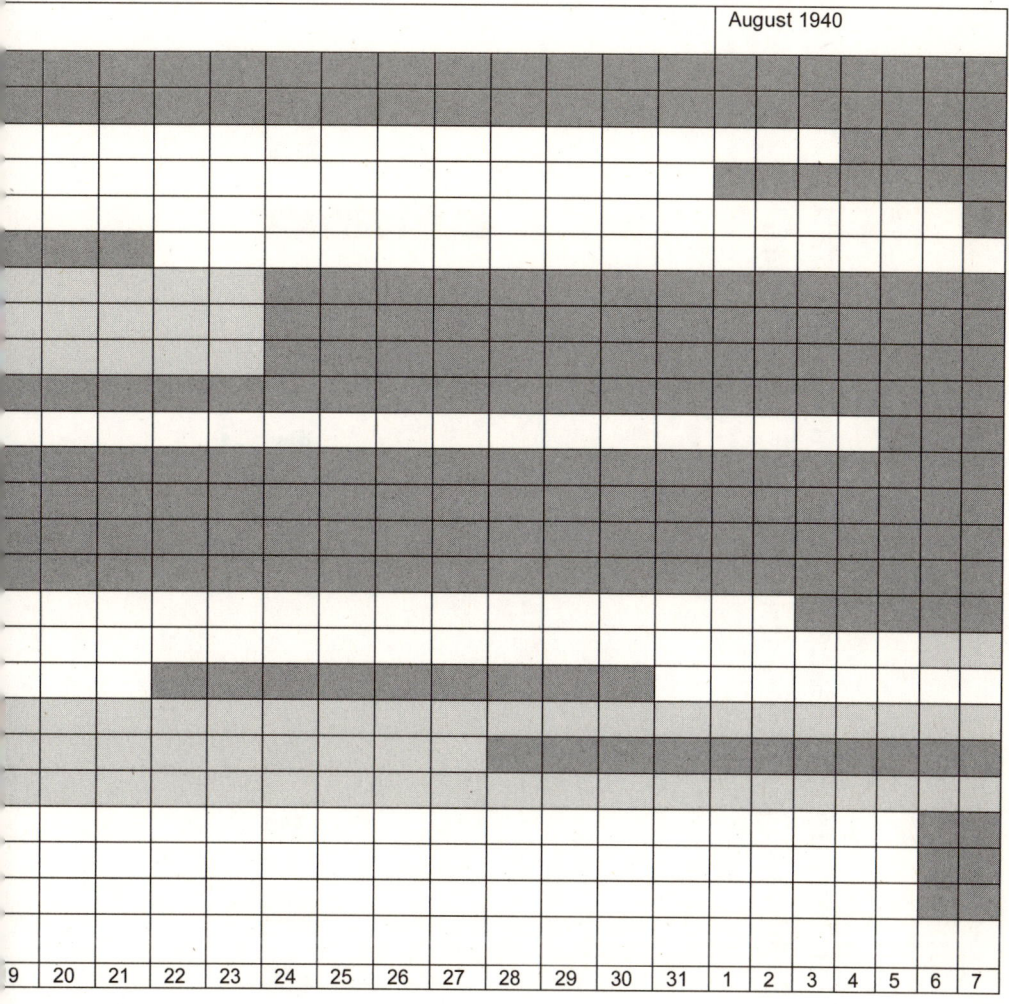

der II. Gruppe des Jagdgeschwaders 52 (Überlingen: self-published, undated);
Bob, Hans Ekkehard, *Grünherzjäger im Luftkampf 1940-1945; Die Geschichte
des Jagdgeschwaders 54: Kriegs-Tagebuch von Hannes Trautloft, Kommodore
Jagdgeschwader 54 Grünherz* (Zweibrücken: VDM Heinz Nickel, 2006); Prien,
Jochen, *Pik-As: Geschichte des Jagdgeschwaders 53, Teil 1* (Illertissen: Flugzeug
Publikations, 1989); Prien, Jochen and Stemmer, Gerhard, *Messerschmitt Bf 109 im
Einsatz bei der II./Jagdgeschwader 3* (Eutin: Struve-Druck, 1996); Prien, Jochen and
Stemmer, Gerhard, *Messerschmitt Bf 109 im Einsatz bei Stab und I./Jagdgeschwader
3* (Eutin: Struve-Druck, 1997).

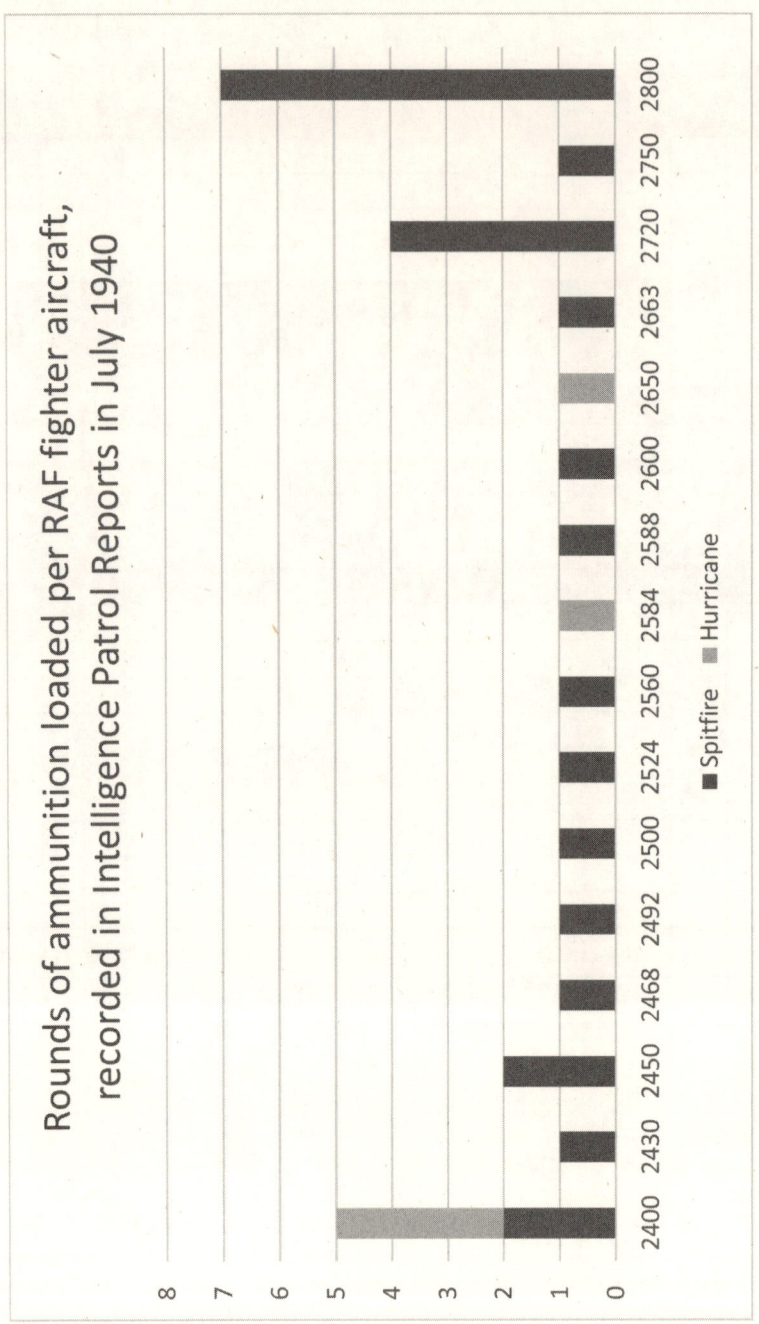

Chart 2. Ammunition loads carried by aircraft of Fighter Command, varying from the 'standard' 2,400 rounds per machine (300 rounds per gun) up to 2,800 rounds; data from Intelligence Patrol Reports (Air 16/955 records, National Archives; details in chapter notes) for period 1 July – 7 August 1940. Values on vertical scale record number of IPRs giving any specific ammunition load.

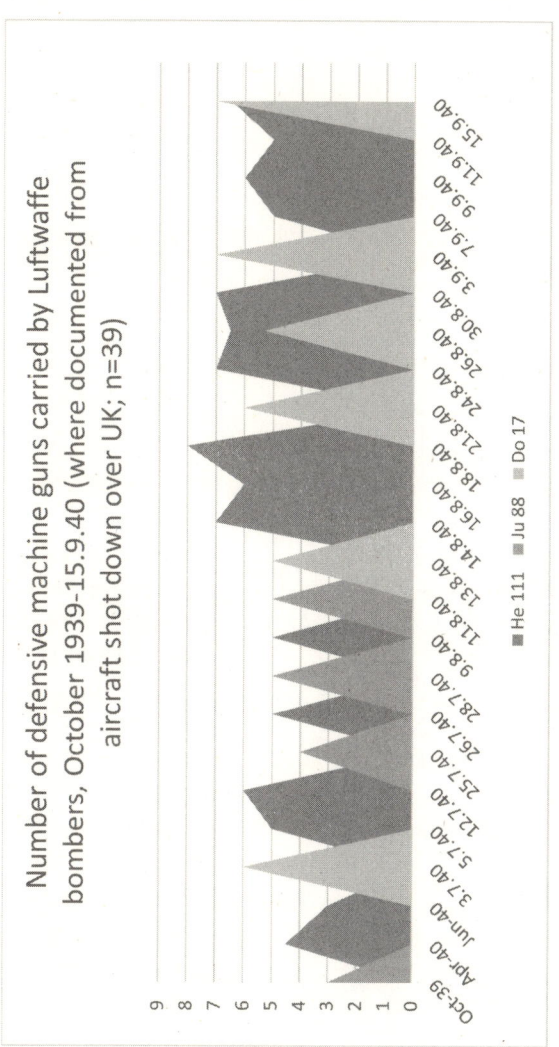

Chart 3. Number of defensive machine guns carried by *Luftwaffe* bombers, data for the period October 1939-15 September 1940 (where documented from aircraft shot down over UK; n=39). Source of data: Parker, Nigel, *Luftwaffe Crash Archive, Vol. 1, 1st September 1939 to 14th August 1940* (Walton on Thames: Red Kite Books, Air Research Publications, 2013); and successive volumes: *Vol. 2, 15th August 1940 to 29th August 1940*, 2013; *Vol. 3, 30th August 1940 to 9th September 1940*, 2013; *Vol. 4, 10th September 1940 to 27th September 1940*, 2014 (full details in Bibliography). Fractions reflect averaging multiple data points for a single day. General trend of increasing defensive armament from beginning of Battle of Britain (1 July 1940) through to 15 September 1940, is better defined for He 111s and Do 17s. These armament enhancements were done at unit level on operational airfields, and were thus individualistic, per *Gruppe* and even per aircraft therein. Not shown are two Do 17s which had 20 mm cannon added in the lower nose (between 26 August and 10 September 1940). Also not included are five reconnaissance machines which carried only three MG 15s until about end of August 1940, increasing to five in one machine on 7 September 1940.

Index

Also available from Amberley Publishing

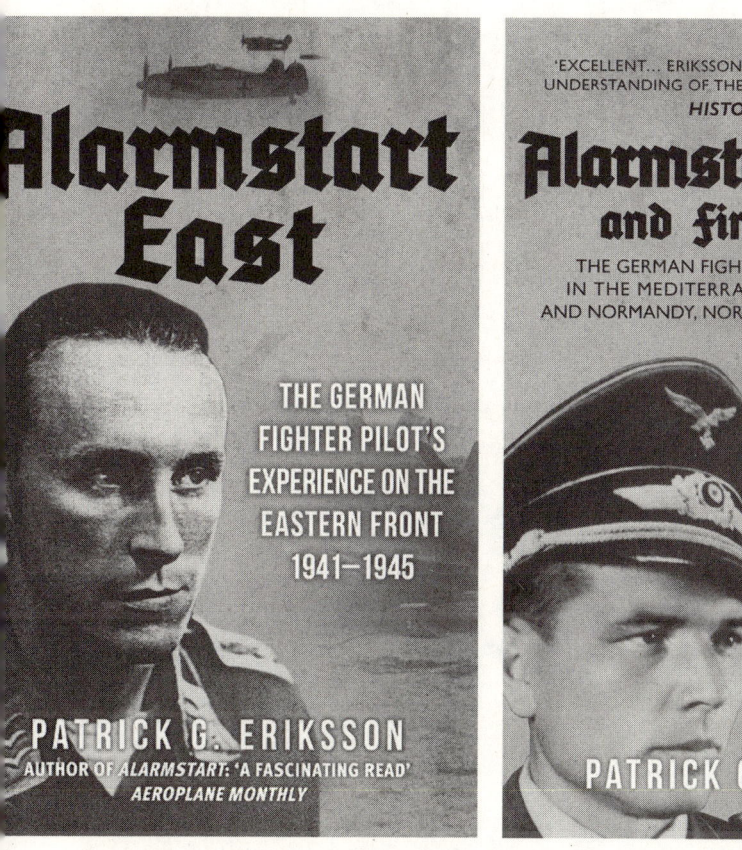

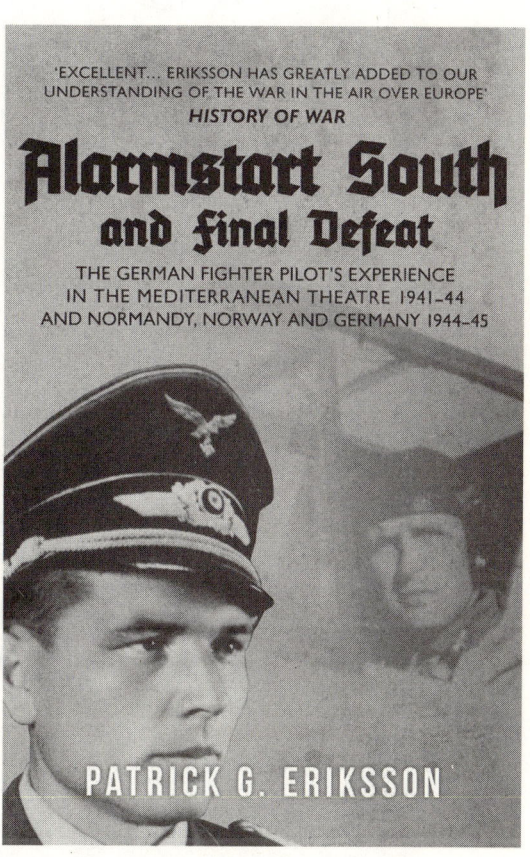

Available from all good bookshops or to order direct
Please call **01453-847-800**
www.amberley-books.com

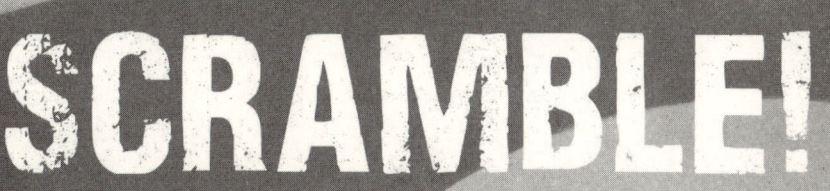

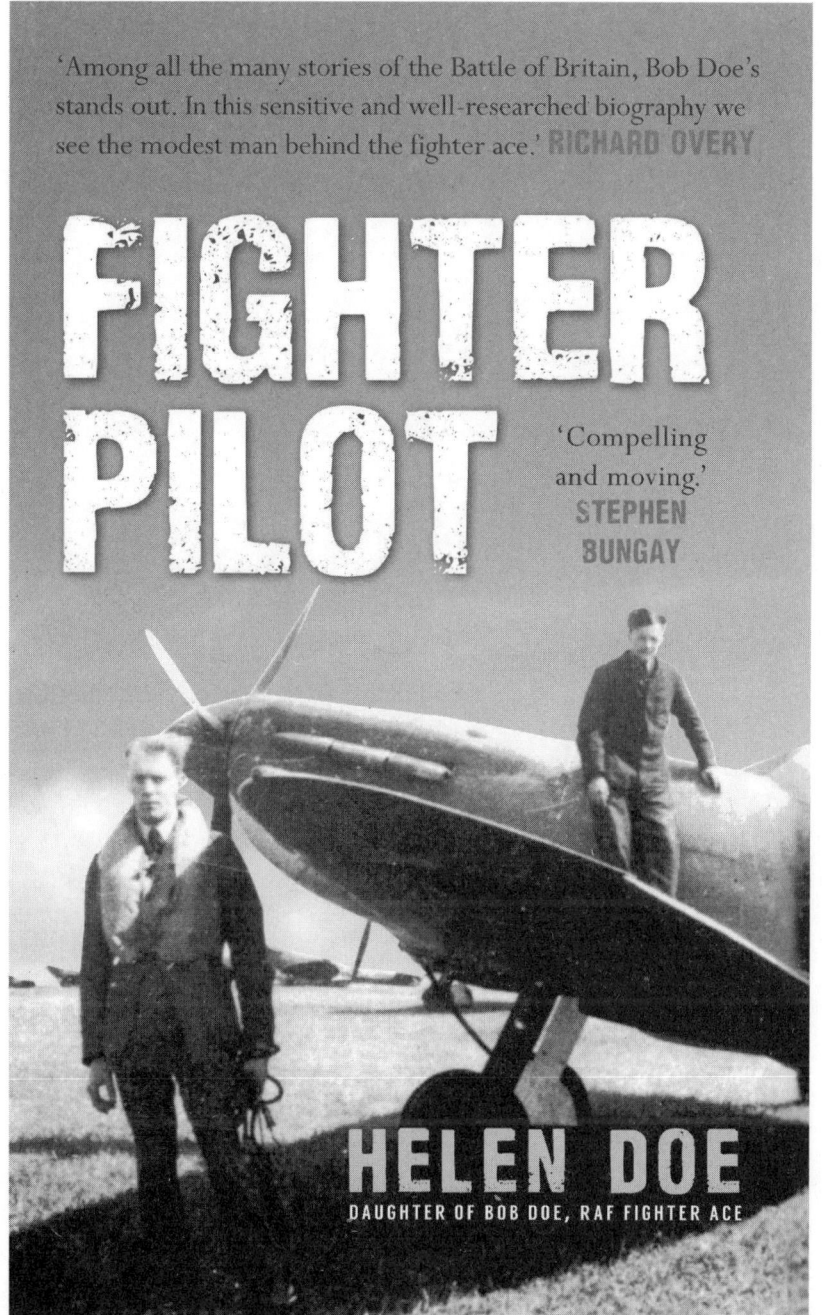